The Structure of Singing

The Structure of Singing

System and Art in Vocal Technique

Richard Miller

Oberlin College Conservatory of Music

Schirmer Books
An Imprint of Simon & Schuster Macmillan
NEW YORK

Prentice Hall International
LONDON · MEXICO CITY · NEW DELHI · SINGAPORE · SYDNEY · TORONTO

Schirmer Books
An Imprint of Simon & Schuster Macmillan
1633 Broadway
New York, NY 10019-6785

Library of Congress Catalog Card Number: 85-11492

Printed in the United States of America

PRINTING   15

Library of Congress Cataloging in Publication Data
Miller, Richard, 1926–
    The structure of singing.

    Bibliography: p.
    Includes index.
    1. Singing—Methods. I. Title.
MT825.M646 1986   784.9'3   85-11492
ISBN 0-02-872660-X

To Mary, who makes possible most of what I do

Primum non nocere
(The first thing is not to do harm)
——Ancient medical dictum

In every field the man who can merely do things without knowing why is at a disadvantage to the one who can not only build but also tell you just why he is building in that way. This is especially noticeable when the prescribed cycle does not obey the laws it is supposed to: then the laborer must sit by with folded hands while the mechanic or engineer comes in and adjusts the delicate mechanism.
——Reuben Fine
(The Ideas Behind Chess Openings.
London: Bell and Hyman, 1981.)

Contents

Preface

As a student, I was intrigued by the many notions about how one sings. I enjoyed descriptions of other singers' voice lessons. As a professional singer, my interest in comparing vocal techniques was strengthened. My singing career has always run parallel with an interest in teaching singing. It has been my experience that helping other people learn to sing contributes to one's own vocal understanding.

Several years on research status and on sabbatical leave were spent visiting hundreds of voice studios and thousands of lessons from a wide range of pedagogic orientations. Very early in the simultaneous careers of singing and teaching, I tried to sort out the confusing array of technical approaches to singing. It seemed clear that it was essential to find how the singing voice functions as an instrument. Much of my "free time" over the years has been spent in reading the growing literature on vocal physiology and acoustics. I found a few scientists and phoniatricians who shared research projects with me and listened sympathetically to my questions. Out of this personal search came the conviction that the best way to maintain "traditional" vocal technique is to use language which communicates concrete concepts regarding efficiency. As in any field, the transfer of information is possible only if a common language exists between writer and reader, teacher and student.

With regard to the current surge in the study of comparative vocal pedagogy in many educational institutions, it is good to know the details of a number of techniques of singing as an intellectual exercise. Digesting those techniques for one's own benefit, or for transmitting information to one's students, however, is entirely another matter. Vocal pedagogy is like a smorgasbord, from which one can sample foods both rich and simple; not everything that can be ingested is equally nutritious. Running from one famous teacher to another, from one master class to the next, from one symposium to yet another, and reading each new "complete" vocal method published, may open some doors. Yet there comes a time when the singer or teacher of singing must stop shopping around and make a choice. An informed choice is possible only if one is aware of what produces free vocal function. Specific vocal sounds may be interesting—perhaps even momentarily thrilling—but if they are not based on reliable, functional principles, they will make the voice sick, just as a continual diet of desserts will adversely affect the constitution.

Technique represents the stabilization of desirable coordination during singing. Technique can be "computerized" in the brain and the body of the singer. No singer ever should be in doubt as to what is going to happen, technically, in public performance, unless illness interferes. Knowing how the singing instrument works, and knowing how to get it to work consistently, is the sum of technical knowledge. That is why a systematic approach to vocal technique is the most successful route to artistic singing. System and art conjoin to produce the professional sounds of the singing voice.

In the end, traditional vocalism is based on efficient vocal production. Artistry cannot be realized without the technical means for its presentation. Systematic vocal technique and artistic expression are inseparable; they comprise the structure of singing.

This book does not answer all the questions about how to sing, but it does provide a basis for vocal freedom in performance through efficient handling of acoustic and physiologic aspects of the singing voice.

Richard Miller

Acknowledgments

If the teachers, colleagues, researchers, and authors who have directly contributed over many years to the shaping of the vocal philosophy expressed in this book were here acknowledged, an endless list would result. I must restrict myself to mentioning only a few of the many persons and sources that have helped me form a system of singing and teaching. I shall ever be grateful for the firm technical foundation in breath management given me by my first voice teacher, Alice Miller, my mother; I also remember with much appreciation two generous teachers of my youth, William Strassner and Ruth Cogan. The latter has been a major influence in my life. Harold Hedgpeth and Harold Haugh were fine performing tenors and excellent mentors who helped me with my young adult voice. Special debts are owed to Maestro Luigi Ricci and to Maestro Mario Basiola, who later set standards of musicianship and vocalism that have remained goals throughout my professional life. The lessons learned from several colleagues who, through their models of freedom and vitality in performance, were also my teachers, have been invaluable. To all of these people, some no longer living, my deepest thanks.

Complementary to these musical and pedagogical influences is a great reservoir of material from many sources, much of which is included in the bibliography of this book. Some of my own early awareness of the importance of disciplines related to the singing voice was sparked by the works of Richard Luchsinger and Godfrey Arnold, Janwillem van den Berg, Peter Ladefoged, Claude Kantner and Robert West, Gunnar Fant, Knud Faaborg-Anderson, and William Vennard. In more recent years, I have greatly benefited from the number of fine published symposia reports listed in the bibliography, particularly those dealing with the care of the professional voice, published by The Voice Foundation. (Wilbur J. Gould, through his vision and leadership of those symposia, has left an indelible mark on professional voice use in this country.) Such other contemporaries as Van Lawrence, Ingo Titze, Harm K. Schutte, Wolfgang Zenker, Minoru Hirano, Willard Zemlin, Stuart Selkin, and Johan Sundberg have influenced my views on how the voice functions, either through the written word or, in several cases, through the generous sharing of ideas and laboratories.

I am indebted to several publishers for permission to use illustrated material (acknowledged where the material appears): Church-ill Livingstone; H. W. Freeman and Company (for *Scientific American,* Inc.); Oxford University Press; W. B. Saunders Company; Springer-Verlag; University of Chicago Press; University of Tokyo Press; Urban & Schwarzenberg; Williams & Wilkins.

To Oberlin College I owe thanks for having made available opportunities to pursue study in this country and in Europe through several sabbatical, faculty development, and research status programs. This book partly grows out of the many invaluable professional contacts and personal experiences such grants made possible.

Thanks go to Dr. Raphael Poritsky, Professor of Anatomy, Case Western Reserve Medical School, for kindly reading the anatomical information found in the appendices and for his helpful suggestions (although he is not to be held accountable for a voice teacher's attempt to describe the anatomy and physiology of the singing instrument!). For some definitions in the glossary, I have paraphrased or quoted from *Webster's New International Dictionary,* 2d edition, and, in a few instances, have relied on Willard Zemlin's *Speech and Hearing Science,* 2d edition, or on William Vennard's *Singing: the Mechanism and the Technic,* 5th edition.

I also want to thank Lynn Poe for his invaluable advice in making some important decisions, and my gratitude is extended to Michael Sander, Associate Editor of Schirmer Books and to Elyse Dubin, Editorial Supervisor, for their patience and help in producing this work.

My daughter Letitia deserves mention for her understanding that our joint stamp collecting activities had to be laid aside until this book was put together.

Introduction

Why This Book Was Written

I have never met anyone who learned to sing by reading a book. On the other hand, my own experience as performer and teacher is that I have been greatly assisted by advice and technical suggestions from a wide range of writers on vocal pedagogy. This fact gives me courage to add yet another volume to that literature. It is my hope to coordinate, as much as possible, what I understand to be the physical and acoustic factors involved in free singing with a detailed system of technical studies for acquiring such freedom.

It is apparent that much of what takes place within an artistically sung phrase can be analyzed only in terms of communication and musical aesthetics. However, a vocal phrase clearly has a beginning and a conclusion, and recognizable physical and acoustic events are responsible for both and for determining what happens in between.

It follows that even though a singer may have a profound understanding of musical style, an imaginative temperament that can serve as a vehicle for artistic expression, and a vocal instrument of promise, these positive attributes cannot be perceived by the listener if the mechanics of technique are faulty. It is not enough for the singer to have something to say; the means for saying it with ease must be present. An understanding of physical function may make the difference between the emergence of a solid technique of singing and a lifelong struggle with the mechanics.

Typically, singers are mostly concerned with the final performance impact (the aesthetic product) and give little thought to the physical and acoustic factors of sound production. Yet any vocal technique involves making assumptions, of varying degrees of specificity as well as of accuracy, concerning the physical production of sound. Differing viewpoints exist with respect not only to aesthetic preference but to the most appropriate physical means for producing the desired sound. The success of any technical approach to singing must be measured by how nearly it arrives at the planned aesthetic result with the least cost.

Freedom of function in singing ought to count heavily in determining which vocal sounds are most pleasing. The highest possible

xix

degree of physical freedom may well be the best indicator of the reliability of aesthetic judgment on the singing voice.

Investigative studies of respiratory–phonatory–resonatory action (the physiologic–acoustic materials of singing) point to four mechanistic functions that unite in breathing and phonating: (1) an energizing system, comprising the mechanism of power, consisting of the inhalatory–exhalatory system housed in the head and torso; (2) a vibratory system, being the laryngeal mechanism itself; (3) a resonator system, made up of a series of cavities in changing relationships with laryngeal tone; and (4) an articulatory system, activated by the lips, the teeth, the cheeks, and the tongue, which must coordinate and modify the activities engendered by the rest of the respiratory-phonatory complex. These systems operate interdependently, so that to examine any one of them alone is to exclude other important considerations temporarily. These four modes of activity and how they may be coordinated to produce beautiful vocal timbre provide the subject matter of much of this book.

Before the second quarter of this century, many books on singing were written either from the subjective experience of the singing artist or from the viewpoint of the scientifically minded person, who explained the basic functions of the vocal mechanism. Beginning in the 1920s, authors applied the new findings of medical science, phonetics, speech research, and speech therapy to singing, in the hope of revolutionizing vocal technique. Since the 1940s, much of what has been written for singers and teachers offers explanations of the physical aspects of singing, designed to support precepts that have evolved from performance experience.

Alongside a number of recent publications on the mechanics of singing exist the numerous older, practical methods of vocalises. Although the daily drilling of that extensive literature may aid in the gradual assembling of a good vocal technique, the teacher is offered no information about how those vocalises relate to the problems common to the singing voice that often stem from a physical cause.

Nor can it be of much help when the great artist requests that I imagine my larynx is suspended from my temples by rubber bands, or suggests that I concentrate on the center of my forehead for high tones. Yet, in like fashion with regard to the dissemination of physiological information, it is doubtful that reading about the function of the cricoarytenoids and the thyroarytenoids has ever proved very decisive in the development of any singing artist.

Why not just put ourselves in the hands of someone who teaches "the old *bel canto* method" and be done with it? We cannot because there is no specific codified system of *bel canto* waiting for the vocal neophyte to pick up and assimilate. Despite some claims that certain teachers have a direct link to "the old Italians," no modern teacher can honestly profess to teach some clearly delineated method that is universally recognized as being "the *bel canto* method."

Anyone who has studied with teachers who trace a historical lineage to other persons often cited as major teachers of *bel canto* (for example, pupils of pupils of Giovanni Battista Lamperti) must admit that the specifics, the actual techniques, of acquiring the art of beautiful singing, are only imprecisely enunciated by them. A careful reading of the pedagogical literature of the historical *bel canto* period must lead to a similar conclusion. The term *bel canto* has become a twentieth-century shibboleth, with opposing methodologies staking out highly suspect claims for its possession. This is because of the indefinability of the term beyond its literal meaning: beautiful singing. Skills of sustaining and moving the voice (*cantilena* and *fioritura*) are required to execute the *bel canto* literature; those skills join to produce "beautiful singing." They call for the most exacting technical accomplishments, in whatever century.

Although it is not possible to claim that the exercises in this book (or any other) comprise the vocalizing material of the *bel canto* tradition, it is fair to state that exercises in this volume, or ones similar to them, existed in the historic Italian School, which in the latter part of the nineteenth and the early decades of the twentieth centuries crossed all national barriers.

It would be pointless here to try to trace each vocalise to some recognizable source, because in all probability such sources would not prove to be the original ones. No doubt most of these vocalises have been in the public domain for centuries.

If it is true that the voice is an instrument that functions best when mechanically most efficient (as the voice scientist assumes), and that one must accomplish a variety of vocal gymnastics in order to be equipped for the exacting demands of literature (as Messrs. Vaccai, Sieber, Concone, Panofka, Garcia, and the Lampertis seem to tell us), then it seems reasonable to devise specific exercises to help achieve the freely functioning voice. That, in fact, is the aim of this book.

Any series of vocalises can be sung in a number of ways, some of which are absolutely without value. Only if freedom can be induced through the use of a vocalise does that vocalise have merit. No vocalise should be sung without some distinct technical intent behind it.

Scale passages, triad patterns, broken arpeggios, and other vocalises built on pyrotechnical rocketry often serve as "warm-up" gestures for singers so that the voice will not be "cold" at the beginning of a performance. The side benefits of such warming up are helpful.

Random vocalization, however, may not necessarily establish the firm technical foundation that permits reliable physical ease (coordinated function) in performance.

Some singers believe that any technical study divorced from the literature itself is extraneous. Established professional singers with ongoing engagements may in part be kept in a state of technical fitness through frequency of performance. But it is unlikely that the range of literature encountered in performance commitments encompasses the gamut of technical skills which a systematic plan of vocalization can offer.

At the same time, a wealth of the best vocalizing material available is to be found in passages from Handel, Purcell, Mozart, Bellini, Verdi, Puccini, Duparc, Fauré, Massenet, Britten, Walton, Barber, and Rorem; phrases from such literatures should be used to supplement the daily vocalizing regimen.

HOW TO USE THIS BOOK

In this book, categories of technical problems frequently encountered in singing are identified. Some explanation of desirable physical action is presented, followed by exercises to assist in establishing the technical skills dependent on optimum physical function.

Additional information on the voice as a physical–acoustic instrument is contained in several appendices. The appendices supplement the briefer descriptions of functions found in chapters where vocal technique is systematically presented.

A singer who reads this book may want to begin with the practical application of the vocalises to an area of technique where improvement is needed. Another reader may wish first to read the background material in the appropriate appendix that justifies the suggested vocal tasks, and then turn to the corresponding chapter or chapters. The appendices serve as references on function, and explain why the recommended vocalises so often produce good results.

Although the art of singing can be learned only through singing, the systematic organization of vocal technique is the most efficient route to the realization of the primary goal: production of beautiful sound. Life being brief and art being long, one should spend only the minimal time each day required to deal with the technique of singing so that one may move on to those much more important aspects of the art that have to do with musicianship, interpretation, and communication.

The
Structure
of
Singing

CHAPTER 1

The
Coordinated Vocal Onset
and Release

Establishing Dynamic Muscle Equilibrium
Through Onset and Release

The way a singer initiates vocal sound is crucial to the subsequent phrase. A good beginning to the singing tone is of prime consideration regardless of the achievement level of the singer. Whether one has been an established performer for years or is about to begin vocal study, every singer should begin the daily vocalizing session with exercises in onset and release. Only if the onset of each phrase demonstrates the principle of nonstatic (that is, dynamic) laryngeal muscle balance and elasticity is the singer assured of freedom. Briess (1964, p. 259) has termed such flexible muscle balance in phonation *dynamic equilibrium.* In the absence of such dynamic, adjustable coordination, hyperfunction (excessive activity) characterizes the action of some muscle or muscle group, with corresponding hypofunction (deficient activity) occurring in some other muscle or muscles. In either case, muscle equilibrium will have been replaced by muscle rigidity. (See Figure 1.1 for positions of the vocal folds during quiet breathing, deep inhalation, normal phonation, one form of whispering, and falsetto. For a description of laryngeal structure and function, see Appendix I.)

THE VARIETIES OF ONSET

There are three types of vocal onset that result from differences in vocal-fold positioning (Luchsinger and Arnold, 1965, pp. 84–85). Although described by various terms, they are best designated as (1) the soft onset; (2) the hard attack; and (3) the balanced onset. (The term *attack* is often used synonymously with *onset.* Because of the connotations of the word *attack,* it may best be used to describe only the hard attack.)

1

Techniques of singing bring attention, directly or indirectly, to the position the vocal folds assume before onset of sound. Such pre-phonatory positioning is supported by the findings of electromyography (EMG), the study of electrical activity in muscle. Faaborg-Anderson (1964, p. 115) reports:

> The action-potential amplitude rises before phonation, both in the crico-thyroid and in the vocal muscles. This means that the intrinsic laryngeal muscles assume the position and degree of tension necessary for production of a tone of a certain pitch even before actual phonation.

Wyke (1974, p. 296) reviews some of the conclusions based on electromyographic studies of laryngeal neuromuscular behavior in both speech and singing just before the onset of phonation and during subsequent utterances:

> Electromyographic studies of the intrinsic laryngeal muscles of normal subjects during phonation (including singing) by numbers of workers have shown . . . that motor unit activity increases briefly but substantially in all the vocal fold adductor muscles just prior to each phonemic utterance (accompanied by an equally brief decrease in the activity of the abductor posterior cricoarytenoid muscles) with an interval that varies (in different individuals and circumstances of utterance) from 50 to 500 msec. Other aerodynamic studies of subjects speaking and singing . . . have shown that the expiratory airflow commences, and that the subglottic air pressure begins to rise, also just prior to each audible utterance—but some 50–100 msec after the prephonatory changes in laryngeal muscular activity described [here] have commenced.

Keeping in mind the activity of the muscles of the larynx before and after onset, we will now view several forms of initial phonation with regard to their ability to induce efficient function (dynamic muscle equilibrium) in singing.

The Hard Attack

Glottal attack, glottal catch, glottal click, glottal plosive, stroke of the glottis, *coup de glotte, colpo di glottide* (also *colpo della glottide*), *Glottisschlag, Knacklaut, Sprengeinsatz,* are terms used to describe the resultant vocal sound when the vocal folds are adducted (approximated) prior to phonation. Electromyography (EMG) shows that in the glottal attack, activity begins early in the vocal muscles and is significantly greater than in the two other forms of onset. Because the glottis firmly closes before phonation in the hard attack, there is a greater degree of pressure below the folds. When phonation begins, the suddenness of the release of this pressure produces the audible catch, the glottal plosive, which is represented by the phonetic symbol [ʔ]. (International Phonetic Alphabet symbols are used in this book. Those symbols are illustrated in Appendix VI.)

The Soft Onset

A singer who consciously feels the flow of breath before vocal sound, is making use of the aspirated onset. Such a sound is represented by the symbol [h]. When this sound is prolonged, the vocal folds are adducted to the paramedian line without firm closure of the glottis (see Figure 1.1d.) Luchsinger and Arnold (1965, p. 85) inform that, in the breathy onset,

> Laryngoscopy reveals an open triangle with the base at the posterior commissure. This intercartilaginous triangle is also known as the "whispering triangle." The audible impression is that of a soft blowing sound, which is transcribed as the sound [h]. A fraction of a second following the aspirate noise the vocal cords begin gradually to vibrate, until the full tone of phonation is heard. This speech sound is not customary in Romance languages.

Studies in progress at the University of Florida, Gainesville, indicate that varying glottal configurations, in addition to the "whispering triangle," may be present in whispering. In some whispering, a lower sound pressure level prevails, with a higher rate of breath flow. Just as the hard attack produces conditions favorable to hyperfunction on the part of certain participating muscles, so the soft onset may result in hypofunction in the same muscle group.

Neither the hard attack nor the soft onset may be endorsed as pedagogical practices for standard use. They result from two opposing errors in phonation, and may be described simplistically as the "grunt" and the "whisper."

When an adult engages in heavy physical activity such as lifting, pulling, or shoving, or even in throwing the arms backward from the torso in an attempt to swing the hands behind the back, an involuntary grunting noise results. One grunts because glottal closure has been extreme and the sudden release of pressure becomes audible with the expulsion of air. The grunt, introduced into phonation, represents reversion to primordial action in laryngeal function (Luchsinger and Arnold, 1965, pp. 118–119).

It can be easily demonstrated that one can go gradually from whispering to speech, controlling the degree of glottal closure. One can whisper softly; one can use a loud stage whisper; one can speak lazily with just sufficient breath mixture in the tone to make speech audible; one can eliminate breath almost entirely, speaking cleanly and firmly. Or one could go a step further and indulge in pressed phonation.

The Balanced Onset (Dynamic Muscle Equilibrium)

If a singer or speaker avoids both the whisper posture and exaggerated vocal-fold closure (the grunt posture), a more balanced laryngeal action is present throughout the phrase. "Prephonatory tuning" of the instrument takes place, and this "tuning" occurs with great rapidity throughout the changing utterances of spoken or sung phonation. It occurs not only during vocal onset, but also during continuous speech or song. According to Wyke (1974, p. 297), "this *prephonatory tuning* of the laryngeal musculature . . . is the principal voluntary contribution to the control of the larynx during speech and singing. . . ." Wyke (1974, p. 300) further points out that

> this prephonatory tuning process involves not only the intrinsic laryngeal muscles, but also the intercostal and abdominal muscles and the external laryngeal muscles . . . as well as the middle ear . . . and the oropharyngeal musculature . . . and is set in train immediately after each voluntary inter-phrase inspiration.

Although Wyke's comments refer not only to the vocal onset but to subsequent utterances within a phrase, "prephonatory tuning" is present in the good onset for singing. Such an onset is accomplished by avoiding either the grunt or the whisper. Glottal closure is modified in the balanced onset by a narrow slit before phonation. This "even onset" is physiologically midway between the hard attack and the soft onset. Without this narrow slit in the glottis just before phonation, the buildup of subglottic pressure results in the glottal plosive, a sound similar to a light cough.

EXERCISES FOR ACHIEVING THE BALANCED ONSET

The desirable condition of balanced muscle equilibrium can be established through the use of several simple exercises.

EXERCISE 1.1

REPEAT THE SPOKEN SEQUENCE "HA, HA, HA, HA, HA" SEVERAL TIMES, SLOWLY AND DELIBERATELY AS A PHRASE UNIT, LINGERING OVER THE INITIAL ASPIRATED [h] OF EACH SYLLABLE. IT IS POSSIBLE TO SENSE WHEN BREATH PASSING OVER THE VOCAL FOLDS IS FOLLOWED BY SOUND THAT RESULTS FROM VOCAL-FOLD APPROXIMATION (THAT IS, WHEN ACTUAL TONE COMMENCES).

EXERCISE 1.2

REPEAT THE SPOKEN SEQUENCE "UH, UH, UH, UH, UH" SEVERAL TIMES, SLOWLY AND DELIBERATELY AS A PHRASE UNIT, LINGERING OVER THE INITIAL GLOTTAL PLOSIVE [ʔ]. ONE CAN SENSE THE MOMENT AT WHICH THE GLOTTIS HAS BEEN SUFFICIENTLY RELEASED TO PRODUCE PHONATION.

EXERCISE 1.3

REPEAT THE SPOKEN SEQUENCE "AH, AH, AH, AH, AH" SEVERAL TIMES, SLOWLY AND DELIBERATELY AS A PHRASE UNIT, IMAGINING A BRIEF [h] BEFORE EACH SYLLABLE BUT NOT ALLOWING IT TO TAKE ON AUDIBILITY. STRIVE FOR THE SUBJECTIVE FEELING THAT WITH THE BEGINNING OF THE PHRASE THE PROCESS OF INHALATION HAS NOT BEEN ALTERED; THERE SHOULD BE NO SENSATION OF BREATH EXPULSION (ALTHOUGH, OF COURSE, AIRFLOW COMMENCES), AND NO SENSATION OF BREATH MOVING BEFORE TONE.

IF PREPHONATORY TUNING IS EXACT (THE RESULT OF DYNAMIC MUSCLE EQUILIBRIUM), THE CORRECT ONSET WILL BE EXPERIENCED. AWARENESS OF THE MOMENT OF ONSET CAN BE EXPECTED, BUT THE ONSET DOES NOT RESEMBLE THE GLOTTAL CLICK OF THE HARD ATTACK. NO VESTIGE OF BREATHINESS OR OF A VOCAL SCRAPE SHOULD BE HEARD. THERE IS A DISTINCT BEGINNING TO THE TONE, BUT ALL SHOCK IS AVOIDED. TONE CAN BE AS LOUD OR AS SOFT AT ITS INCEPTION AS AT ITS CONCLUSION.

In singing, the coordinated onset occurs only when the glottis has been fully opened with the preceding inhalation. This full abduction of the vocal folds (see Figure 1.1b) is followed by clean and precise closure (see Figure 1.1c, and 1.2). A *partially* opened glottis, as in normal as opposed to deep breathing, does not produce the subsequent clean onset demanded for skillful singing. The onset vocalises drill the quick juxtaposition of the fully opened and the efficiently closed glottis, in immediate response to frequency, vowel, and amplitude (see Figure 1.2).

In this regulated onset lies the germ of all good vocalism. Preparatory to the onset of phonation there must be proper inhalation,

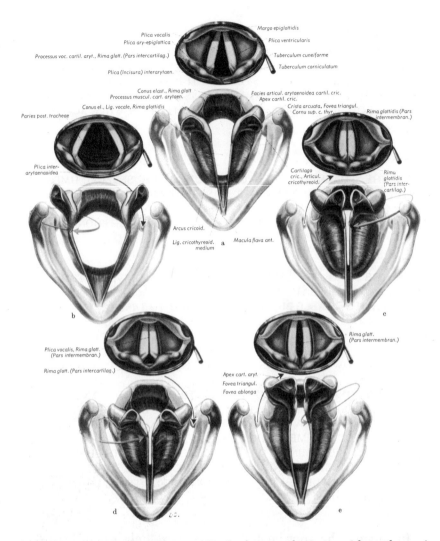

Figure 1.1. The vocal folds viewed by the laryngeal mirror, with a schematic design beneath, in (a) quiet breathing, (b) deep inhalation, (c) normal phonation, (d) one form of whispering, and (e) falsetto. (From Eduard Pernkopf, *Atlas der topographischen und angewandten Anatomie des Menschens*, ed. by Helmut Ferner, Vol. 1, 1963. Munich: Urban & Schwarzenberg. By permission.)

then appropriate vocal-fold positioning (not achieved through conscious effort or laryngeal sensation); breath activates vocal-fold vibration, which remains relatively constant throughout the duration of the phrase to be sung; the release terminates the sound as cleanly as it began; the cycle then resumes. *(The release is the new breath.)*

Nothing in technical accomplishment in singing is more beneficial to the vocal instrument than the proper positioning of the vocal folds for the clean onset. Such prephonatory tuning of the laryngeal muscles in combination with the exact degree of subglottic pressure and airflow provides the basis for good singing.

Should the singer then be permitted only the use of the imaginary [h], always avoiding the audible [h] and the plosive [ʔ] as well? The answer in both cases is probably negative. Although one of the three forms of onset is physiologically most efficient (the balanced onset) and aesthetically pleasing to most, but not all, listeners, pedagogical benefits may derive from the other two.

USES OF THE ASPIRATED ONSET

Especially among the athletically young there is a tendency toward a higher rate of muscle activity in the vocal onset than among more phlegmatic persons, whose psychological and physiological mainsprings appear less tightly wound. The aggressive personality, whose active approach to life makes little use of introspection and repose, will tend to display a greater degree of laryngeal tension and of subglottic pressure than the less visceral personality. Physical aggressiveness in singing is often an outward expression of a particular category of human spirit. Especially among the young, it can also be learned in imitation of some mature artist, in which case aggressive singing may emerge from an otherwise docile personality.

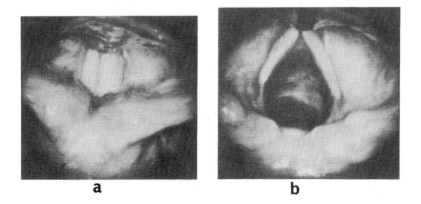

a   **b**

Figure 1.2. Laryngoscopic view for (a) normal phonation and (b) deep inspiration. (From *Vocal Fold Physiology*, ed. by Kenneth N. Stevens and Minoru Hirano, 1981. Tokyo: Tokyo University Press. By permission.)

Whatever the cause, too much tension in vocal-fold positioning prior to and during phonation is a common error among singers at all levels of technical advancement. When the grunt, the initial "bite" into the tone, or the scraped attack make habitual appearances, the most productive antidote is the aspirated onset. By its very fault of excessive airflow and reduced pressure, the aspirated onset may be exactly what is temporarily needed to combat tense vocal production. When a singer begins a phrase with a pressed attack, there will be some retention of that laryngeal function throughout the remainder of the phrase. The wisest move, then, is to make use of the short aspirated onset over a period of time.

USES OF THE GLOTTAL ATTACK

Human personality is delightfully diverse, and vocal instruments mirror that diversity. The teacher may have to instruct the raw, overly energized young male voice (and occasionally the female) as well as the ectomorphic male and the female who, either through genes and chromosomes or as a result of cultural conditioning, remains physically somewhat uninvolved during singing. In such cases, breathiness and physical detachment characterize the vocal sound. It may then be wise to introduce the slight glottal attack so that excess breath is eliminated. It surely need not be urged that no exaggeration of glottal closure should ever be requested. Overcorrection is not in order.

PHYSIOLOGICAL BENEFITS OF THE COORDINATED ONSET

The coordinated onset, which results from dynamic equilibrium of the participating musculature and of subglottic pressure, produces healthy vocalism. The electromyographic (EMG) techniques developed in 1950 at the Phonetic Institute of Zurich (Switzerland) University, make clear that the balanced onset avoids the irregular wave patterns associated with the breathy onset and is free of the erratic initial waves that indicate the explosive character of the hard attack (Luchsinger and Arnold 1965, p. 86). Similar evidence exists for the several types of vocal release.

ONSET VOCALISES WHICH INDUCE
DYNAMIC EQUILIBRIUM

The pitch at which any group of exercises in this book should be sung is determined by the vocal category and by the registration events of the individual instrument. For exercises in Groups 1 and 2 in this chapter, the following pitch ranges generally should be kept in mind[1]:

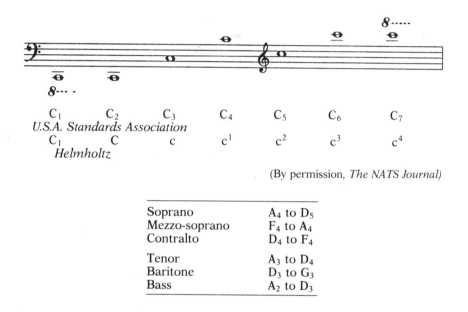

	C_1	C_2	C_3	C_4	C_5	C_6	C_7
U.S.A. Standards Association							
	C_1	C	c	c^1	c^2	c^3	c^4
Helmholtz							

(By permission, *The NATS Journal*)

Soprano	A_4 to D_5
Mezzo-soprano	F_4 to A_4
Contralto	D_4 to F_4
Tenor	A_3 to D_4
Baritone	D_3 to G_3
Bass	A_2 to D_3

Transposition of the vocalises, as necessary, is assumed. They should be sung in a number of keys. Strict rhythmic adherence is important, and the final note must be given full rhythmic value.

At each onset, the singer should produce a vibrant tone, avoiding any straight quality, maintaining vibrancy throughout the duration of the pitch, no matter how brief it may be (see Chapter 14). The release must be sudden and clean.

---

[1] All pitch indications, other than those quoted from other sources, are based on the system devised by the Acoustical Society of America, endorsed by the U.S.A. Standards Association, in which middle C is represented as C_4. Most international acoustic research relies on this system for pitch designation. The pitch designations beneath the U.S.A. Standards Association system indicate the Helmholtz system, which for many years enjoyed international use, in which middle C is represented by c^1.

Breath renewal is indicated by a comma (**9**) in all of the exercises.

The momentary silence between each release and new onset should be absolute. We are as interested in the silence as in the sound. Any noise resulting from the intake of breath between syllables indicates improper involvement of either the vocal folds or other parts of the vocal tract. (For example, to portray fear on the stage, one constricts the vocal tract upon inhalation, creating resistance to the inspired air. Inspiratory phonation as found in some non-Western languages and as an occasional expressive device in the Teutonic languages and in French, no matter how slight, should be avoided by the singer.)

A common error in executing any onset exercise is the tendency to gradually draw inward the epigastric–umbilical region (that area between the sternum and the navel) with each rhythmic impulse or detached syllable. (For imaginary surface lines indicating areas of the torso and abdomen, see Figure 1.3)

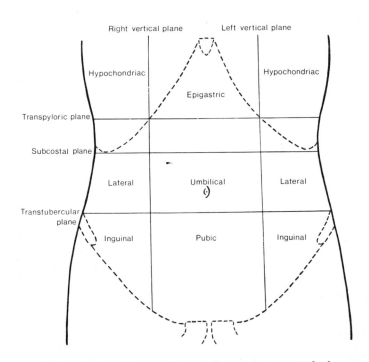

Figure 1.3. Planes of subdivision of the abdomen proper, with the names of the nine abdominal regions. (From *Cunningham's Manual of Practical Anatomy*, 14th ed., ed. by G. J. Romanes, Vol. 2, 1967. Oxford: Oxford University Press. By permission.)

Group 1 Exercises

No specific vowel has been designated for use in the vocalises that follow. All vowels should be used; care should be taken to alternate between front and back vowels. First, a single vowel may be used throughout the series; subsequently, a different vowel should be used on each rhythmic group.

EXERCISE 1.4

(any vowel)

EXERCISE 1.5

(any vowel)

EXERCISE 1.6

(any vowel)

EXERCISE 1.7

(any vowel)

EXERCISE 1.8

(any vowel)

EXERCISE 1.9

(any vowel)

In Exercises 1.4 and 1.5, breath is taken after each note. Whether breath is taken after a single note or following a series of notes, expansion is experienced in the abdominal region. Yet, *this replenishment of the breath may be so slight as to give the singer the impression of having scarcely breathed at all.*

In Exercise 1.6, which is in triplet pattern, breath is renewed only after the completion of the triplet figure. In this exercise, the onset impulse in the umbilical region occurs on the second and third notes, but *without inhalation* (glottis abducts but inhalation does not take place). In Exercises 1.4, 1.5, and 1.6 the vocal folds are engaged and relaxed, sometimes in response to inhalation and sometimes independent of inhalation (as between the first two notes of the triplet pattern). The same principle of repeated vocal onset with regulated rhythmic breath renewal, as in Exercises 1.7 and 1.8, may be drilled after the briefer patterns of Exercises 1.4, 1.5, and 1.6 become easy to execute. Exercise 1.9 combines the entire series into one task, requiring inhalation between varying rhythmic patterns. This process of coordinating laryngeal and abdominal impulses is a major vehicle for achieving vocal-fold approximation, glottal flexibility, and rapid silent breath renewal.

Up to this point there has been no consideration of changes in pitch. Changing pitches should not upset the exact balance of airflow and vocal-fold approximation, yet the basic actions of technical coordination presented in these onset vocalises should be well established before the singer proceeds to exercises requiring greater skill in vocal onset.

STACCATO AND ONSET

Staccato has already been experienced in the execution of the exercises on single pitches (1.4 through 1.9). In the exercises built on intervallic patterns (1.10 through 1.14) the goal is clean approximation, and involves the principle of quick alternation between vocal-fold adduction and abduction on single pitches, then on longer patterns.

There must be no excess of airflow (whisper factor) and no excess of subglottic pressure (grunt factor). Brodnitz (1953, p. 84) remarks:

> In staccato singing a form of glottal stroke is used to produce the sharp interruptions of sound that characterize it. But in good staccato the glottal stroke which starts each note is well controlled and done with a minimum of pressure. . . .

A peril of quick staccato passages is the tendency to remove vibrancy by singing without vibrato, with a straight-tone quality. Such straight-tone timbre indicates a lack of vitality. As an interpretative, coloristic alternative to vibrant timbre, straight-tone may have a reason for being; its presence during technical study should be limited to a few special circumstances (see Chapter 14).

Exercises in Group 2 are useful in applying the principles of dynamic muscle equilibrium and prephonatory tuning to patterns of increasing rapidity in the onset, and are restricted to limited pitch alteration.

Group 2 Exercises

EXERCISE 1.10

(any vowel)

EXERCISE 1.11

(any vowel)

EXERCISE 1.12

(any vowel)

EXERCISE 1.13

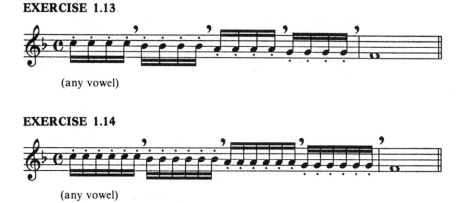

(any vowel)

EXERCISE 1.14

(any vowel)

When the exercises of Group 2 have been thoroughly drilled, additional patterns such as those in Group 3 should be introduced. The Group 3 vocalises are of progressive difficulty; it is not wise to use them all, initially. Nor is it necessary to make all of them a part of the daily routine. Exercises involving a series of four or six notes should not be attempted until those of triplet nature have been digested. In those vocalises where rhythmic patterns shift with subsequent groups of notes (as in Exercises 1.25–1.28), exactitude in rhythm must be maintained if the benefits of the exercises are to be realized.

The series of exercises should be executed in accordance with the following guidelines:

1. Each exercise is to be accomplished in a series of key progressions; transposition within a comfortable medium range should be made for each vocal category, gradually expanding that range as technical facility increases.

2. Although all of the cardinal vowels are eventually to be used, until an exercise can accurately be executed with a vibrant quality and a clean onset, the front vowels [i], [e], and [ɛ] should be preferred to the back vowels [ɔ], [o], [ʊ], and [u], in almost all cases.

3. In general, the onset should be preceded by an imaginary, nearly audible aspirate [h] as occurs in the rapid "ha-ha-ha" of well-supported laughter. The singer must feel subjectively that the aspirate sound has been eliminated, and that the flow of breath and the emergence of tone occur simultaneously. It may seem that singing begins on *the gesture of inhalation* (why get out of the position of singing for breath renewal?). Of course, it does not.

4. In cases where vocal-fold approximation is slack, with resultant breathiness, the attack should incorporate a slight glottal stroke. However, any firm *coup de glotte* should be reserved for extreme cases, and solely as a temporary corrective device.

5. In cases where conditions of vocal tension impair freedom in the onset, the aspirate [h] should be consciously introduced. Exercises 1.15 through 1.28 have similar purposes. Because of shifting rhythmic values, they should be carefully executed only after the breath-pacing skills required in the earlier exercises have been well established.

Group 3 Exercises

EXERCISE 1.15

(any vowel)

EXERCISE 1.16

(any vowel)

EXERCISE 1.17

(any vowel)

EXERCISE 1.18

(any vowel)

EXERCISE 1.19

(any vowel)

EXERCISE 1.20

(any vowel)

EXERCISE 1.21

(any vowel)

EXERCISE 1.22

(any vowel)

EXERCISE 1.23

(any vowel)

EXERCISE 1.24

(any vowel)

EXERCISE 1.25

(any vowel)

EXERCISE 1.26

(any vowel)

EXERCISE 1.27

(any vowel)

EXERCISE 1.28

(any vowel)

THE RELEASE

Even for persons who can initiate a balanced onset, the release of sound may cause technical complications. The proper release of any phonation is as much a factor of technique as is the balancing of vocal sound at the outset. The character of the vocal release contributes to the response the mechanism will make at the subsequent onset. The release must be rhythmically related to the rest of the phrase, with an exact point of termination. Indeed, the type of release a singer uses will generally be dictated by the onset. On the other hand, it is possible to begin the onset efficiently and to terminate it badly.

The Soft Release

When the glottis is gradually opened at the termination of phonation, breathiness will characterize vocal timbre. This quality is usually not restricted to the last note of the phrase, and represents insufficiency of breath coordination below the glottis throughout the pitch, or throughout the phrase. In such cases, the release at the termination of the phrase forces the subsequent onset to be inefficient unless some radical adjustments are quickly made. The collapse of the breath mechanism visibly changes the posture of the torso. Such an inefficient release can be best described as the *soft release*.

The Hard Release

Suddenly increasing the degree of glottal closure (vocal-fold approximation) at the termination of a vocal utterance will produce a phonatory event reminiscent of the grunt. The grunt results from the unskillful attempt to loosen the too tightly occluded vocal folds, and is not appropriate to artistic singing. It is only fair to say that, as an expressive device, especially at rare moments of dramatic intensity, the hard release may be both effective and desirable. However, its overuse can become the annoying hallmark of the singer who customarily sings at a higher dynamic level than is necessary, simply because the art of dynamic variation has not been mastered. The vocal instrument, in this instance, is geared to one level of loudness, and the only way to terminate the concluding note is to give an ample grunt.

To excuse the frequent use of this animalistic noise by claiming it is an "operatic release" is to call a ragweed a rose and hope that no one notices the difference in smell. In addition to being an ugly sound, the hard release requires a difficult readjustment if freedom in singing is to be regained; the subsequent onset will have small opportunity to be anything other than "hard," because of prevailing hyperfunction.

The Balanced Release

In the properly executed onset–release cycle, the quality of vocal sound will be consistent from beginning to end. The glottis neither tightens nor remains in any of the whispering postures at the onset of phonation, nor does it assume those postures at phrase termination.

In order to achieve a balanced release, it is not necessary to change dynamic level, although musical factors may at times convince one to do so. Furthermore, there is no need to diminish dynamic level in order to avoid the hard release. The perfectly balanced release can be demonstrated in the following exercise.

EXERCISE 1.29: COORDINATING THE RELEASE

GIVE A GENUINE "HA-HA-HA-HA-HA" TYPE OF LAUGH, LISTENING CAREFULLY TO THE TERMINATION OF EACH INDIVIDUAL SYLLABLE; EVERY SYLLABLE SHOULD END AS DISTINCTLY AS IT BEGAN. WITHIN THIS LAUGHTER VOCALISE (ON EACH OF ITS SYLLABLES) ARE FOUR IMPORTANT ASPECTS OF GOOD SINGING: (1) BALANCED ONSET OF PHONATION: (2) CONSISTENCY OF QUALITY THROUGHOUT THE DURATION OF THE TONE, HOWEVER BRIEF: (3) BALANCED RELEASE: AND (4) OPTIMUM CONDITION FOR THE CONTINUATION OF EFFICIENT PHONATION.

Separate exercises for the release are unnecessary because, as has been seen, preparation for succeeding onset requires giving equal attention to the release. One of the most practical aspects of the onset–release vocalise is that it can be used under adverse vocal conditions (unless irritation occurs directly within the larynx). When the singing range is curtailed by the common cold, by upper respiratory infections, or by other physical ailments not related to the singing voice but which diminish physical energy and preclude normal practicing and performing, the onset and release vocalises can be the means by which the voice is kept in good form. Breathing itself is schooled and balanced. Freedom in sustained singing and in agility is a direct outgrowth of the free onset and release.

CHAPTER 2

The Supported Singing Voice

Breath Management in Singing

When the body is at rest, the normal inspiration–expiration cycle is brief, about 4 seconds. The inspiratory portion generally takes 1 second, or slightly more; the expiratory portion occupies the remainder. When dealing with the aerodynamic events of breathing, in either speaking or singing, it is important to recognize that, unless restricted in some fashion, air will flow from a region of higher pressure to one of lower pressure. *Gray's Anatomy* (1980, p. 551) states:

> In inspiration the intrapleural and the intrapulmonary pressure fall below atmospheric. At the end of inspiration the intrapulmonary pressure is equal to the atmospheric. During inspiration the air which flows into the lung is not evenly distributed. Regional differences occur in both the ventilation and blood flow. The ventilation is greater in the lower than in the upper lobes of the lung. This accords with the fact that the movement of the upper chest in quiet respiration is inconspicuous, whereas that of the lower chest is greater, affecting principally the transverse diameter. These regional differences may also be related to the varying elasticity of different parts of the lungs and the dimensions of the air passages leading to them. . . .

(For a schematic representation of the mechanism of breathing, see Figure 2.1; for a description of the structure and mechanics of the breath apparatus, see Appendix II.)

In deep inspiration, as in preparation for singing, the diaphragm, and the thoracic and abdominal muscles increase their activity. Phonation and physical effort modify the pace of the breath cycle. In singing, phrase upon phrase will occur in which the breath cycle is drastically prolonged, especially in its expiratory phase. To accomplish skillful control of breath management for singing, special coordination of the phases of the breath cycle (inhalation, onset, phrase duration, release) must be learned.

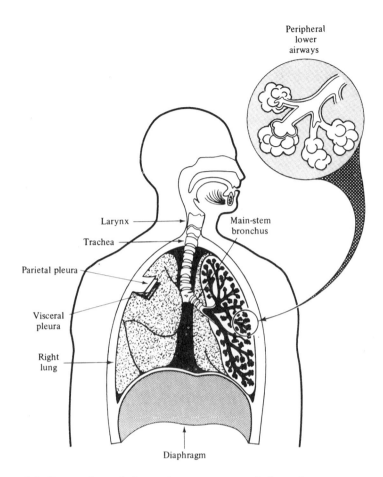

Figure 2.1. Front view of the major structures of the pulmonary system. A small section of the double-walled pleural lining is cut away from the right lung. The left lung is sliced obliquely to reveal the lower airways, a small segment of which is shown greatly magnified. (From *Normal Aspects of Speech, Hearing, and Language,* ed. by Fred D. Minifie, Thomas J. Hixon, and Frederick Williams, 1973. Englewood Cliffs, NJ: Prentice-Hall, Inc. By permission.)

SUBGLOTTIC PRESSURE AND GLOTTAL ACTIVITY

In a summary of a frequently encountered viewpoint on air pressure below the vocal folds, Ladefoged (1962a, p. 248) creates the following analogy:

The four factors affecting the pressure of the air below the vocal cords may be considered by an analogy with a pair of bellows which has (1) a mechanism to pull the handles apart, corresponding to the inspiratory activity of the diaphragm and the external intercostals; (2) an opposing mechanism which will pull the handles together, corresponding to the expiratory activity of the internal intercostals and other muscles; (3) a variable orifice, corresponding to variations in the constrictions at the glottis, and in the vocal tract; and (4) a spring between the handles, corresponding to the relaxation pressure, which will exert a considerable force on the handles when they have been pulled wide part, with continually increasing force, as soon as the bellows have been closed beyond their normal unsqueezed position (which corresponds to the position of the lungs at the end of a normal expiration).

Ladefoged's bellows analogy is equally applicable to a description of the regulation of subglottic pressure and airflow rate in singing. However, the breath cycle in singing is almost always of longer duration than in speech. Following deep inspiration for the requirements of singing, the expiratory portion of the breath cycle is retarded through an acquired coordination of the muscles of the torso and the larynx. Agostoni (1970, pp. 105–106) details glottal response to subglottic pressure in the phonatory contest:

The breathing pattern during phonation consists of rapid inspirations and prolonged expirations. During the expiration the vocal cords are drawn together by the adductor muscles: the subglottic pressure pushes them apart, while their elastic recoil and the decrease of the lateral pressure due to the increase of kinetic pressure (Bernoulli principle) close them again, thus generating a periodic flow. This produces longitudinal vibrations of the air above the glottis at the frequency of the fundamental tone of the voice. . . .

To produce a tone of constant loudness and pitch the subglottic pressure must increase, while the vocal cord tension must decrease in order to keep pitch constant. Phonation requires therefore a fine coordination between the laryngeal and the chest wall muscles. . . .

The Bernoulli principle mentioned in the quotation holds that when a gas or a liquid is in motion, less than normal pressure is exerted on the surrounding environment. During the vibratory cycle, the vocal folds draw closer to each other, thereby narrowing the air passage sufficiently, so that the Bernoulli principle draws them together, if breath is flowing. Vennard (1967, p. 40) likens the trachea and larynx to an atomizer, to illustrate the suction force that results from the reduction in pressure caused by the flow of air or water. Although the arytenoids may be closing at a nearly constant rate, the vocal folds pull apart after the suction of the air brings them toward each other again.

This principle is of major importance in understanding the mechanics of phonation. In exhalation, the velocity of the air stream increases as it passes through the constriction of the glottal chink, and the vocal folds are sucked toward each other. The release of air results in a sudden decrease in pressure, and "the elasticity of the vocal-fold tissue, plus the Bernoulli effect, causes the vocal folds to snap back again into an adducted posture." (Zemlin, 1981, p. 185.)

Technical skill in singing is largely dependent on the singer's ability to achieve consistently that fine coordination of airflow and phonation—the vocal contest—which is determined by cooperation among the muscles of the larynx and the chest wall, and diaphragmatic contraction, a dynamic balancing between subglottic pressure and vocal-fold resistance. Von Leden (1968, p. 56) mentions that "fundamental investigations at different laryngeal research institutions support the contention that laryngeal efficiency is based mainly upon an interplay between two physical forces, a fine balance between subglottic pressure and the glottal resistance." In cultivated singing, thoracic, diaphragmatic, and abdominal aspects of respiration must be coordinated (dynamic muscle equilibrium) without exaggerated activity in any one of the three areas. How strange to ignore breath management if one is a teacher of singing!

THE TECHNIQUE OF *APPOGGIO*

There is an amazingly uniform concept of breath management in the international Italianate school, which has dominated serious twentieth-century vocalism. *Appoggio* cannot narrowly be defined as "breath support," as is sometimes thought, because *appoggio* includes resonance factors as well as breath management. *Appoggio* may be translated as "support" *(appoggiarsi a,* "to lean upon"). The historic Italian School did not separate the motor and resonance facets of phonation as have some other pedagogies. *Appoggio* is a system for combining and balancing muscles and organs of the trunk and neck, controlling their relationships to the supraglottal resonators, so that no exaggerated function of any one of them upsets the whole. As defined by *Enciclopedia Garzanti della musica* (1974, p. 17):

Appoggio, in the terminology of vocal technique, refers to the point of appoggio, whether it be of the abdominal or the thoracic region where the maximum muscular tension is experienced in singing (appoggio at the diaphragm, appoggio at the chest), or the part of the facial cavity where the cervical resonances of the sound are perceived (appoggio at the teeth, palatal appoggio, appoggio at the nape of the neck, and so forth). The points of appoggio vary according to the type of emission used.

With regard to breath management, *appoggio* maintains for a remarkable period of time a posture near that which pertained at the beginning of the inspiratory phase of the breath cycle. This initial posture ensures cooperative muscle activity in the pectoral, epigastric and umbilical regions, and diaphragmatic control. The total torso is involved. The powerful abdominal musculature undergirds the breath mechanism.

A practical description of *appoggio* follows. In *appoggio* technique, the sternum must initially find a moderately high position; this position is then retained throughout the inspiration–expiration cycle. Shoulders are relaxed, but the sternum never slumps. Because the ribs are attached to the sternum, sternal posture in part determines diaphragmatic position. If the sternum lowers, the ribs cannot maintain an expanded position, and the diaphragm must ascend more rapidly. Both the epigastric and umbilical regions should be stabilized so that a feeling of internal–external muscular balance is present. This sensation directly influences the diaphragm.

In the latter half of the nineteenth century, Francesco Lamperti (n.d., p. 33) described the resultant vocal contest (*lotta vocale*, also *lutta vocale*, and in French, *lutte vocale*) by which the inspiratory muscles (termed "respiratory muscles" by Lamperti) strive to retain their initial posture against the action of the expiratory muscles, thereby establishing, for a time, something close to an equilibrium:

> To sustain a given note the air should be expelled slowly; to attain this end, the respiratory [inspiratory] muscles, by continuing their action, strive to retain the air in the lungs, and oppose their action to that of the expiratory muscles, which is called the *lotta vocale*, or vocal struggle. On the retention of this equilibrium depends the just emission of the voice, and by means of it alone can true expression be given to the sound produced.

In *appoggio* the region between the sternum and the umbilicus moves outward on inspiration, but the chief outward movement occurs in the lateral planes (see Figure 1.3). This action does not correspond to the pushing outward of the lower abdominal wall (hypogastric, or pubic area; see Figure 1.3 for designated areas of the torso and abdomen), which is to be found in some breathing techniques. Following the initial expansion, a nearly imperceptible inward motion commences unless consciously resisted internally by counterbalancing pressure, experienced in the navel region, at the flanks, and in the lower back regions. The torso remains stable, with almost no movement in the area of the lateral planes; at the close of a long phrase, of course, some inward abdominal movement is apparent. There should be an awareness, when inhaling, of transverse expansion, the result of antagonism of the anterolateral muscles. These muscles include those of the rectus sheath, the rectus abdominis, the external and internal obliques, and the transversus abdominis. (See Figures 2.2, 2.3, and 2.4.)

Lateral distention is experienced at the level of the tenth rib and immediately below, between the tenth rib and the crest of the ilium (the hip bone). Balance of muscular action is felt both in the frontal regions (thoracic, epigastric and umbilical) and in the lateral–posterior (also lumbodorsal) areas (see Figures 2.2, 2.3, and 2.4).

In the technique of *appoggio* little or no feeling occurs in the pectoral region in inspiration, even though the pectoral muscles contribute to the supportive framework. Although the lower abdomen (hypogastric, or pubic, region) does not distend, there is a feeling of muscular connection from sternum to pelvis (see Figure 2.3). However, to move out the lower abdomen either during inspiration or during the execution of a phrase, as some singers are taught to do, is foreign to *appoggio* technique. Equally alien is the practice of pulling inward on the pubic area as a means of "supporting" the voice.

Whether the singer is breathing or singing, the same general posture should apply. As breath is expelled, some slight modification of posture ensues, but the singer's intent is to keep such postural changes to a minimum. This stabilized position would seem to be what Giovanni Battista Lamperti (1931, p. 36) had in mind when he asked, "Why should you get out of position while adding more energy to your breath power?"

The "position of singing" must remain throughout the act of singing. "Sing in the position of breathing—breathe in the position of singing" expresses this postural attitude. Posture need not be altered for the renewal of the breath.

No initial sensation of grabbing or holding the breath should be associated with singing. When a singer feels extreme muscle resistance to inhalation, in either pectoral or abdominal regions, a "full"

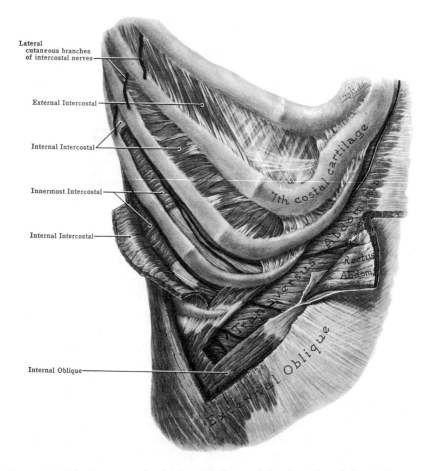

Figure 2.2. The intercostals, the lower ribs, and the muscles of the abdomen, showing the common direction of the fibers of the external intercostal and external oblique muscles, and the continuity of the internal intercostal with the internal oblique muscles at the anterior ends of the 9th, 10th, and 11th intercostal spaces. (From J. C. Boileau Grant, *An Atlas of Anatomy*, 5th ed., 1962. Baltimore: Williams & Wilkins Company. By permission.)

or "deep" breath is not the cause; unnecessary muscle antagonism is taking place. In primitive valvular function, glottal closure is the normal response to tension in the costal and abdominal regions. It is to be avoided in singing.

In inspiration for singing, the lungs should never feel crowded—only satisfied. Ewald Hering and Joseph Breuer were pioneers in the study of the reflex control of breathing. They drew attention to the sensory aspects of the reflex pathways to and from the lung during the respiratory cycle. With regard to lung distention:

[T]he prevailing degree of distention of the lung contributes

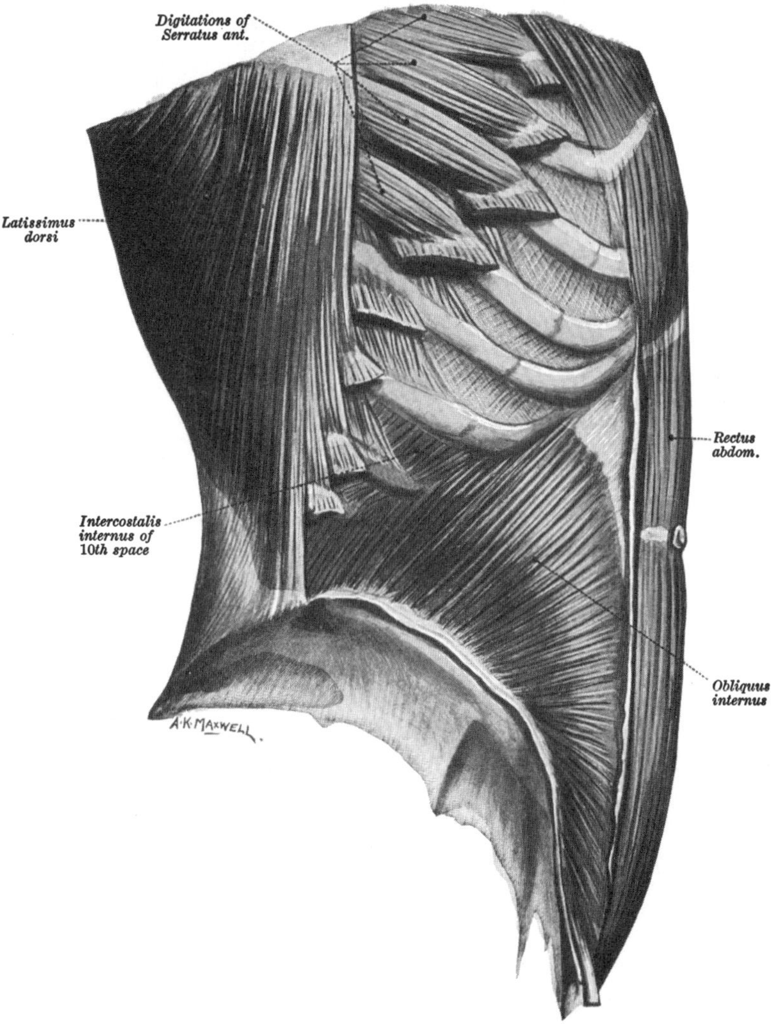

Figure 2.3. Dissection of the muscles of the right side of the trunk. The external oblique has been removed to show the internal oblique, but its digitations from the ribs have been preserved. The sheath of the rectus has been opened and its anterior wall removed. (From *Gray's Anatomy*, 36th ed., 1980, ed. by Peter L. Williams & Roger Warwick. Edinburgh: Churchill Livingstone. By permission.)

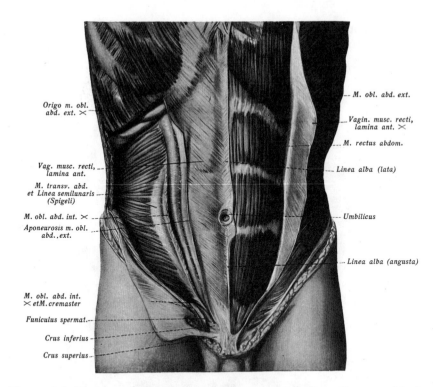

Figure 2.4. Muscles of the abdomen. (From O. Schultze, *Topographische Anatomie*, 4th ed., ed. by Wilhelm Lubosch, 1935. Munich: J. F. Lehmanns Verlag. By permission, Springer-Verlag.)

a modifying influence on the movements of breathing. . . . The lung, when it becomes more expanded by inspiration, or by inflation, exerts an inhibitory effect on inspiration and promotes expiration, and this effort is the greater the stronger the expansion. (Hering, 1868, p. 361).

"Crowding" the lungs will induce a quicker rate of expiration. The singer who takes an "easy" breath, who thereby merely "replenishes" the breath that has been used, will have a longer breath supply than does the singer who "crowds" the lungs with breath. Even in the case of the long phrase, expiratory reflexes will be under better control if the singer avoids exaggerated expansion. Breathing clavicularly gives the impression that the lungs are filled with breath, when actually the sensation the singer is experiencing is muscle tension, not lung expansion. Therefore, the proper "low" breath may at first seem less complete to the singer who is unaccustomed to transferring the sensation of a full breath from the pectoral region to the region of the tenth rib. However, in order to *avoid* high-chest (clavicular) breathing, the chest and sternum must be relatively high so that the muscles of the torso may move outward. (No expanding of the pectorals should occur with the intake of breath; they are positioned rather high, but they do not "feel" further expansion with inspiration.) A complete, not a "crowded," inspiration is appropriate.

Silent inspiration is the hallmark of *appoggio*. Noise, it should be recalled, results from resistance of the throat to inspired air. Whether taken in quickly or spread out over a period of time (however paced), whether through nose (which requires more time) or through mouth, the process of inspiration remains the same in the *appoggio* technique. Above all, the breath for singing must be inaudible.

It might be logically presumed that all techniques of singing embrace this functionally efficient approach to breath management, and that persons dealing professionally with singers recognize noiseless inspiration as part of correct vocal production. To the contrary, there are teachers of singing who hold that a noisy inspiration indicates an "open throat" ("Let's *hear* you open that throat!") and there are coaches and conductors, as well as accompanists, who find themselves disoriented unless the singer inhales noisily. Such viewpoints indicate serious lapses of technical knowledge regarding both good vocal function and good singing.

The exercises that follow are based on functional efficiency as induced by the *appoggio* technique.

Breath Management Exercises without Phonation

Phonation cannot take place until adduction of the glottis occurs. However, learning how to manage the breath efficiently for singing can be assisted through silent breathing exercises that prepare for the proper prephonatory position.

EXERCISE 2.1

RAISE THE ARMS ABOVE THE HEAD. RETURN THE ARMS TO THE SIDES WHILE RETAINING THE MODERATELY HIGH POSTURE OF THE STERNUM AND RIB CAGE. IF THE CHEST, AT THIS POINT, CANNOT BE RAISED SOMEWHAT HIGHER WITH AN UPWARD THRUST OF THE STERNUM, THE BASIC THORACIC POSTURE IS TOO HIGH; IF THE CHEST SINKS DURING EITHER INSPIRATION OR EXPIRATION, THE INITIAL THORACIC POSTURE WAS NOT SUFFICIENTLY HIGH.

BREATHE IN AND OUT, EASILY AND SILENTLY, MAKING CERTAIN THAT

THE STERNUM DOES NOT FALL AND THAT THE RIB CAGE DOES NOT
COLLAPSE. THE EPIGASTRIUM AND THE UMBILICAL REGION, AS WELL AS
THE RIB CAGE, MOVE OUTWARD WITH INSPIRATION. AT COMMENCEMENT
OF EXPIRATION, A SLIGHT INWARD MOVEMENT IS EXPERIENCED IN THE
UMBILICAL AREA, BUT NEITHER THE STERNUM NOR THE RIBS SHOULD
CHANGE POSITION. THE EXERCISE SHOULD BE ACCOMPLISHED BY
BREATHING THROUGH THE NOSE. FOLLOWING SEVERAL
INSPIRATION-EXPIRATION CYCLES OF NOSE BREATHING, THE SAME CYCLE
SHOULD THEN BE PRACTICED BY BREATHING THROUGH THE MOUTH. IT IS
ESSENTIAL THAT THE STRUCTURAL SUPPORT (POSTURE) AND THE
QUIESCENT VOCAL TRACT REMAIN UNCHANGED, WHETHER BREATH IS
TAKEN THROUGH THE NOSE OR THROUGH THE MOUTH. THERE SHOULD BE
COMPLETE SILENCE DURING BOTH INHALATION AND EXHALATION.

EXERCISE 2.2

RECLINE ON A FLAT SURFACE. BE CERTAIN THE HEAD IS NOT TILTED
BACKWARD WITH ELEVATED CHIN (HEAD AND SHOULDERS SHOULD BE IN
LINE). USUALLY, DEPENDING ON HOW THE HEAD SITS NATURALLY ON THE
SHOULDERS, IT WILL BE NECESSARY TO PLACE A BOOK UNDER THE HEAD
TO AVOID BACKWARD TILTING. BREATHE QUIETLY THROUGH PARTED LIPS,
THE FLAT HAND BRIDGING THE EPIGASTRIC AND UMBILICAL REGIONS (THE
AREA BETWEEN THE NAVEL AND THE STERNUM). OBSERVE THAT THE
EPIGASTRIC-UMBILICAL AREA MOVES OUTWARD BUT THAT THE LOWER
ABDOMEN (HYPOGASTRIC, OR PUBIC AREA) DOES NOT, UNLESS PURPOSELY
PUSHED OUTWARD. (FOR A MOMENT, MOVE OUT THE LOWER ABDOMINAL
WALL; NOTICE THE INWARD COLLAPSE OF THE RIB CAGE WHEN ONE
THRUSTS OUT THE LOWER ABDOMEN. THE FALSENESS OF LOW ABDOMINAL
DISTENTION AS A PART OF INHALATION WILL BE APPARENT AT ONCE.) THE
CHEST NEITHER RISES NOR FALLS DURING THE BREATH CYCLE (OR ONLY
SLIGHTLY), BECAUSE OF THE POSTURAL ALIGNMENT OF THE BODY IN THIS
RECUMBENT POSITION. BREATH INTAKE IS TOTALLY QUIET, AS IS BREATH
EXPULSION. MAINTAINING THIS RELATIONSHIP OF HEAD, NECK, AND
SHOULDERS, RISE TO A "NOBLE" STANDING POSITION. ALTHOUGH THE
DIAPHRAGM IS NOT IN EXACTLY THE SAME POSITION IN STANDING AND
LYING, THE AXIAL ALIGNMENT OF THE BODY IS SIMILAR IN BOTH
POSITIONS.

In both of these exercises there should be no sensation of
"crowding" the lungs, nor should there be any sensation of "holding"
or "storing" the breath.

The following exercises prolong the events of the breath cycle.
Many teachers of singing believe that Exercise 2.3 was used by the
famous castrato Farinelli. Although there is no written historical cor-
roboration, tradition maintains that Farinelli daily practiced this
exercise for long periods of time. He did so, it is thought, because he

could train the breath musculature essential to singing without tiring the voice. Some teachers attribute Farinelli's reputed astounding breath control, and his ability to renew breath silently and imperceptibly, to this exercise. If tension occurs during the suspension–exhalation aspect, the exercise is not being properly executed.

EXERCISE 2.3:

INHALE WHILE MENTALLY COUNTING FROM 1 TO 5 AT A MODERATE TEMPO, MAINTAINING ABSOLUTE SILENCE. KEEP PRECISE RHYTHM BY TAPPING A FINGER OR PENCIL. A METRONOME ALSO MAY BE HELPFUL. LIPS SHOULD BE PARTED THROUGHOUT THE THREE PARTS OF THE EXERCISE. COMPLETE BUT UNFORCED EXPANSION OF THE RIBS AND OF THE MUSCLES OF THE UMBILICAL-EPIGASTRIC AREA AND OF THE LUMBAR AREA SHOULD BE REALIZED.

SUSPEND THE BREATH WITHOUT ANY SENSATION OF HOLDING IT (GLOTTIS REMAINS OPEN, AN ACTION SOMETIMES TERMED "THE VAN DEN BERG MANEUVER" IN THE FIELD OF PHONIATRICS), WITHOUT ANY MUSCULAR TENSION IN EITHER THE VOCAL TRACT OR THE TORSO. THE POSITION OF THE RIB CAGE AND THE ABDOMINAL WALL IS RETAINED WHILE SILENTLY COUNTING FROM 1 TO 5 AT THE ORIGINAL TEMPO.

EXHALE SILENTLY, MAINTAINING AS FAR AS POSSIBLE THE SAME POSTURE OF STERNUM AND RIB CAGE, COUNTING 1 TO 5. THERE SHOULD BE RHYTHMIC CONTINUITY BETWEEN THE THREE PHASES OF THE EXERCISE (INHALATION, SUSPENSION, AND EXHALATION). IMMEDIATELY FOLLOWING COMPLETION OF THE THREE-PART BREATH CYCLE OF 1 THROUGH 5, MOVE WITHOUT PAUSE TO A CYCLE OF 1 THROUGH 6, PASSING THROUGH THE THREE SUCCESSIVE PHASES OF THE EXERCISE; IN THIS FASHION, INCREASE THE NUMBERS UNTIL 9, 10, OR PERHAPS 12 COUNTS HAVE BEEN ACHIEVED.

Exercise 2.3 may be graphed in this way:

```
     Inhale              Suspend              Exhale
   1 2 3 4 5 ─────────▶ 1 2 3 4 5 ─────────▶ 1 2 3 4 5
  1 2 3 4 5 6 ────────▶ 1 2 3 4 5 6 ───────▶ 1 2 3 4 5 6
 1 2 3 4 5 6 7 ───────▶ 1 2 3 4 5 6 7 ─────▶ 1 2 3 4 5 6 7
 1 2 3 4 5 6 7 8 ─────▶ 1 2 3 4 5 6 7 8 ───▶ 1 2 3 4 5 6 7 8
 1 2 3 4 5 6 7 8 9 ───▶ 1 2 3 4 5 6 7 8 9 ─▶ 1 2 3 4 5 6 7 8 9
1 2 3 4 5 6 7 8 9 10 ─▶ 1 2 3 4 5 6 7 8 9 10 ─▶ 1 2 3 4 5 6 7 8 9 10
```

As the numerical count is increased, inhalation will of necessity be paced over a period of time so that "partial breaths" must be introduced. The inhalatory process will be momentarily suspended at several points before complete lung capacity has been reached; inhalation will not be one continuous gesture. There will be several inspiratory phases without any intervening exhalation during the mental counting to, for example, 10. These additional inhalations alternate with brief moments of suspension of the breath, all within the single inspiratory gesture. There may be several such suspensions before full expansion is reached. This terraced inspiration is the "half breath," the "partial breath," what Giovanni Battista Lamperti (1931, p. 65) termed "thimbles-full" of breath.

Breath Management Exercises with Sibilants and Fricatives

EXERCISE 2.4: PROLONGATION OF THE SIBILANT [s]

CONTROL OF MUSCLES OF THE TORSO DURING EXHALATION CAN BE GAINED BY THE USE OF THE PROLONGED SIBILANT. SOUND IS INTRODUCED, BUT SUSTAINED PITCH IS NOT. A "NOBLE" CHEST POSTURE SHOULD FIRST BE ESTABLISHED. FOLLOWING SILENT INSPIRATION, BREATH IS EXHALED VERY SLOWLY WHILE SUSTAINING A CONSTANT SIBILANT NOISE. THE SOUND SHOULD BE BARELY AUDIBLE.

ONE HAND IS PLACED ON THE EPIGASTRIC–UMBILICAL REGION, THE OTHER HAND ON THE FLANKS JUST BELOW THE RIB CAGE. THE ABDOMINAL WALL GIVES NO INITIAL INWARD IMPULSE NOR DOES IT MOVE INWARD DURING THE EXERCISE UNTIL THE LAST FEW SECONDS. THE AIM OF THE EXERCISE IS TO MAINTAIN THE RIB CAGE AND THE ABDOMINAL WALL NEAR TO THE INSPIRATORY POSITION THROUGHOUT MOST OF THE EXERCISE. EVENTUALLY THE ABDOMEN MUST MOVE INWARD, AT THE CLOSE OF THE EXPIRATION, BUT THE RIB CAGE REMAINS LONGER IN THE POSTURE OF INSPIRATION, AND THE STERNUM DOES NOT LOWER.

The exercise should take 40 to 50 seconds. (Time it with a watch that has a second hand.) Subsequent cycles, consecutively executed with a quick but silent breath, may at first be difficult. The exercise goes to the heart of inspiratory–expiratory control. Longer breath cycles become possible with practice.

EXERCISE 2.5: THE AUDIBLE PANT

PANT AUDIBLY, THOUGH GENTLY. SUPPLE, FLEXIBLE, AGILE MOTION OF THE ABDOMINAL MUSCULATURE IS FELT BY THE HAND PLACED ON THE UMBILICAL–EPIGASTRIC REGION. THE SURFACE MOVEMENT INDICATES RAPID INHALATION–EXHALATION PATTERNS. IF GLOTTAL ADDUCTION WERE INTRODUCED, RAPID ONSET VOCALISES WOULD RESULT.

EXERCISE 2.6: THE SILENT PANT

PANT SILENTLY AND AS RAPIDLY AS POSSIBLE. ESTABLISH THE PATTERN OF UMBILICAL–EPIGASTRIC MOTION PRESENT IN THE AUDIBLE PANT, WITHOUT

SOUND, AND WITHOUT ACTUAL INHALATION AND EXHALATION TAKING PLACE. EPIGASTRIC MUSCLE ACTION IS NOW INDEPENDENT OF THE BREATH CYCLE.

The ability to induce this abdominal muscular movement, independent of breath action, is essential when agility and rapid intervallic articulation are required. Such umbilical–epigastric motion is sometimes termed (too narrowly) "the bouncing diaphragm." (see Chapter 3.)

EXERCISE 2.7: RAPID EXECUTION OF THE VOICELESS LABIODENTAL FRICATIVE CONTINUANT [f]

THIS EXERCISE IS BASED ON THE EPIGASTRIC IMPULSE NECESSITATED BY HIGH-FREQUENCY VIBRATIONS THAT RESULT WHEN AIR PASSES THROUGH THE NARROW APERTURE OF THE LABIODENTAL ORIFICE. THE EXPENDITURE OF BREATH MUST BE AT A SOMEWHAT HIGH LEVEL, YET EMISSION OF THE BREATH IS CONTROLLED BY THE ABDOMINAL MUSCULATURE AND, IN TURN, BY THE RESULTING IMPACT ON THE NARROWED LABIODENTAL ORIFICE (KANTNER AND WEST, 1960, P. 145).

ONE HAND SHOULD BE PLACED ON THE UMBILICAL–EPIGASTRIC REGION, THE OTHER JUST BELOW THE RIBS AND ABOVE THE ILIAC CREST (UPPERMOST PORTION OF THE PELVIS), AT THE SIDE OF THE BODY. A QUIET BREATH SHOULD BE TAKEN, PACED OVER SEVERAL SECONDS, FOLLOWED BY A SERIES OF RAPID, LABIODENTAL FRICATIVE CONTINUANT NOISES, REPRESENTED PHONETICALLY BY THE SYMBOL [f].

SUFFICIENT IMPULSE SHOULD BE GIVEN EACH FRICATIVE IN THE SERIES SO THAT ABDOMINAL MOTION IS DISTINCT. YET THE EXIT OF THE BREATH MUST BE SO CONTROLLED THAT A SERIES OF SHORT EXPULSIONS CAN OCCUR ON ONE BREATH WITHOUT ANY COLLAPSE OF THE RIB CAGE, WITH NO LOWERING OF THE STERNUM, AND WITH MINIMAL INWARD MOTION OF THE UMBILICAL–EPIGASTRIC REGION.

EXERCISE 2.8: SLOW EXECUTION OF THE VOICELESS LABIODENTAL FRICATIVE CONTINUANT [f]

THIS EXERCISE IS A VERY OLD ONE, LONG ASSOCIATED WITH THE INTERNATIONAL ITALIANATE SCHOOL. THE SINGER IS REQUESTED TO "BLOW OUT SIX OR EIGHT CANDLES SUCCESSIVELY WITH ONE BREATH, BUT WITH SEPARATE ABDOMINAL IMPULSES." THE EXERCISE SHOULD BE DONE IN SUCCESSIVE PHASES, PERHAPS FOUR TIMES IN A ROW, WITH A DEEP AND SILENT INHALATION AFTER EACH SERIES:

[f f f f f f]⁹ [f f f f f f]⁹ [f f f f f f]⁹ [f f f f f f]⁹

DURING THE STACCATO EXECUTION OF THE PHONEME [f], NO PART OF THE ANTEROLATERAL WALL SHOULD BE DRAWN INWARD; AN INTERNAL-EXTERNAL BALANCE OF THE ABDOMINAL MUSCULATURE SHOULD BE THE AIM. STERNUM AND RIB CAGE REMAIN STATIONARY.

Breath Management Exercises Involving Phonation

Control over three specifics of breath pacing (breath management) is essential to efficient function in singing: (1) the rate and ease of each initial inhalation; (2) the variable rate of breath emission (in response to phrase demand); and (3) the quiet renewal of breath energy (replenishment of the source of power).

The exercises that follow systematically drill these three aspects of control. They establish the appropriate prephonatory tuning, the dynamic muscle equilibrium appropriate to subsequent phonation. Comments by van den Berg (1968d, p. 140) at a symposium for the New York Academy of Sciences seem to verify the need for the respiratory precision these vocalises attempt to establish. (Previous discussion had been concerned with possible actions of laryngeal and intercostal muscles, the diaphragm, the accessory muscles of the upper torso, and the mechanical relationships of the rib cage and diaphragm in phonation):

> [T]he trained singer and the trained speaker achieve their fine control by means of a balance between expiratory and inspiratory muscles. . . . In this respect I might suggest that all these muscles enter into this balance; otherwise there would be a weak place somewhere. I might compare this balance with a balance of forces when one measures the reaction time of a finger that is to press a button for an acoustic signal. This reaction time is long if one activates the agonists [contracting muscles opposed in action by other muscles called antagonists] after the receipt of the signal; i.e., if all muscles are inactive before the signal. The reaction time is much shorter when both the agonists and the antagonists are already active before the signal, the antagonist releasing and the agonist becoming more active upon receipt of the signal.

Most of the exercises that follow are easy and do not have to be practiced in order to be mastered. However, their value lies in their function as systematic material for coordinating fast respiration-phonation responses.

These vocalises may be sung on any vowel. An initial metronomic marking of ♩ = 50 is in order, but tempo should be varied. There should be no "overstuffing"; the ability to relax the glottis, and to take a silent breath, is essential for accomplishing fine respiratory-phonatory control. Regardless of the speed with which breath is renewed, each inspiration must be totally inaudible.

Pitch level should be lower middle voice, adjusted to keys

appropriate to each category of voice. As skill increases, pitch levels may both rise and lower from the medium pitch level. (Keys here indicated are for lyric soprano and tenor voices.)

Rhythmic accuracy should be carefully observed, including the duration of the final note of each vocalise.

EXERCISE 2.9: RENEWAL OF BREATH ENERGY DURING EXTENDED PAUSES

(any vowel)

EXERCISE 2.10: MODERATELY-PACED RENEWAL OF BREATH ENERGY

(any vowel)

INHALATION IS PACED OVER TWO BEATS, TAKEN NEITHER TOO EARLY NOR TOO LATE FOR THE SUBSEQUENT ATTACK.

EXERCISE 2.11: QUICKLY-PACED RENEWAL OF BREATH ENERGY BETWEEN ONSETS

(any vowel)

IT IS APPARENT THAT THE SINGER DOES NOT NEED TO RENEW BREATH BETWEEN THE FOURTH AND FIRST BEATS OF THE BAR. THE PURPOSE IS TO DEVELOP THE ABILITY TO RELAX THE GLOTTIS WITH THE BREATH, REGARDLESS OF LUNG CAPACITY, AND TO DO SO WITHOUT "OVERCROWDING."

EXERCISE 2.12: QUICKLY-PACED RENEWAL OF BREATH ENERGY WITHIN A CONTINUING PHRASE

(any vowel)

IN THIS VOCALISE, THE SINGER MUST LEARN TO REGULATE RELATIVELY
QUICK INHALATIONS WITHOUT ALTERING THE "POSITION OF SINGING,"
THAT IS, THE PREPHONATORY TUNING OF THE LARYNGEAL MUSCULATURE,
AND OF THE SUPRAGLOTTAL VOCAL TRACT DURING RENEWAL OF THE SO-
CALLED "PARTIAL" BREATHS.

EXERCISE 2.13: ALTERNATION OF FULL AND "PARTIAL" BREATH ENERGY RENEWAL

(any vowel)

THIS VOCALISE HAS VALUE ONLY IF THE PHRASE AND BREATH
INDICATIONS ARE STRICTLY OBSERVED. THE QUICKLY-PACED BREATHS IN
BAR 4 MAY AT FIRST APPEAR EXCESSIVE; THEY PURPOSELY DEMAND A
DELICATE ADJUSTMENT OF SUBGLOTTIC PRESSURE AND OF GLOTTAL
RELAXATION. *THE FREEDOM TO RELAX THE GLOTTIS AND TO REPLENISH
THE BREATH (NO MATTER HOW QUICK A TRANSACTION) IS INDICATIVE OF
PRECISE INSPIRATORY–PHONATORY COORDINATION.*

EXERCISE 2.14: RENEWAL OF BREATH ENERGY WITHIN BRIEFER AND LONGER PHRASES

(any vowel)

THE SMALL, SILENT ACTIONS OF BREATH RENEWAL MAKE THIS VOCALISE
IMPORTANT FOR ACHIEVING CORRECT POSTURAL AND LARYNGEAL
RELATIONSHIPS, WHILE ADDING TO BREATH ENERGY.

**EXERCISE 2.15: RENEWAL OF BREATH ENERGY IN
ALTERNATING BRIEF AND EXTENDED PHRASES**

(any vowel)

The ability to relax the glottis, and to renew breath capacity at whatever rate of occurrence, is fundamental to dynamic, flexible muscle adjustments in singing. To avoid static hypogastric or epigastric distention, the delicate balancing of the muscular activity in the anterolateral abdominal wall and the laryngeal muscular response should be drilled through such traditional vocalises as these.

BREATH-PACING VERSUS "MORE SUPPORT"

Almost any vocalise is a breath-management exercise. Vocalises indicated in this book as useful in developing precision in the onset are equally concerned with breath management. Exercises devoted to the development of agility and sostenuto are also breath-management vocalises. Any error in vocal technique, or any accomplishment of technical skill in singing, usually can be traced to techniques of breath management; control of the breath is synonymous with control of the singing instrument.

Perhaps this explains why the most frequent expression in vocal pedagogy seems to be "more support." To the poor voice student, such advice must appear a catchall nostrum that automatically surfaces when the teacher's ingenuity fails. (Can it be denied that this perception may be accurate?)

Unless the singer, either student or professional, understands the delicate physical balances appropriate to the shifting demands of breath management, to call for "more support" only complicates the task of balancing subglottic pressure, airflow rate, and vocal-fold approximation. In fact, it may well be that too much muscle activity is present in the torso; requesting "more support" may only exacerbate problems of dynamic muscle equilibrium.

Such directions as "fill out the rubber tire," "expand the balloon," "open out the spine," and "squeeze the dime" usually result in unnecessary pressure on the viscera; thrusting out the abdominal wall another inch, pushing or stretching with the dorsal muscles, and a still heavier anal sphincteral closure are actions that inhibit freedom of breath control.

In opposition to "more support," *pacing of the breath* is recommended. Control over the speed and ease of inhalation, and over the expiratory rate, can be acquired in a systematic manner, as indicated in the previous vocalises.

Contrary to what is sometimes assumed, exercises aimed at increasing the time during which breath can be "held" have questionable value as aids in breath control. Such exercises are based on an extreme degree of subglottic pressure and static laryngeal function; they tend to induce earlier breath expulsion. Breath-holding exercises are often thought to increase vital capacity, but lung *capacity* does not necessarily relate to the art of singing. The important factor is that, through training, the singer can learn a more efficient use of expanded capacity (W. J. Gould, 1977, p. 4).

By now it must be clear that systems of breath control which consciously induce the collapse of the rib cage, request a "relaxed" sternum, promulgate lower abdominal distention, or require inward movement of the abdomen in inspiration, are contrary to functionally efficient practices of breath management for singing.

In summation:

1. Breath management is partly determined by the singer's concept of what takes place physiologically during the inhalation–exhalation cycle. The singer ought not to base a method of "support" on incorrect information regarding the physical processes involved in singing.

2. The same breath coordination of the *appoggio* technique occurs whether a complete breath is taken within a split second or paced over a longer period, whether through nose or mouth.

3. Cultivation of the so-called "partial" breath is as essential to good vocal technique as the ability to take the "full" breath.

4. Good physical condition is necessary to proper coordination, but breath capacity and management are largely determined by skill and not through the enlargement of organs or muscles. Breath-holding exercises teach one to hold the breath and have little to do with lung expansion or with muscle coordination during phonation.

5. In order for inhalation to be efficient (avoiding maladjustment of any part of the vocal tract), it must be silent. (In cumulative phrases, minimal sound of breath intake may be heard occasionally even in skillful singing, but such noise should be kept to the barest minimum.)

6. Tension is not "support." Increased muscle resistance is not necessarily an indication of better breath management.

7. "Relaxation" is a relative term; breathing involves muscle antagonism (and synergism) just as does any other physical activity. Energy for the singing voice demands muscle coordination between the breath source (the motor) and the larynx (the vibrator).

8. During the "vocal contest" *(la lotta vocale)*, suppleness, agility, and flexibility characterize the activity of the diaphragm and the epigastrium and the muscles of the thorax and neck. A noble posture permits such activity. Prephonatory exactitude combines breath and phonation. Such precision may be acquired through the systematic drill of breath management—breath pacing—exercises.

Agility in Singing

Flexible Application of Breath Power

Passages that move swiftly—*fioriture, Rouladen,* rapid melismas, embellishment, and trill—are not decorations on the surface of vocal technique. The same umbilical–epigastric control that permits the precise onset, the staccato, the pant, and the execution of velocity or coloratura passages also produces the sostenuto (the sustained line) in singing. Both staccato and legato articulation require prephonatory muscle activity, which Astraquillo et al. (1977, p. 516) term MAP (muscle action potential):

> With both staccato and legato articulation, muscle activity is seen preceding the onset of the voice. MAP phasic activity is evident . . . in the following instances: (1) in staccato exercises at high pitch and high intensity, (2) in rapid legato and agility exercises for all types of voices executed in three dynamic levels, and (3) in air depletion at the end of a phrase.

Agility and sostenuto are opposing poles of vocal proficiency, but both are produced by the same muscle participants. Dynamic muscle balance is determined by synergism of muscles of the torso, consisting of alternating movements of engagement and disengagement at a rapidly occurring rate, and the responding supple adjustments of the muscles and tissues of the larynx. Strength and flexibility are brought into balance.

It is essential to any vocal category, whether or not the literature of that vocal type demands it, that agility be part of the singer's daily practice. A basso profundo is as much in need of the technical facility of agility as is the coloratura soprano. Unless the singer, regardless of vocal classification, is able to negotiate running passages and melismas cleanly, sostenuto passages will lack ease of production.

In spite of skillful technique that retards the upward coursing of the diaphragm during expiration, such diaphragmatic ascent begins, to some degree, soon after the inspiratory phase of the breath cycle is completed. Much of the technique of singing is to delay the rate of expiration (the first two chapters of this book are largely devoted to establishing that capability), but muscle rigidity cannot efficiently accomplish such a delaying action. Alternation of muscle tension and relaxation depends on the presence of flexibility. Good singing combines both power and flexibility.

There is a danger during sustained singing, especially when the tessitura is high and the writing is dramatic, to fix an energy level. At such moments, the imagination is kindled, the flow of adrenaline increases, the body is keyed up, and the full athleticism of the singer is brought into play. Such passages risk introducing tension and subsequent vocal fatigue. How can a singer reveal the powerful, expressive sweep of the voice and still remain free? The answer lies in the agility factor. Even if the climactic phrase consists of a series of whole notes at slow tempo, *agileness* must be present.

Although the sensation of agile dynamic muscle balance must be subjectively experienced, certain of its hallmarks can be identified: abdominal muscle antagonism *(appoggio)* feels both firm and supple; power and energy are not static conditions; breath renewal remains easy.

The feeling of suppleness in fast-moving melismatic passages is akin to the umbilical–epigastric movement experienced in rapid, silent panting. (See Chapter 2.) This movement in the anterior abdominal wall resembles quick staccato onset activity, incorporated, however, into the articulated legato.

Although there is a relationship between the function of properly articulated legato passages and staccato articulation, all tendency toward aspiration as a device for articulating moving pitches must be avoided. The amateur chorister may resort to interpolated "ha-ha-ha-ha" syllables as a means for achieving clean moving passages, but the skilled singer may not.

Equally undesirable is the substitution of straight-tone for vibrant timbre, simply because the pitches move quickly. Melismas must be sung with the same vibrancy as in sustained passages.

The four parts that make up the mechanism of singing—energizing, vibratory, resonatory and articulatory—can be systematically drilled into an integrated whole. Astraquillo et al. (1977, p. 499) identify these factors as part of "the instantaneous body–voice coordination" of the singer:

> The singer coordinates the resonating space, vocal cord vibration, and the volume of the total phonatory tract with the expiratory effort which produces the pressure and flow of air needed to drive the larynx. During phonation, in the production of a tone of constant pitch and loudness, the subglottic pressure and the airflow through the larynx

remain constant. . . . [T]he entire mechanism described [here] for singing depends upon the instantaneous body–voice coordination as determined by abdominal muscular control.

Agility patterns play an important role in inducing efficient coordination among the separate parts of the vocal mechanism. Such patterns are to be alternated with exercises still to be considered, such as those that deal with sostenuto, registration, resonator adjustment, vowel modification, and dynamic control.

EXERCISES FOR THE ACQUISITION OF AGILITY

Because of the necessity to organize the technical factors of singing in some systematic way, agility patterns are grouped here together. They are progressively difficult (some patterns are more difficult for one singer than for another). In the following exercises, the direction of pitch is often altered, rhythmic patterns are varied, and narrow and wide intervallic leaps are juxtaposed, sometimes within the same vocalise. Only after mastery of the less-complicated agility vocalises should the singer move on to the more difficult exercises. Each vocalise is to be sung in several neighboring keys, series-wise. Usually, they should be first sung in middle voice; range is to be expanded as ease develops. Exercises 3.21 through 3.24 are for the technically advanced singer.

EXERCISE 3.1

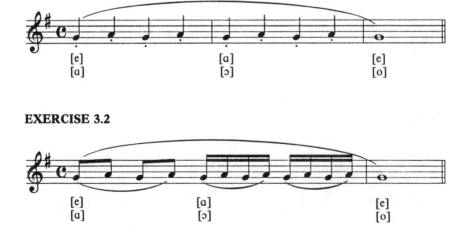

EXERCISE 3.2

EXERCISE 3.3

[i]	[e]	[a]
[e]	[a]	[i]
[o]	[a]	[u]

EXERCISE 3.4

[i]	[e]	[a]
[a]	[e]	[i]
[o]	[ɔ]	[u]

EXERCISE 3.5

[i]	[e]	[a]
[e]	[a]	[i]
[o]	[o]	[u]

EXERCISE 3.6

| [i] | [e] | [a] |
| [o] | [a] | [u] |

EXERCISE 3.7

[a]	[e]	[i]
[i]	[o]	[a]
[o]	[a]	[u]

EXERCISE 3.8

[i]	[e]	[ɑ]
[u]	[e]	[i]
[o]	[i]	[u]

EXERCISE 3.9

[i]	[e]	[ɔ]	[ɑ]
[o]	[ɛ]	[e]	[i]
[ɑ]	[u]	[e]	[o]

EXERCISE 3.10

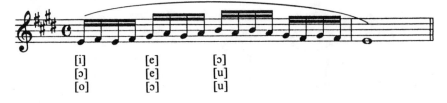

[i]	[e]	[ɔ]
[ɔ]	[e]	[u]
[o]	[ɔ]	[u]

EXERCISE 3.11

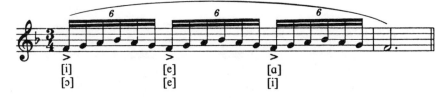

[i]	[e]	[ɑ]
[ɔ]	[e]	[i]

EXERCISE 3.12

[i]
[e]
[ɔ]

EXERCISE 3.13

[i]   [e]   [a]
[a]   [e]   [i]

EXERCISE 3.14

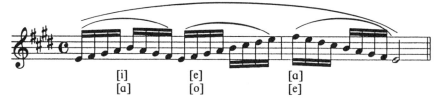

[i]   [e]   [a]
[a]   [o]   [e]

EXERCISE 3.15

[i ——————————————————]
[e ——————————————————]
[a ——————————————————]

EXERCISE 3.16

[i ——————————————————]
[e ——————————————————]
[a ——————————————————]

EXERCISE 3.17

[i]   [e]   [a]
[a]   [e]   [i]
[o]   [a]   [ɔ]

EXERCISE 3.18

[a ————————————————]
[e ————————————————]
[o ————————————————]

EXERCISE 3.19

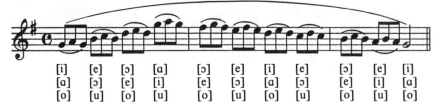

[i]	[e]	[ɔ]	[a]	[ɔ]	[e]	[i]	[e]	[ɔ]	[e]	[i]
[a]	[ɔ]	[e]	[i]	[e]	[ɔ]	[a]	[ɔ]	[e]	[i]	[a]
[o]	[u]	[o]	[u]	[o]	[u]	[o]	[u]	[o]	[u]	[o]

EXERCISE 3.20

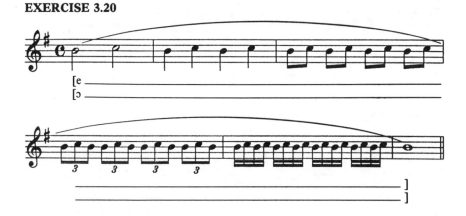

[e ————————————————————————
[ɔ ————————————————————————

————————————————————————]
————————————————————————]

EXERCISE 3.21

[a ————————————————]
[o ————————————————]
[e ————————————————]
[i ————————————————]

EXERCISE 3.22

[e ———————————————————————————————————]
[ɔ ———————————————————————————————————]

EXERCISE 3.23

[i ———————————————————————————
[e ———————————————————————————
[ɔ ———————————————————————————

————————————————————————]
————————————————————————]
————————————————————————]

EXERCISE 3.24

[e ————————————————————————————————
[ɔ ————————————————————————————————
[ɑ ————————————————————————————————

—————————————————————————————]
—————————————————————————————]
—————————————————————————————]

CHAPTER 4

The Resonant Voice

Supraglottic Considerations in Singing

Systematic exercises for coordinating the respiratory and the phonatory systems have been suggested thus far. Two other systems of the singing instrument remain to be considered: the resonatory and the articulatory. No clear division exists between the latter two systems. Articulation, to some extent, controls resonance.

Laryngeally-produced sound (the result of airflow and vocal fold approximation) is modified by a mechanical acoustic filter, the vocal tract (see Figure 4.1). Minifie (1973, p. 243) points out that the shape and size of the vocal tract determines the nature of the filtering properties. Baer et al. (1978, p. 49) state that laryngeal sound "depends on the acoustic properties of the filter that are excited by the source." They suggest that, although there are basic acoustic principles which apply to both speaking and singing, singing involves different patterns of control over the source and the filter. Clearly, in both speech and song (Baer et al., 1979, p. 51)

> (1) [M]ovements of the articulators affect tube or cavity dimensions in the vocal tract; (2) these shapes affect the resonances (that is, the filter function) of the vocal tract; (3) this change in the filter function affects what we hear.

The vocal tract resonator tube consists of the pharynx, the mouth, and at times the nose, (see Figure 4.1). By skillfully combining the resonating cavities, vocal timbre can be controlled (see Appendix III

Figure 4.1. The voice organ is composed of the lungs, the larynx, the pharynx, the mouth, and the nose, shown in longitudinal section (a). The larynx is a short tube at the base of which are twin in-foldings of mucous membrane, the vocal folds (b). The larynx opens into the pharynx; the opening is protected during swallowing by the epiglottis. The larynx, pharynx, and mouth (and in nasal sounds also the nose) constitute the vocal tract. The vocal tract is a resonator whose shape, which determines vowel sounds, is modified by changes in the position of the articulators: the lips, the jaw, the tip and body of the tongue, and the larynx. The vocal folds are opened for breathing and are closed for phonation by the pivoting arytenoid cartilages. (From Johan Sundberg, "The Acoustics of the Singing Voice," *Scientific American*, March 1977, Vol. 236, No. 3. By permission.)

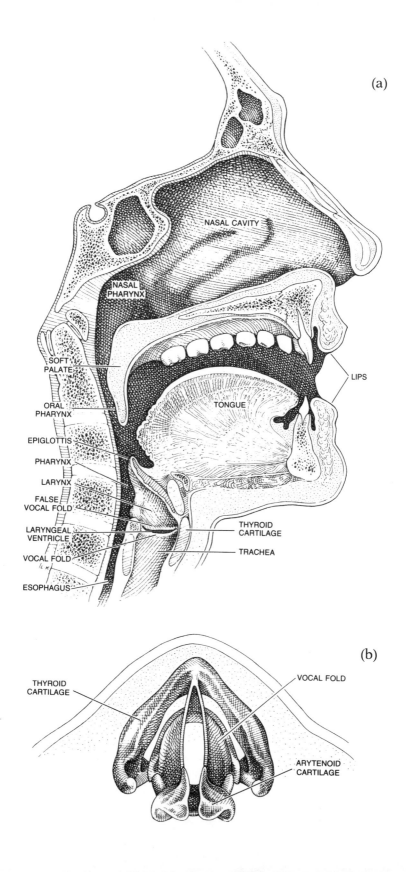

(a)

NASAL CAVITY

NASAL
PHARYNX

SOFT
PALATE

ORAL
PHARYNX

EPIGLOTTIS

PHARYNX

LARYNX

FALSE
VOCAL FOLD

LARYNGEAL
VENTRICLE

VOCAL FOLD

ESOPHAGUS

TONGUE

LIPS

THYROID
CARTILAGE

TRACHEA

(b)

THYROID
CARTILAGE

VOCAL FOLD

ARYTENOID
CARTILAGE

for the physiology of the vocal tract resonator system). The tube responds to the demands of articulation presented by vowels and consonants.

VOWEL FORMANTS

Complex tones, such as those generated by the larynx, are composed of frequencies that are integral multiples of the lowest frequency. The first component is the fundamental frequency (the first harmonic), and the others are overtones. A partial is a harmonic component of this complex tone, and the sound spectrum is made up of the resonance frequencies, which produce peaks, called formants.

Kantner and West (1960, p. 68) describe how resonance patterns produce recognizable vowels:

> All vowels, per se, have resonance but each vowel has its own distinct pattern of resonance that is the result of the number, frequencies and energy distribution of the overtones that are present. It is by means of these differences in the overall patterns of resonance that we are able to hear and discriminate one vowel from another. These changing resonance patterns are produced by altering shape and size of the discharging orifice.

The shaping of the resonator tube produces prominent distributions of acoustic energy, a phenomenon that has led to the identification of two frequency maxima called formants, for each vowel sound (Luchsinger and Arnold, 1965, p. 462). Although frequencies vary from voice to voice on the same vowel, the formants tend to appear in a fairly predictable manner (see Figure 4.2).

When the resonance cavities match the shape for a particular vowel, a pitch is determinable even without complete vocal-fold approximation, as can be illustrated by loudly whispering the cardinal vowels [i, e, ɑ, o, u] in sequence. A descending pitch pattern results (Aikin, 1910, p. 50). Regardless of the raising or the lowering of pitch, harmonic partials that match shapes of mouth and pharynx (vocal tract configuration) identify the vowel. We hear the same vowel, determined by its typical acoustic spectrum, even though the pitch of the voice may traverse the scale.

Minifie (1973, p. 243), in an exposition of speech acoustics and vowel formation, identifies the physical factors that produce the front vowels, the central vowels, and the back vowels:

> If the major constriction of the airway during vowel production is the result of elevating the tongue tip and blade so that

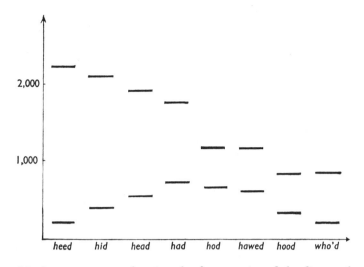

Figure 4.2. A spectrogram showing the frequencies of the first and second formants of some of the English vowels. (From Peter Ladefoged, *Elements of Acoustic Phonetics,* 1962. Tenth impression, 1974. Chicago: The University of Chicago Press. By permission.)

the point of vocal tract constriction occurs near the alveolar ridge, the vowel is called a front vowel. Included in this category are vowels [i, ɪ, e, ɛ, æ, a]. If the major constriction of the airway is between the dorsum of the tongue and the velum or between the dorsum of the tongue and the posterior pharyngeal wall, the vowel is called a back vowel. Included in this category are the vowels [u, ʊ, o, ɔ, ɑ]. The remaining vowel sounds are produced with either no obvious points of vocal tract constriction, or with the major point of constriction occurring at the region of the hard palate. These sounds are called central vowels and include [ʌ, ə, ɚ, ɜ].

Specific vocal tract configurations, therefore, can be directly associated with vowel differentiation (see Figure 4.3). These include the posture of the hump of the tongue in the vocal tract; the extent of constriction between the tongue and the velum; length of the tongue in regard to constriction at certain points in the vocal tract; lip separation; lip rounding, jaw separation; velopharyngeal posture; and tongue constrictions which occur in some phonetic postures, as in the retroflex [ɚ] and [ɝ]. These variables can be joined, as, for example, in the extent of lip separation or rounding related to tongue or palate constrictions (see Figure 4.4).

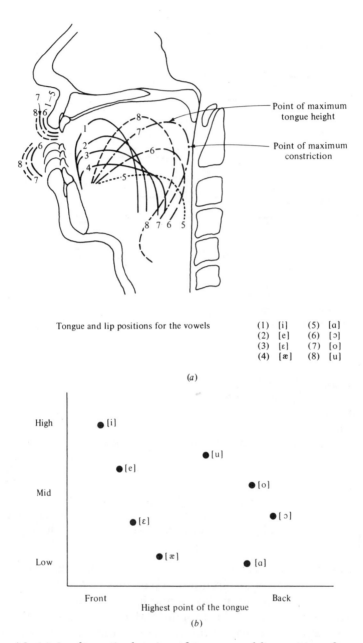

Tongue and lip positions for the vowels

(1)	[i]	(5)	[ɑ]
(2)	[e]	(6)	[ɔ]
(3)	[ɛ]	(7)	[o]
(4)	[æ]	(8)	[u]

(a)

(b)

Figure 4.3. (a) A schematic drawing of tongue and lip positions for certain vowels. (b) Location of the high point of the tongue for various vowels. (From *Normal Aspects of Speech, Hearing, and Language,* ed. by Fred D. Minifie, Thomas J. Hixon, and Frederick Williams, 1973. Englewood Cliffs, NJ: Prentice-Hall, Inc. By permission.)

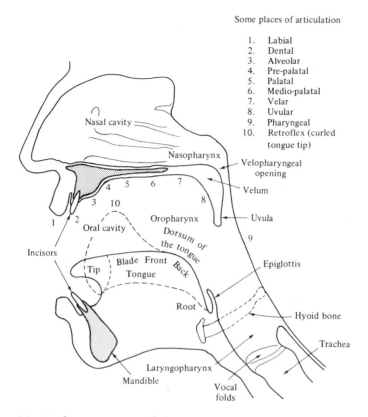

Some places of articulation

1.	Labial
2.	Dental
3.	Alveolar
4.	Pre-palatal
5.	Palatal
6.	Medio-palatal
7.	Velar
8.	Uvular
9.	Pharyngeal
10.	Retroflex (curled tongue tip)

Figure 4.4. A schematic view of the articulators, vocal tract cavities, and places of articulation. (From *Normal Aspects of Speech, Hearing, and Language,* ed. by Fred D. Minifie, Thomas J. Hixon, and Frederick Williams, 1973. Englewood Cliffs, NJ: Prentice-Hall, Inc. By permission.)

Much of the technical work in singing is given to the balancing of the extremes of acoustic configuration of the vocal tract. Obviously, the upper partials essential to the front vowels require a higher forward tongue posture than do the back vowels. The front vowels demand a narrower channel in the forward area of the mouth, thereby creating more room in the pharynx than is present with back vowel configurations (see Figure 4.5). Bloomer (1953, p. 239) notes that palatal elevation, which contributes to pharyngeal dimension and over-all vocal tract length, is also higher on the front vowels than on the back vowels. Acoustic distortion of the vowel will result if the tongue is held low and flat in the oral cavity when the acoustic shaping of the vowel is determined by a quite different

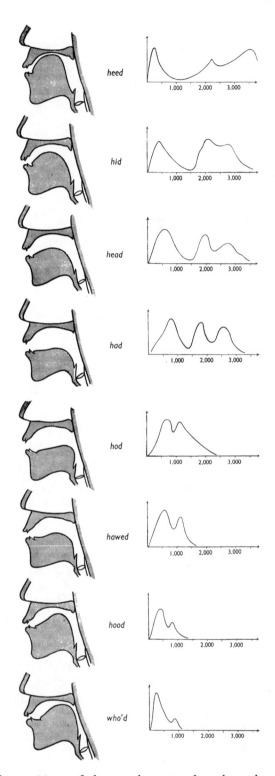

Figure 4.5. The positions of the vocal organs (based on data from X-ray photographs) and the spectra of the vowel sounds in the middle of the words *heed, hid, head, had, hod, hawed, hood, who'd.* (From Peter Ladefoged, *Elements of Acoustic Phonetics,* 1962. Tenth impression, 1974. Chicago: University of Chicago Press. By permission.)

tongue position. Acoustic distortion is audible if the tongue is held high when it ought to be low, or vice versa.

THE SINGER'S FORMANT

Formant frequencies are peaks that determine the shape of the acoustic spectrum (spectral envelope) of a vowel. However, in singing, another factor of spectral energy is displayed in the area of 2500 to 3200 Hz (see Figure 4.6), which usually is present in "resonant" singing, regardless of the vowel (Sundberg, 1977a, pp. 84–85). There is a long history of interest in the singer's formant (also, "the singing formant"). This phenomenon is by no means a recent discovery. Vennard (1967, p. 128) dubbed this resonance factor the "2800 factor," and suggested that the ringing quality of "2800" results when the resonators are in tune with the vibrator. Vennard based his

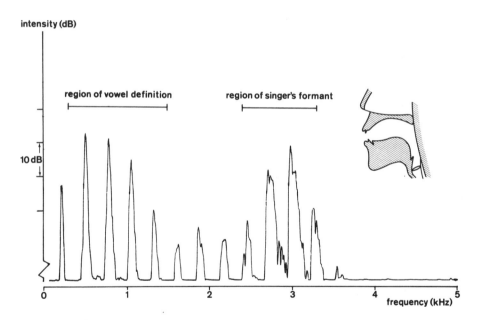

Figure 4.6. The vowel [ɔ] (as in "hawed") sung at approximately 262 Hz (C₄). The spectral envelope indicates desirable vowel definition and singer's formant. Note the favorable balance in sound energy between the region of vowel definition and that of the singer's formant. (From Richard Miller and Harm Kornelis Schutte, "The Effect of Tongue Position on Spectra in Singing," *The NATS Bulletin*, January/February, 1981, Vol. 37, No. 3. By permission.)

assumptions on much earlier studies by Paget, Delattre, and Bartholomew. Attention to the same phenomenon can be found in another early (although undated) source: Pelsky's treatment of the spectra in singing classifies the characteristic formant in resonant singing according to vocal category—for male voices, between 2500 and 3200 (Pelsky made no differentiation, apparently, between tenors and basses); for mezzos and contraltos, around 3200; and up to 4000 for sopranos. Pelsky's work from the late 1930s anticipates much of the current interest in the singer's formant. Sundberg has added significantly to the literature on the singer's formant in a series of publications detailing the relationship of the formants in the singing voice (1981, p. 13):

> Acoustically, it [the singer's formant] can be described as a peak in the spectrum envelope appearing somewhere in the neighborhood of 3 kHz. In this frequency range, then, the partials radiated from the lip opening are particularly strong. Articulatorily, the singer's formant can be generated by adjusting the pharynx width so that it is considerably wider than the area of the entrance to the larynx tube. If this is done, the formants number three, four, and probably five are clustered and the ability of the vocal tract to transport sound in this frequency is much improved. The result, of course, is that the voice source partials in this frequency range gain in amplitude. . . .
>
> However, it will be clear that the amplitude of the partials underlying the singer's formant are dependent not only on the vocal tract sound transfer characteristics, or, in other words, the initial amplitude of the partials as they enter the vocal tract . . . this initial amplitude depends on the rate of change from maximum to minimum airflow value. An interesting question is how this rate can be manipulated . . . it increases as vocal effort is increased. Vocal effort is raised primarily by increasing subglottic pressure, so this pressure seems important. The rate of decrease in the airflow is also influenced by some other factors. . . .

All of these sources suggest that "good singing tone" displays the "ring," the result of desirable formant balancing. Sometimes this technique is described as the tracking of the laryngeally produced vowel by the resonator tube.

THE SINGER'S PERCEPTION OF TIMBRE

A major source of misunderstanding with regard to "resonance" in singing stems from confusing the source of sound with the sensation of sound. Some singers experience sensation largely in the posterior half of the head or, if in the forward regions, solely in the forehead. Other singers, oriented to quite different pedagogical goals, experience sensation in the mask *(masque)*, the sinuses and the forward half of the skull, particularly in the facial regions. These sensations relate to specific physical postures of the vocal tract. It is important for any sensation in singing to accord with efficient physical and acoustic function.

The singer's own sound may reach the Eustachian tube (which runs from the nasopharynx to the inner ear) before it enters the external ear. The difference in time between outer and inner hearing is not of significance; significant is the fact that internal sensation is conveyed from the nasopharynx, the oropharynx, and the mouth, to upper areas of the head.

Speech, which passes through the larynx, the pharynx, and the mouth, brings the bones of the skull into vibration. Froeschels (1957a, pp. 630–631) recounts that Rethi, using an electrically stimulated tuning fork, demonstrated that sound waves pass through the hard and soft parts of the mouth and pharynx into the bones of the skull. Froeschels concludes that vocal band sound stimulates the whole head to vibrate, and that such sound also enters the Eustachian tube.

According to von Békésy (1960, p. 187), the hearing of one's own voice by bone conduction is of the same order of magnitude as by air conduction. Vibrations of the skull are caused not only by the vibrating vocal bands but also by the sound pressure in the mouth. Von Békésy adds that, perceptually, the sound pressure in the mouth cavity produces about the same amount of loudness as does the vibration of the vocal bands (1960, p. 189).

The timbre of vocal sound produced by the singer obviously varies. Differences in timbre have corresponding locations of resonance sensation. (Singers generally mean vocal timbre when they speak of "resonance.") The relative dimensions of the resonators of the vocal tract constantly change in response to phonetic articulation. Flexible adjustment of a resonator is more important than the resonator's absolute dimension. Taylor (1958, p. 31) finds that, beyond comfortable conductivity passages between the resonating cavities, there is no point in making the connecting channels larger: "cavities of the mouth and throat opened or closed beyond a certain optimum or normal usage is useless effort." In fact, it is pointless to try to direct attention solely to the mouth or the throat, because air vibrates in the entire tract, not separately in each of its parts. Vocal timbre is determined by resonator coupling and by the modifying actions of other parts of the vocal machine. The frequencies of the formants and the shapes of the resonators match.

THE OPEN THROAT *(GOLA APERTA)*

It would be hard to find a voice teacher who recommended singing with a closed throat. "Open the throat" is almost as frequently heard as "support the voice," "sing on the breath," or "place the voice." These expressions have the potential for inducing malfunction in singing, because they are imprecise. Just as the singer must concretely understand how the tone is "supported" (how the rate of breath emission is determined), so must the singer know what to experience as "the open throat." At best, subjective expressions can be but vague indicators of specific concepts. Such adages can mean many things to many persons. Vocal pedagogy could probably take a major step forward if these and other subjective terms were replaced with, or augmented by, more exact language.

Although to some extent singing is an extension of speech (Hammer, 1978, pp. 61–64), the special requirements of the singing voice demand resonator shaping and coupling that transcend those of speech. The dimensions of the buccopharyngeal cavity respond to those special requirements.

The pharynx is accustomed to sensations of distention, largely through the normal and beneficial actions of the yawn. In describing the yawn, we use language suggesting relaxation. We feel that the throat has widened, we can see in the mirror that the soft palate is high with the uvula elevated, we notice that the tongue lies low and flat, all producing a sensation of "openness." In yawning, we see the larynx lower and the jaw hang. Surely, one might think, this is the position of "the open throat." Some singers do believe erroneously that in the widest pharyngeal distention, in laryngeal depression and velar elevation (all present in a hearty yawn), we are near the optimum position for singing. This claim must be considered with regard to the interrelationships of the resonating cavities, to vowel formation and differentiation, to the articulation of consonants, and to muscle activity.

We often stretch our arms and yawn at the same time, particularly when weary, or when we have been maintaining one physical posture for some time and feel cramped by it. The muscular stretch feels good, and it is good for us. We conclude the yawn and the stretch by allowing the participating musculature to return to conditions of normal function. We would not attempt physical activity of a sustained sort with the arms and legs while also stretching them. Nor would we aim at this dimension of oral and pharyngeal distention for extended periods of speech, although we may occasionally lapse among friends, with apologies. Yet, in the literature of vocal pedagogy can be found sources that advocate as the ideal position for singing exactly the fully distended pharyngeal and buccal posture found in the yawn. Other sources recommend a modification of the sensations of yawning. How do these sensations correspond to those of *gola aperta*, long advocated by the historic Italian School?

A sensation of openness is essential in singing, but such sensation need not be chiefly felt in either the laryngopharynx or the oropharynx. When one breathes deeply through the nose, as, for example, when filling the lungs with fresh, clean air following an electrical storm, or when one inhales a pleasant fragrance, there is a feeling of considerable openness in the nasopharynx, some in the oropharynx, and to some extent in the laryngopharynx. The position of the tongue does not alter (it will, if the breath is grabbed noisily), the jaw does not hang, the larynx is not radically depressed, and the velum is not rigidly raised. Although spatial relationships among the resonators now have changed from those of "normal speech," neither of the chief resonators (mouth and pharynx) has become subservient to the other in this coupling. Yet, there is a favorable arch to the fauces, the velum is raised, and the connecting channel between the resonators is open and free. The same sensation of openness can be experienced whether one breathes through the nose or through the mouth.

By breathing in this fashion, the singer achieves a position of the resonators that feels open, without, however, the muscle tension that must occur in the throat with the yawn posture. Throat tension inherent in the yawn can be verified externally by placing the fingers flat under the jaw between the chin and the larynx. This tension can also be internally felt, and externally seen, in singers who believe they have "opened the throat."

The nasopharynx is capable of playing a major role in sensations of open-throatedness. One often experiences openness in the region of the oropharynx and in the region of the nasopharynx (as opposed to concentrated sensation in the laryngopharynx) in moments of heightened emotion in speech. When we are happily excited, when surprised by pleasant circumstances, when physically alert for undertaking an unusual activity, when viewing a thrilling event, when greeting a long-absent loved one, when about to smile or laugh—we breathe with this sense of openness in the regions of the nasopharynx and the oropharynx. Do we drop the jaw, lower the tongue, depress the larynx, and yawn at those moments? The yawn, which produces pharyngeal enlargement and laryngeal depression, plays no part in those joyous moments of life; it has no role in active athletic movement, and it is not part of the imaginative, alert, creative moments of daily life. Why then assume a need for the yawn in singing when the open throat can be accomplished in singing by the same means as in other heightened situations in life? The yawn is an action that belongs to the tired, to the bored, an attitude of the weary spirit and body.

It is understood, of course, that persons advocating the yawn posture admit some modification of that posture for the necessities of articulation in singing. However, even when only slightly yawning during speech, one hears a resulting timbre distortion. The same distortion is present when even the *slight* yawn is maintained in singing. What of "opening the throat" by "breathing through the yawn," but then dropping the yawn sensation? An unnecessary pharyngeal distention is momentarily introduced, a tension that hinders freedom.

For some persons, the yawn quality in singing is perceived as enriched and enlarged; for some other persons, the yawn quality in singing is considered to be manufactured and undesirable. Such preferences are aesthetic judgments often based on cultural histories (Miller, 1977, pp. 87–88). However, if freedom (functional efficiency in singing) produces the most beautiful sound (a premise of this book that may be accepted or rejected, of course), any form of functional tonal distortion is not a thing of beauty.

To breathe as though inhaling deeply the fragrance of a rose is to accomplish the buccopharyngeal position of *gola aperta*, in direct contrast to techniques of the open throat achieved through the yawn. (The incipient yawn produces similar sensations to those felt in breathing as though inhaling a lovely fragrance, but it is less useful pedagogically because its extent is difficult to regulate. All too often the *incipient* yawn develops into the full-blown yawn.) The rubric of the rose is a favorite device of the international school; an open sensation is present during inspiration, and that sensation remains throughout the subsequent phrase. No functional distortion is involved in this method of resonator coupling. The open throat *(gola aperta)* is efficient, and it produces vocal timbre that listeners find fully resonant and balanced, without artificiality.

"PLACEMENT" OF THE VOICE *(IMPOSTAZIONE DELLA VOCE)*

Impostazione della voce (also *imposto*) means "voice placement" (also "tone placement"). It is doubtful that teachers who use placement imagery believe that the singer literally places tone. Placement imagery is meant to help the singer discover desirable vocal timbre ("resonance") through sensation. Vocal pedagogies are not in agreement as to what these sensations should be. "Forward placement" is the aim of some teachers: "into the *masque* (mask)," "into the mouth," "into the upper jaw," "out in front," "behind the eyes," "into the sinuses," "at the end of the nose," "on the lips," etc. Other teachers believe the tone should be directed posteriorly: "down the spine," "at the back of the throat wall," "up the back of the throat wall, then over into the forehead," "into the body," "into the back half of the head," etc.

Although most teachers are committed to one, or to some limited number of "places" to which tone is to be directed and where sensations of resonance are to be felt, there are other teachers who use most or all of these expressions in an experimental way, depending on what they consider to be the need of the singer. Regardless of what theory of "placement" a teacher may embrace, there is always the peril that the student may not experience the sensation that the teacher's terminology means to elicit. A wise route, it might seem, would be to understand the acoustic principle of resonator coupling in singing, and to find some objective technical language to communicate this information.

Both breath management and resonance factors are included in the term *appoggio;* although *imposto,* or *impostazione,* refers to placement sensations, these sensations are not considered apart from breath management. *Imposto* does not narrowly indicate a localized "place," but rather expresses the more general concept of resonance in singing as a result of *appoggio.* "In the terminology of vocal technique, *impostazione* (or *imposto*) indicates the manner by which the vocal organs cooperate in phonation during singing" (*Enciclopedia Garzanti della musica* 1974, p. 277).

Impostazione produces distinct and recognizable sensations of resonator coupling. Whereas pedagogies that strive for localized placement also localize sensation, in the historic Italian School resonator coupling permits sensation in all parts of the vocal tract. The resonance balance (placement) relies neither on the pharynx nor on the mouth as chief resonator, but on a combination of both. Sensation centers neither in the throat nor in the face. Resonator coupling becomes resonance balancing without functional or acoustic violation of any single part of the vocal tract. Hanging the jaw and spreading the pharynx will produce marked *sensations* of openness in the throat, but an imbalance of the resonator tube at the expense of higher frequencies in some vowels; concepts of mask placement will produce the opposite result, unnecessary thinning of the timbre and an increase in upper partials. *Imposto* technique avoids both the heavy, dull vocal production and the shrill, blatant production.

EXERCISES FOR ESTABLISHING RESONANCE BALANCE *(IMPOSTAZIONE)* IN SINGING

EXERCISE 4.1

WITH LIPS CLOSED, BREATHE THROUGH THE NOSE AS THOUGH SLOWLY INHALING A PLEASANT AROMA; MAINTAIN A PLEASANT EXPRESSION ON THE FACE WITHOUT ACTUALLY SMILING.

KEEPING THE SAME SENSE OF OPENNESS, EXHALE ON THE EXCLAMATION "HM!" SLOWLY, WHILE SUSTAINING THE SOUND. BE AWARE OF THE BALANCE OF SENSATION IN NASAL, BUCCAL, AND NASOPHARYNGEAL AND OROPHARYNGEAL CAVITIES.

EXERCISE 4.2

ESTABLISH THE "NOBLE" POSTURE; BREATHE THROUGH THE NOSE AS THOUGH INHALING THE FRAGRANCE OF A ROSE AND HUM THE PATTERN IN SEVERAL KEYS OF EASY RANGE. BE CERTAIN THAT THE HUM IS PRODUCED WITHOUT TENSION IN THE TONGUE, THE VELUM, OR THE JAW. STRUM THE LIPS LIGHTLY AND QUICKLY A FEW TIMES WITH THE FOREFINGER. UNLESS A DISTINCT "MUM-MUM-MUM" RESULTS, THE PROPER NEUTRAL POSTURE OF THE ARTICULATORY MECHANISM IS NOT PRESENT.

EXERCISE 4.3

THE HUM ON THE TRIAD IS FOLLOWED WITHOUT INTERRUPTION BY THE INDICATED VOWELS.

EXERCISE 4.4

THE HUM ON THE TRIAD IS FOLLOWED WITHOUT INTERRUPTION BY A SERIES OF VOWELS AS INDICATED.

EXERCISE 4.5

[ɑ _____]
[with occluded nostrils]

BREATHE THROUGH THE NOSE. WITH THE FINGERS LIGHTLY PINCHING THE
NOSTRILS CLOSED, SING THE VOWEL [ɑ].
    THIS EXERCISE IS AN ANCIENT ONE FOR CHECKING ON THE PRESENCE
OF UNWANTED NASALITY, BUT IT IS ALSO AN EXCELLENT DEVICE FOR
ACHIEVING PROPER RESONANCE BALANCE BETWEEN THE MOUTH AND THE
PHARYNX.

Exercises that juxtapose the hum and closed nostrils during non-nasals often produce dramatic improvement in resonance balance in the singing voice. Sensation then moves out of the throat. Although the pharynx continues to serve as a major resonator, sensation tends to be equally experienced in the nasopharynx and in the frontal areas. These sensations attest to a balance among the components of the resonator tube; no single part of the vocal tract is given pre-eminence.

EXERCISE 4.6

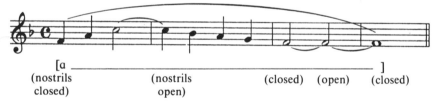

[ɑ _____]
(nostrils   (nostrils   (closed) (open) (closed)
closed)   open)

PARTS OF THE PHRASE ARE SUNG WITH THE NOSTRILS CLOSED GENTLY BY
THE FINGERS, OTHER PARTS WITHOUT CLOSURE OF THE NOSTRILS. THE
SINGER MUST BE CERTAIN THAT NO CHANGE IN TIMBRE OCCURS WHEN
THE NOSTRILS ARE RELEASED IN MID-PHRASE. RESONANCE SENSATIONS,
EITHER WITH MOUTH OPEN OR CLOSED, OR WITH NOSTRILS OCCLUDED OR
FREE, REMAIN THE SAME.

VELOPHARYNGEAL CLOSURE

From ordinary X-ray sagittal projections, it is difficult to determine the extent of velopharyngeal (palatopharyngeal) closure in non-nasal sounds. Tomography provides pictures of sharper contrast and records a more accurate cross section. On the basis of tomographic studies, Bjork (1961, supplement 202, pp. 1–94) concludes that velo-pharyngeal closure may be less complete than X-ray photographs show. His study indicates marked narrowing of the nasopharyngeal opening, both from lateral and from anterior–posterior aspects. Fant (1964, p. 231) suggests that the elevated velum as viewed tomographi-cally may not occlude the velopharyngeal opening to the extent phoneticians often assume. Zwitman et al. (1973, p. 473) find that "[T]he degree of lateral pharyngeal wall movement varies among normal individuals. . . . Conflicting descriptions of lateral wall move-ment probably are attributable to differences among individuals."

Zwitman et al. (1974, pp. 368–370) established that several fac-tors contribute to pharyngeal closure:

1. Lateral walls move medially and fuse, resulting in a purse-string closure as the velum touches the approximated section of the lateral walls.
2. Lateral walls almost approximate, with the velum contacting the lateral walls and partly occluding the space between them. A small medial opening is observed in some cases.
3. Lateral walls move medially, filling the lateral gutters and fusing with the raised velum as it contacts the posterior wall.
4. Lateral walls move slightly or not at all. Velum touches posterior wall at midline, and lateral openings are observed during phonation.

Nearly half of the 34 normal subjects examined in this study showed incomplete velar closure on non-nasals. Fritzell (1979, pp. 93–102) also suggests that muscular action in velopharyngeal closure varies among normal subjects. Such studies are of impor-tance in providing probable factual support for theories of "the open nasal port" in some form in singing.

The possibility of at least some coupling of the nasal resonator to the buccopharyngeal resonator has also been recognized by Sund-berg (1977a, p. 90) in dealing with the acoustics of the singing voice: "It is just possible . . . that the nasal cavity has a role in singing of vowels that are not normally nasalized." It should be kept in mind that there may well be considerable individual physiological varia-tion with regard to nasopharyngeal coupling.

Implications for the technique of singing are significant. Limited degrees of nasopharyngeal coupling (some aperture of the port) seem to be induced by the numerous vocalises that make use of nasal con-sonants as "placement" devices. The perception of nasality in non-nasals is always, of course, to be avoided. However, vocal sound perceived by the listener as resonant but non-nasal may in fact result from some degree of nasopharyngeal coupling (House and Stevens, 1956, p. 218). The ratio in balance between oral and nasal resonance may depend on how the posterior apertures into the nasal cavities relate to the size of the oral cavity. Nimii et al. (1982, p. 250) comment that

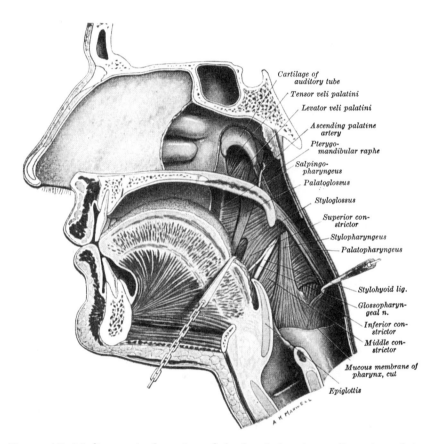

Figure 4.7. Median sagittal section of the head showing a dissection of the interior of the pharynx after the removal of the mucous membrane. (In order that the structures may be displayed satisfactorily, the bodies of the cervical vertebrae have been removed and the cut posterior wall of the pharynx then drawn backward and laterally. The palatopharyngeus is drawn backward to show the upper fibers of the inferior constrictor, and the dorsum of the tongue is drawn forward to display a part of the styloglossus in the angular interval between the mandibular and the lingual fibers of origin of the superior constrictor. (From *Gray's Anatomy*, 36th ed., ed. by Peter L. Williams and Roger Warwick, 1980. Edinburgh: Churchill Livingstone. By permission.)

[I]t is apparently quite usual for velar elevation to vary during connected speech, with changes in velar position, and thus in velopharyngeal port size, produced to enhance or prevent nasal coupling, as needed, for the segments in the phonetic string . . . [V]elar elevation varies directly with the oral cavity constriction of oral segments.

This group of researchers concludes that one must expect "some individual differences, even among normal speakers" as to the mechanical means for velopharyngeal closure (1982, p. 255).

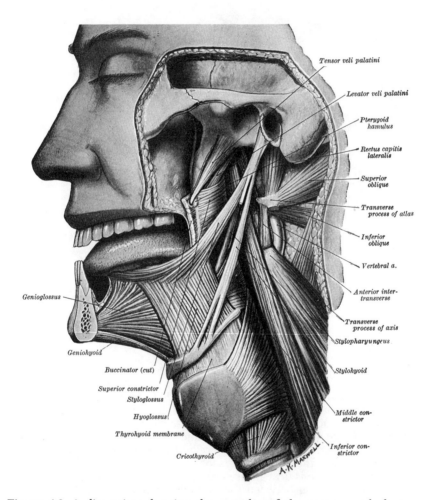

Figure 4.8. A dissection showing the muscles of the tongue and pharynx. (From *Gray's Anatomy*, 36th ed., ed. by Peter L. Williams and Roger Warwick, 1980. Edinburgh: Churchill Livingstone. By permission.)

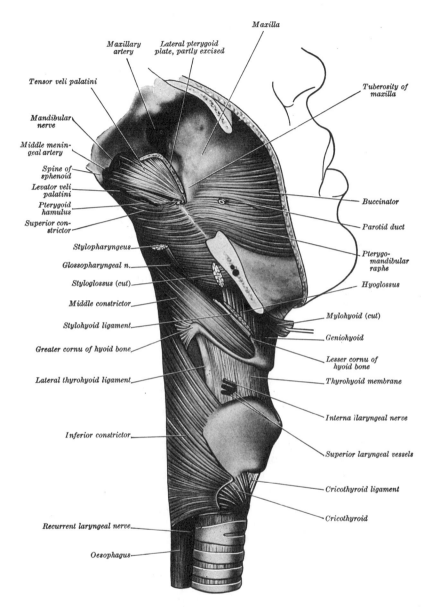

Figure 4.9. The buccinator and the muscles of the pharynx. (From *Gray's Anatomy*, 36th ed., ed. by Peter L. Williams and Roger Warwick, 1980. Edinburgh: Churchill Livingstone. By permission.)

The answers are not all in, regarding the mode by which velo-pharyngeal closure may be modified. According to Nimii et al. (1982, p. 253):

> There is general agreement that the velum is elevated and retracted primarily by the levator palatini muscle. . . . The point of controversy revolves around the putative role of other muscles in the velopharyngeal port region in bringing about movement of the lateral pharyngeal walls at various levels relative to the point of velopharyngeal closure.

This piece of research concludes:

> We believe that the levator palatini is the muscle primarily responsible for the medial movement of the lateral pharyngeal wall from the level of velopharyngeal closure (which varies with the type of phonetic segment produced) to the superior limit of that movement. That the interpretation that the levator palatini is responsible for both the lateral wall and velar movements is a valid one is supported by the data. . . .

How one conceives of "opening the throat" and "placing the voice" leads directly to specific kinds of muscle activity in the velo-pharyngeal area. The levator veli palatini (levator palatini), the tensor veli palatini, the palatoglossus and palatopharyngeus, and the musculus uvulae (see Appendix III and Figures 4.7, 4.8, and 4.9) respond to such concepts. The presence or lack of "resonance" in the singing voice is closely tied to adjustments made in the velopharyngeal region. The extent to which the nasal cavities are united with the rest of the resonator tube partly determines the perception of "resonance." As with the exact character of velopharyngeal closure itself, not all the answers are clear regarding the degree to which velo-pharyngeal closure may be modified in singing. Additional attention to balanced resonator adjustment through the use of consonants (including the nasals) will comprise the material of other chapters. However, the resonant, well-balanced vowel in singing must first be considered.

CHAPTER 5

The Well-balanced Vowel

Vowel Differentiation in Singing

The acoustic postures associated with vowels easily fall prey to the transition sounds of speech. Continual movement of the articulatory mechanism prevents precise postures of the vocal tract. Nevertheless, clean articulation and good diction in singing require vocal tract movements that can be recorded by exact phonetic symbolization.

The adjustments of the tongue, the lips, the mandible, the velum, and the resonators can define a recognizable phonetic position more precisely during singing than they do in speech, because of the duration factor. Although vowel postures, represented by specific phonetic symbols, are not static or set postures in singing, they tend to resemble the "model" postures described by the phonetician. Such a high degree of acoustic exactitude in vowel definition can occur in singing that the production of the "pure" vowel is a realizable goal.

THE ACOUSTIC AT-REST POSTURE

Phonetic characteristics of vowels relate to a constant landmark. We do not have to hypothesize such a position, because, unless we are phonating at this moment, we are probably at that posture. When one is in a state of repose, without exaggerated respiratory activity, the tongue is relaxed in the mouth, with its blade (both the tip and the forward sides) in easy contact with the lower teeth. (If you are lying down as you read this, the tongue may well be resting against the upper teeth just forward of the alveolar ridge.) The upper and lower rows of teeth are slightly parted, regardless of whether or not the lips are separated. The upper and lower jaws are separated (although the mouth may remain closed) because the mandible obeys the law of gravity. Unless one consciously "relaxes" the mandible, it will not be in a hanging position. This central position of the tongue and the mandible is home base for the speech mechanism (see Figure 4.4). It is also the position of the neutral vowel [ʌ].

THE VOWEL POSTURES

Vowels are continuants, capable of maintaining a specific vocal tract configuration and sustaining phonation. In singing, such a configuration of the vocal tract may extend through an entire expiratory phase of the breath cycle, if so desired. Unless vowels are improperly produced, no friction noises intrude during the sound. The characteristic quality of the vowel depends on the vowel formants, which have fixed values for each particular shape of the vocal tract (see Chapter 4, and Figures 4.3, 4.4, and 4.5). Some of these vocal tract formations follow.

Formation of the Neutral Vowels [ʌ] and [ə]

The most neutral, the most primitive, vocal expression is represented by the vowel [ʌ]. This is the sound heard in groaning, in the audible sigh, and in emotional phonation without words. The same sound occurs when one "thinks out loud," before speech has been formulated. The lips part for [ʌ], but they remain unshaped; there is a slight lowering of the mandible.

Closely related to [ʌ] is a sound represented by the symbol [ə] called the *schwa*. Originally a Hebraic phonetic formation, the *schwa* now has general phonetic usage and refers to the neutralized vowel, the unaccented syllable that so frequently concludes a word. Some phoneticians view the *schwa* as a vowel tendency toward neutralization rather than as a distinctly identifiable phoneme. In unskillful singing, other vowels tend to drift toward [ə], causing unintentional blurring of vowel differentiation. The neutral vowel serves as a device for essential vowel modification in some circumstances in singing. (Significantly, the neutral vowel is not found in formal Italian.)

In singing, the *schwa* functions as the unaccented corollary of [ʌ]. Although the symbols [ʌ] and [ə] represent differences in duration in speech, the temporal distinctions between them disappear in singing, where the brief sounds of spoken language are frequently elongated.

Both of the neutral vowels are produced with minimal vocal tract constriction; the tip and the blade of the tongue are not elevated, and constriction exists neither between the dorsum of the tongue and velum nor between the dorsum of the tongue and the posterior pharyngeal wall (Minifie, 1973, p. 245). Neutral retroflex tongue postures are usually avoided in cultivated singing, so that no consideration is given to them here.

Formation of the Vowel [ɑ]

When singing [ɑ], the lips part, the mandible lowers, and the tongue lies flat on the floor of the mouth cavity. With regard to the extent of buccal aperture, the vowel [ɑ] is farthest removed from the central posture of the neutral vowel [ʌ] (perhaps much less distant than some singers realize). The vowel [ɑ] is sometimes classified as the first of the back vowels because of its particular combination of frequencies and the shape of the resonator tube during its production. However, the attraction of the vowel [ɑ] for many singers lies in its avoidance of tongue constriction of the vocal tract.

Vocalization based solely on [ɑ] does not deal with the more exacting principles of vowel differentiation encountered in singing both front and back vowels. In any technique of singing, if other vowels are less comfortable in execution than the vowel [ɑ], articulatory flexibility is lacking.

Formation of the Vowel [i]

For purposes of contrast, we move now to the most frontal of all the vowels (the closest, regarding forward tongue posture), represented by the symbol [i]. The buccal orifice is narrowed in the vowel [i], and is horizontally elongated as in a pleasant facial expression. The mandible is in a posture that shows limited space between the two rows of teeth. What makes the [i] vowel most distinctive acoustically is the high, close position of the tongue. With the exception of the apex of the tongue, which contacts the lower teeth, the front of the tongue is elevated so that the tongue arches almost to the roof of the mouth. The highest degree of tongue elevation occurs in front of the middle point of the hard palate. The tongue contacts portions of the hard palate on either side.

Investigating front cavity resonances in speech, Kuhn (1975, p. 430) concludes that the shape of the forward part of the buccal cavity determines the overall spectral shape of the vowel, and has an effect on frequency and on the extent of higher formants.

What does front cavity resonance frequency accomplish with regard to total resonator adjustment in singing? Obviously, the singer feels less space in the front of the mouth in the vowel [i] than in the vowel [ɑ]; some singers find the narrower position of [i] intolerable. Desiring the frontal mouth space for "resonance," the singer may try to "open the throat" by opening the buccal cavity.

In the vowel [i], total resonator space has not been diminished, but rearranged. The acoustic nature of the vowel [i], with its considerable pharyngeal room, plays a significant role in vocalises devoted to vowel differentiation and to resonance adjustment. Because of the nature of front cavity shape, tongue posture, and increased pharyngeal room, the vowel [i] is useful in developing the full timbre of the voice. It should be noted that a number of researchers comment that soft palate elevation is higher in [i] than in any other vowel (Hirano et al., 1966, p. 377).

Formation of the Vowel [e]

The vowel [e] is more closely related to [i] than any other sound. (The vowel [ɪ] enjoys an acoustic position in between [i] and [e].) Sensations resulting from the distribution of buccal space found in the vowel [i] can be felt in singing [e]. However, most singers are aware of the increased lateral contact of the tongue with the teeth on [e]. A slightly lower jaw posture than in [i], and the wider shape to the oral cavity, result in more frontal spaciousness in [e] than in [i].

The vowel [e] is an important member of the front vowel series. With both [i] and [e], the elevation and forward postures of the tongue evoke sensations in the mask. The high formant distribution of the vowels is mainly responsible for these sensations.

Formation of the Vowel [ɛ]

Progressing through the series of front vowels (also known as close vowels), we next encounter the vowel [ɛ]. By pronouncing out loud the series [i, e, ɛ, ə] several times as a continuous phrase, the gradual opening of the mouth from the frontal [i] to the more central, neutral [ə] may be demonstrated. A marked lowering of the tongue is noted at the point in the vowel series where the front vowel is modified to a neutral posture. Even greater awareness of this change in shape and sensation is experienced if one concludes the same vowel progression with [ɑ] (Kantner and West, 1960, p. 105).

X-ray evidence shows that the hump of the tongue moves progressively into the pharynx in the series [u, o, ɔ] (Peterson, 1951, p. 548). This vowel progression narrows the pharyngeal cavity and increases the buccal cavity. Ladefoged et al. (1979, p. 1027) remark that "Whenever a speaker produces the vowel /i/ as in "heed," the body of the tongue is always raised up towards the hard palate. Whenever anyone produces the vowel [ɑ] as in "father," the tongue is always low and somewhat retracted."

Formation of the Vowel [ɔ]

Moving away from the centrally located vowels, we encounter the back vowels, beginning with the vowel [ɔ]. This vowel is commonly met in all Western languages; it is a difficult sound for American singers to execute (less problematic for the British singer), because in most American speech the vowel [ɔ] is insufficiently differentiated from the vowel [ɑ]. Americans are lazy about moving the lips and the tongue, and about changing the shape of the oral cavity.

The vowel [ɔ] requires buccal rounding. The buccal dimension for [ɔ] is smaller than for [ɑ]; there is a slight pout for [ɔ]. The mouth is slightly less open in [ɔ] than in [ɑ]. The acoustic definition of [ɔ] requires some elevation of the back of the tongue, which places the vowel squarely in the back vowel series.

Formation of the Vowel [o]

The lips are separated with [o], but they are more rounded than with [ɔ], and they protrude somewhat more. However, it is easy to exaggerate the physical distance from [ɔ] to [o] in singing. In executing [o], the tongue is depressed in its anterior portion; elevation of the posterior part of the tongue, characteristic of all back vowels, is also present.

Formation of the Vowel [u]

With the vowel [u] we reach the opposite end of the vowel series from the vowel [i]. Whereas in [i] the front portion of the tongue is at its highest, in [u] it is the back portion of the tongue that elevates, leaving little space between the tongue and the soft palate. In [i], more space exists in "the back of the mouth," coupled directly with the pharynx. In [u], there is little space in the posterior buccopharyngeal area because more room exists in the forward part of the mouth.

MOUTH POSITION FOR VOWELS IN SINGING

Two pedagogical extremes can be cited in regard to mouth position for vowels in singing. Teacher A hangs the jaw for all vowels, regardless of the acoustic properties. Teacher B inserts a pencil (even chopsticks) between the singer's teeth, requesting that all vowels be produced within the resulting narrow buccal aperture. Patently, both

techniques cannot be equally correct from the standpoint of phonetic efficiency. That some listeners prefer the kinds of sounds that
result from one or the other of these opposing techniques is unques-
tionable, inasmuch as both flourish as living pedagogical examples.
In such practices, the system of vowel formants is seriously disturbed, and vowel distortion is unavoidable. Appelman (1967, p. 230)
admonishes:

> When a sung sound has migrated away from the phoneme
> necessary for proper pronunciation to a position near the
> neutral vowel [ʌ] or an adjacent phoneme that is not the
> quality alternate, it is no longer a pure vowel. The integrity
> of the phoneme, which gives meaning, has been lost. . . .

It is not possible to set a basic posture of mouth, lips, tongue, and
jaw through which all vowels are to be sung, without distorting most
(or all) of them. The jaw and the tongue are not in the same positions
throughout all vowel sounds in speech; a hand placed lightly on the
jaw will register considerable jaw mobility during speech; observation with a mirror will verify that the tongue is not equally flat, low,
and grooved throughout the sequence of vowels. Why, then, could
one basic posture be appropriate for singing?

Cantare come si parla (to sing as one speaks) attests to a commitment to vowel formation in singing based on rapid adjustments
of the vocal tract. The ideal is acoustic mobility rather than acoustic
stabilization. Balancing resonance factors is best accomplished
through timbre uniformity, not through uniformity of buccopharyngeal positioning. Unification of vowel timbre results when each
vowel is permitted, in freedom, to assume its own distinctive acoustic shape while "tracking" the frequencies that provide the voice with
its carrying power.

In such a request as "Can you *help* me find my book?", the
mouth will be opened only moderately on the vowel [ɛ] in the word
"help." If one were in desperate straits and wildly cried out "Help!" at
a high pitch, the mouth would be considerably more opened in the
vowel [ɛ]; the mouth would probably be even more widely opened on
the same pitch were the emotive word "Ah!"

Opening the mouth for ascending pitch answers the need to
match frequencies when the fundamental frequency in singing is
higher than the first formant in most spoken vowels. Sundberg
(1977a, pp. 89–90) has given an explanation of this phenomenon, here
briefly summarized. By moving up the first formant frequency (by
opening the mouth), the singer allows the formant to enhance the
amplitude of the fundamental. The result is that there is a minimum

of variation in loudness from pitch to pitch and from vowel to vowel (see Figure 5.1).

Along with lowering the mandible as a means of enlarging the buccal cavity, lifting the maxillary area of the face finds acoustic justification in Sundberg's findings (1977a, p. 90): "Opening the jaw, however, is not the only way to raise the first formant frequency. Shortening the vocal tract by drawing back the corners of the mouth serves the same purpose, and that may be why some teachers tell their students to smile when they sing high notes."

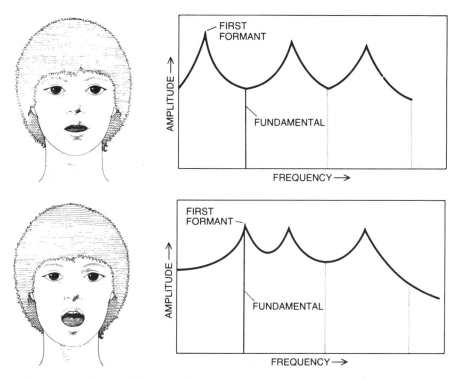

Figure 5.1. The need for a wider jaw opening in the upper range arises from the fact that a soprano must often sing tones whose fundamental (which is actually the lowest partial) is far higher in frequency than is the normal first formant of the vowel being sung. When that is the case, the amplitude of the fundamental is not enhanced by the first formant, and the sound is therefore weak. Opening the jaw wider raises the pitch of the first formant. When the first-formant frequency is raised to match that of the fundamental, the formant enhances the amplitude of the fundamental, and the sound is louder. (From Johan Sundberg, "The Acoustics of the Singing Voice," *Scientific American*, March 1977, Vol. 236, No. 3. By permission.)

EXERCISES FOR VOWEL DIFFERENTIATION

Potential pedagogical benefits derive from acoustic differences between front and back vowels. The singer begins a vocalise with a front vowel characterized by a high second formant, then alternates the front vowel with a back vowel having a lower second formant (what some teachers call double formant and single formant vowels). Subsequent alternation between front and back vowels is then drilled using changing vowel combinations and changing pitch levels, with the aim of maintaining the same vocal resonance. Fortunately, vowel differentiation is an aspect of vocal technique that can be seen as well as heard. Movements of mouth, lips, tongue, and jaw can be observed. In all of the vowel differentiation exercises that follow, it is recommended that for at least part of each session a hand mirror be used by the singer. Three perceptual elements are coordinated: hearing the sound, seeing the movements of tongue and mandible, and feeling the resonance factor in the vocal tract and in the head.

Group 1 Exercises

EXERCISE 5.1

(A) [ɑ, o, i, o, e]
(B) [i, o, ɑ, o, e]

(1) PRONOUNCE THESE TWO PATTERNS ALTERNATELY, AT NORMAL SPEECH LEVEL, IN LEGATO FASHION, ALLOWING LIPS AND JAW TO MOVE NATURALLY, WITHOUT EXAGGERATION. (2) THERE SHOULD BE NO ATTEMPT TO HOLD ONE POSITION OF LIPS, JAW, TONGUE, OR MOUTH. (3) NO ATTEMPT SHOULD BE MADE TO DIFFERENTIATE THE VOWELS BY EXCESSIVELY MOUTHING OR SHAPING THEM. (4) OBSERVE THE LIMITED BUT DISCERNIBLE MOVEMENT OF THE MOUTH AS THE VOWELS ARE ARTICULATED. (5) INCREASE TEMPO SO THAT THE VOWELS MUST BE QUICKLY ENUNCIATED, BUT AVOID SLURRING OR TRANSITION SOUNDS. THE SAME ARTICULATION OCCURS, REGARDLESS OF SPEED.

The flexibility of buccal aperture should be equally present in singing the exercises that follow as in these spoken patterns. Tempo should alternate between slow and fast.

EXERCISE 5.2

[ɑ   o   i   o   e]

EXERCISE 5.3

EXERCISE 5.4

EXERCISE 5.5

Group 2 Exercises

EXERCISE 5.6

EXERCISE 5.7

EXERCISE 5.8

EXERCISE 5.9

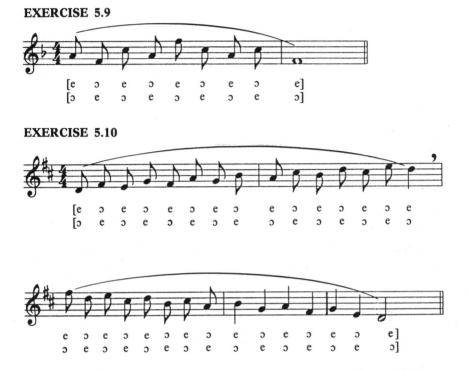

By using the progressions [e, ɔ] and [ɔ, e] the articulatory process is readily demonstrated. Other vowel combinations can be helpful in achieving accurate vocal tract flexibility and clean articulation. Alternation between front and back vowels should include combinations taken from the cardinal vowels.

CHAPTER 6

Resonance Balancing through Nasal Consonants

The Influences of Nasal Continuants on Resonator Adjustment

Vowels seldom stand alone, either in speech or in singing. The ubiquitous consonant alters and adjusts the shape of the resonator tube. The consonant adjacent to a vowel is largely responsible for transition sounds that occur. Transition sounds (also known as *glides*) result from the constantly changing positions of the vocal organs as they approach the subsequent phoneme *(on-glide)*, or as they leave a phoneme *(off-glide)* (Carhart et al., 1961, pp. xxiv–xxxi). Such intermediate positions of the resonators, so common in speech, must be minimized in singing if voice timbre is to remain uniformly resonant.

Consonants need not be considered unwelcome intruders that impede good vocalization. If each consonant is permitted to enjoy its brief but exact phonetic location and is allowed a clean departure when its stint is over, the singer's ideal of the "pure" vowel will not be violated.

PEDAGOGICAL USES OF CONSONANTAL PHONEMES IN GENERAL

Singers have long recognized the value of prefacing vowels with some specific consonant that improves subsequent timbre. Even those consonants that require concerted action from tongue, lips, and velum may assist the ensuing vowel.

Several consonants already have been identified as useful for producing desirable resonator coupling and for assisting in a coordinated onset: the glottal fricative [h] and the glottal plosive [ʔ] help determine the nature of vocal-fold approximation; [s] and [f] heighten awareness of abdominal control in breath management; prolongation of [m], as in the hum, is a good technique for accomplishing favorable resonance balance. A look at additional uses of several consonants is now in order (see Appendix V for influence of various voiced and unvoiced consonants on resonator adjustment).

USE OF THE NASALS IN BALANCING
RESONATOR COUPLING

Phoneticians sometimes refer to the nasal continuants as "nasal vowels." Although there is a lower incidence of "nasal vowels" in speech in comparison with "oral vowels," the nasal continuants are prominent phonemes in some 28 languages (Björn et al., 1977, p. 486).

The four nasals, [m, n, ŋ] and [ɲ] are useful for improving resonance balance in vowels that follow them (see Figure 6.1a and b). In all four nasals, the oral cavity has some degree of closure; the soft palate assumes postures that determine the degree of coupling of mouth, pharynx, and the nasal cavities. The four nasals differ in quality as a result of the extent to which the oral cavity is excluded as a resonating chamber. Wood Jones (1940, cited in *Gray's Anatomy*, 1980, p. 1308) concludes that "the nasal part of the pharynx" is actually a part of the nasal cavities, with the velum separating the pharynx from the chamber of the nose. Whatever its anatomic designation, the velum, assisted by the extent of tongue elevation,

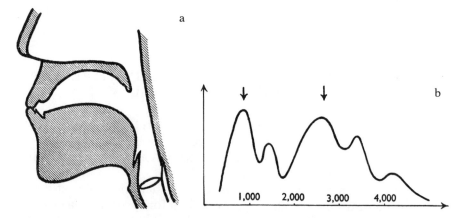

Figure 6.1. (a) The position of the vocal organs during the [m] in *mat.* (b) The resonance curve of the vocal tract during the pronunciation of the first sound in the word *mat.* (From Peter Ladefoged, *Elements of Acoustic Phonetics*, 1962. Tenth printing, 1974. Chicago: University of Chicago Press. By permission.)

determines the character of the nasal phonemes by the postures it assumes in relation to the oral cavity.

SOME USES OF THE VOICED BILABIAL STOP [m]

In the production of [m] the full length of the buccal cavity is used as a resonating chamber (see Figure 6.1a). The tongue lies in the mouth in a neutral position. Tensions of the tongue and velum often are eliminated by vocalises that use [m].

EXERCISE 6.1

[m a   m a   m a   m a   m]
[m i   m i   m i   m i   m]

(1) EXECUTE THE VOCALISE ON A SINGLE PITCH, SLIGHTLY ABOVE NORMAL SPEECH RANGE, AT MODERATE TEMPO, IN ONE CONTINUOUS PHRASE, ALTERNATING [m] AND [a]. **(2)** PROGRESS BY HALF STEPS THROUGH SEVERAL KEYS. NO SHAPING OF THE BUCCAL TRACT, OTHER THAN THE NECESSARY PARTING OF THE LIPS FOR THE VOWEL, SHOULD OCCUR. **(3)** USE THE SAME PROCEDURE AS IN THE BEGINNING OF THIS EXERCISE, EXCEPT ALTERNATE [m] AND [i].

Because the lips are closed, and because the mouth, pharynx, and the nostrils are now connected cavities, distinct vibratory sensations are felt in regions of the pharynx, the nose, the mouth, and the area of the sinuses. The quality of the sound is nasal. When the lips are parted, no continuance of actual nasality should be present in the tone, but the same *sensation* should pertain in the nasal and sinusal areas (sympathetic resonance experienced by the singer largely through bone and cartilage conduction).

The [m] is sung vibrantly, without any pinching of the lips. The tongue must not be raised to the alveolar ridge as in the [n] position, nor should it assume any transition posture between [m] and [n]. With singers who tend to pull the tongue back with the hum, the tongue tip should then rest forward on the top of the lower front teeth. In any event, the tongue must not be pulled back from contact with the teeth. The teeth are parted behind closed lips. It is essential that the tongue be in contact with the lower teeth without dropping down to the floor of the mouth at the roots of the teeth. Failure to do so may distort the vowel spectrum and defeat the purpose of the exercises (Miller and Schutte, 1981, pp. 26–27, 34).

EXERCISE 6.2

(The symbol (+) indicates occluded nostrils.)

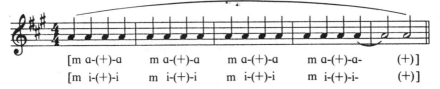

[m a-(+)-a   m a-(+)-a   m a-(+)-a   m a-(+)-a-   (+)]
[m i-(+)-i   m i-(+)-i   m i-(+)-i   m i-(+)-i-   (+)]

BEGIN WITH THE HUM ([m]) AS IN EXERCISE 6.1. ADDITIONALLY, BEATS ARE INTRODUCED, DURING WHICH TIME THE NOSTRILS ARE CLOSED BY THE FINGERS (INDICATED IN EXERCISE 6.2 BY THE SYMBOL [(+)]), THEN ALLOWED TO REOPEN WITH NO CHANGE IN VOCAL QUALITY. THIS IS TO ENSURE THAT THE VELUM DOES NOT INTERFERE WITH THE PROPER COUPLING OF NASOPHARYNX AND ORAL CAVITIES IN THE QUICK CHANGE FROM [m] TO [a] (OR [i]). BEAT 1 OF EACH BAR IS DEVOTED TO [m], BEAT 2 TO [a]; BEAT 3 [(+)] CHECKS THE DEGREE OF RESONANCE BALANCE BY LIGHTLY PINCHING THE NOSTRILS CLOSED WHILE CONTINUING TO SING [a]; BEAT 4 RETURNS TO THE UNOCCLUDED NOSTRILS. NO QUALITY CHANGE SHOULD BE EXPERIENCED BETWEEN BEATS 2, 3, AND 4.

Because of the simplicity of these vocalises, the singer should not assume that, once accomplished, the vocalises have served their purpose. They are a means of checking on that acoustic balance so essential to what singers term "resonance." It is recommended that these vocalises be practiced at least a few minutes each day.

The nasal [m] also helps produce optimum resonator balance when momentarily introduced as a study aid before some problematic syllable in a text during singing (see Figure 6.1a and b). The same vowel quality that is present following the hum is retained when the singer returns to the original offending consonant.

The nasality of [m] must not continue over into the vowel (unless dictated by the French nasal vowels, and even then with but the slightest soupçon!). The singer should never be advised to continue singing "on the hum."

EXERCISE 6.3

(a)

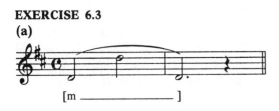

[m ———————]

(b)

Exercise 6.3 is quatrefoliated. The four parts of it form the single exercise. Although it is here presented among the group of exercises on the [m] hum, the nasals [n] and [ŋ] should be used as well.

EXERCISE 6.4

(a)

Exercise 6.4 is a version of Exercise 6.3 extended to the leap of a tenth. It should also be executed as an exercise in four parts, with only enough time between parts for the breath.

Both Exercises 6.3 and 6.4 should be done first on the vowel [ɑ], followed by the vowels [ɔ], [e], and [i], each in the sequence of four.

USES OF THE ALVEOLAR-NASAL CONTINUANT [n]

Whereas the sensation of [m] is more directly located on the lips and in the sinusal area, the sensation of [n] is located higher, in the region of the upper jaw and maxillary sinuses. This sensation has important ramifications for singing; buccal sensation diminishes, and increased sensation is felt in the region singers call the *masque* (mask).

When singers fail to experience sufficient frontal sensation, [n] may be a better key to its accomplishment than [m]. Sometimes the stopped position of the lips in [m] causes problems for singers when they open the mouth for the next vowel sound, particularly if they have been accustomed to dropping the jaw excessively for most syllables. The phoneme [n] is produced with an already opened mouth, lips slightly parted.

For singers who feel that the tone "falls back" from a resonant position when they proceed from [m] to an open vowel, [n] can often be beneficial as a substitute for [m]. (Exercise 6.1 under [m] may be used to advantage on [n].)

EXERCISE 6.5

An exercise to heighten awareness of the difference in sensation between [m] and [n] juxtaposes them, alternates the juxtaposition, and then separates them with the vowel [o] (Exercise 6.5.).

As just indicated, the [m] exercises should be used on [n] as well.

The uses of consonants in achieving resonator adjustment will be examined in a systematic way as each group is separately considered. However, at this point the close relationship between [n] and the plosive lingua–alveolar [d] should be mentioned.

Some singers with inflexible tongue action, or with too strong a tongue thrust, do not find freedom through the [n] vowel in initial attempts. In such cases, an exercise that alternates [n] and [d] should be tried. It can be quickly noted that mouth, tongue, lips, and jaw are in similar positions for both phonemes. (Location of both [d] and [n] varies somewhat from person to person and language to language, of course.) Among native Italian singers, who tend to touch only briefly the nasal consonants (unless they are doubled), [n] in singing is often only slightly discernible from [d], which is indicative of the closeness of their postural relationship.

EXERCISE 6.6

[da - na - da]   [na - da,   da - na,   da - na - da]

SOME USES OF THE VOICED
LINGUAVELAR STOP [ŋ]

When suffering from a head cold, one is made aware of the relationship between the formation of [g] as in "rug" and of [ŋ] as in "rung." The velar plosive [g] is produced in a position similar to that which forms the nasal continuant [ŋ], but the latter maintains an open port into the nasopharynx not enjoyed by [g].

Many phoneticians believe that in [ŋ] the mouth cavity does not contribute to the sound because of close contact between the soft palate and the tongue. Some other phoneticians question such complete occlusion of tongue and palate during the execution of [ŋ].

The pedagogical merit of [ŋ] has long been acknowledged by singers as a means of achieving an improved resonance balance. Although Thomas Fillebrown (1911, pp. 58–59) did not invent the use of [ŋ] for resonance balancing in singing, he popularized it through his now-famous "Hung-ee" series of vocalises.

For most singers, the velar nasal posture of [ŋ] produces a sensation located high in the *masque*. Vibratory sensations in the frontal area of the face are often intense. This is the sensation of "forward resonance" associated with the singer's formant.

The next vocalise is patterned after those of Fillebrown and his Italian contemporaries (if oral tradition can be trusted), but here [h] will be replaced with the sibilant [s]. The vocalise becomes "Sung-ee." This preference for the sibilant over the glottal fricative [h] is based on the sudden deflection of the stream of air into the mouth cavity as opposed to the possibility for more gradual entrance with [h].

EXERCISE 6.7

sung [i   e   ɑ   e   i]

In the first phase of the vocalises, prior to the emergence of the vowel, there should be an acute awareness of nasality, sensation now having progressed beyond that induced by the use of [n]. With the second phase of the vocalise (vowel replaces the nasal continuant), the quick discontinuance of lingua–alveolar contact should be complete. The coupling of the nasopharyngeal and buccal resonators is immediate.

EXERCISE 6.8

sung [i   e   ɔ   e   i   e   o]

SOME USES OF THE LINGUA–PALATAL–NASAL CONTINUANT [ɲ]

In describing the pedagogical uses of the nasal continuants, it was mentioned that the entire oral cavity serves as a resonator in the execution of [m] (while remaining in a lateral position). It has also been shown that in [n] the oral cavity is altered so the portion lying behind the conjunction of tongue and alveolar ridge acts as a resonator without contribution from the forward area between the teeth and the lips, and that in [ŋ] the mouth cavity (with the exception of the faucial area) is probably excluded as a resonator.

Still another nasal continuant, the lingua–palatal-nasal continuant [ɲ], can be useful. It is found in such words as *"ogni"* and *"gnocchi"* in Italian, and even in English words such as *"onion"* and *"union."*

The ultimate location of high "head sensation" is often experienced with the phoneme [ɲ], pinpointing a feeling of "resonance" squarely in the center of the *masque,* or behind the nose, the eyes, or in some related area of the face, depending on subjective responses of the singer.

EXERCISE 6.9

It will be seen at once that these syllables are based on the Italian word *ogni,* and that the exercise stems from the Italian School. The syllables, at the repetition on the vocalise, are reversed, the initial sound then being the lingua-palatal-nasal one.

The next two exercises are built upon alternation of nasal continuants and front and back vowels. (Exercise 6.10 may very well be an "everyman" vocalise in more than one sense. Exercise 6.11 expands the practice of the lingua-palatal-nasal continuant in alternation with vowels, and the singer must "vowelize" from front to back on *ignudo,* making this a very revealing exercise.)

EXERCISE 6.10

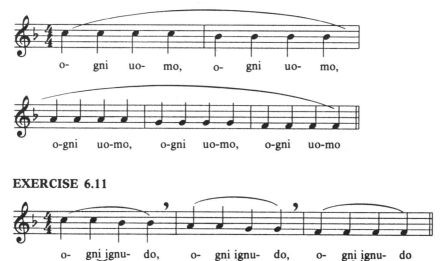

EXERCISE 6.11

It is occasionally useful to run the series of four nasal continuants in sequence on a single pitch, as an exercise in quickly experiencing variations of the sensation of *masque* "resonance." Some singers like to massage in circular motion the maxillary area of the face while singing the nasal continuants. The value of such an exercise may be largely psychological, but it is possible that the additional physical action on the face heightens perception of *masque* sensations.

SOME GENERAL CONSIDERATIONS ON THE NASAL CONTINUANTS

Many people come from regions where nasality is characteristic of speech (a phenomenon not restricted to midwestern or southern Atlantic seaboard America), especially whenever a nasal continuant occurs in the phrase. Lingering nasality becomes habitual for phonation. Uses of nasal continuants take on added relevance for singers with speech backgrounds where such rhinolalia (excessive or constant nasality in speech) is an accepted mode of speech. Consciousness of the comparative locations and accompanying sensations in the four nasal continuants, and how they can be produced, often has a salubrious effect on speech problems. Fricatives, plosives and sibilants, and consonants that close off the nose and direct sound into the oral cavity, may be alternated with nasal continuants.

Much of the problem with "placement" terminology in singing is that singers attempt physical actions which they assume will produce certain desirable "resonance" results, but which have other functional ramifications. In trying to "place" sound, they falsely adjust parts of the vocal tract, thereby hampering flexibility. One of the best ways to develop good acoustic function in resonator adjustment is through the use of the nasal continuants.

Sometimes a singer's production is based on exaggerated muscle stretching to achieve velar elevation, excessive laryngeal depression, and a hanging jaw (as unaesthetic to look at as it must be difficult to accomplish!). With that kind of vocal technique, the postures essential to the formation of the nasal continuants are difficult to execute. The nasals can be used therapeutically, because during their production the soft palate must remain, to some extent, in a more relaxed position, with the port into the nasopharynx remaining open and tone being directed into the nasal cavities. In some of the nasals, as has been seen, the mouth has little or no participation, or participates from a narrow lateral position. The problem of excessive jaw dropping (under the assumption that to hang it is to relax it) may be attacked through the nasal continuants. (Of course, it is possible to use [ŋ] with the jaw forced downward. When that is the tendency, replace it with [n].)

In techniques of singing which avoid the postures essential to the production of nasals, nasal continuants and humming are out. On the contrary, any freely produced voice should be able to vocalize on the nasals throughout most of the effective range of the instrument. It is difficult to do so with [m] in the upper range, because the mouth should open in ascending pitch. Even in that range, however, [m] can be a useful corrective exercise. In the upper voice, the [n] and the [ŋ] hum are preferable for vocalization.

In the give and take of language, whether in speaking or singing, the acoustic postures assumed by the resonators in the nasals must quickly alter to comply with the phonetic sequences that follow them. The principle of total flexibility of the shaping potential of the resonator tube is inimical to some vocal pedagogies in which one ideal resonator shape is advocated. Eminent Italian laryngologist and authority on the singing voice, Carlo Meano (1964, p. 156), refers to this dichotomy among teaching techniques when admonishing that,

> Especially in singing, it is necessary that the voice have the maximum sonority, for which all the parts of the resonance cavities must participate in the sonorous production, particularly the *nasal cavity,* any impediment of which constricts the throat, causing the voice to become excessively dark, as can often be verified among singers of northern origin.

The main route of vocal pedagogy to which most professional singers of international stature adhere is based on resonance precepts of the historic Italian School as articulated in the second half of the nineteenth century and the early decades of the twentieth century. Nasal continuants play a major role in those concepts.

Additional benefits from using "humming" sounds are found in the heightened "support" sensations experienced in the torso, which are the result of total or partial closure of the mouth that occurs during the production of nasals.

CHAPTER 7

Resonance Balancing through Non-nasal Consonants

The Influence of Non-nasal Consonants on Resonator Adjustment

USES OF THE VOICED LINGUA-ANTERIOR-PALATAL CONTINUANT [j]

The voiced lingua-anterior-palatal [j] is clearly discernible in the English word "yes," and in the "double vowel" of the Italian word *ieri*. In singing, [j] is best treated as a quickly occurring version of the vowel [i], joined to the oncoming vowel. The [j], sometimes termed a semi-vowel or a liquid consonant, is a useful pilot sound.

When pitch begins on a word introduced by the vowel [u], many singers sense a loss of "focus," a lack of "resonance." The phoneme [j] often is coupled with the back vowel [u], as in the word "you." By substituting "you" for a word such as *luna, Uhr,* or "soon," as a momentary exercise, improvement in the resonance of the syllable containing [u] will result. The original word is then sung with the same "resonance." In so doing, we juxtapose vowels [i] and [u] (at opposite poles of the vowel series), then we quickly unite them in a single syllable. Because of the initial high tongue posture, which begins with the mouth in a lateral position, followed by low posture (from [i] to [u]), the sense of "focus" remains throughout the diphthong.

The word "yes" also serves as a splendid pilot word for locating a sensation of balanced resonance in singing. Diphthongization occurs quickly in speech but may require much more time in singing, in which case some recognition of the rhythmic relationships of the two parts of the diphthong must remain. The phoneme [j] then becomes the vowel [i] in words like "you" and "yes." A five-note descending scale, sung in medium range, illustrates the exercise.

EXERCISE 7.1

you,   you,   you,   you,   you

Similar help may be found by coupling a nasal continuant with [j] using the combined sound as a pilot device for locating sensations of balanced resonance, as in the word "new" (pronounced [n i u], and not to be confused through regional speech habits with "gnu").

EXERCISE 7.2

new,   new,   new,   new,   new

Each singer can devise words of this sort as aids temporarily substituted for syllables that cause problems. A particularly helpful vocalise that makes use of [j] is built on the phrase *ieri l'altro*, in which the vowel sequence (when sung slowly) is [i ɛ i ɑ o].

EXERCISE 7.3

ie- ri l'al-tro,   ie- ri l'al-tro,   ie- ri l'al-tro

USES OF THE LINGUA-ALVEOLAR CONTINUANT [l]

As with the nasal continuants, the consonant [l] can be vocalized as a syllable of extended duration. The [l] is a fickle sound, behaving sometimes as a semivowel and sometimes as a consonant. An obvious relationship exists between [n] and [l] in the position of the tongue at the alveolar ridge. (When singing the nasals, sound passes through the nasal cavities, and there is a tendency to nasalize [l] as well, because of its formation at the alveolar ridge. It is wise to close off the end of the nostrils occasionally while singing [l] to be certain that nasality does not intrude.)

The consonant [l] shares yet another characteristic with the nasal continuant [n], in that the mouth is partially opened. Greater freedom is experienced by some singers in phonetic–acoustic situations where the mouth is partially opened; buccal closure in the youthful, unskilled singer may induce too much glottal resistance.

Because the consonant [l] requires an upward stroke of the tongue as it moves toward the alveolar ridge from the acoustic at-rest posture, [l] is capable of producing an inordinate number of transition sounds, especially in combination with ensuing vowels and consonants. Sometimes [l] is a detrimental influence on clean articulation in singing. On the other hand, when properly executed, [l] is one of the most favorable consonants for achieving facile tongue action, the key to good articulation. The blade of the tongue should move quickly from its position of contact with the lower front teeth to the alveolar ridge, where it must be fully forward in direct contact with the inner surfaces of the upper front teeth. In singing, [l] should never rest at the posterior edge of the alveolar ridge. Both in approaching this phonetic position and in taking leave of it, the tongue must avoid the slow motions that are typical of this consonant in most American and British speech. In the English language, [l] tends to be formed farther back up the alveolar ridge (indeed, at times behind it) than in the Latin languages, producing a lazy, liquid consonant that encourages transition sounds. The continuant [l] should be executed with a light flick of the tongue; following the production of [l], the tongue should quickly return to the position of phonetic rest, with absolutely no transition sounds permitted.

When properly harnessed, [l] helps acquire the quick tongue action essential to free articulation. A sluggish [l] destroys all hope for good diction. The consonant [l] can serve as a model for all other alveolar consonants when the singer has mastered it. Even the doubled consonant, although long in duration in several languages, must be sharply enunciated.

EXERCISE 7.4: "LA-LA-LA-LA-LA"

(1) REPEAT A PATTERN OF CONSECUTIVE [l] SYLLABLES IN A COMFORTABLE RANGE OF THE SPEAKING VOICE; VARY THE TEMPO OF THE SERIES OF SYLLABLES, MAKING CERTAIN THAT THE TONGUE BLADE PERFORMS ITS ACTION QUICKLY, RETURNING AT ONCE TO THE CENTRAL "AT-REST" POSITION. (2) AT SOME MODERATE PITCH LEVEL, SING THE SAME SERIES IN A LEGATO FASHION, BEGINNING AT SLOW TEMPO, GRADUALLY ACCELERATING.

EXERCISE 7.5

la   la   la   la   la   la   la   la   la

The phoneme [l] should scarcely interrupt the vowel flow. Alternation between two notes on one syllable and one note per syllable permits the singer to check that the vowel is not truncated and that it does not succumb to any change of timbre because of transition sounds.

EXERCISE 7.6

la la la   la,   la   la   la la la,   la

la la la   la la la   la la la   la

The consonant [l] should be of as brief duration as possible; the tongue leaves the central phonetic posture at the lower teeth only momentarily, quickly returning there.

USES OF THE ALVEOLAR SINGLE [ɾ] AND THE ALVEOLAR ROLLED [r̆]

In the single flip (single-tap) [ɾ], a fast flap of the tongue point against the alveolar ridge is caused by breath emission, which produces a quickly executed fricative sound uniquely its own. This is followed by an immediate return of the tongue to its "home base," in contact with the lower teeth.

Properly executed forms of r in singing bear some similarities to the consonant [l] and to several of the nasal continuants, in that the mouth remains somewhat opened but partly closed off by the forward tongue position (lingual closure) (Hirano et al, 1966, p. 377). If the single flip [ɾ] is difficult to manage, substitute the consonant [d].

The singer should never confuse the single tap [r] with the tongue-point trill (rolled) [r̆]. (The symbol [r̆] is used in this work, and in many phonetic sources, to represent the alveolar rolled r, because the IPA symbol for the trilled r, [r], is used indiscriminately in many American sources to indicate any form of r.) The tongue-point trill is one of the most important of all technical devices for inducing looseness of the tongue *at both its frontal and its hyoidal extremities*. In order for the flapping motion of the tongue blade to take place, no tension may exist within the muscle bundles that make up the body of the tongue. In the freely trilled (rolled) [r̆], there can be no tension at the points of tongue contact at the upper teeth and the alveolar ridge. Nor can the tongue-point trill be properly executed if there is tension in the hyoidal musculature. (The larynx is suspended by the thyrohyoid membrane from the hyoid bone, to which the tongue also is attached. See Figures 4.8 and 4.9). Another advantage of the tongue-point trill is that it prevents excessive spreading of the buccal–pharyngeal cavity (which is occupied by the mass of the tongue). This is especially the case during rapid pitch changes within a phrase sung on the sustained tongue-point trill.

EXERCISE 7.7

SUSTAIN THE SPOKEN SYLLABLE "BRRR!" DURING ASCENDING AND DESCENDING PITCHES OF APPROXIMATELY AN OCTAVE, PORTAMENTO FASHION.

EXERCISE 7.8

[ř ———————————————————]

SING THE TONGUE-POINT TRILL ON A DESCENDING FIVE-NOTE PATTERN.

EXERCISE 7.9

[ř ———————————————————]

SING THE TONGUE-POINT TRILL ON A PHRASE OF MODERATE DURATION.

The tongue-point trill (tongue blade trill or flutter) exercises have two specific goals: (1) to induce freedom in larynx and tongue and (2) to increase awareness of good breath management, which is essential for lingual vibration. The consciousness of the trunk as the source of breath control is heightened by the use of the tongue point flutter. There is a marked sensation in the anterolateral abdominal wall during the execution of the prolonged tongue blade trill, as is also the case with nasal continuants.

To represent r as a single consonant without suggesting the number of variations on the r theme is confusing. The single tap [r] and the tongue point trill [ř] are two such phonemic variants. Others include sounds omitted in cultivated singing. The retroflex speech sounds [ɝ] and [ɚ], in which the tongue curls backward toward the center of the mouth in much of American and some regional British speech, is *never* used in artistic singing. The retroflex [ɚ] is heard in folk, pop, jazz, soul, rock, and (especially) in country western literatures; the extremely retroflexed r is indicated by [ɻ]. It contributes more to vowel distortion than any other phoneme in Western languages. Americans who are untrained singers rely almost entirely on the sounds [ɝ] and [ɚ] of regional speech for the proper r. (In speech, factors of duration and stress, and the degree of retroflexing, determine which symbol is accurate; in singing, these differences tend to merge.) The so-called "midwestern r" ([ɻ]), prominent in many geographical regions of North America, makes difficult the execution of either the single tap [r] or the rolled [ř].

The uvular rolled [Ř] and the velar fricative [ʁ], characteristic of spoken French and (in some regions) of spoken German, are avoided in well-schooled singing in both French and German.

The consonants thus far considered have the dangerous tendency to induce *on-glides* and *off-glides* (transition sounds) which upset clean vowel definition. Exercises have been devised as a systematic way of eliminating such distortion of subsequent vowels. This group of consonants demands quick tongue movement. Tongue and jaw flexibility cannot coexist with the stationary hung jaw and the overly distended pharynx. The "setting syndrome" of hung jaw and spread throat techniques is corrected through these exercises.

At a later point, benefits to be gained from coupling [l], [r], or [ř] to other consonants in singing will be considered.

USES OF THE VOICED LABIODENTAL FRICATIVE CONTINUANT [v] AND THE VOICELESS LABIODENTAL FRICATIVE CONTINUANT [f]

In the [v] the upper incisors meet the bottom lip. The continuant [v] and its voiceless counterpart [f], as well as a neighboring continuant [z] and its voiceless paired consonant [s], recall the central position of phonation, the at-rest posture previously described. Certain modifications of the central phonetic position must take place in order to arrive at the exact physiological postures essential to the production of [v] and [f], but those modifications are slight: some mandibular adjustment, contact between the upper incisors and the lower lip (as was just seen), some closure of the nasopharyngeal port, and approximation of the vocal folds. In singing, it is significant that in executing [v] and [z], and their voiceless mates [f] and [s], the tongue need not move from its acoustic, at-rest posture.

In the production of [v], the lips assume something of the horizontal smile position, avoiding any vertical buccal posture. The external orifice is narrowed, and the laryngeal sound is deflected directly into the oral cavity. The consonant [v], being a continuant, demands no change in posture within the vocal tract throughout its duration. (The consonants [v] and [f] are both fricative and labiodental.)

Singers learn a great deal about the process of resonator coupling when [v] precedes vowels. That mouth position, with parted lips, closely resembles the posture associated with pleasure and repose. The physical location of [v] encourages sensations in the *masque* area of the face.

EXERCISE 7.10

(1) AT A COMFORTABLE PITCH LEVEL, RECITE THE SYLLABLES [*vi-ve-va-vo-vu*].
(2) RECITE THE SYLLABLES [*fi-fe-fa-fo-fu*].

EXERCISE 7.11

AT A COMFORTABLE PITCH LEVEL, ON A SINGLE PITCH, SING THE SYLLABLES [*vi-ve-va-vo-vu*]. THEN SUBSTITUTE THE CONSONANT [f] for [v].

EXERCISE 7.12

```
[vi- ve - va- ve - vo - ve - vu - ve -  vi]
[fi - fe - fa - fe - fo - fe - fu - fe -  fi ]
[vi- fe - va- fa - vi - fi - vo- fo -  vi]
[fe- va- va- fa - fe - va- va- fa -  fe]
```

ALTERNATE THE SYLLABLES INITIATED BY [v] AND [f].

USES OF THE VOICED BILABIAL STOP PLOSIVE [b] AND THE VOICELESS BILABIAL STOP PLOSIVE [p].

Consonants [b] and [p] are called bilabials because both lips are involved in their formation; they are also classified as stop plosives. Because the nasopharynx is closed and the vocal folds approximated, the airstream, when released from bilabial stop-plosive impedance, flows directly into the buccal cavity. Lip posture during [b] and [p] remains in the central, at-rest position, although occluded, occasioning an increase of air pressure in the mouth. The lips meet firmly; as they release, the mouth opens quickly, so that the airstream is suddenly permitted to exit.

The consonant [b] is a voiced consonant, while its companion [p] is a surd (that is, a voiceless consonant). The [b] shares a certain characteristic with the nasal continuant [m] in that both are produced by a closure of the lips. However, quite different conditions prevail in the velar area during the production of the two consonants, as a moment's demonstration will prove.

In all bilabial acoustic events, breath is stopped by the lips, with breath pressure accumulating behind them. The sudden release of the lips often brings the perception that "tone" has been directly produced at the lips, and this has psychological (as well as physiological) implications for persons whose attention has been excessively directed toward the pharyngeal or laryngeal areas. On the other hand, the very occlusion of the lips serves to identify sharply for the singer a resonance chamber comprised of both mouth and pharynx.

EXERCISE 7.13

(1) SILENTLY FORM THE LIPS IN POSITION FOR THE PRODUCTION OF [b], BEING CONSCIOUS OF BUCCOPHARYNGEAL SPACE. **(2)** SUBSTITUTE [p] FOR [b] IN THE SAME MANNER. **(3)** SING [b] and [p] ALTERNATELY, COUPLING THEM WITH A VOWEL AT MODERATE PITCH LEVEL. REMAIN ON THE SAME COMFORTABLE PITCH, ONCE AGAIN NOTING THE SPATIAL ARRANGEMENT OF THE RESONATOR CAVITIES.

EXERCISE 7.14

[be- pe- be- pe, pe- be- pe- be, pe be pe be]

ALTERNATE THESE PAIRED CONSONANTS, OBSERVING THE SENSATION AT THE LIPS, AND BE AWARE OF THE CONTRAST BETWEEN VOICED AND UNVOICED CONSONANTS.

EXERCISE 7.15

[be- pe- be, pe- be- pe]

USES OF THE VOICED LINGUA-ALVEOLAR FRICATIVE CONTINUANT [z] AND THE VOICELESS LINGUA-ALVEOLAR FRICATIVE CONTINUANT [s]

Another consonant which has considerable merit in assisting the singer to experience desirable resonator balance is [z]. It has been seen that this voiced lingua-alveolar fricative is a continuant that requires little alteration from the central acoustic position, and therefore illustrates the possibility of minimal technical entanglement in singing. Breath passes between teeth and tongue, the tongue being elevated and nearly, or lightly, flattened against the hard palate, producing a narrow orifice. A small stream of air passes over the edge of some of the teeth, generally the incisors; this explains the presence of a hissing noise which accompanies the laryngeally produced tone in [z].

The lips are parted, and mandibular movement is slight. The close relationship between buccal cavity and upper jaw contributes to the frontally located sensation of [z] and [s]. As pilot consonants for subsequent vowels this pair of consonants often helps the singer find that ideally balanced tone which is composed of fundamental and upper partials in correct proportions. The consonants [z] and [s] are especially useful in correcting hollow and unfocused vocal quality.

EXERCISE 7.16

[z _____]

A VOCALISE ON [z] HELPS IDENTIFY ITS CHARACTERISTIC PRODUCTION.

EXERCISE 7.17

za-	za-	za-	za-	za-	za-	za-	za-	za
ze-	za-	ze-	za-	ze-	za-	ze-	za-	ze
za-	ze-	zi -	zo-	za-	ze-	zi -	zo-	za

SING SYLLABLES INTRODUCED BY [z] WITH TONGUE ENGAGEMENT AT THE LOWER TEETH AND WITH LATERAL POSTURE OF THE MOUTH.

EXERCISE 7.18

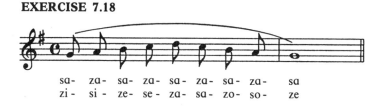

sa- za- sa- za- sa- za- sa- za- sa
zi - si - ze- se - za- sa- zo- so - ze

ALTERNATE [z] AND [s].

USES OF THE VOICED LINGUADENTAL FRICATIVE CONTINUANT [ð] AND THE VOICELESS LINGUADENTAL FRICATIVE CONTINUANT [θ]

The pitch consonant [ð], as in "thy," further exaggerates sensation in the upper jaw which was already somewhat experienced in [z]. The linguadental consonant [ð] is produced with elevated tongue, although the tongue is flattened and protruded so that its lower surface is in contact with the edges of the lower teeth, its superior surface in contact with the edges of the upper teeth. The accompanying "buzzy" feeling that results from sustaining the consonant [ð] is generally strongly felt in the upper jaw and *masque* areas. Through exercises involving this consonant, the singer becomes aware of the desirable balances among buccal, nasal, and pharyngeal resonators.

EXERCISE 7.19

[ð ———————————————]

EXERCISE 7.20

ðai- ðai, ðai, ðai, ðai- ðai, ðai
(thy- thy, thy, thy, thy- thy, thy)

A counterpart to the voiced consonant [ð] is its paired voiceless linguadental fricative continuant [θ], as in the word "think." Although [θ] is closely related to the voiced analogue [ð], and its relationship to the central acoustic position is identical with that of [ð], the vocal folds are not approximated with [θ], so that air is directed suddenly into the oral cavity.

The advantage of prefacing a vowel sound with the unvoiced linguadental fricative is that it encourages a loose glottis and a narrow buccal aperture, and it helps in releasing tension with some singers who make too much use of subglottic pressure and who distend the jaw.

EXERCISE 7.21

[ðai-   θai-   ðai-   θai-   ðai]
(thy,   thigh,   thy,   thigh,   thy)

EXERCISE 7.22

θai   θai   θai   θai   θai
(thigh, thigh, thigh, thigh,   thigh)

USES OF THE VOICED LINGUA–ALVEOLAR STOP PLOSIVE [d] AND THE VOICELESS LINGUA–ALVEOLAR STOP PLOSIVE [t]

In singing, the voiced lingua–alveolar stop plosive [d] may resemble the phoneme to which some phoneticians give the symbol [ḍ]. Singers have a tendency on [d] to press the tongue against the inner surfaces of the upper teeth, to increase subglottic pressure, and then to remove the tongue from the alveolar position with a very sluggish movement. Empirically, one senses that in the sound [d] the stream of air is blocked by the pressure of the tongue. In a badly produced [d], there are many possibilities for vocal tension, because the vocal folds are approximated, the port into the nasopharynx is probably closed, and tongue elevation prevents the escape of air through the mouth.

By moving the tongue toward the [ḍ] posture and by enunciating with a quick, light motion, glottal or lingual tension can be avoided. (In this instance, as in all consideration of the effect of consonants on resonator adjustment, it is not presumed that every singer encounters the same kinds of problems with each consonant. However, a systematic pedagogy must be at hand to deal with faulty function wherever it occurs in the singing instrument.)

The desirable [d] in singing is the dentalized [d̪], which lies close to the sound heard just prior to [z] in the word "adz."

EXERCISE 7.23

PRONOUNCE THE WORD "ADZ" AND REPEAT IT; PAUSE ON THE PHONEME [d̪], MOMENTARILY DROPPING THE SECOND CONSONANT [z]. REPEAT, REPLACING [z] WITH [ɑ].

EXERCISE 7.24

RETAINING THE SAME LINGUAL LOCATION FOR [d̪] AS ENCOUNTERED IN EXERCISE 7.23, REPEAT THE PHRASE "DA-DA-DA-DA-DA." (MOST INFANTS MAKE USE OF THE PHONEME [d̪] WHEN LEARNING TO SAY "DADDY," BEFORE THE EAR HAS BECOME CONDITIONED TO THE HARDER, MORE POSTERIORLY LOCATED ALVEOLAR [d] ASSOCIATED WITH THE ENGLISH LANGUAGE.)

The consonant [t] is produced in a manner similar to its voiced counterpart [d], with the exception that it is unvoiced; the vocal folds do not approximate in its production. Therefore, there is less tendency to squeeze the plosive [t] in singing than the plosive [d]. Although [d] and [t] may be produced in nearly identical locations in spoken English, when singing [t̪] in most European languages the blade of the tongue avoids the strong percussive sound of [t] as it is heard in the English language. In fact, the difference between tongue position in [d̪] and in [t̪] when produced in the "European" manner (a necessity when singing much of the great vocal literature) is often minimal.

When glottal closure is desired together with a forward tongue posture and a relatively moderate mandibular distention, [d̪] is often very useful. If there is evidence of too much glottal pressure, as is often the case when beginning a word such as "day" on a high pitch, the momentary substitution of [t̪] for [d] will tend to release tension. After practicing the passage with [t̪] a few times, [d] is made easier.

EXERCISE 7.25

(1) AT A MODERATE SPEECH LEVEL, WITH TONGUE WELL FORWARD, REPEAT [dɑ-te-de-te-do-te-dɑ-te]. (2) SING THE SAME COMBINATION OF SYLLABLES (OR ALTER THEM) BY USING ANY CONVENIENT VOWEL COMBINATION WHILE RETAINING THE ALTERNATION OF [d] AND [t̪] ON ONE PITCH AT A MEDIUM RANGE LEVEL.

EXERCISE 7.26

```
[da   te   da   te   da]
[te   da   te   da   te ]
```

ALTERNATE THE LINGUA-ALVEOLAR STOP PLOSIVES.

EXERCISE 7.27

```
[de   de   de   de]
[te   te   te   te ]
[te   de   te   de]
[de   te   de   te ]
```

ALTERNATE THE LINGUA–ALVEOLAR STOP PLOSIVES.

EXERCISE 7.28

```
[te   de   te   de   te ]
[de   te   de   te   de]
[te   de   de   te   te ]
```

ALTERNATE THE LINGUA–ALVEOLAR STOP PLOSIVES.

Many singers have a tendency to preface [d] with an additional sound such as [m], probably in an attempt to avoid the glottal closure (and the lack of immediate sound). Sometimes "ha" is also intruded. We hear such interpolations as "[m]Bald aber küsst sie," "[n]Du Ring an meinem Finger," "[h]deh! non cessar!" etc. (One recalls the classic example of the Italian singer of great fame who insisted he could not sing "The Hills of Home" except as "The Ills of Ome," because there is no [h] in the Italian language, but in his concluding Tosti song, sang "La-*ha*-mor!") An excellent counteraction of this vicious habit, which is very widespread, is to make use of such vocalises as those in the previous exercises, concentrating on sensations of forward acoustic position. (Of course, as with all of these vocalises, other pitch patterns may be used.)

USES OF THE VOICED LINGUAVELAR STOP PLOSIVE [g] AND THE VOICELESS LINGUAVELAR STOP PLOSIVE [k]

Another consonant that incites the wrong laryngeal involvement for many singers is [g], particularly when it occurs on a note of onset in an area of the vocal range which is not yet comfortable for the singer. As its location clearly shows, the voiced linguavelar stop plosive [g] brings total closure. The elevated back of the tongue touches the velum and presses against the rear portion of the hard palate. Yet, precisely because of this occlusion, [g] has merit for the singer.

Air, when finally released from the stoppage involved in the consonant [g], explodes directly into the buccal cavity, producing a condition of openness in the channel between the oropharynx and the oral cavity. The sensation from that event is very distinct and extremely useful. When a singer habitually suffers from a lowered velar posture, with resultant nasality and thinness of quality, the use of [g] can prove to be a valuable antidote. Even when such faults are not present, [g] has great worth as a conditioner of proper resonance balancing.

The consonant [k] provides an even more dramatic illustration of the release from linguavelar occlusion. The strong sensations between closure and openness of the nasopharyngeal passage and the mouth can be realized even in whispering.

EXERCISE 7.29

WHISPER "BIG GOAT," LINGERING OVER THE STOP PLOSIVE [g]; REPEAT THE WORDS AT A FAIRLY HIGH DYNAMIC LEVEL.

WHISPER "SICK CAT," LINGERING OVER THE STOP PLOSIVE [k]; REPEAT AT A FAIRLY HIGH SPOKEN DYNAMIC LEVEL, IN THE SAME RHYTHM.

SLOWLY SPEAK THE PHRASES "BIG GOAT; SICK CAT," LINGERING OVER THE TWO STOP PLOSIVES.

AT A MODERATE PITCH, SING THE PHRASE "BIG GOAT, SICK CAT," LINGERING OVER THE STOP PLOSIVES. BE AWARE OF THE ACOUSTICAL POSTURES OF [g] AND [k] AND OF THE IMMEDIACY OF THE SUBSEQUENT VOWEL SOUNDS.

This prefatory spoken exercise should serve as an introduction to other exercises that cultivate a sense of openness (following closure) in the nasopharynx, and result in the *gola aperta.*

The exercises that follow establish an awareness of the raised velum in singing. Because of that action, they are ideal for eliminating nasality in the singing voice.

EXERCISE 7.30

[ge,	go,	gaw,	ge - go - ge-go, ge,	go,	ge]
[ke,	ko,	kaw,	ke- ko- ke-ko, ke,	ko,	ke]
[gi,	ge,	ke,	gi - ge - ki -ke, gi,	ki,	ge]
[ga,	ga,	ka,	ga- ka - ga-ka, ga,	ka,	ga]

EXERCISE 7.31

[gi -	ge-	gi -	ge,	gi - ge- gi - ge- gi - ge- gi - ge-	gi]
[ki -	ke-	ki -	ke,	ki - ke- ki - ke- ki - ke- ki ~ ke-	gi]
[go-	ge-	go-	ge,	go- ge- go- ge- go- ge- go- ge-	go]
[ko-	ke-	ko-	ke,	ko- ke- ko- ke- ko- ke- ko- ke-	ko]
[gi -	ke-	gi -	ke,	gi - ke- gi - ke- gi - ke- gi - ke-	gi]

EXERCISE 7.32

| [ki - ke- ki-ke- ki, | gi - ge-gi - ge- gi, | ki- ke- ki-ke- ki] |
| [gi - ke- gi -ke- gi, | ga- ka-ga- ka- ga, | gi- ke- ki-ke- gi] |

USES OF VOICELESS CONSONANTS IN GENERAL

Phonetic symbols representing speech sounds in a number of languages can never cover the full range of acoustic events of which the vocal mechanism is capable. Many of these postures are easier than others to produce. This depends on the language background of the individual. During the development of language, certain sounds have been selected while others have been suppressed, as a result of cultural environment. (There is no biological reason why the clicks of certain South African tribes should not have been incorporated into the speech patterns of Western European languages.)

The presence or absence of certain phonemes in a speaker's own language may explain difficulties encountered in another language. For example, the sounds of the French, Germanic, and Slavic languages are not easily caught and imitated by many English-speaking tongues, and the reverse is equally true, yet singers must regularly deal with the sounds of several branches of language. Good singers do so remarkably well. There is a direct correlation between the singer's ability to be phonetically precise, even in foreign languages, and the ability to produce desirable vocal timbre.

Frequently, the voiceless consonant appears to be unfriendly to the singer. Languages that display a high incidence of unvoiced consonants are sometimes disparaged by singers. Despite their lack of pitch orientation, there is no need for the voiceless consonants to be detrimental to the production of a good vocal line. They can be comfortably incorporated in such a way that they do not break the flow of sound.

The best way to deal with voiceless sounds in singing is to isolate them and analyze them phonetically. Later, when they appear separately or when they group in clusters, even in quickly delivered recitative or soaring vocal line, they will be met as manageable acquaintances.

Drilling of coupled consonants is essential for establishing agile tongue action. The same problem-solving principle, of course, applies to any "diction" difficulty that may come up in the vocal literature. If the tongue stumbles on some phonemic combination, those sounds may be extracted and made into an exercise.

Flexibility of tongue, lips, jaw, and the entire resonator tube can become so well routined that the singer has no problems with any consonant combination. If the singer possesses an articulatory ease far beyond the norm, time should not be wasted in practicing the remaining exercises in this chapter. There are singers who sing all languages well. They also have techniques that allow them to produce free vocal sounds. The free voice has no diction problems!

The exercises that follow are based chiefly on voiced and unvoiced consonants combined with the consonants [l], [r], and [ɾ]. This is because of the inherent problem of transition sounds connected with the approach of the tongue to the alveolar ridge. However, flexible execution of the consonant, whether it has pitch or is pitchless, can often be the key that unlocks proper resonator balance.

The suggested useful pitch patterns may be altered, but they or others similar in nature should be used to drill combinations of coupled consonants, vowels, and diphthongs.

USEFUL PITCH PATTERNS

Pattern 1

Pattern 2

Pattern 3

Pattern 4

VOWEL AND DIPHTHONG PATTERNS

These patterns may be altered, of course, but they or others similar in structure should be used to drill some combinations of coupled consonants, and vowels and diphthongs.

Vowel Patterns	Diphthong Patterns
[i]	[ɑo]
[e]	[ou]
[ɛ]	[eɪ]
[ɑ]	[ɔɪ]
[ɔ]	[ɑɪ]
[o]	
[u]	

COUPLED CONSONANTS

These consonants are to precede the vowels and diphthongs, sung on the indicated patterns.

[ml]	[mr]
[nl]	[nr]
[vl]	[vr]
[zl]	[zr]
[dl]	[dr]
[tl]	[tr]
[pl]	[pr]
[fl]	[fr]
[gl]	[gr]
[kl]	[kr]
[θl]	[θr]
[ðl]	[ðr]
[sl]	[sr]
[ʃl]	[ʃr]

If the acquisition of a thorough technique of singing is a desirable goal, a singer should be willing to master the kind of acoustical detail these vocalises represent. On the other hand, an occasional run-through should be sufficient. The singer may then select any problematic ones for special attention.

It is questionable that either literature or technique can be successfully undertaken without some knowledge of the acoustic basis of vocal sound. The artist–singer must be capable of executing the many sounds of several languages and must know how they are differentiated. Unless singers are aware of the way in which vowels and consonants adjust the resonator tract, through either empirical or factual knowledge, they will not be able to find freedom in singing.

Any phonetic exercise that induces heightened localized sensation is valuable only if it activates participation from some neglected portion of the tripartite resonator system, the pharynx (including its three divisions—laryngo–oro–naso), the buccal cavity, and the nasal cavities. (For additional information as to the influence of voiced and unvoiced consonants on resonator adjustment, see Appendix V.)

CHAPTER 8

Sustaining the Voice

Sostenuto

Until singers master the onset, the brief phrase, and the skillful release, and can sing agilely, they will experience cumulative strain and fatigue on sustained phrases. If the singer is unable to articulate vowels without distortion and cannot manage rapid consonantal adjustment freely, the vocal instrument is certain to tire when those factors occur in sustained phrases.

There is a body of vocal literature whose chief characteristic is *sostenuto*. Almost none of this literature is appropriate to the technically insecure singer. Songs and arias of a sustained character, coupled with a high-lying tessitura, must be avoided until technique is relatively stabilized. Singing the great sweeping Brahmsian or Verdian line is not a logical expectation if the torso periodically collapses at phrase endings. Many lingering problems with singers can be traced to introducing sustained literature too early. The best road to the long-sustained phrase is to elongate progressively the breath-pacing exercise of short duration (see Chapter 2).

The ultimate test of technical ability lies in sustained singing. Energy and power are frequently required, but these attributes of the good singer must be balanced by freedom. The problem in sustained singing is that primitive sphincter action, which ordinarily prevails in such heavy activities as lifting and pulling, is often carried over into energized singing. During powerful sustained singing, the larynx is subjected to subglottic pressure. The singer must learn to be schizophrenic, engaging the respiratory musculature for heavy duty while not pressing the laryngeal valve. Indeed, freedom at the glottis can be present in the long phrase only if breath emission is controlled in the epigastric–umbilical and costal regions.

In attempting to avoid tensions that inadvertently result from the application of power, there is the perilous temptation to produce "relaxed" vocalism built on breath mixture. Breath mixture is the result of inefficient vocal-fold occlusion, which, in turn, is the result of poor breath management.

Often, the most precarious part of a mounting, sustained line is found not in approaching the climactic notes, but in descending from them. Breath energy has been expended improperly on the dramatic "high" note, with nothing left in reserve. Muscular support should increase following a vocal climax, especially when one is redescending through the *passaggio* zone.

Sostenuto vocalises should be begun as soon as basic techniques have been established. Sustained exercises of progressive difficulty are then gradually introduced. At each practice session, sostenuto is interspersed among onset, breath pacing, and agility vocalises. Giovanni Battista Lamperti's axiom (as recorded by Brown, 1931, p. 49) must always be kept in mind: "Power either builds or destroys."

Sostenuto has just such potential. Where voice technique is founded on systematically acquired skills, sostenuto fills its role as a builder of the instrument. Sustaining power will increase vocal stamina and ensure vocal health.

EXERCISES FOR DEVELOPING SOSTENUTO

Sostenuto is the culmination of all the technical aspects of singing. Therefore, a number of vocalises of a sustained nature are presented here. As in all technical areas of singing, passages from the literature should supplement this material. Pitch and tempo are adjusted in the vocalises to match the technical capacity of the individual. As facility increases, range should extend, and slower tempos may also be introduced.

Group 1 Exercises

EXERCISE 8.1

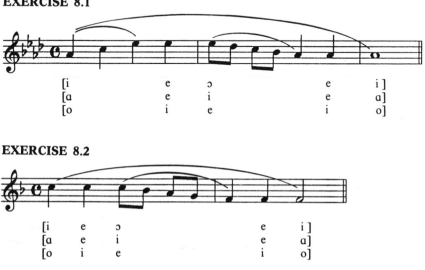

[i   e   ɔ   e   i]
[a   e   i   e   a]
[o   i   e   i   o]

EXERCISE 8.2

[i   e   ɔ   e   i]
[a   e   i   e   a]
[o   i   e   i   o]

EXERCISE 8.3

```
[i    e    ɔ              e    i ]
[ɑ    e    i              e    ɑ]
[e    i    ɔ              i    e]
```

EXERCISE 8.4

```
[ɑ    e    i              e    ɑ]
[i    e    ɔ              e    i]
[ɔ    o    u              o    ɑ]
```

EXERCISE 8.5

```
[i    e    ɑ                   e    i ]
[ɑ    e    i                   e    ɑ]
[o    i    e                   i    o]
```

EXERCISE 8.6

```
[i    e    ɑ                   e    i ]
[ɑ    e    i                   e    ɑ]
[ɔ    o    u                   o    e]
[u    o    ɔ                   o    u]
```

EXERCISE 8.7

```
[i           e    ɔ            e    i ]
[ɔ           e    i            e    ɔ]
[u           o    ɔ            o    u]
```

Group 2 Exercises

EXERCISE 8.8

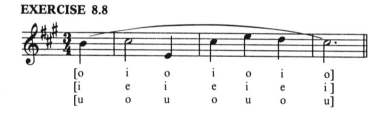

```
[o    i    o    i    o    i    o]
[i    e    i    e    i    e    i]
[u    o    u    o    u    o    u]
```

EXERCISE 8.9

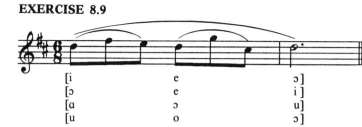

```
[i         e         ɔ]
[ɔ         e         i]
[ɑ         ɔ         u]
[u         o         ɔ]
```

EXERCISE 8.10

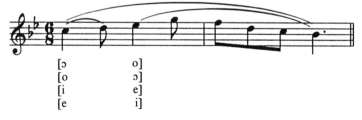

```
[ɔ         o]
[o         ɔ]
[i         e]
[e         i]
```

EXERCISE 8.11

```
[e    ɔ]
[ɔ    e]
[i    o]
[ɛ    ɑ]
```

Group 3 Exercises

EXERCISE 8.12

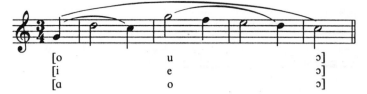

[i	e	ɔ	o	i	e]
[ɔ	e	i	e	o	ɔ]
[ɑ	o	e	o	e	ɑ]

EXERCISE 8.13

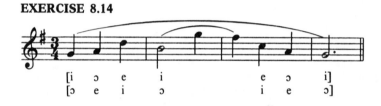

[o	u	ɔ]
[i	e	ɔ]
[ɑ	o	ɔ]

EXERCISE 8.14

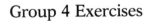

[i	ɔ	e	i	e	ɔ	i]
[ɔ	e	i	ɔ	i	e	ɔ]

Group 4 Exercises

EXERCISE 8.15

[ɔ	e	ɔ	e	ɔ]
[e	ɔ	e	ɔ	e]

EXERCISE 8.16

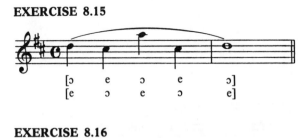

[e	ɔ	o	e	ɔ]

EXERCISE 8.17

Exercise 8.17 consists of a slow turn on every note of the scale. It may be sung at a moderately slow tempo (♩= 60–70), in a comfortable range. Gradually transpose by half steps throughout most of the singing range.

A single vowel is used (keep a balance between front and back vowels), or vowels may be varied by the phrase or by the beat. Consonants may be introduced before syllables on each phrase. The exercise is intended only for the technically secure professional singer, or for use under careful supervision of the teacher.

In order to secure the fully opened glottis and the immediate response among the great muscles of the torso, which ensure deep and precise inhalation, it is often wise to precede the sostenuto phrase with a bar of quick onset vocalises. The inhalation just before the sostenuto phrase is taken in exactly the same quiet, efficient, quick manner as in the onset vocalise. Equally important is to practice the sostenuto exercises with slow rhythmic breath pacing (inhalation) between the phrases of a consecutive series. In this manner, onset and sostenuto functions are combined.

Group 5 Exercises

EXERCISE 8.18

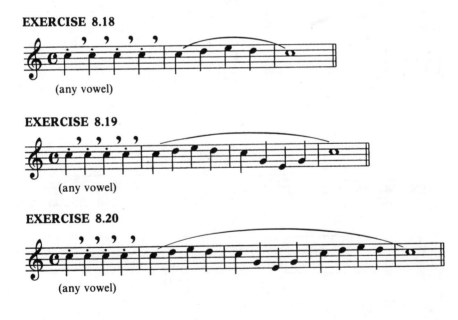

(any vowel)

EXERCISE 8.19

(any vowel)

EXERCISE 8.20

(any vowel)

CHAPTER 9

Unifying the Registers of Male Voices

REGISTER TERMINOLOGY

Register terminology should be carefully chosen. "Breaks" and "lifts" may well refer to existing register phenomena in a voice, but psychologically they tend to point up the divisions between registers rather than their unification. Although it is obvious that in the terminology of the Italian School there are also reminders of divisions, that terminology takes on a more gentle implication with its reference to register transition points as *primo passaggio* and *secondo passaggio*, with the *zona di passaggio* (the passage zone) lying between. (It is customary to use the terms "lower *passaggio*" and "upper *passaggio*" when dealing with the female voice.) Since many musical terms are in Italian, there seems no reason to avoid these terms in vocal registration. They are no longer restricted solely to the historic Italian School of singing, but are by now international in usage. Several decades ago, an attempt was made by a few American singing teachers to abandon the classic register terminology of the singing voice and to substitute for it the terminology of speech investigators, thereby designating only "modal" and "loft" registers. These terms, however, ignore the subtle differences in a number of register timbres recognized in traditional schools of singing. This limiting terminology is less frequently encountered, currently, even in investigative studies of the singing voice. There is a reemergence of interest in historic register phenomena, because they are a fundamental part of the art of elite vocalism.

By placing a hand on the chest of an adult male who is speaking, one becomes aware of sympathetic subglottic resonance (largely of the trachea and the bronchi). A rumbling sensation is felt against the hand as long as the speaker remains in a comfortable speech range. As the voice is sharply inflected upward, the vibratory rumble diminishes or ceases. (The same phenomenon occurs in the female chest voice— *voce di petto*—but women speakers tend not to use that register in speech with as much frequency as do male speakers.) (For a discussion of physical factors in voice registration, see Appendix IV.)

115

Primo passaggio (First Register Transition)

The speaking voice encompasses more than an octave of easy negotiation. Untrained singers have few problems in singing the pitches that lie within the speaking range. When adolescent males and untrained male singers approach the termination of the comfortable speech range, they reach a point in the ascending scale where they often involuntarily raise the chin and the larynx. The corresponding pitch is the *primo passaggio* (first register transition). The vibratory sympathetic chest rumble of the voice tends to lessen or stop. The untrained singer produces pitches beyond this pivotal point, but often resorts to laryngeal elevation to do so.

Secondo passaggio (Second Register Transition)

As the untrained singer continues to ascend the scale, quality change becomes more audible. At pitches about the interval of a fourth above the top of the comfortable speaking range (the point at which the need to elevate the larynx was originally felt), the untrained voice will either break off or resort to a sudden falsetto. This point is the *secondo passaggio* (second register transition).

Zona di passaggio (zona intermedia) (The Passage Zone)

Between the *primo passaggio* and the *secondo passaggio* register points lie pitches often used in the calling voice, that require an increase in breath energy, as well as heavier mechanical action than takes place below the *primo passaggio*. In the singing voice, this area is termed *zona di passaggio* (register transition zone), or *zona intermedia* (intermediate zone). (Any tendency to carry the unmodified "call" of the speaking voice over into the singing voice must be completely negated, however.)

REGISTRATION EVENTS OF MALE VOICES

Male voices of every category experience registration events of similar nature, at correspondingly higher and lower pitches. The *basso profondo* relies on the same principles of registration as does the *tenore lirico*, albeit at lower pitches. Differences in location of the *passaggi* reflect differences of structure and timbre between the bass and tenor voices. This viewpoint is in conflict with the following assumption that basses sing chiefly in chest voice, and that tenors sing in chest until F_4 or $F\sharp_4$, after which they pass into head (Vennard, 1967, p. 73):

Most authorities agree that basses sing largely in "chest," with some use of "head" for very high tones, but that their falsetto is acceptable only for comic effects and that there is probably no transition to it without yodeling. Tenors sing in "chest" up to F_4 or $F\sharp_4$, passing into "head," which they carry at least to A, above which theorists dispute. Some call the quality from there on up a "reinforced falsetto"; others deny the use of falsetto. The baritone, of course, is midway between, but more like a bass in quality.

On the contrary, a bass who relies largely on chest, although his chest voice may be somewhat longer than the tenor's, will exhibit a troublesome upper range; the tenor who waits until F_4 or $F\sharp_4$ to "pass into head" will produce those qualities of the "call" of the voice that technical studies in registration ought to eliminate. There is no single, arbitrary pitch in the scale below which chest is sung and above which head predominates, with all vocal categories rotating around it. Such an assumption must follow if it is postulated that basses sing chiefly in chest, tenors in head, with baritones somewhere in between. The germ of this error lies in confusing falsetto with head voice.

The approximate register events are fairly predictable for all categories of voice, although individual variations should not be ruled out.

Approximate Register Events		
Category of Voice	*primo passaggio*	*secondo passaggio*
tenorino	F_4	$B\flat_4$
tenore leggiero	$E_4,(E\flat_4)$	$A_4,(A\flat_4)$
tenore lirico	D_4	G_4
tenore spinto	$D_4,(C\sharp_4)$	$G_4,(F\sharp_4)$
tenore robusto (tenore drammatico)	$C_4,(C\sharp_4)$	$F_4,(F\sharp_4)$
baritono lirico	B_4	E_4
baritono drammatico	$B\flat_4$ *mixed*	$E\flat_4$ *head*
basso cantante	A_3	D_4
basso profondo	$A\flat_3,(G_3)$	$D\flat_4,(C_4)$

Voce di petto (Chest Voice)

Ordinarily, *voce di petto* (chest voice) corresponds to the comfortable speaking range and terminates in the region of the *primo passaggio*. For the baritone, the normal use of the speaking voice lies from B_3 downward, and that of the lyric tenor at about the interval of a minor third higher, near D_4. The baritone, using his speaking voice to call out loudly, extends the chest range to E_4; by pushing his voice through added breath pressure and sustained thyroarytenoid function, he may manage an additional half-tone extension. In the process, he will experience considerable vocal discomfort. The tenor, unless he is a high-pitched *leggiero,* seldom inflects the speaking voice much above D_4, although he is able to "yell" up to G_4, or even a semitone or two beyond. The tenor also experiences vocal discomfort in so doing. Neither the baritone nor the tenor makes shouting sounds in speech much above the *secondo passaggio,* unless resorting to a loud falsetto production.

Voce mista (Mixed Voice)

The male middle voice *(zona di passaggio)* is the crucial area in determining whether or not smooth register negotiation will take place from the lowest to the highest range of the singing voice. If the thyroarytenoids continue unabated in their action as pitch rises, the vocal quality known as chest voice will be carried up into the middle voice register. In contrast, introduction of the timbre known as *voce mista* brings about early balanced mechanical action between the thyroarytenoid and the cricothyroid muscles. Proctor (1980a, p. 30) speaks to this point:

> There is some controversy over the nature of the so-called "break" in the voice. One can raise the pitch of the voice considerably by increasing vocal-cord tension alone, and without lengthening the vocal folds. In my opinion, the elimination of this troublesome vocal problem, this "break," requires that one learn how gradually to bring in the vocal-fold lengthening process at a lower pitch than it ordinarily would come into play. Thus, as a scale is sung, there is a smooth transition from increasing vocal-fold tension to vocal-fold lengthening.

Voce mista is not restricted to the *zona di passaggio;* although fully operative in middle voice, *voce mista* descends into the low range to modify heavy mechanical action, thereby ensuring gradual timbre transition throughout the scale.

Voce di testa (Head Voice)

Above the second pivotal point *(secondo passaggio)* lies the legitimate head voice *(voce di testa),* a range extending a fourth or fifth in most male voices. Increased cricothyroid action, vocal-fold elongation, diminution of vibrating vocal-fold mass, and constantly changing contours of vocal-fold edges—all are more completely realized in the uppermost region of the voice. Loud shouting at these high pitches occurs at risk to the voice, yet these pitches are delivered with comfort in the singing voice.

Voce finta (Feigned Voice)

In *voce finta* (feigned voice) timbre, two conditions prevail: (1) slight laryngeal elevation, and (2) some breath mixture. (The first condition will produce the second.) Laryngeal adjustments for ascending pitch in singing are normally undergirded by corresponding adjustments in the torso; in *voce finta*, these adjustments are avoided. Depending on the extent of laryngeal elevation and breath admixture, *voce finta* sounds disembodied. This "feigned" timbre can be sung as early as the *primo passaggio*, where increase in breath energy is essential if normal registration events are to happen. Most successful in the *zona intermedia*, *voce finta* is seldom sung more than a semitone or two above the *secondo passaggio*.

Used for emotive coloration in literature demanding moments of quietude or introspection, *voce finta* is a favorite device among light tenors in particular, and is often used to excess among some baritone *Lieder* singers.

Less skill is required for singing *voce finta* than for *mezza voce*. All too often, *voce finta* is substituted for *mezza voce*. In the 1860s, Francesco Lamperti (n.d., p. 27) upheld the viewpoint that piano singing should not be disembodied, or "feigned":

> *Piano* should, in all respects, with the exception of intensity, resemble the *forte;* it should possess with it in equal degree, depth, character and feeling; it should be supported by an equal quantity of breath, and should have the quality of tone, so that even when reduced to *pianissimo* it may be heard at as great a distance as the *forte.*

These characteristics of legitimate piano singing are vitiated by the *voce finta* timbre.

Although pleasing to the ear when recorded in the studio, transferred live to the concert hall *voce finta* is generally inadequate. On the opera stage, *voce finta* appears mannered and sterile. Its excessive use becomes cloying. However, there are moments when *voce finta* provides interesting vocal coloration.

No specific exercises will be suggested for the cultivation of *voce finta*, because it verges on the unskillful, unsupported tone so common to many unaccomplished singers. Pedagogically, the use of *finta* should be frowned on until piano can be sung with legitimate *mezza voce* timbre in the *zona intermedia.*

Falsetto

Eighteenth and early nineteenth century treatises on singing frequently are misread with regard to the meaning of the term *falsetto* as it was used in a prescientific age. Discussing the history of registers in the singing voice, Mori clarifies the historical use of the term *falsetto* (1970, p. 76):

> Every epoch in one way or another has indicated the existence of registers. Singers of the medieval period cite head voice and throat voice, and the famous Caccini, Tosi, and Mancini also mention two registers: chest and falsetto. *The falsetto for them, however, was the head register.* But whether falsetto or chest, they refer to the preponderance of one of the two cavities of resonance, not to the exclusive dominance of one or the other. [Emphasis added]

Large et al. (1972, p. 19), in discussing head register in the male singing voice, comment:

> The head register in the male singing voice is often one of the most difficult vocal adjustments to acquire and to maintain. Cultivated especially for opera, *it should not be confused with the falsetto, a much thinner-sounding register.* A well-developed operatic head register ("Vollton der Kopfstimme") is the hall-mark of the accomplished tenor, but it is used in the upper range, spanning a musical interval of approximately a fourth or a fifth, by all well-trained male singers—tenors, baritones and basses. Some singers report subjective sensations of several different adjustments in the full head voice. *In contrast to the more robust-sounding head register, the falsetto is usually characterized as weak and effeminate and is used in legitimate Western vocal music culture mostly for special, particularly comic, effects.* [Emphasis added]

Brodnitz, after defining the chest, mixed, and head registers, comments on the falsetto (1953, p. 32):

> The male voices have on top of the head register the *falsetto,* which even to the untrained ear has a distinctive quality of its own. The Italian masters of the early Bel Canto thought of it as an unnatural and therefore false voice—thence the name. ... It has less brilliance than the sounds of the head register. It can be used occasionally, but its continuous employment gives the voice an effeminate character.

The mechanical action of falsetto is not identical to that of legitimate head voice—indeed, it exhibits quite different behavior. The mechanics of falsetto production are described by Zemlin (1981, p. 214):

> High-speed motion pictures of the larynx during falsetto production reveal that the folds vibrate and come into contact

only at the free borders and that the remainder of the folds remains relatively firm and nonvibratory. Furthermore, the folds appear long, stiff, very thin along the edges, and somewhat bow-shaped.

Brodnitz also discusses vocal-fold function during falsetto: "The falsetto is sung with only the foremost parts of the cords left free to vibrate at the margins, the rest being damped." (Brodnitz, 1953, p. 82.)

Mori (1970, pp. 97–98), on the avoidance of the use of falsetto in the historic Italian School, presents information to substantiate that Garcia (who located falsetto *between* chest and head) did not intend to equate falsetto *with* head. Mori quotes Garcia as saying, "The falsetto voice constitutes a particular register, different at the same time from the chest register . . . and from the head register." (". . . la voce di falsetto costituisce un particolare registro, differente al tempo stesso e dal registro della voce di petto . . . e dal registro di testa. . . .") Mori comments that the Italian School, from at least Garcia onward, considers falsetto and head voice to represent two different principles of vocal color. She states that falsetto is an artificial voice in cultivated singing to be used only therapeutically, or when the voice is very tired or in poor condition, or as a special interpretative effect of characterization or insinuation. "Per le voci maschili è artificio in via assoluta" (it is absolutely false for male voices). She further mentions that it is allowable, and was used by some great singers, for effects on an occasional extremely high note beyond the range of the singer, as for example, the high D♭ (D♭$_5$) at the end of the cadenza in "Cujus animam" from the Rossini *Stabat Mater*.

The term *falsetto* as used by some persons to describe events of both speaking and singing cannot be carried over to vocal pedagogy without confusion. In the international language of singing, falsetto describes that imitative female sound that the male singer is capable of making on pitches that lie above the normal male speaking range. With practice, the singer can bring these sounds down into the lower range. To term any sound not produced in the chest voice as falsetto is to obfuscate pedagogical meaning. To speak of Jussi Bjoerling's operatic sound from G$_4$ and above as falsetto is to confuse both language and the practice of vocalism. The beauty of Bjoerling's fully resonant head voice is an example *par excellence* of traditional head voice in cultivated singing. Because the issue of falsetto versus legitimate head voice is so often raised in discussions concerning the tenor voice, it is appropriate to cite further examples. Alfredo Kraus, in a public master class in Fiesole in June, 1984, stated that he is completely opposed to the practice or use of falsetto. Certainly the ringing sounds of Placido Domingo and Luciano Pavarotti (or any other great tenor voices of this century, excluding occasional uses of falsetto by Beniamino Gigli and Ferruccio Tagliavini for musical and interpretative effects) cannot be described as falsetto! Nicolai Gedda, in an interview given Jerome Hines (1982, p. 123), says, "Falsetto . . . it's very high-pitched, but a tone I cannot do anything with." He describes falsetto as an unsupported tone, and cites a pianissimo that can be crescendoed as the desirable route for the high voice.

Were we to turn word symbolism upside down and call a dog a cat, and were we all to understand that change in meaning, there would be no resultant problems: my St. Bernard is a cat. However, outside the limited circle in which this special word symbolism operates, it would be difficult not to cause confusion when I walk my cat and it barks at people. Falsetto should not be called head voice.

It is incorrect to group into one category all persons who find some value in falsetto singing, and to pronounce equal sentence on them all. There is a big difference between designating falsetto as head voice and recommending limited pedagogical uses for falsetto. It is doubtful that any but a few persons who sing or teach traditional solo literature for voice advocate falsetto timbre as a performance sound. Some, however, conclude that laryngeal conditions are similar in head and falsetto, and, therefore, the key to developing head voice lies in the falsetto. They believe that mechanical benefits accrue from exercising the falsetto voice.

It should be pointed out that vocal-fold occlusion is not the same in head and falsetto; vocal-fold approximation is less complete in the falsetto production. Further, nodules can result from continued lack of good vocal-fold closure.

Some psychological benefit perhaps derives from the occasional use of falsetto as a means of avoiding tension. However, few singers, other than those of very light vocal categories (often voices of less than professional potential), succeed in "reinforcing" the falsetto sound. When the sound is "reinforced," the muscular coordinations that produce legitimate head voice must be introduced. Improved vocal-fold occlusion, and the vital character of the sound, indicate that falsetto has been replaced by legitimate head voice.

Occasional falsetto can be useful for "marking" in rehearsals, when for some temporary physical reason the singer wishes to conserve energy on certain passages, but caution should be exercised.

In some voices, the transition from falsetto to full voice *(voce piena)* may occur without any demarcation between the two timbres. Seldom is this a learned skill. Generally, it has to do with the size of the vocal instrument and the vocal category, and is either there or it is not. This facility is frequently present in the young *tenore leggiero* and almost never there in the heavier categories of tenor or in the baritone and bass voices. (Rarely, a baritone of lyric character will also have this ability as a natural phenomenon.)

Limited usage of falsetto may be productive, in some voices, in the *zona di passaggio*, between the *primo passaggio* and the *secondo passaggio*. For male singers who lack easy entrance into upper middle voice, vocalises that begin in light falsetto may be practiced, with the singer increasing breath energy, thereby moving into legitimate middle voice.

The purpose is not to "blend" the falsetto into the legitimate sound of the male voice (such a skill has merit as a coloristic device, but for that very reason may be a Trojan horse to legitimate vocalism in the upper range), but to build on the perception of effortlessness that accompanies the falsetto just prior to the full vocal-fold approximation that then occurs in legitimate voice.

EXERCISE 9.1

THE SINGER SHOULD BEGIN DIRECTLY ON THE *PRIMO PASSAGGIO* PIVOTAL NOTE, IN PIANO FALSETTO, CRESCENDOING TO *VOCE PIENA* AND THEN BACK TO FALSETTO. (IT DOES NOT MATTER IF REGISTER TRANSITION POINTS ARE HEARD.) IMMEDIATELY, A NEW ONSET IN LEGITIMATE VOICE SHOULD BE MADE ON THE SAME PITCH. PROGRESS BY HALF-STEPS (OVER A PERIOD OF WEEKS OR MONTHS) THROUGH THE *SECONDO PASSAGGIO* PIVOTAL POINT.

EXERCISE 9.2

FALSETTO AND LEGITIMATE VOICE ARE ALTERNATED ON THE SAME PITCH, CROSSING BACK AND FORTH BETWEEN THE TWO TIMBRES. BEGIN AT *PRIMO PASSAGGIO*, AND OVER A PERIOD OF TIME, PROGRESS BY HALF STEPS THROUGH THE *SECONDO PASSAGGIO*.

The Male Falsettist

A performance phenomenon that must be dealt with in any serious consideration of contemporary singing is the male falsettist. The solo counter-tenor is here to stay. It is unrealistic for teachers of singing to regard him as a nonlegitimate performer. The counter-tenor should be taught, and he should be taught seriously.

There are, however, several approaches to the production of counter-tenor timbre, and although cultivated falsetto singing plays a role in almost all of them (probably to some extent, *all*), falsetto is not the only vocal register in use throughout the counter-tenor range. Those counter-tenors who are chiefly male falsettists make use of that same falsetto sound which is readily available to almost all male voices. An aesthetic and artistic choice has been made, in such cases, to develop skill in the falsetto voice in preference to cultivation of other vocal registers. Not infrequently, such counter-tenor singers do not have remarkably beautiful voices in the traditional male ranges, but are able to produce admirable timbre as falsettists. Why not? The reason such persons can perform more skillfully in falsetto is that falsetto production does not require the subtle register equalization demanded in the traditional upper male register involving dynamic muscle balancing.

Almost any musical male can more easily produce running passages and pianissimo dynamic levels in falsetto than he can accomplish in his full voice in head *(voce piena in testa)*. The vocally uninformed listener often is astounded at the "ease" of florid singing displayed by the counter-tenor. Such persons somewhat naively believe that the counter-tenor is a rare breed of vocal category with a special native endowment. Although that is not the case, a number of excellent male musicians wisely have made the decision to perfect those skills that are relatively easily acquired in the falsetto register. The impressive part of a fine counter-tenor's technique is his ability to maintain sustained lines and long phrases, because he must learn additional breath-management skills to compensate for the open chink that characterizes the glottal shape in falsetto singing and permits a higher rate of breath seepage than in the non-falsetto voice. The agility, the ability to decrescendo on very high tones, and the displays of florid singing are pleasurable, but they do not represent great heights of technical prowess over other male voices. The counter-tenor often encounters difficulties in the technical area of breath management, and a good voice teacher should be able to assist him. There is a literature appropriate to the counter-tenor voice, and there is an audience for that category of male singer. It should be noted that several international vocal competitions now have a separate category for the counter-tenor voice.

The reasons for choosing to sing counter-tenor rather than to perform the traditional timbres of the male voice are complex and most often highly personal. They involve considerations that extend beyond the confines of this discussion. Special techniques of extending the falsetto range and in blending it (in most counter-tenor voices) with the traditional low male register are required. However, teaching the counter-tenor voice should be no more difficult than teaching any other vocal category. One of the most important steps to be taken in providing proper instruction for counter-tenors is to rid the voice-teaching profession of the notion that the counter-tenor instrument is in some way structurally unlike other male instruments. A second important step, which might well follow were the first to be taken, would be the removal of a certain amount of prejudice against nontraditional vocal timbres. Counter-tenoring, badly done, can be vocally hazardous. An understanding of vocal function is imperative in the teaching of the counter-tenor voice. The systematic drill of vocalises suggested in the preceding chapters applies to all categories of singer, including the counter-tenor.

Strohbass

Strohbass (the literal English translation, "straw bass," is seldom used) is a register that lies below the normal male speech range. The length of the *Strohbassregister* varies from four or five whole steps in most males to more than an octave in others. *Strohbass* is often cited, together with falsetto, as one of two "unused" vocal registers that must be developed in order to achieve a complete singing instrument. That assumption should not go unquestioned.

Because the cricothyroids have been thought to show increased activity in extremely low pitches (Zenker, 1964b, p. 25) as well as in ascending pitch, *Strohbass* exercises are sometimes recommended for the development of the upper range. The faulty assumption that singing in *Strohbass* produces extension in upper voice may be due to the fact that range normally expands at both extremities of the voice when proper registration practices are incorporated. In any case, laryngeal muscle balance in upper register is very unlike the heavy mechanical action of *Strohbassregister*.

Just as an occasional falsetto note is intruded in legitimate upper range for some specific coloration, so an occasional *Strohbass* tone may be introduced in the lowest range of the voice. "Straw bass register" occurs in low voice for the same reason falsetto often occurs in high voice—it is the only secure way some singers have of producing those particular pitches. (Perhaps that literature should be avoided!) *Strohbass*, if used at all, should be used judiciously. Exercises for the development of this register phenomenon should be undertaken *only* with a teacher, and never for more than a few brief moments. When the note that seems only minimally present in the voice—often a phrase end, or a note touched briefly—must be called on, a conscious lowering of the larynx beyond its normally stabilized position will assist. This technique should be reserved for only a few occasions. The register should not be drilled as a means of "strengthening the vocal ligaments." It is hard on the voice, and ideally should never be used. However, when a baritone sings an aria with great ease and beauty of tone but discovers low $A\flat_2$ escapes him, there is no problem in resorting to *Strohbass* for that single pitch. Exercise 9.3 may be used by half-tone progressions, with only the bottom note produced in *Strohbass* register. (It is a well-known fact that in certain Eastern liturgical choirs, some low male voices have developed the *Strohbass* register for supplying weightiness to the ensemble, with the result that other registers of the voice are no longer operable.)

EXERCISE 9.3

Schnarrbass (growl bass, literally) is a term used interchangeably with *Strohbass*, in some cases. However, *Schnarrbass* is used at times to describe *vocal fry* (vocal rattle or vocal scrape). The term can also mean the bass drone in another connotation. *Growl register* is an equally descriptive term for the sounds that can be produced in the limited range extending below pitches normally used in speech. At times, a moderate use of *vocal fry* may help a young, low-voiced male develop a "feel" for additional pitches at the lower extension of his range. *Vocal fry* encourages an imprecise onset and should not be relied on as a standard vocalizing technique.

EXERCISES FOR ACHIEVING AN EVENLY REGISTERED SCALE IN LOWER AND MIDDLE VOICE

The *zona di passaggio* is the key to the evenly registered scale. Exercises should induce light mechanical action in the pivotal area between low and middle registers. Vocalises should begin in the easy speaking range of the voice and proceed only slightly above the *primo passaggio;* other vocalises should begin just above the *primo passaggio,* then descend. Care should be taken that neither chin nor larynx be raised on the pitches above the easy speaking range. An increase in breath support, in accordance with *appoggio* practice, should be felt in the trunk.

The suggested vocalises (9.4 through 9.11) should be transposed to accommodate each vocal category. They are to be executed in series, in neighboring keys, both ascending and descending.

Nasal continuants produce sympathetic facial vibration of the sort associated with balanced laryngeal muscle action. Closely-knit intervallic patterns that commence on pitches in the upper range of the speaking voice are hummed by half-step progressions into the *zona di passaggio.* The nasals are followed by vowel sounds.

Group 1 Exercises

The exercises indicated for promoting an evenly registered scale in the middle and lower voice can also be transposed by half-step progressions into upper middle voice and into the region of the *secondo passaggio.*

EXERCISE 9.4

[m   a]

EXERCISE 9.5

[m   e]

EXERCISE 9.6

[m]   [a]   [m]   [a]
[m]   [e]   [m]   [e]

EXERCISE 9.7

[m]   [ɔ]   [m]   [ɔ]

EXERCISE 9.8

[m]	[a]	[m]	[a]	[m]	[a]
[a]	[m]	[a]	[m]	[a]	[m]

EXERCISE 9.9

[na	ne	na	ne	na]
[mo	me	mo	me	mo]

EXERCISE 9.10

[nai,	nai,	nai,	nai,	nai]
[nau,	nau,	nau,	nau,	nau]

EXERCISE 9.11

[me]	[me]
[nɔ]	[nɔ]
[me]	[me]

All voices are not at the same level of facility with regard to easy entrance into the *zona di passaggio*. In general, the more robust the instrument (with the greater probability of professional potential), the more problematic is entry into middle voice. Some singers, particularly the late adolescent of college age, will require a considerable period of "ironing out" the passage from lower to middle voice. Yet middle voice must be freely produced before the singer can find ease in the upper voice. However, it is disastrous to avoid upper voice entirely until all the problems of middle voice have been solved. Although it is true that the upper range must be "built" upon middle voice, functional differences between the two are largely a matter of degree. The dynamic muscle balance needed to ensure entrance into upper range can be acquired only by singing pitches at the upper end of the *zona di passaggio*. To work at parts of the voice, rather than to use the total instrument, is to misunderstand unity of function. Nevertheless, much work must take place in balancing upper–middle voice before any remarkable results can be expected in the upper voice.

EXERCISES FOR ACHIEVING AN EVENLY REGISTERED SCALE IN UPPER AND MIDDLE VOICE

In successful vocal registration, head voice is of one substance with the rest of the voice, yet sensations experienced above the *secondo passaggio* are in considerable contrast to those felt below the *primo passaggio*. Sensations of the lighter mechanical action (decrease in activity of the thyroarytenoids and increased action of the cricothyroids) are very apparent commencing at the *primo passaggio*, becoming more prominent at the *secondo passaggio*. In reverse direction, in the descending scale, there is *no* sudden chest sensation below the *primo passaggio*, because the muscular coordination that determines pitch does not jump from one static state to another, but is a graduated process (there is no feeling of "changing gears"). Indeed, some feeling of "head" must always be present throughout the scale of the male voice, regardless of vocal category, whether one begins or ends in lower voice.

Exercises 9.12 through 9.21 (Group 2) are recommended as a systematic approach to equalization in register transition. Some of the vocalises begin below the *primo passaggio* and extend into the area of the *secondo passaggio*; others deal more directly with the passage from *voce intermedia* into upper voice. These exercises should be transposed to accommodate any category of voice. The exercises are executed in half-step progressions, in series fashion, in several neighboring keys, both ascending and descending.

Group 2 Exercises

EXERCISE 9.12

[i]	[e]	[ɔ]
[ɔ]	[i]	[e]
[e]	[ɔ]	[i]

EXERCISE 9.13

[i]   [e]   [ɔ]   [o]

EXERCISE 9.14

[ɑ]   [e]   [ɔ]

[o]   [ɛ]

EXERCISE 9.15

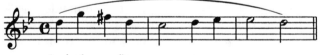

(a single vowel)

EXERCISE 9.16

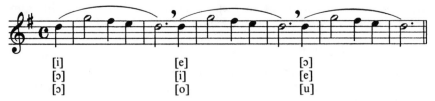

(a single vowel)

EXERCISE 9.17

[i]   [e]   [ɔ]
[ɔ]   [i]   [e]
[ɔ]   [o]   [u]

EXERCISE 9.18

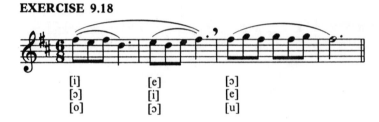

[i]   [e]   [ɔ]
[ɔ]   [i]   [e]
[o]   [ɔ]   [u]

EXERCISE 9.19

EXERCISE 9.20

EXERCISE 9.21

An exercise previously recommended for the study of sostenuto (Exercise 8.17) is equally well suited as a registration vocalise, treating as it does neighboring pitches at the pivotal points of both the *primo passaggio* and the *secondo passaggio*. In progressive half-step transposition, this sustained vocalise points up subtle but important differences in factors of resonance and breath management encountered either in ascent or descent.

It should be repeated that the use of *passaggio* vocalises depends on the technical accomplishment of the singer. These vocalises should not be attempted until some considerable degree of technical proficiency has already been demonstrated.

CHAPTER 10

Unifying the Registers of the Female Voice

Structural differences in male and female adult larynges are obvious, even externally. The male larynx grows considerably more during puberty, roughly 30%, than does the female (Kahane, 1978, pp. 11–20; Titze, 1980, p. 20). The adult male has a membranous portion of the vocal fold that is longer than the adult female's, while the cartilaginous portion of the male fold is proportionately smaller than hers. The more radical events of puberty cause the male to speak largely in chest voice. Female chest is less extensive in speech, especially in voices of a light, lyrical quality. Decisive change in the size of the male larynx in early adolescence often results in uncertainty of pitch control; nothing comparable is experienced by the female larynx. (For a discussion of physical factors in voice registration, see Appendix IV.)

Register pivotal points do not directly correspond in the scales of female and male voices. In the lower female vocal categories, chest voice does not have the same extension as in low male vocal categories; middle registers of male and female voices do not have exact range correspondence. It is coincidental that the *passaggi* for certain female and male voices occur at similar pitches, as for example, the *passaggi* of the *soprano lirico* and the *tenore lirico* (an octave apart). The female is capable of making a shift in registers from chest to head, in the lower range of her voice, but she cannot produce the marked transition sound from middle voice into head voice that the male can make through the use of falsetto.

It is confusing to describe as falsetto all of the sounds of the female voice not sung in chest, particularly if the term falsetto is at the same time used to designate the legitimate male head voice. The upper register of the female voice does not correspond functionally with the imitative female sound that male singers are capable of making. Further confusion results from calling the flageolet voice "female falsetto," or from terming the laryngeal whistle the "female falsetto." Zemlin (1981, p. 216) remarks:

> High female voices do not exhibit a falsetto, however, but a laryngeal whistle, which is not produced by vibration of the

132

vocal folds, but by the whistling escape of air from between them.

The term "falsetto" should be reserved to designate the imitation of female vocal quality by the male voice.

REGISTERS OF THE FEMALE SPEAKING VOICE

Speech habits of females tend to fall into three types: (1) head voice is almost exclusively used; and chest voice may be nearly nonexistent; (2) both chest and head voices are used for speech inflection, with a preponderance of head; and (3) chest voice is chiefly used. The size of the female larynx, and cultural influences, perhaps, determine register preferences in speech. Not all may be well (from the standpoint of healthy function) with the speaker who excludes all chest voice, or with her colleague who never uses head voice. Serious vocal literature cannot be sung by any category of female singer who avoids using all adjustments of vocal registration. (Omitted from this consideration are popular vocal idioms that purposely violate registers.) Singers who tend to avoid a given register in speech need to develop that unused register for singing. The coloratura has less need of chest than does the dramatic soprano, but the coloratura may be seriously handicapped without the ability to sing in some form of chest. The contralto and the mezzo-soprano cannot function without head voice ability.

COMBINING FEMALE SINGING REGISTERS

It is pedagogically convenient to call a vocal register in which the thyroarytenoids are predominant, the *heavy mechanism*, and to call those registers in which the cricothyroids are predominant, the *light mechanism*, so long as it is understood that there are not actually two separate mechanisms, but changing, dynamic balances among the laryngeal muscles. Separation of registers as a means of strengthening them is contrary to the aim of vocal registration in singing: the achievement of gradual register transition. Separating the chest register from the head register results in driving up chest voice beyond the *primo passaggio* terminal point through heavy thyroarytenoid action; such action produces the condition of hyperfunction found in pathological vocal conditions. However, bringing the head voice downward into the low register is not an act of register separation, but rather a technique for register combining (Proctor, 1980a, p. 30).

REGISTRATION EVENTS OF FEMALE VOICES

As with male voices, location of pivotal points of register demarcation provides indications of female vocal categories. Such pivotal points may vary somewhat within the individual voice, depending on how lyric or how dramatic the voice. (See Figures 10.1, 10.2, and 10.3).

The soprano category embraces voices of wide diversity, from coloratura to dramatic. The dramatic soprano instrument is closer in character to the dramatic mezzo than to the light soprano; registration events reflect these relationships. Vocal classification must take into account the location of pivotal points, without, however, relying solely on them.

Overlapping of registers indicated in the charts designates those areas in which certain pitches can be sung in several ways. There is

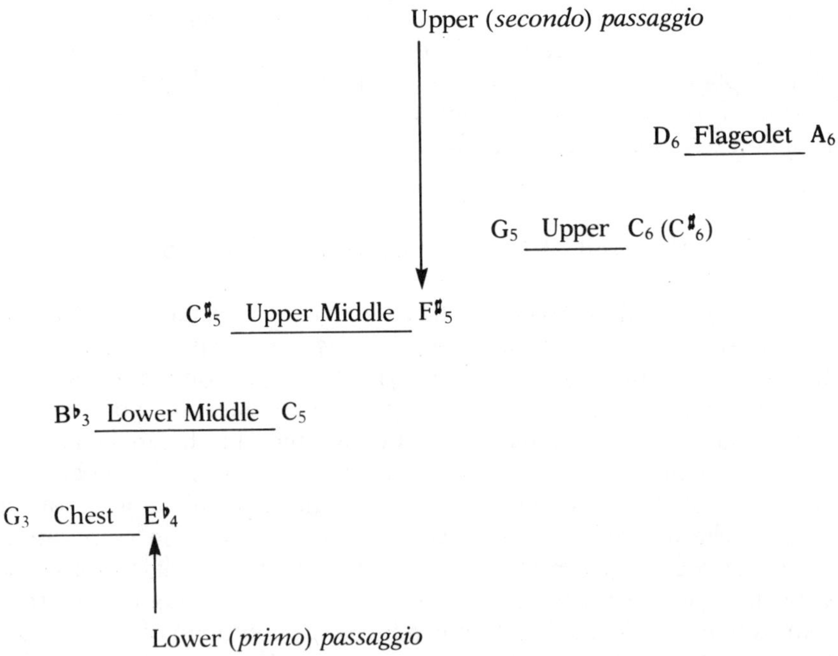

Upper (*secondo*) *passaggio*

D_6 Flageolet A_6

G_5 Upper C_6 ($C^{\sharp}_6$)

$C^{\sharp}_5$ Upper Middle $F^{\sharp}_5$

$B^{\flat}_3$ Lower Middle C_5

G_3 Chest $E^{\flat}_4$

Lower (*primo*) *passaggio*

Figure 10.1. Soprano *passaggi* and Register Zones

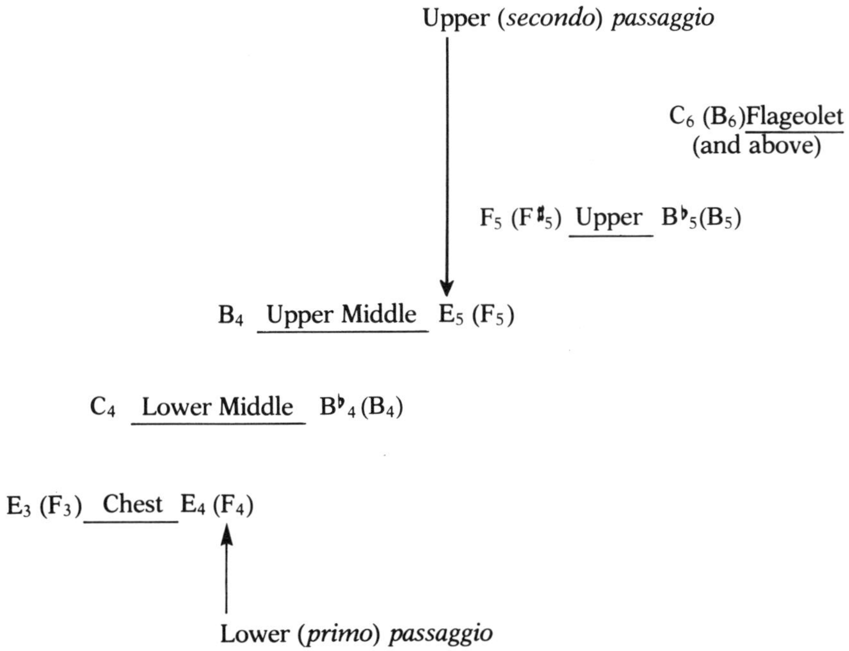

Upper (*secondo*) *passaggio*

C_6 (B_6)Flageolet
(and above)

F_5 ($F\sharp_5$) Upper $B\flat_5$(B_5)

B_4 Upper Middle E_5 (F_5)

C_4 Lower Middle $B\flat_4$ (B_4)

E_3 (F_3) Chest E_4 (F_4)

Lower (*primo*) *passaggio*

Figure 10.2. Mezzo-soprano *passaggi* and Register Zones

Upper (*secondo*) *passaggio*

A_5 Flageolet (seldom
developed)

$E\flat_5$ Upper $A\flat_5$

Upper
$B\flat_4$ Middle D_5

Lower
F_4 Middle A_4

D_3 Chest G_4 ($A\flat_4$)

Lower (*primo*) *passaggio*

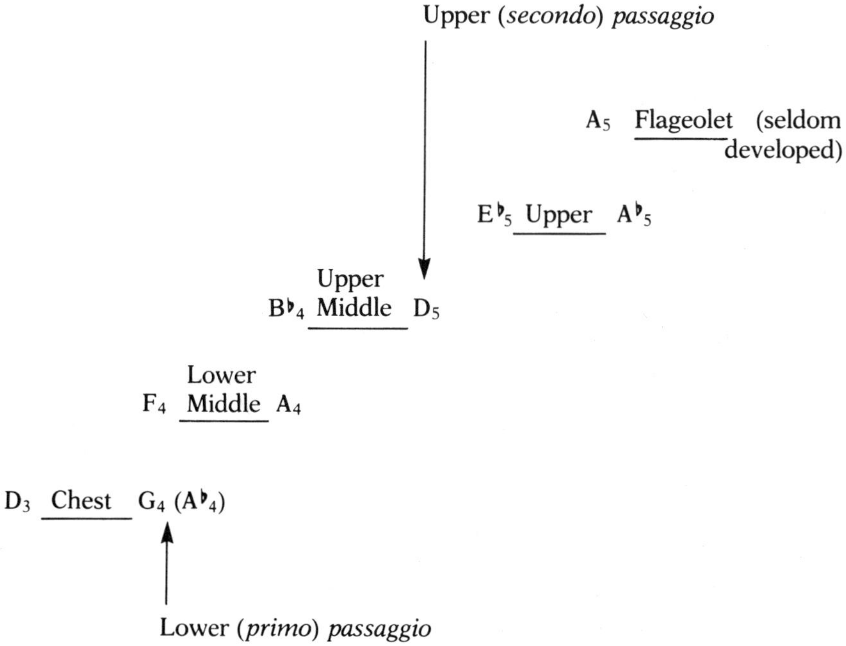

Figure 10.3. Contralto *passaggi* and Register Zones

135

actually no overlapping of mechanical functions without mixing of timbres, except in those rare cases where a particular vocal coloration that does not match neighboring tones is purposely intruded.

CHEST IN FEMALE VOICES

The chest voice in the light soprano is shorter than in the female voice of dramatic proportions. Some females possess laryngeal structures that are larger than the norm; these singers have low voices and long chest registers.

OPEN CHEST

The term chest *(voce di petto)* includes several distinct timbre possibilities within the female singing voice: open chest and chest mixtures. Open chest is characterized by a certain masculinity, because its execution is similar to production of the male chest voice: heavy action from the thyroarytenoid muscles; wider amplitude of vibration; thicker and shorter folds. Open chest timbre should be completely avoided in pitches above the *primo passaggio.*

CHEST MIXTURE

Chest mixture avoids the vulgarity of timbre often present in open chest; in skillful singing, it is a timbre more frequently encountered in low register in the female voice than is open chest.

Some of the vocal literature written especially for female voice takes into account the timbre known as chest mixture. The need for vocal coloration associated with chest mixture extends to the soprano, as well as to the mezzo and contralto voices. It is usually the lighter soprano voice that lacks this important timbre.

A soprano whose voice is of fair size will most probably never need to sing any open chest sound in the lower range; she might well be more useful in performance if she has the ability to sing some or all of the pitches below Eb_4 in chest mixture. Inability to use chest mixture is an indication that the singer may suffer from hypofunction of the thyroarytenoids on those pitches, with a corresponding hyperfunction of the cricothyroids. Chest mixture will strengthen the soprano's lower–middle range. Almost every female can make some chest timbre sounds, no matter how insecure, in the lowest part of her range. These notes should be sung in short, intervallic patterns, transposing by half steps upward, as more sound emerges.

EXERCISES FOR THE DEVELOPMENT OF THE LOWER RANGE

The following exercise should be practiced by females who have a limited sound in either open chest or chest mixture in the lower range. Pitch may be adjusted to the needs of the singer.

EXERCISE 10.1

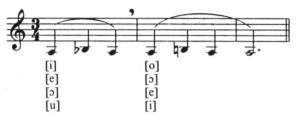

[i]	[o]
[e]	[ɔ]
[ɔ]	[e]
[u]	[i]

In some cases, it may take a period of time before chest mixture makes an appearance. Attempts must be limited to no more than five minutes, scattered throughout a practice session.

Most singers discover that they can produce chest timbre very low in the speaking voice, even though unaccustomed to its use in normal speech. From the speech pitch to the sung pitch is an easy transition. Occasionally, chest mixture will come more readily at the lowest part of lower–middle voice, rather than in the lowest register. As some chest quality appears, the entire lower and lower–middle registers will gain in projection.

Female singers not accustomed to the use of chest in the speaking voice may feel they must "produce" it in the singing voice; in all probability they are not used to giving much attention to breath management in the lower speaking voice. No force should accompany these sounds, but increased "support" may make the difference between failure and success.

Exercise 10.2 is important for developing control over degrees of chest mixture. The suggested keys are appropriate for soprano voices of a lyric character. Dramatic sopranos and mezzo-sopranos should transpose the vocalise *up* a half tone, contraltos a full tone. Within each of the keys, the transition note should be executed as smoothly as possible, avoiding any sudden change in timbre.

The sequence must be carefully observed if the purpose of the exercise is to be realized: all seven steps, key by key.

EXERCISE 10.2

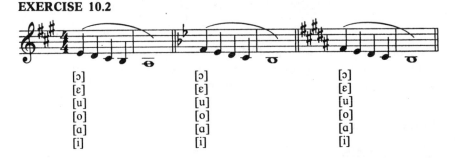

```
[ɔ]          [ɔ]          [ɔ]
[ɛ]          [ɛ]          [ɛ]
[u]          [u]          [u]
[o]          [o]          [o]
[ɑ]          [ɑ]          [ɑ]
[i]          [i]          [i]
```

(1) SING THE FIVE-NOTE DESCENDING PATTERN ENTIRELY IN *HEAD*. **(2)** SING THE FIVE-NOTE DESCENDING PATTERN WITH ONLY THE FINAL NOTE IN *CHEST MIXTURE*, THE REST IN *HEAD*. **(3)** SING THE FIVE-NOTE DESCENDING PATTERN WITH THE LAST TWO NOTES IN *CHEST MIXTURE*, THE REST IN *HEAD*. **(4)** SING THE FIVE-NOTE DESCENDING PATTERN WITH THE LAST THREE NOTES IN *CHEST MIXTURE*, THE REST IN *HEAD*. **(5)** SING THE FIVE-NOTE DESCENDING SCALE WITH THE LAST TWO NOTES IN *CHEST MIXTURE*, THE REST IN *HEAD*. **(6)** SING THE FIVE-NOTE DESCENDING PATTERN WITH ONLY THE FINAL NOTE IN *CHEST MIXTURE*, THE REST IN *HEAD*. **(7)** SING THE FIVE-NOTE DESCENDING PATTERN ALL IN *HEAD*.

Other useful vocalises for developing an awareness of chest function and sensation are those based on descending intervallic patterns. These vocalises should be transposed a half step higher for mezzos and a whole step higher for contraltos. Any vowel may be used.

EXERCISE 10.3

(any vowel)

(1) SING PITCHES 5 AND 3 IN *HEAD*, 1 IN *CHEST MIXTURE*. **(2)** SING PITCH 5 IN *HEAD*, 3 AND 1 IN *CHEST MIXTURE*. **(3)** SING PITCHES 5 AND 3 IN *HEAD*, 1 IN *CHEST MIXTURE*. **(4)** SING PITCHES 5, 3, AND 1 IN *HEAD*.

EXERCISE 10.4

(any vowel)

(1) SING PITCHES 8, 5, AND 3 IN *HEAD*, 1 IN *CHEST MIXTURE.* **(2)** SING PITCHES 8 AND 5 IN HEAD, 3 AND 1 IN *CHEST MIXTURE.* **(3)** SING PITCHES 8 AND 5 IN *HEAD*, 3 IN *CHEST MIXTURE*, 1 IN *OPEN CHEST.* **(4)** SING PITCHES 8, 5, 3, AND (IF POSSIBLE) 1 IN *HEAD*. **(5)** SING PITCHES 8 AND 5 IN *HEAD*, 3 IN *CHEST MIXTURE*, 1 IN *OPEN CHEST.* **(6)** SING PITCHES 8 AND 5 IN *HEAD*, 3 AND 1 IN *CHEST MIXTURE.* **(7)** SING PITCHES 8, 5, AND 3 IN *HEAD*, 1 IN *CHEST MIXTURE.*

EXERCISE 10.5

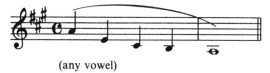

(any vowel)

(1) SING THE PATTERN (ON ANY VOWEL) IN *HEAD.* **(2)** SING PITCHES 8, 5, 3, AND 2 IN *HEAD*, 1 IN *OPEN CHEST.* **(3)** SING PITCHES 8, 5, 3, AND 2 IN *HEAD*, 1 IN *CHEST MIXTURE.* **(4)** SING PITCHES 8, 5, AND 3 IN *HEAD*, 2 AND 1 IN *CHEST MIXTURE.* **(5)** SING PITCHES 8, 5, AND 3 IN *HEAD*, 2 IN *CHEST MIXTURE*, AND 1 IN *OPEN CHEST.* **(6)** SING PITCHES 8 AND 5 IN *HEAD*, 3 AND 2 IN *CHEST MIXTURE*, AND 1 IN *OPEN CHEST.* **(7)** SING PITCHES 8 AND 5 IN *HEAD*, 3 IN *CHEST MIXTURE*, 2 AND 1 IN *OPEN CHEST.*

EXERCISE 10.6

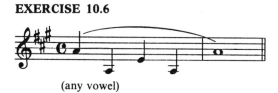

(any vowel)

(1) SING THE PATTERN (ON ANY VOWEL) ENTIRELY IN *HEAD*, IF POSSIBLE. **(2)** SING PITCH 8 IN *HEAD*, 1 IN *CHEST MIXTURE*, 5 IN *HEAD*, 1 IN *OPEN CHEST*, 8 IN *HEAD.* **(3)** SING PITCH 8 IN *HEAD*, 1 IN *CHEST MIXTURE*, 5 IN *HEAD*, 1 IN *CHEST MIXTURE*, 8 IN *HEAD.* **(4)** SING PITCH 8 IN *HEAD*, 1 IN *OPEN CHEST*, 5 IN *HEAD*, 1 IN *OPEN CHEST*, 8 IN *HEAD.* **(5)** IF POSSIBLE, SING THE PATTERN ENTIRELY IN *HEAD.*

EXERCISE 10.7

(any vowel)

(1) IF POSSIBLE (ON ANY VOWEL), SING THE ENTIRE PHRASE IN *HEAD.* **(2)** SING PITCH 8 IN *HEAD*, 1 IN *OPEN CHEST*, PITCHES 5, 4, 3, AND 2 IN *HEAD*, 1 IN *OPEN CHEST*, 3 IN *CHEST MIXTURE*, AND 8 IN *HEAD.* **(3)** SING PITCH 8 IN *HEAD*, 1 IN *CHEST MIXTURE*, PITCHES 5 AND 4 IN *HEAD*, 3 AND 2 IN *CHEST MIXTURE*, 1 IN *CHEST*, 3 IN *CHEST MIXTURE*, 8 IN *HEAD.*

EXERCISE 10.8

(any vowel)

(1) IF POSSIBLE (ON ANY VOWEL), SING THE ENTIRE PHRASE IN *HEAD.* **(2)** SING PITCH 8 IN *HEAD*, 1 IN *OPEN CHEST*, 5 IN *HEAD*, 3 IN *CHEST MIXTURE*, 5 IN *HEAD*, 1 IN *OPEN CHEST*, 8 IN *HEAD.* **(3)** SING PITCH 8 IN *HEAD*, 1 IN *CHEST MIXTURE*, 5, 3, AND 5 IN *HEAD*, 1 IN *CHEST MIXTURE*, 8 IN *HEAD.* **(4)** SING PITCH 8 IN *HEAD*, 1 IN *CHEST MIXTURE*, 5, 3, AND 5 IN *HEAD*, 1 IN *CHEST MIXTURE*, 8 IN *HEAD.*

HEAD MIXTURE IN FEMALE LOWER RANGE

Mixture describes any timbre that is neither entirely head nor entirely chest; the shade of mixture in any pitch depends on laryngeal action. Breath management and resonator response are not uniformly experienced in all ranges of the voice. In the lowest range of the voice, a lack of head sensation accompanies chest timbre. A limited amount of head sensation is present in chest mixture. *Head mixture* in lower–middle voice produces a somewhat "headier" feeling than is felt in chest mixture. An increase in "headiness" characterizes upper–middle voice. An even more decisively "heady" sensation occurs above the upper *passaggio.* In all of these sensations, with the exception of pure chest, some elements of the "light mechanism" are operative.

EXERCISE 10.9

[i]
[e]
[ɛ]
[ɔ]
[o]
[u]

EXERCISE 10.10

[i]
[e]
[ɛ]
[ɔ]
[o]
[u]

EXERCISE 10.11

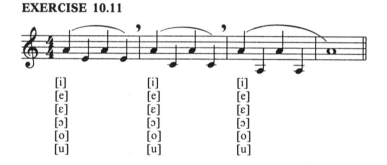

[i]   [i]   [i]
[e]   [e]   [e]
[ɛ]   [ɛ]   [ɛ]
[ɔ]   [ɔ]   [ɔ]
[o]   [o]   [o]
[u]   [u]   [u]

EXERCISE 10.12

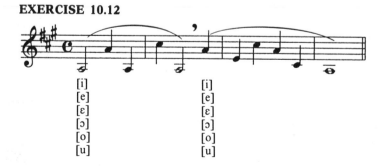

[i]   [i]
[e]   [e]
[ɛ]   [ɛ]
[ɔ]   [ɔ]
[o]   [o]
[u]   [u]

HEAD MIXTURE IN FEMALE MIDDLE RANGE

The action of the heavy open chest mechanism should terminate relatively early in the ascending scale. However, it is confusing to term everything that lies above the *primo passaggio* "head voice"; head voice should be identified as the range lying above the *secondo passaggio*. The long middle register that lies between the lower and upper *passaggi* should then be termed mixed voice, head mixture, or simply, middle voice. This middle register is more extensive in the female than in the male because of laryngeal structural differences. In the lyric soprano, middle voice extends from $E\flat_4$ to $F\sharp_5$. Although the lyric soprano may be able to carry chest mixture above the $E\flat_4$ pivotal point, she should rarely do so, for reasons of vocal health.

Many sopranos experience an additional pivotal point midway in the long middle register, around $C\sharp_5$, with lower–middle register lying below that pitch, and upper–middle register above it. Sometimes the entire long middle register is identified as *voce mista* (mixed voice); at times, *voce mista* designates the predominant head sensation from $C\sharp_5$ to $F\sharp_5$. The least confusing terminology identifies these two divisions of the long middle voice as lower–middle and upper–middle. Heavier voices have a more distinct midpoint division than do lighter voices. These differences result not only from structure but also from speech habits, factors that vary among vocal categories. Some coloratura and soubrette singers perceive no timbre or resonance changes at all at any point in the middle register, between chest and head.

EXERCISES FOR INDUCING HEAD MIXTURE IN MIDDLE VOICE

The following group of vocalises is suggested for achieving resonance balance in head mixture:

EXERCISE 10.13

i   e   ɔ   i   e   ɔ   i

EXERCISE 10.14

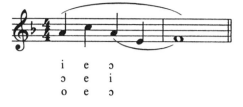

```
        i    e    ɔ
        ɔ    e    i
        o    e    ɔ
```

EXERCISE 10.15

(any vowel)

EXERCISE 10.16

(any vowel)

EXERCISE 10.17

(any vowel)

EXERCISE 10.18

(any vowel)

FEMALE *VOCE DI TESTA*

A distinct head sensation is felt at the F♯₅ transitional point for the lyric soprano. The gradual thinning of the vocal-fold edges, which has taken place gradually over the ascending scale, now becomes pronounced; much less vocal-fold mass is available to offer resistance to subglottic pressure.

EXERCISES FOR INDUCING *VOCE DI TESTA* SENSATIONS THROUGHOUT THE VOICE

Voce di testa sensation, markedly experienced above the *secondo passaggio,* should be carried down throughout the voice. A group of exercises is designed to unify the registers of the voice. This series begins in descending passages from above the *secondo passaggio* pivotal point; then the direction is reversed, with arpeggiated patterns beginning in lower or lower middle voice and ascending. Still others begin in middle voice. The series may be sung with varying tempos and vowels.

EXERCISE 10.19

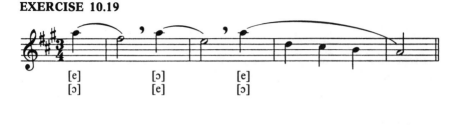

EXERCISE 10.20

EXERCISE 10.21

(any vowel)

EXERCISE 10.22

(any vowel)

EXERCISE 10.23

[e]
[ɔ]
[i]
[o]
[ɑ]
[u]

EXERCISE 10.24

[e]
[ɔ]
[o]

EXERCISE 10.25

(any vowel)

EXERCISE 10.26

(any vowel)

EXERCISE 10.27

(any vowel)

EXERCISE 10.28

(any vowel)

Additional exercises are built upon the vocal glissando (often called the portamento), which includes both low and high pitches. *Voce di testa* sensation is present even in the low pitch, assuring uniform resonance balance throughout the subsequent glissando. The quick glissando should be accomplished through [m], [n], and [v], often followed by a vowel in a descending scale passage. This group of glissando vocalises should be alternated with the previous group of *voce di testa* exercises.

EXERCISE 10.29

[m]   [m]   [ɑ]
[n]   [n]   [ɑ]
[v]   [v]   [ɑ]

EXERCISE 10.30

[m]   [ɑ]
[n]   [ɑ]
[v]   [ɑ]

EXERCISE 10.31

[m]   [m]   [ɑ]
[n]   [n]   [ɑ]
[v]   [v]   [ɑ]

EXERCISE 10.32

[m]   [ɑ]
[n]   [ɑ]
[v]   [ɑ]

EXERCISE 10.33

[m]   [ɑ]
[n]   [ɑ]
[v]   [ɑ]

Occasionally, a young female will have a "hole" in upper-middle voice, a brief area of weakness consisting of one or more pitches. Vocalises should start above the upper *passaggio* point, and descend through the area of weakness. Two examples follow.

EXERCISE 10.34

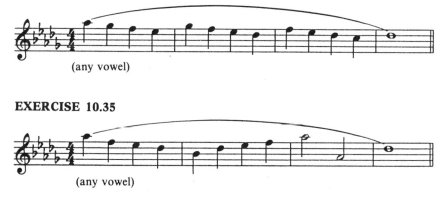

(any vowel)

EXERCISE 10.35

(any vowel)

FLAGEOLET REGISTER

Above upper voice *(voce di testa)* lies a register with a distinctive timbre. This register has acquired descriptive names in several languages: flageolet register, bell register, flute register, piccolo range, echo voice; *registre de flageolet, flute registre; die hohe Quinta, die zweite Höhe; voce di campanello.* This high-lying register is also sometimes called the whistle register, the short register, *le petit registre,* and *die Pfeifestimme.* However, these last four terms are best avoided because they are also used to describe the laryngeal whistle.

The muscle activity within the larynx that produces head voice becomes more acute in the stratospheric flageolet range. Flageolet timbre has been described as reminiscent of the ringing of a small, high-pitched bell, or of the echo of a high, distant pitch. The flageolet voice has a high rate of longitudinal tension of the vocal ligaments, considerable damping of the posterior portion of the vocal folds, limited vibrating mass of the vocal folds, and high subglottic pressure and airflow rate (see Appendix IV for additional comment).

Because muscle coordination of the light mechanism is at its most extreme in flageolet register, there are advantages in using flageolet vocalises for developing the upper register that lies immediately beneath the flageolet register. A singer often produces the extremely high pitches with a sound that seems to her childlike and tiny; these pitches feel relatively effortless. A comfortable opening of the mouth modifies the flageolet timbre, and an increase in breath support assists in uniting the flageolet range to the upper voice. Excessive dependence on resonance sensations associated with the flageolet voice can produce undesirable thinness and shrillness in the upper register. However, to ignore the flageolet register is to cast aside a useful tool for working in the upper female voice, especially in soprano categories. Flageolet register should not be confused with the short register, in which breath is forced through a narrow chink of the glottis, producing the high-pitched shriek made by lusty, furious infants or hysterical adults. According to Zemlin (1981, p. 216): "Many children are able to produce a very clear, flute-like, laryngeal whistle. The vocal folds are *extremely* tense and the glottis appears as a very narrow (about 1 mm) slit through which the air flows." Sounds of the whistle register are not subject to control, are not of pleasing timbre, and are not useful to the singer.

For the coloratura and the soubrette, vocalization in the flageolet register is essential. The lyric soprano voice and, in some instances, the heavier soprano voice, should practice rapid arpeggios and quickly moving scale passages that ascend into flageolet register. The exercises should be sung only after other areas of the voice have been vocalized. A few minutes per practice session is an adequate amount of time to spend on the flageolet range.

EXERCISES FOR DEVELOPING THE
FLAGEOLET RANGE

EXERCISE 10.36

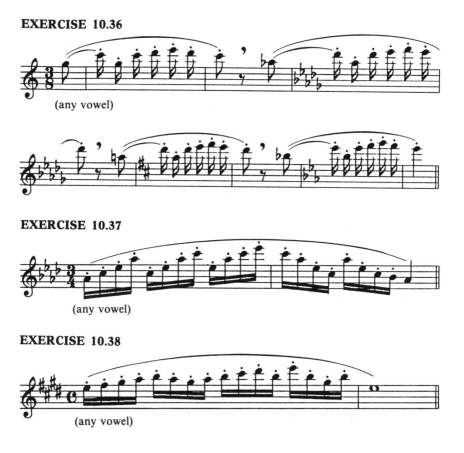

(any vowel)

EXERCISE 10.37

(any vowel)

EXERCISE 10.38

(any vowel)

CHAPTER 11

Vowel Modification in Singing

aggiustamento

There are no timbre demarcations in the scale of a good singer, unless introduced for coloristic purposes; the skillful singer appears to have but *one* register. Neither the demands of articulation nor the search for resonance sensations must be permitted to fragment the scale. Appelman (1967, p. 90) cites vowel modification as an aim of the *bel canto* period:

> One of the objectives of the singers of bel canto was the development of a vocal scale that was pure, unbroken, and uninterrupted. The transition of registers—either up or down the scale—demanded a modification in the tonal color of the topmost notes to prevent them from becoming disagreeable and harsh and to preserve the quality of the vowel sound as well as an even tonal line.

The front vowels (singers often call them "high") have formants that produce brilliance and "ring." Back vowels (singers frequently term them "low") have lower formants and strike the ear as being less brilliant (see Figures 4.2 and 4.5). The combination of rising pitch and high formant vowel in singing results in spectral patterns that produce "open" or "white" quality.

To counteract the tendency toward "open" sound, front vowels may be modified in rising pitch so as to reduce the incidence of higher harmonic partials. Pedagogical opinions vary as to how aesthetic demands can be met by this modification. Some singing teachers locate a spot in the ascending scale of each category of voice at which the tone must be "covered."

"Covering" encourages fundamental changes in the mechanical function of the larynx, and alteration of the shape of the resonators, accompanied by a sensation of additional spaciousness in the pharynx, by a high velum, a low tongue, and a lowered larynx, thereby increasing "depth" in the tone. These actions alter the harmonic spectra, and the tone is darkened by the heavier mechani-

150

cal action of the entire vocal instrument. Pedagogies that already tend toward overuse of the heavy mechanism recommend "heavy and early cover." Pronounced "cover" may be dangerous.

Brodnitz (1971, p. 36) comments:

> Singing with pronounced covering requires more air under increased pressure, and it involves considerable muscular tension. Moderate use of covering is part of the necessary and not harmful technique of the dramatic singer. Unfortunately, it is often used in excess, particularly by singers who try to sing dramatic parts with basically lyric voices. In that instance it is very dangerous and may lead to a permanent deterioration of the voice.

There can be little doubt that in desirable "closed voice" *(voce chiusa)*, a timbre that should prevail throughout the singing voice regardless of range, as opposed to "open voice" *(voce aperta)*, there is a stabilized laryngeal position—relatively low—and a somewhat widened pharynx. These conditions together with proper vowel modification *(aggiustamento)* produce the so-called "covered" sound of the upper range.

However, because of the tendency to make too much of a good thing (overcorrection is a major pitfall in the teaching of singing), and because of the diversity of meanings attached to the term "cover," it may prove useful to avoid the term and to speak of *vowel modification* rather than "cover" as the *passaggio* zone is reached. Some understanding of the underlying physiologic and acoustic factors of such modification certainly will help in removing nonmatching timbres in the vocal scale.

Often teachers of singing assume that "openness" characterizes all good singing, when in fact, the lowering of the epiglottis may be part of the "covering" action. No extensive study on the contribution of the epiglottis to "covering" has yet been undertaken. However, fiberoptic observations seem to indicate that where there is the omega-shaped epiglottis (the so-called "infantile" epiglottis) there is frequently an inability in the adult male to achieve *voce coperta* ("covered voice") with ease. It is probable that limited participation of the epiglottis (at a nonproprioceptive level, of course, just as is the case in vowel differentiation) is necessary to filter out the strident timbre traditionally associated with *voce aperta (voce bianca)*. Some low-voiced males who exhibit the omega-epiglottic structure seem never to negotiate the upper regions of the voice in satisfactory manner. Before definitive conclusions can be reached, a large number of subjects must be studied.

When subglottic pressure and airflow are commensurate with the need for balanced, resonant sounds in the singing voice, some epiglottic participation in general sphincteral activity may unconsciously take place. (One of the reasons the laryngologist asks patients to sing a falsetto "ee" is that the epiglottis is positioned perpendicularly and does not get in the way of an examination of the vocal folds as it does in the back vowels. Obviously, "covering," with its introduction of vowel modification in the direction of the back vowels, has some relationship to epiglottic position.)

How does one interpret the limited scientific information on "covering"? Are researchers aware of tonal ideals different from those exhibited by their subjects? Do we approve of the sounds made by the subjects? Do we agree with the aesthetic demand that fosters the pedagogy which has produced those results? For example: "The general impression is that the quality of the voice is 'darker' in singing, somewhat as it is when a person yawns and speaks at the same time; voice teachers sometimes describe the effect as covering."

The same source (Sundberg, 1977a, p. 84) goes on to say that "It is interesting to note that voice teachers tend to agree that the pharynx should be widened in singing, and some of them mention the sensation of yawning. In other words, a low larynx position and an expanded pharynx are considered desirable in singing."

However, the extent of pharyngeal distention and of laryngeal depression varies from school to school. Indeed, it may be that the *prevailing* viewpoint among teachers of singing is that pharyngeal expansion and a relatively low-positioned larynx occur as a consequence of proper inhalation and remain during the well-managed breath cycle, and are *not* induced by conscious localized actions. Stretching the pharynx and forcefully depressing the larynx are considered by many teachers to be artificial means of vocal production, contributing to that much "darker" voice of the Nordic schools, a coloration that a large segment of the singing profession wishes to avoid. One does not question the research methods but rather the narrowness of the field from which subjects may have been chosen.

Sundberg continues: "The lowering of the larynx, then, explains not only the singing formant peak but also major differences in the quality of vowels in speech and in singing."

He adds (1977a, p. 88), perhaps in response to auditory experiences: "The singer does pay a price however, since *the darkened vowel sounds deviate considerably from what one hears in ordinary speech.*" [Emphasis added] But *should* vowels have major differences in quality from speech to singing? Which aesthetics do we follow?

The oft-quoted statement of Pacchierotti, "Pronunciate chiaramente, ed il vostro canto sarà perfetto" ("Pronounce clearly and your singing will be perfect") is a basic tenet of the historic Italian School; it would appear to endorse a different aesthetic viewpoint from that which produces the "dark" voice. To claim that "open" or "white" timbre was then the aim is to ignore evidence from the literature itself. (Nor should one accept the highly questionable notion that a singer uses one approach for dramatic literature and another for lyric singing.) Heavy "covering," as found in northern schools, is to be avoided not only because it causes language and diction distortion, but because it distorts vocal timbre.

Is it possible to remain free during singing while constantly depressing the tongue, spreading the pharyngeal wall, maintaining an extreme velar elevation, and lowering the larynx excessively—all concomitant with the yawn? Is the text intelligible in any part of the voice? Despite the need for vowel modification in upper range, language sounds should always remain defined in artistic singing. A fault of vowel distortion should not be raised to a pedagogical tenet. Teachers of singing, except in certain Nordic schools, tend not to want a "dark" voice that resembles the timbre one hears when a person "yawns and speaks at the same time."

The alternative to the depressed larynx is by no means a high laryngeal position. Slight laryngeal descent with initial inspiration for singing is normal. If the singer is already in the "noble" position, very little descent of the larynx takes place upon inhalation. In any event, following the slight descent that accompanies inspiration, the larynx should then remain in a stabilized position. It should neither ascend nor descend, either for pitch or power, beyond the minimal requirements of vowel and consonant articulation. It should stay "put." The singer's physique determines the degree of depression.

Researchers Frommhold and Hoppe (1966, p. 89) did a series of experiments devoted to laryngeal movements during singing, relating the larynx posturally to the cervical vertebrae. A summary of their findings underscores the need for a stabilized laryngeal position during singing:

> In an investigation of the problem of voice production in trained singers, the movements of the cervical vertebrae were studied by means of tomograms, as providing a fixed bony point of attachment for the extrinsic laryngeal musculature. Important postural differences were found dependent upon the level of training and ability of the singer. *Outstanding international artists were conspicuous without exception for a constant posture over the entire vocal range,*

whilst students showed increasing tension resulting in kyphosis (changes in the angle of the axis between the vertebrae II and VI), isolated distortions and also gliding movements in individual segments. [Emphasis added]

It should be noted that some drawings of "low larynx production" in pedagogical treatises show the cricoid cartilage in an exceedingly low position. Sometimes, in these techniques, laryngeal depression is practiced apart from phonation, to "strengthen the depressor muscles" and to "anchor" the larynx. As a result of such postures, very little space remains between the mandible and the sternoclavicular joint, with the larynx wedged between them. The larynx can be retained in this posture only through the antagonistic activity of muscles of the neck and upper torso. Can this produce freedom in the singing voice?

Before leaving the subject of conscious laryngeal depression, it may be well to take a more direct look at sensation within the larynx itself during singing, as experienced in several pedagogies.

Most singers, regardless of pedagogical allegiance, are aware of even the slightest sensation within the larynx (as every laryngologist who deals with singers knows). Even normal phonation and phonemic articulation may be registered in the consciousness of the trained singer. These sensations often are interpreted (perhaps not without some basis in fact) as stemming from "resonance" within the larynx. It is not yet clear to what extent the ventricles of the larynx contribute to the singing tone, but there is evidence from tomographic studies that "covering" the voice while retaining the "ring" may have to do with increasing the ventricular space.

Some of the laryngeal sensations during singing may probably be disregarded, but any excessive awareness of sensation in the larynx is the result of unnecessary antagonism of the intrinsic and extrinsic laryngeal muscles. Sensation in the larynx means lack of freedom in the larynx. It should be the perceptions of the ear, not the kinesthetic perception of muscle setting within the laryngeal area, that occupy the singer's consciousness.

There is an appealing kind of false logic to conscious throat adjustment for the accomplishment of "covered" tone. The separate actions of "roominess" complement each other. A summary of this faulty viewpoint follows: A deep groove in the tongue runs to the back of the pharynx so that the tongue seems to have been gotten out of the way, permitting emergence of pharyngeal tone: As a result of the deep tongue trough, the soft palate is stretched upward revealing a large area of the oropharynx, sometimes described as heart-shaped; the descending larynx, via the hyoid bone, pulls down on the root of the tongue, an action which has been termed "the downward pull of the yawn"; the pillars of the fauces (which connect with both the tongue and the palate) are stretched, an action thought to be an asset inasmuch as muscular tension may contribute in producing the right kind of "twang" in the timbre.

Can this "logic" withstand the test of freedom of action, of functional efficiency? Do such techniques correspond to what is known about the action of the articulatory mechanism? Can the demands of language, agility, ease in breath management, and the dynamic events of registration be accomplished with freedom? What are the results of this vocal philosophy?

In the male voice, trained by the premises just outlined, such heavy throat adjustments as a means of "covering" produce a dark vowel sound already at the *primo passaggio* (see chapters on registration); by the *secondo passaggio*, vowels have been modified to a neutral condition, or to a back vowel, even if they are front vowels. For example, a baritone trained in this "heavy production," when singing an arpeggio on [ɑ] in the key of E♭, may well have "covered" the vowel to [o] by the time the fifth pitch of the scale (B♭) is reached, and may be singing something close to [ʊ] or even [u] on arrival at the top of the arpeggio at E♭₄, producing an effect of [ɑ, ɔ, o, u, o, ɔ, ɑ], although the vowel [ɑ] is indicated throughout the passage.

In contrast to this radical phonemic shift in vowel structure and mechanical adjustment in the pharynx, in the historic Italian School concentration is on graduated vowel modification. Flexible adjustment of the vocal tract must be permitted in order to define all vowel form. In the best singing of the international school, adjustment of acoustic postures defines vowels at any level of pitch.

The sole purpose of *aggiustamento* is to *modify* the formation of ascending vowels so that upper pitches may match the over-all timbre of the unified scale; adjustment of the vocal organs necessary to rising pitch (and power) automatically occurs when the acoustic laws of vowel differentiation are allowed to function without mechanical falsification of the vowel.

TIMBRE TERMINOLOGY

In considering the role to be played by vowel modification, some terminology relating to vocal timbre should be examined.

Voce bianca (*voix blanche*, white voice) results from an excess of upper harmonic partials in the sound, and is not an acceptable quality in any vocal range.

Voce aperta (open voice) indicates a general imbalance among resonance factors in all ranges of the voice, especially apparent in upper–middle and upper voice. *Voce bianca* contributes to *voce aperta.*

Voce chiusa (closed voice) describes a timbre in all parts of the range with a desirable balance of low and high harmonic partials. *Voce chiusa* produces the *chiaroscuro* (light–dark) timbre in which both brilliance and depth are present in any area of the vocal scale.

Voce coperta (suono coperto) occurs in rising pitch without engendering mechanical changes associated with *Deckung,* and without the kind of mechanistic action represented by some uses of the term "cover." Although *copertura* might literally be translated as *Deckung,* or "covering," the physiological events are not necessarily identical. *Deckung,* or "covering," as it is sometimes understood, cannot be managed without introducing heavy thyroarytenoid activity in parts of the vocal range where other muscle balances should prevail. A healthier and more aesthetically pleasing alternative (of course, not to ears that have been culturally conditioned otherwise) may be found in almost imperceptible modification, at the *primo passaggio,* which does *not* completely neutralize the vowel at the *secondo passaggio* pivotal point (Miller, 1977, pp. 82–83).

Voce coperta is part of the *voce chiusa* concept and avoids *voce aperta* through *aggiustamento* of the vowel. Such *copertura* forms a major technical accomplishment in artistic singing. As mentioned, it is not equatable with some uses of *Deckung* (or "covering"). It is also inaccurate to translate directly the terms *gedeckt* and "covered" as *voce coperta.* The *aggiustamenti* of *copertura,* a technique also known as *arrotondamento* (rounding), are much more graduated in the historic schools than in some other twentieth-century systems. *Aggiustamento* is of much importance for high pitches *(le note acute)* of the voice.

Some singers tend toward an open quality of sound because they lack the proper energization and physical involvement needed to achieve unified timbre in the mounting scale. On reaching upper voice or encountering the *secondo passaggio,* they suddenly "cover," producing a markedly "woofy" sound. Therefore, although avoiding the perils of early *Deckung,* they violate function as the scale rises; they then force sudden adjustments on the larynx, and dark, unsupported tone results. To ignore vowel modification *(aggiustamento)* throughout the ascending scale is to lay the ground for unwanted register demarcation.

THE TECHNIQUE OF *AGGIUSTAMENTO* (THE VOWEL SERIES IN MODIFICATION)

Characteristic attributes of the even scale can be determined only by a professional ear attuned to properly balanced vocal timbres. Yet certain guidelines for modifying the vowel can be suggested. By approaching a neighboring vowel, either toward neutralization or away from it, the harmonic spectra (the balance of fundamental and overtones) can be kept in proportion throughout the scale. This *aggiustamento* is often illustrated by a chart such as Figure 11.1.

The least degree of modification of the laryngeally produced sound is to be found in the neutral vowel, expressed phonetically by [ʌ], and in the *schwa* vowel, [ə]. The *schwa* represents the neutral sound that must often be modified when singing in most foreign languages and in English as well. The vowel [ɑ], lying midway in the vowel series, with possible modification approaching from either front or back vowels, can often serve even more appropriately as a central modifying vowel than can the *schwa*, which sometimes becomes lost in indeterminate timbre.

How does vowel modification work in actual practice in singing? In vocalizing an arpeggio on the vowel [i] into the upper regions of the voice, some modification toward neutralization must take place as a means of balancing out additional upper partials that result from the conjoining of high pitch and front vowel. The vowel [i] must therefore modify toward the vowel [ɪ]. Actually, the very act of opening the mouth somewhat wider to accommodate mounting pitch and

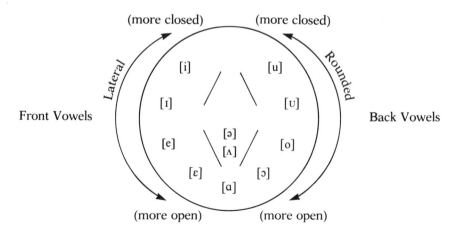

Figure 11.1. Vowel Modification *(aggiustamento)* Chart

power will very nearly accomplish this vowel adjustment. Indeed, *natural modification of the vowel* will inevitably result in the mounting scale in response to this subtle modification of the chambers of the resonator tube, with any specific conscious mechanical change at the level of the larynx unnecessary. (Of course, laryngeal configuration will change with vowel definition. Additional muscular action is not a conscious goal).

This principle of *arrotondamento* is especially important, of course, in *voce acuta*, with [ɑ] modifying toward [ɔ]; [e] toward [ɛ]; [ɛ] toward [ɑ]; [ɔ] toward [o]; [o] toward [ʊ]; and [ʊ] toward [u]. However, in the methodology of the historic Italian School, it is not suggested that all vowels modify to the *schwa* (which does not "officially" exist in the Italian language), or to some other designated phoneme at a specified pitch below the *secondo passaggio*, nor even in those pitches that lie above it. That suggestion, however, is made in some other schools of singing (Miller, 1977, pp. 137–141).

Exercises in vowel modification can be useful only so long as the singer (along with the teacher) has a concept of well-balanced, resonant sound, based on what actually happens when the vocal tract is in tune with laryngeal vowel definition while maintaining the presence of the singer's formant.

Vowel modification may well be the most subtle of all technical aspects in the teaching of singing. Perhaps because most singers in the early phases of study tend to err on the side of open singing without sufficient modification of the vowel, it is a pedagogical problem not to "close" the voice excessively.

Open singing (lack of modification of vowels) in the upper voice is detrimental to vocal health. However, it is often overlooked that carrying the weight of the heavy mechanism into upper–middle or upper voice (under the assumption that such action modifies the vowel) is at least potentially as disastrous. Brodnitz warns against the hazards of excessive "covering": "Covering has to be used with great care, because in its extreme form it is hard on voices" (1953, p. 83). He states that the danger in heavy covering lies "in the greater tension of the outer laryngeal muscles as well as of the inner ones, both of which tense the cords." When too much modification is experienced by the singer in the mounting scale, the reverse process of neutralization may be necessary: The vowel [u] tends toward [ʊ], [o] toward [ɔ], etc. Never should any form of vowel modification draw attention to itself ("Watch me 'cover' this one!").

In achieving proper modification of the vowels *(aggiustamento)*, distinct advantages are to be gained by alternating neighboring vowels on the vowel series, always examining them to be certain they retain a common quality of resonance and projection.

Although the vocalises devised for vowel adjustment in the rising scale are useful in establishing that technique, they should be undertaken by the nonprofessional or youthful singer only under the guidance of a practiced ear. Every practicing professional singer should devote time in the daily regimen to vocalises of this category. In addition, spot passages from one's repertory should be worked over with the same principles in mind.

EXERCISES FOR ACHIEVING *AGGIUSTAMENTO*

Vocalises are to be transposed to accommodate the vocal category; they should be sung as a series, in several neighboring keys.

EXERCISE 11.1

EXERCISE 11.4

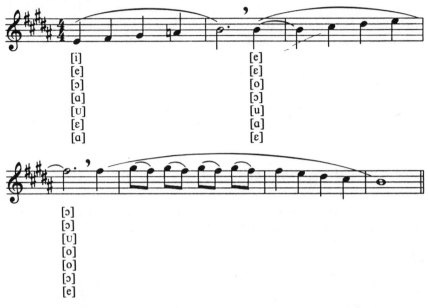

[i]	[e]
[e]	[ɛ]
[ɔ]	[o]
[a]	[ɔ]
[ʊ]	[u]
[ɛ]	[a]
[a]	[ɛ]

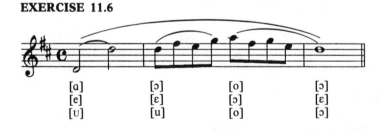

[ɔ]
[ɔ]
[ʊ]
[o]
[o]
[ɔ]
[e]

EXERCISE 11.5

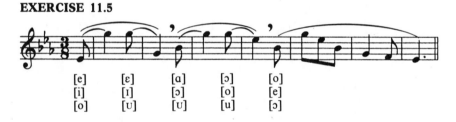

[e]	[ɛ]	[a]	[ɔ]	[o]
[i]	[ɪ]	[ɔ]	[o]	[e]
[o]	[ʊ]	[ʊ]	[u]	[ɔ]

EXERCISE 11.6

[a]	[ɔ]	[o]	[ɔ]
[e]	[ɛ]	[ɔ]	[ɛ]
[ʊ]	[u]	[o]	[ɔ]

CHAPTER 12

Range Extension and Stabilization in Singing

For each category of voice there are rather precise range expectations. Singers must restrict themselves to literature of a specific vocal range, determined by their category (termed *Fach* in the international language of the theater). On the other hand, a limited range within a category is a serious disadvantage to a performer. Inability to negotiate the full range of the voice has halted some promising careers. The topic of range limitation is a much more pressing one than the general silence that prevails on the subject indicates.

Some female singers have the curious problem of being able to sing pitches that encompass the ranges of both mezzo-soprano and coloratura voices. Unfortunately, an extensive range is not a primary determinant in evaluating a voice—quality is. The agile "nightingale" voice, with fantastic range extension but small in size, is not uncommon; sometimes it is uninteresting. Such instruments fall into the "normal" soprano category. Unless some highly individualistic facet of artist imagination or vocal timbre is characteristic, such a voice will remain undistinguished from hundreds of others, despite technical facility.

The opposite problem may plague the individual with "everything but the top voice." A successful singer must be able to perform most of the rangy literature of the *Fach*; "short" voices are seldom given a chance at major professional assignments, regardless of other positive attributes.

However, more than one singer has been disturbed to read that a professional singer ought to possess a performing range of three octaves. A look at the literature for the singing voice, or an evening at recital or the opera, reveals that this is almost never the case. An interesting experiment may be made by taking a vocal score (opera, oratorio, or song literature—it makes no difference which), leafing through it page by page, and tabulating the number of notes that lie either above or below the staff (bass or treble). An amazingly high percentage of all vocal writing for any category of singer is contained within the range of a tenth. It so happens, however, in most categories, that the notes lying on either side of that tenth are exactly the pitches needed at the few moments of emotional and dramatic impact (yet, almost never encompassing three octaves).

Conventions of vocal composition reflect physiological fact; range demands for the light soprano, for example, generally are considerably greater than for any other vocal type, and logically so. Anatomically, the light soprano larynx is slight, sometimes being only two thirds the size of the lower female larynx. By using the possibilities of the flageolet and chest registers, the light soprano voice may extend from G_3 to G_6 with, in some cases, a few additional pitches on either end. There is no need for astonishment at those additional pitches that lie above High C, when it comes to the light soprano categories. They are routine, and, if not present, technical deficiency is the probable cause. Many highly successful professional light soprano voices do not have all of those pitches (three octaves) in their publicly performable range.

Most factual material presented on singing ranges is of little value in helping singers make judgments about their own professional qualifications, because such material is often without differentiation of subcategories within the over-all *Fach*. Ranges shown in encyclopedic sources are often repeated from source to source without real verification.

Equally unreliable, in general, are the charts included in some works on singing, showing the "normal" range-extent of a particular vocal category; professional voices often do not correspond to such indications, frequently exceeding them on both ends. It is not unusual, for example, to encounter tenor voices of lyric as well as of dramatic proportions (but seldom *leggieri* or *tenorini*, of course) who have many pitches below C_3. Tenor voices appropriate to the opera house often negotiate a low G_2, with good quality and with comparative ease. Knowing this to be the case, more than one tenor has been amused at the continuing awe expressed down through the years by some critics and vocal aficionados for Caruso's much-publicized feat of singing the bass aria "Vecchia zimarra, senti," from the last act of *La Bohème*, during an onstage performance. Although it is clear that no other tenor would manage the unique Caruso timbre in that or any other vocal range, almost *any* current professional Rodolfo could sing Colline's aria very successfully, inasmuch as it extends only from C_3 to $E\flat_4$, a quite manageable range for the tenor voice. The incident is remarkable not because Caruso "had such a strong low voice that he could sing bass arias," but because his native timbre permitted him to do so with such good results that some members of the audience assumed his bass colleague was actually singing.

Much of the material regarding the range and character of the tenor voice has little to do with the professional operatic tenor. Studies of the high-voiced male, on which generalities about the singing voice are often based, frequently deal with pathologically high speaking voices, or with amateur ensemble singers. Measurements of the vocal folds, pyknic physical characteristics, gonadal contributions to vocal development, and psychological attitudes help determine vocal category, no doubt. The problem with much published information about the high-voiced male is that many of the subjects encountered by speech therapists or medical examiners do not correspond to the professional tenor, yet in some studies these voices are termed "*true* tenor voices." The laryngologist, when initially seeing the larynx of the professional tenor, may assume him to be a baritone because much of the "scientific" literature describes the tenor larynx as being remarkably small.

The same point may just as readily be made about the contralto voice. To state that "the low female voice suffers from virilization due to hormonal secretion" (a comment typically found in some literature devoted to voice categories), producing a larger larynx, may be quite true with regard to, say, the low-voiced, bearded lady of the circus; it is questionable that such observations apply to most professionally low-voiced female singers.

RANGE AND VOICE CATEGORIZATION

Ability to negotiate range has an obvious relationship to vocal structure and to categorization, but much care is needed in judging which limitations are truly congenital and which are technical. In recent decades, methods for determining the probable range (and therefore vocal category) of a voice by mechanical measurement have gained some limited acceptance. Although such correlations are of interest, it is doubtful that any pedagogically useful information lies in that direction. Voices are housed in physiques that to some extent dictate categorization, but general vocal environment and the specific vocal training a singer encounters will provide the decisive factors in determining voice category and range. A fair case may be made in support of the hypothesis that cultural attitudes serve as crucible in many vocal matters, and that national preferences in vocal quality may at times provide the essential factor for determining voice classification.

When range is allowed to serve as the chief consideration in vocal classification, many potential professional voices of one category are mistakenly classified early as belonging to some other category. The tenor with full, resonant low voice, the soprano with the temporarily short top, the singer whose range is limited because of a lack of energy, often mislead as to true vocal category, especially with regard to range expectation from the respective categories.

The events of register demarcation serve as indicators of vocal categorization; if these events are overlaid with technical encumbrances, range may be curtailed. The upper range is highly vulnerable to such limitation. Discovering the *passaggi* pivotal points of the voice, and avoiding classification based chiefly on how high or how low a singer can sing at some early stage of vocal development, is wise procedure.

The world is full of singers who possess phenomenal high notes, but whose timbre below the upper ledger lines bores the listener. Few opportunities are then forthcoming to display those remarkable high pitches. They take on the character of a circus act, or a parlor trick. (Incidentally, shining high notes on top of an otherwise dull instrument usually indicate a technically handicapped instrument in need of resonator adjustment.)

Much of the work of extending and stabilizing the vocal range has to do with casting aside certain attitudes and replacing them with other more positive ones. Most of our vocal experiences as singers are tied to word symbols, which construct a continuing pattern of performance responses for us. Very often if we substitute one set of symbols for another, we help change the physical response. Isn't this pure empiricism? Of course it is, and it is fine as long as it is based on an understanding of free physical action. (Certainly no singer should ever attempt to perform only mechanically, in any range of the voice!) The singer must be certain that the word symbols that are chosen incite the *correct* physical responses. Much of the imagery of vocal pedagogy is directed toward localized control, which inhibits freedom in singing.

Furthermore, it is precisely in the area of physical function that *all singing experience must rely on psychological climate.* Appropriate word symbols (imagery!) that create a prevailing psychological aura (or at least give it verbal utterance) can be intelligently expressed only in response to what has actually been experienced *physically.*

Success in developing acceptance of the physical possibilities of the top voice (in the healthy instrument) is often achieved by attention to several concepts:

1. *Continuity.* Within the extensive range requirements of vocal literature, nearly every climactic note in the upper range of the voice has one or more connecting notes that *unite* it with the rest of the voice. The high pitch belongs to the rest of the phrase.

2. *Unity of the Musical Phrase.* Not only is there the physical connection of one pitch to another delivered by an instrument skilled in legato, there is the concept of singing through a phrase, of incorporating every note within the phrase into one whole. No note is isolated, regardless of its pitch or its duration; it is constantly moving within the sweep of the phrase; the pitch on which it happens to occur becomes immaterial when attention is riveted on *directing the phrase*, pointing it ahead. (Legato as an expressive device in communicative singing will be discussed in Chapter 15.)

3. *Centeredness* (also *centering*). Concerns about high and low pitch can be replaced by a feeling of central location of all pitch; pitch is incorporated into a sense of collected focus, a mental and physical process. There is an elimination of "up and down," and there is no sense of shifting location of either pitch or attention. (With some singers who have been accustomed to think in terms of high and low, a decisive shift to horizontal thinking and feeling may be helpful.) Out of this centering comes compactness of energy and concentration, of both the body and the artistic imagination. The singer should *consciously cultivate* a sense of physical and mental well-being. (This is exceedingly hard to do if the poor singer is trying to yawn, achieve the idiot jaw, make space in the pharynx, distend the abdomen, etc.!) This centering can be acquired, it can be practiced, and it can become a habitual way of thinking and performing. It is, without doubt, closely related to ancient exercises of both East and West that unite mental and physical responses (mind and body).

4. *Function.* Physical action—the functional part of singing—is best controlled through indirect suggestion, but it must be efficiently established before freedom can be expected to occur. Behind all of the artistic–psychological (the spiritual, perhaps?) lies the physical and acoustic instrument. The determination of pitch throughout the voice, including the extremes of high and low, is fundamentally a functional matter. Alteration of pitch in the human voice depends on physical factors within the larynx. Yet, this "function" is closely related to several ideas already presented. It is the result of the coordinated mechanism, and it is one graduated mechanical process. No sudden new action is ever introduced into any area of the voice, including the top voice (centeredness need not be subjected to any sudden disruption). Mastery of the technical facility of *aggiustamento* is a functional matter dictated by the aesthetic demands of the ear.

5. *Commitment to Textual Immediacy.* Singing is not vocalization, but communication. High pitches are not isolated exemplars of technical principles; they are almost always emotive moments in vocal literature, and they must be incorporated into that immediacy of expression that results from believing totally the situation of word and drama as it transpires (see Chapter 15). Although some part of the mind monitors on a technical level, in singing, everything must be subservient to the imagination if performance is to occur on an artistic plane. Commit yourself to believing what you are singing at the moment you sing it, and the high note will join with you in that conviction!

As just pointed out, high pitches mostly occur within the contour of the general phrase shape, and they must be incorporated into the phrase. Occasionally, a note must be attacked or released (perhaps both) at the top of the range. Regardless of how that pitch is approached (à la Puccini or à la Babbitt), fear of high notes can be eliminated by avoiding vertical thinking and by keeping the complete structure of the passage in mind, no matter how disjunct it may appear. (The addition, mentally, of pitches on either side of the pitch may temporarily assist.)

Fear is not foolish if it derives from intelligent experience; fear *is* foolish if experience consistently proves there is no basis for it. It is, however, not sufficient to advise the singer to give up the foolish habit of being frightened about high notes; only when the singer has had good experiences in singing high notes under all kinds of circumstances will fears be replaced by confidence in performance situations. (The way to do that is to make every practice session a performance. If you can consistently do it in the practice room, you can consistently do it on the stage. If you cannot, then review these five suggestions.)

Despite positive thinking, unless singers have a technique that permits freedom of function, they have no right to expect freedom in the upper range of the voice. When proper coordination is routined and established, confidence in the upper range results. (It will not result if the vocal mechanism is not in line with physical and acoustic laws that govern its function.) If your technique is a patchwork of tricks and does not add up to a complete system of freely functioning parts, you have no reason to expect ease in the upper voice. If you jut your jaw and raise your larynx for high pitch, you will never have freedom in the upper range, for example. Nor will you have it if you depress the larynx.)

EXTENDING THE VOCAL RANGE

Earlier in this chapter the need for a three-octave range for every singer was questioned. Now the problem of the truly limited range must be raised.

A free voice is a rangy voice. Despite good technical coordination and healthy vocal production, some singers continue to suffer range limitations. The teacher must first determine that no pathological causes are present; if there are none, and the voice answers to the various indicators of a specific vocal classification but falls short of the range expectations of the category, the singer probably suffers from acquired anxiety regarding high pitches. The best way to approach that problem is head on, by systematically working on the upper range.

Although singers have no right to expect nonproblematic entrance into upper voice if problems abound below it, it is not necessary to have every aspect of vocal technique well in hand before turning to range extension, which must form a part of normal technical development. Sometimes surprising vocal advances occur through exercising the upper range even when problems still remain in middle voice, but this is rare. In general, the upper range only develops gradually as a part of the equalized scale.

Proper coordination can replace anxiety over high pitches. The series of vocalises that follow are culled from the nineteenth-century and early twentieth-century Italian School. Some have sweeping lines, some are presented as isolated pitches, and others terminate abruptly. In executing the vocalises both female and male singer must be willing to risk something, be willing to accept even the possibility of an occasional sound that fails. Anyone who undertakes these vocalises should be convinced that the imagination which germinates the performance ideal, and the mechanics of the responding physical–acoustic instrument, are subject to unification by the will of the performer.

EXERCISES FOR EXTENDING AND STABILIZING THE VOCAL RANGE

Because the vocal literature is rich in challenging examples for each category of high-lying passages, it is not necessary to contrive a comprehensive series of vocalises for range extension. Several kinds of patterns may be isolated. When they have become routine, they provide a road map to other demanding phrases encountered in the literature.

The exercises that deal with range extension must be transposed as necessary for each vocal category. (In their present keys they are intended for the lyric soprano and the lyric tenor.) They may be sung on any single vowel, and tempo should be varied. Most of the exercises will be limited to a few neighboring keys for each category of voice.

They may appear strenuous at first. These vocalises are not intended for the singer who does not already have a fair degree of technical facility. They are for young professionals, not for beginners. The exercises are reasonable examples of passages that demand range, and serve as models for daily practice by the advanced singer.

EXERCISE 12.1

(any vowel)

EXERCISE 12.2

(any vowel)

EXERCISE 12.3

(any vowel)

EXERCISE 12.4

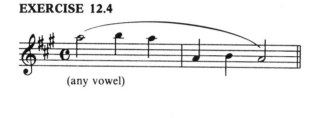

(any vowel)

EXERCISE 12.5

(any vowel)

EXERCISE 12.6

(any vowel)

EXERCISE 12.7

(any vowel)

EXERCISE 12.8

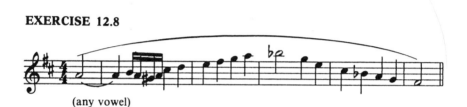

(any vowel)

EXERCISE 12.9

(any vowel)

Vocalises indicated for the development of the flageolet register (see Chapter 10) for the female voice are as directly concerned with range extension as with registration. In addition, a number of agility exercises (see Chapter 3) are equally useful in expanding and securing range. The development and extension of lower range also has been given earlier consideration (see Chapters 9 and 10). Exercises in this chapter deal with some of the specific demands of extended range.

CHAPTER 13

Messa di voce *and* *Dynamic Control*

Controlling the quantity of sound is a major requirement of good singing. Without mastery of dynamic contrast, the best vocal production becomes inexpressive and uninteresting. Most composers have in mind the mosaic-like possibilities of the entire dynamic palette when writing for voice. Vocal coloration and dynamic level are inseparable. Even when no dynamic markings are present in the vocal line, markings in the piano or orchestral score often are intended for the singer as well.

The singer must be able to

"Sing high and low,
Fast and slow,
Loud and soft also!"

General dynamic level and variable dynamics are an interpretative and artistic concern. The singer who unwisely maintains a constant volume throughout a song (or an evening) may be doing so because of technical limitations, not because of insufficient artistic sensitivity. Many of the problems connected with breath energy and sustained tessitura come from improper approaches to dynamics, both at soft and loud levels.

The technical means by which a singer varies dynamic level is another of those watersheds that divide vocal pedagogies. A singer who has been instructed to "build upon the soft" as a general approach to vocal technique involves different muscle controls than the singer who has been taught that dynamic muscle equilibrium should be present throughout *all* levels of volume or range. The vitalized *voce piena*, in the latter case, is the ideal, to be varied dynamically without vitiating the kernel of the sound.

Techniques built upon the soft onset often have difficulty in eliminating an admixture of breath from the tone, unless subglottic pressure is suddenly increased at some point in the mounting dynamic level. In such techniques there is a tendency to revert to breath in the tone as a means of diminishing volume and projection.

171

Breath admixture becomes the hallmark of some singers when they attempt piano singing. (Just as unfavorable is the unmitigated loud dynamic level of certain singers whose ears seem to demand feedback at high amplitude at all times. They mistake dynamic level for "resonance.")

The same *character* of tone should be possible for the singer in both loud and soft passages, unless there is purposeful intent to change the timbre for coloristic reasons. The traditional international school adheres to such timbre consistency. (The belligerent bellowing of insensitive singers who are convinced that a constant fortissimo is appropriate for operatic literature is best ignored.)

Breath admixture, in some other pedagogies, is admittedly appealing in that it requires less energy, and less time and skill to acquire. Then why not do what is easiest? Because when examined in the light of the freely coordinated instrument, "soft, sighing piano" is an enemy that enters the citadel of vocal technique to erode its foundations by literally removing its supportive pillars. It introduces into vocalism a number of destructive possibilities. Sustained piano singing should cause neither a higher mixture of breath in the tone nor an increase in glottal pressure as a device for diminishing volume. Dynamic variation should not be dependent on sudden shifts in vocal timbre caused by a series of static adjustments. Dynamic equilibrium, not static settings, produces the capability for contrasts within the basic timbre.

Bouhuys (1977, p. 275) reports that in tests comparing trained and untrained singers, the frequency spectra of the trained singer suggest that the air pulses through the glottis have a similar waveform in soft and loud tones. In the untrained singer, louder tones show excessively high frequencies, producing shrillness and a more peaked glottal air pulse. The untrained singer has a decisive air leak through the glottis that is not in evidence in the trained singer. On the other hand, the untrained singer tends to make more efficient use of the airstream in louder passages than when singing softly. "The untrained singer is unable to adduct the vocal folds completely, or nearly so, when he sings softly. This results in a 'breathy' character of these soft tones" (Bouhuys, 1977, p. 275).

It is clear that a good singer uses efficient, lower airflow rates when singing softly than does the untrained singer. The "sighing, yawning" piano permits high airflow rates because the vocal folds are not efficiently approximated. "Building on the soft," and concentrating on the soft onset, are concepts that produce high airflow rates. Mechanical efficiency in singing, Bouhuys (1977, p. 278) and Schutte (1980, pp. 147–162) assure us, is dependent on skillful breath management, which reduces breath leakage. Excessive breath passing over the vocal folds is the mark of the poor singer. The balanced onset is essential at *all* dynamic levels.

Messa di voce is the classic device for achieving mastery of a wide range of dynamic contrasts. One begins at pianissimo level with a sustained tone, crescendoing to fortissimo, then decrescendoing back to pianissimo *while maintaining uniform timbre.* Ideally, the whole dynamic range of *messa di voce* should be possible on every pitch within the entire vocal compass, yet it is doubtful that more than a handful of great singers have ever achieved that goal, in any generation.

EXERCISES FOR DEVELOPING DYNAMIC CONTROL

The following vocalises are for singers with advanced technical proficiency. Beginning in lower–middle voice, the singer may cautiously extend these vocalises into upper–middle and upper range levels over a period of months and years. At the outset, crescendo and decrescendo portions of the *messa di voce* are interrupted with a quiet breath, as indicated:

EXERCISE 13.1

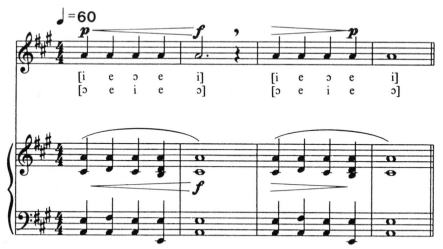

Initially, extremes of dynamic contrast should not be the aim. Piano and forte levels can later be developed into greatly contrasted pianissimo and fortissimo levels. Although begun at piano, initial sound should conform to that balanced onset (see Chapter 1) previously acquired. The aspirated onset and the glottal plosive must both be avoided or the exercise will not prove beneficial. Above all, there must be no point within the phrase at which "softness" is replaced by "kernel"; the "core" of the tone must be present from the start. No "entering wedge" should be audible, as has sometimes been suggested (Vennard, 1967, p. 213), and there must be no sensation that "as you crescendo, drive in the wedge."

During the course of any sustained phrase, maintaining a steady epigastric–umbilical balance requires increased attention to breath management. In *messa di voce* there should never be sudden conscious increase in breath pressure; a sense of gradual energization within constant stability of timbre should be experienced as the dynamic level changes. The concluding pianissimo will require the highest levels of control. Such control is the result of having earlier developed the sensation of breath "suspension" discussed in Chapter 2.

The male singer should avoid the tendency to resort to falsetto as the *messa di voce* technique is extended upward into middle voice. (Although the falsetto may be used in a limited way under the circumstances described in Chapter 9, it must not normally make its appearance in the *messa di voce* exercise. Falsetto encourages faulty vocal-fold approximation and an increase in airflow that the *messa di voce* is intended to correct.) The female singer must never indulge in the "tiny" adolescent sound that reduces amplitude but vitiates timbre.

It must be mentioned emphatically that the suggestion to "go from 'chest voice' to 'head voice'" in the *messa di voce* exercise is to be avoided at all costs (although recommended in some pedagogies). The ability to crescendo is not related to registration of the voice. No fundamental altering of muscle participation occurs at some precise moment during sustained pitch; *messa di voce* involves no abrupt change in cricothyroidal–thyroarytenoidal balances. (How could such action possibly be considered appropriate to a sustained note in the upper region of the voice, for example?) Sudden drastic shifts in muscle balance among the internal adjustors of the vocal bands are to be shunned. Stability is the key.

The viewpoint that *messa di voce* vocalises are exercises in sudden alternation of the heavy and the light mechanisms of registration on a single pitch is not in line with the traditional concept of that skill. Indeed, *messa di voce* can be accomplished within any register timbre. However, its most valuable contribution consists in *unification*, practiced in all but the most extreme ranges of the voice. It is not solely an exercise in dynamic control.

EXERCISE 13.2

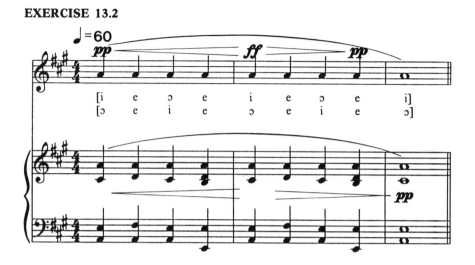

No singer should despair if early tries at the *messa di voce* are less than perfect. The singer should be happy to manage the vocalises even in a limited part of the range. Yet, the importance of the exercise as a technical device for gaining control of the entire singing instrument can hardly be overestimated. *Messa di voce*, in fact, is the ultimate test of a coordinated technique of singing. *Messa di voce* lets us know how we stand as singers. It instructs us as to what still remains to be accomplished technically, in the task of unifying the singing instrument. *Messa di voce* is a skill both technical and artistic; it is a facility that should be treated with great respect by the singer.

Attempts to achieve the highly controlled *messa di voce* must wait for general technical stability. As was noted with regard to the sostenuto vocalises, caution should be exercised by any singer who does not yet possess a high degree of technical prowess. Only the singer who has fundamentals of vocal technique well in hand should attempt these vocalises.

In contrast to changing vowel sequence, a single vowel is sung throughout the *messa di voce* pitch. Great care should be taken that the individual vowel remains unaltered. Clear vowel definition must always be present. For most singers, certain vowel formations are easier than others. Good judgment must be exercised in determining which vowels offer the most favorable results and which need to be subjected to more careful handling; a balance should then be maintained among them all, in daily practicing.

EXERCISE 13.3

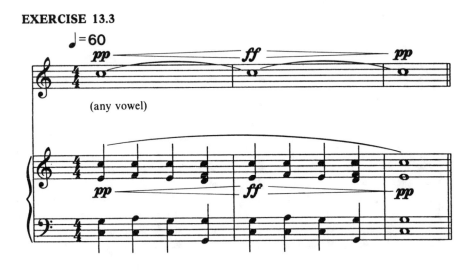

(any vowel)

DETERMINING DYNAMIC LEVELS

Dynamic levels indicated in a musical score often are designations not only of amplitude, but of quality and mood. Instrumental and vocal textures are as much a part of dynamic perception as are degrees of softness and loudness, a musical subtlety overlooked by many musicians. All dynamic markings are relative to the basic dynamic scope of the individual composition and to the character of the performing instrument. Should any fortissimo in Mozart equal that of Berlioz, Strauss, or Mahler? A good reviewer looks for an understanding of the composer's intent when evaluating a performance, as in the following (Löbl, 1977, p. 9):

> [Conductor X] takes Verdi at his word. In the *Requiem* he permits himself to play with those dynamic extremes which are indeed indicated in the score. There one finds quintuple fortissimi [fffff] as well as cumulative piano indications. In the realization, this means [dynamic] eruption as well as extinction.
> The question is whether Verdi meant so literally such orgies of fortissimo as occurred in this performance; one questions the accuracy of the conception of [Conductor X]. I believe that Verdi in his dynamic indications had in ear more matters of quality, clarity and severity than the actual brutalization of an entire chorus.

Young singers, particularly those who still exhibit characteristics of late adolescence (a vocal condition that extends considerably beyond the late teens), cannot be expected to display as much skill in dynamic control as do more mature voices. In fact, insistence on exact dynamic reading of much of the vocal literature (the *Lied* in particular) will serve only to compound existing problems in the young voice, and to produce other problems. It is pedagogically unwise to ask a robust immature voice to sing Schumann's "Mondnacht," or Schubert's "An die Nachtigall" (Claudius); both are exercises in dynamic subtlety. (Of course, if the voice is light and lyric in character [especially if a soprano], there should be little problem.)

Perhaps one of the most treacherous areas of the teaching of singing lies in determining appropriate dynamic levels within each vocal category. Many voices of potentially dramatic proportions may be permanently impaired by well-meaning teachers who, in attempting to avoid "pushing," advocate breath mixture and a general reduction of energization in singing. The voice can be "pushed" in more than one way: (1) Breath pressure at the glottis can be so intense that muscular tension in singing becomes unavoidable, and (2) breath energy can be so lax that the laryngeal mechanism must unsuccessfully strive to meet the demands of pitch and amplitude without sufficient muscular support. The second mode of "pushing" is just as pernicious as the first.

The result of pedagogical attitudes, in some cases, is to make all voices small, regardless of the actual category of voice. Equally dangerous is the opposite tendency, to make every voice into a big voice. Some voices are sizable and others are modest. Each vocal instrument must arrive at its own dimension through freedom of action.

The majority of errors regarding determination of dynamic level, in early vocal training, can be laid to the account of the conscientious teacher who hopes to avoid "pushing" the young voice, and who thereby falls into the trap of under-energizing for singing. The chief pedagogical problem among young students of singing is not that they "push" the voice, but that they have not learned how to apply physical energy while remaining loose and free.

Furthermore, there is a great deal of misunderstanding about what ought to comprise the dynamic range within each category of singer. The voice studio can become a very isolated, confining laboratory of idealism, remote from the actualities of the professional performance world. There are teachers of singing who tend to suspect *all* dramatic voices. For them, only the *Lieder* singer (or perhaps the oratorio soloist) stands *in parte dextra*, because in that viewpoint everyone else "pushes" and suffers from "hyperfunction." There is confusion as to why the world-renowned tenor who sings Radames or Don José (or who did a generation ago, at least) so splendidly, does not "spin out the concluding high $B^\flat$ pianissimo." Why is it that the dramatic soprano who has delivered Elektra thrillingly for many decades does so at such a high dynamic level, and why does she not sing certain other literatures as does the "sensitive" recitalist who "floats" her tone? These examples are drawn from life, and illustrate that it is sometimes difficult not only for the sheltered voice teacher (who easily grows accustomed to dealing with the college-age singer), but for the supposedly knowledgeable critic to recognize that all of those subtle sounds so musically appealing in the voice studio and the small recital hall may be more readily achieved by voices of lighter category, and under limited acoustical circumstances. To expect the same vocal style and behavior from a dramatic instrument is to show ignorance of the several categories of the singing instrument. As Titze has noted (1980, p. 20), there are sprinters and long-distance runners among singers as well as among athletes.

Informed contest judges expect the late-adolescent female to possess more technical polish than her male contemporary, particularly with regard to dynamic control. (Anyone who judges contests at college level ought to be aware of the maturation continuum of the male and female instruments.) Those who adjudicate should demand that soubrettes, coloraturas, and lyrics display characteristics of their respective *Fächer*, attributes that are by no means identical to those expected of the *dramatic* female categories. Vocal adjudicators who serve on panels heavily weighted with instrumentalists sometimes watch a coveted prize go to a small soprano voice of limited professional potential, singing literature that for her category is by no means demanding, while a dramatic voice loses because it does not yet exhibit the same degree of *dynamic* control. These statements must not be misunderstood as an endorsement of the all-too-frequent practice of entering young students in contests with literature much too dramatic for their years and skills, nor of that uninteresting howling that sometimes passes for dramatic singing in vocal competitions. However, teachers of singing easily become enamored of singing that is "musical" and dynamically varied, but which actually is mannered, limited vocalism. Professional potential should never be overlooked.

This may be an appropriate place to insert an encouraging word for the young male singer who regards his twenty-one-year-old female counterpart (particularly if she is a soubrette or a coloratura) with awe for her technical ease. He should realize that if his female friend does not sing considerably more skillfully than he at this developmental point in her career, she is probably the possessor of a problematic voice. Despite technically rough edges, his own instrument may later prove to be the superior one of the two.

Many teachers of singing, when candid, admit that teaching the female voice at the college- and university-age level is far more satisfying musically than dealing with the male voice of a corresponding age, simply because vocal skill is inevitably linked at that age with laryngeal history (her voice is 21 years old, his only 7—give or take a year). The teacher of the potentially professional male voice in this age category should be extremely cautious about covering up lack of skill through the use of quick solutions, such as dependence on *voce finta*, falsetto, or breath-mixture practices. Each passing year (each passing six-month period, in fact) will bring greater maturity to the male voice, which at college age still exhibits strong mutational signs. (Some male voices, especially those of the lighter categories, have physical growth well behind them at age 21. Late maturation is, however, the rule for the sturdy male voice.)

The problems of dynamic variance become acute with young males who have an appreciation for the subtleties of vocal art, who are musically, linguistically, and interpretatively well equipped to do highly advanced vocal literature, and who feel a need to perform publicly (they are rare, but they do exist). Teacher and pupil have to face facts, recognize what is feasible (and resist vocal coaches who have little awareness of the maturation continuum of singers), and strike a compromise as to what is acceptable performance literature. The compromise should avoid vocal gimmickry, which might temporarily permit a wider range of literature than would free vocalism.

Excellent vocal literature exists for any healthy voice without resorting to the almost impossible demands found in some parts of the literature (both operatic and song). Because of physical maturation differences, it is much easier to find appropriate study material for the young female than for the young male voice.

On the other hand, if the young singer, male or female, is incapable of negotiating some fair amount of the less-demanding song literature by the time those requirements are to be met in either academic or professional programs, it may be necessary to conclude that singing talent is not sufficiently present to justify continued professional hopes. Some young male voices are of potentially professional caliber, but their vocal development is slower than the norm. If they have the time, the money, and the emotional fortitude, it may be advisable to keep at it. Yet it is part of the responsibility of the voice teacher to give frank appraisal of the probability of professional success and to weigh it against other life interests of the young singer. (Throughout this discussion, the "young" singer refers to the late adolescent of roughly 18–23 years of age.)

Let us return to our young male singer of average developmental level, and consider approaches to the dynamic requirements of the literature he must sing. Above all, it should be repeated, studio idealism should not set up requirements that do not exist outside the studio walls! The "studio" *piano* that the ears of some teachers (and coaches) insist on, would never be heard (at any age) across the orchestra pit even during a general pause, let alone with the orchestra playing. It should also be kept in mind that *piano singing* is frequently a technical refinement that increases gradually with the physical maturation of the vocal instrument. To demand that a 20-year-old baritone sing pianissimo on F_4 because the composer asks for it, may be to request an impossible technical feat for him; if the *pianissimo* marking is the crucial factor for the performance of the composition, and our young baritone cannot possibly manage it legitimately, then he probably should not be publicly singing the song or the aria at all. If he continues to study it, he should be permitted to sing the F_4 a bit louder than he or his teacher (and the composer) would like, with the understanding that over a period of time he will work to diminish the volume.

In addition to essential differences among categories of professional singing voices with regard to the expectations of dynamic range, any dynamic level (either soft or loud) is only understandable within the general volume and dimension of a particular instrument. All dynamic levels are relative to the size of the instrument that produces them. To request the large dramatic instrument, as we have seen, to sing as soft a pianissimo in actual amplitude as can the leggiero instrument, is as nonsensical as to require the leggiero to match the fortissimo of the dramatic voice. An unwillingness to realize this proportional relationship of dynamic level within each instrument is partly the reason why *falsetto* and *finta* practices have increasingly crept into vocal pedagogy the past decade or so. A trumpet is not expected to produce the piano dynamic level of a recorder. (As to the naive viewpoint that the vocal instrument should try to match its accompanying instrument—that is, "color the voice to match the accompanying instrument"—silence is best. A comparable argument would be that the string and the oboe should imitate the vocal sound. What nonsense! Each instrument, including the voice, has its own timbre, regardless of historical period. (Stylistic factors must be taken into account, but not at the expense of the health of the instrument or of producing a wretched sound!).

This argument is not to be understood as granting license to those singers of whatever weight or size who seem convinced that if they don't sing their loudest they will not be duly appreciated. For some singers the "resonant" sound means nothing more than loud singing. *Every* voice must accomplish the full dynamic range appropriate to its size and weight if the demands of professional skill are to be met. (But don't ask that of every male singer at age 21!)

Messa di voce vocalises, taken together with carefully selected passages from the vocal literature (always appropriate to the singer's capabilities at the current stage of development), are the best means for acquiring dynamic control in the singing voice.

The maturing young artist and the seasoned professional should regard the *messa di voce* vocalise as an essential part of each day's technical work. Younger singers should not attempt that skill until they have acquired a thorough grounding in vocal technique.

CHAPTER 14

Vibrancy in Singing

Vibrato and Vocal Timbre

The phenomenon of vibrato contributes to perception of pitch, intensity, and timbre of the vocal sound. Subjective terminology describing the quality of vocal tone, such as "warm," "vibrant," "resonant," "dull," "lifeless," or "hollow," often refers to the presence or absence of vibrato.

The term *vibrato* is used somewhat loosely to describe several kinds of pitch fluctuation that may occur during a sustained tone. In the following considerations, its use will be restricted to the terminology of the historic Italian School, which differentiates between *vibrato, oscillazione, tremolo,* and *trillo.*

Most persons who work with singers are aware of the studies of Seashore and his associates, and of his by now classic definition of the vibrato (1936, p. 7): "A good vibrato is a pulsation of pitch, usually accompanied with synchronous pulsations of loudness and timbre, of such extent and rate as to give pleasing flexibility, tenderness and richness to the tone."

Three parameters are generally determinable in vibrato, being the fluctuation of pitch, variation of intensity, and the number of undulations per second. Most authorities tend to agree that 6 undulations per second seem to represent the normal vibrato in singing; studies using singers of international reputation indicate that 6.5 may be a truer figure, with 7 per second not being unusual (6.2 is common for the male, 7 for the female). When undulations exceed 7.5 (or, at most, 8) per second, the resultant sound is perceived by most ears as being tremulous; the timbre suffers from *tremolo.* When the vibrato rate is below 6 fluctuations per second, the Italians say that *"la voce oscilla"* or *"la voce balla,"* and the term *oscillazione* (oscillation) describes the unfavorable wobble. The rate of the vibrato varies within an instrument, depending on coordination and tonal concept. Vibrato can be the distinguishing feature between good and bad vocal timbre.

Some singers demonstrate a vibrato rate that is rather constant at 4 per second (exceedingly slow and wide), while others have been recorded as high as 12 per second (narrow, fast, and tremulous).

182

Some voices regularly average a semitone oscillatory pattern; in very slow oscillation, the pitch variant can be as wide as a whole tone or a minor third.

In techniques where heavy vocal production prevails, oscillation rate is usually well below 6 times per second, with 5 being closer to the norm. The pitch variant, then, becomes wider. Studies that deal with vibrato rates in the range of 4 have no value for the singer; most musicians' ears would not accept such a slow vibrato as having aesthetic value, other than in uncultivated vocal styles. When reports on vibrato are published, the informed reader must take into account the pedagogies by which the subjects in those studies have been trained.

In well-regulated vibrato, the pitch variant is seldom as large as a semitone; its undulation pattern averages about a third of a whole tone. This variation of pitch is perceived by the ear as a quality characteristic, not as pitch vagaries.

PHYSICAL CAUSES OF VIBRATO

A considerable amount of investigative work over a number of years has been directed to the phenomenon of vibrato (Smith, 1972, pp. 28–32). The following range of assumptions has resulted:

1. Muscle synergism within the supralaryngeal area accounts for frequent fluctuation in the vocal folds.
2. Pitch fluctuations are caused by tremors in the laryngeal suspensory system, with intensity variations having their origin in the base of the tongue.
3. Vibrato rate can be correlated with oscillations in the musculature of the thorax.
4. Pitch and intensity variations are affected by the basic repetition rate of nerve impulses.
5. Pitch and intensity regulatory processes are probably influenced by an out-of-phase relationship between the cricothyroid and the mylohyoid muscles.
6. Correlations exist between the phases of pitch vibrato and energy peaks in the intrinsic and extrinsic muscles of the larynx.
7. The intermittent supply of nerve energy provided for the vocal mechanism determines vibrato rate.

8. Vibrato results from the rapidly alternating contractions in the laryngeal muscles during phonation.

9. Normal frequencies of nerve impulses have different rates of discharge depending on the dominance of coordination centers affecting the laryngeal as well as other groups of muscles.

10. The vocal folds are continually energized as a result of their own motion, at least partly in response to auditory feedback.

Some of these theories may at first appear to be mutually exclusive, but the following closer look will show that the correlation of nerve impulses with laryngeal muscle action, which figures prominently in most of them, is significant.

The tremors in the suspensory system of the larynx which produce a shaking tongue are not desirable. They are the result of an unsupported laryngeal mechanism. Fiberoptic examination indicates that a shaking tongue means a shaking epiglottis. In fact, the whole laryngeal system shakes at the same rate as the tongue. Usually, this vibrato approaches a tremolo.

The vibrato applied externally to the larynx by the musculature of the thorax (the "abdominal" vibrato) is responsible for the shake that plagues many singers, and is a direct result of failure to apply *appoggio* technique to singing. The muscles of the epigastric–umbilical region produce an oscillatory motion that produces this "false" vibrato, which is generally perceived as a wobble. Some sympathetic movement may occur in the epigastric–umbilical region, but must not function as an externally-applied oscillatory force.

The neurological source of vibrato, and its superiority over the externally-applied oscillatory motion from the abdomen, is well presented in some extemporaneous comment by Shipp (1981, p. 70) as a panelist discussing supraglottal aspects of voicing. His remarks were in response to the query, "I wondered about the rapid oscillation of the larynx, often synchronous with vibrato. Would you comment on that?":

> This goes into the model of what vibrato is and how it is produced. If we can stay with frequency vibrato which from everything that I can determine is really this oscillation produced by the cricothyroid muscle, innervated by the superior laryngeal nerve, then I think that's a normal physiologic thing. Everybody potentially has vibrato, *if they can allow their vocal folds to get into a place where they can really have enough slackness so that this overriding wave of contraction at about five or six cycles per second can take effect,*

and if they can inhibit other neural pathways to other structures of the vocal tract.

Another way to produce vibrato would be to have an external force applied to the abdominal wall and thereby rapidly change the driving force at the same rate. We've all seen people's tongues move at that rate, we've seen jaws shake at that rate. The pharynx and the larynx move up and down at that rate. I won't make a judgment as to whether all this is good or bad technique, but I think the point is that it does represent failure to be able to inhibit certain elements, certain neural pathways of this normal physiological tremor, to allow it to come through others. (Emphasis added)

In answer to the question as to where, anatomically, vocal vibrato is generated, Shipp (1983, p. 132) responds:

It seems reasonable to suppose that the singer thinks of a note in terms of absolute or relative pitch, not as the two pitches bounding the target note. *The singer's brain,* or more specifically a motor neuron pool, *organizes a neurologic impulse pattern to contract the cricothyroid muscle by an amount that the singer has learned will cause the vocal folds to vibrate at the target frequency.* This pattern is sent down the motor pathway to the involved muscles. At some point along this transmission line, perhaps at the cerebellar level, *this relatively steady impulse pattern is modified to a rhythmic undulating one that causes the muscles to contract and relax so that the vocal folds vibrate at frequencies just above and below the target.* The extent of this oscillation is monitored by the singer through the auditory pathways principally, and voluntarily adjusted to the extent of the vibrato range from "straight" tones to exaggerated vibrato. (Emphasis added)

Shipp's comments point out two significant facts. Vibrato has a neurological source which activates the cricothyroid muscles, and vibrato involves a relaxant principle in laryngeal action.

USES OF THE VIBRATO

No one can dictate nerve impulses through consciously exercised controls; no one, through direct conscious effort, can control laryngeal muscle synergism so as to produce specific responses that determine vibrato rate. Yet these controls can to some extent be realized and routined in response to timbre concepts.

A valuable pedagogy device lies in developing awareness of vibrancy as a constant and desirable characteristic of vocal timbre. If a common character of vibrancy does not exist throughout all the notes and syllables of a vocal phrase, legato is not possible (Miller, 1966b, pp. 18–21). One of the marks of a good singer is the ability to match tonal quality from note to note. If vibrato frequencies are slow on one pitch, to be followed by a quicker vibrato rate on the subsequent pitch, then totally absent in the next, the quality of the sound will appear uneven, destroying any impression of legato.

A singer can very quickly recognize the presence of *oscillazione* (wobble), or of *tremolo*, often being disturbed by them but not knowing how to be rid of them. These disturbing aberrations may be present in certain vowels and not in others, or they may be restricted to some limited area of the voice.

The assertion that it is dangerous to direct a singer's attention to the vibrato rate (a commonly expressed pedagogical viewpoint) is totally without foundation. The singer is almost always aware of the presence of an undesirable wobble or a tremolo, and is looking for any assistance in the elimination of either in as direct a fashion as possible. The problem of an undesirable vocal oscillation should no more go unidentified than the problem of pitch vagaries (of which it is a part).

Countermeasures can be taken against both *oscillazione* and *tremolo*. There are those who claim that vibrato rate should be ignored in teaching, that it will emerge as a natural phenomenon when everything else in the act of singing is coordinated. So will the breath, the vowel, registration factors, articulation, and all other facets of vocal technique. Naturally, when singing is fully coordinated, nothing is a problem, including vibrato rate.

An awareness of the vibrato rate can be helpful pedagogically through comparing the kinds of sensation and physical coordination that accompany a vibrant sound in the voice with those which pertain when vibrancy is disturbed. A problematic vibrato rate may serve as a major indicator of technical problems in a voice.

CORRECTING OSCILLATION ("WOBBLE")

Slow vibrato rate (oscillation) usually results from slackness of the vocal folds due to insufficient resistance to airflow. Under conditions of aging or of physical debility, muscle tonus lessens and the vibrato rate is retarded. A similar muscle slackness can be present at any age when the natural structural support is removed from the larynx.

If subglottic pressure and the balance between the intrinsic laryngeal musculature and external supportive musculature of the neck prove insufficient, vibrato rate will mirror those conditions. It is not yet clear how those factors relate to the neurological events of vibrato. Empirical experiences of the seasoned singer indicate that the kind of physical coordination expressed by the *appoggio* technique can provide the structural support for the larynx that will permit desirable vibrato to be present. Wobble is largely a "support" problem.

Each individual voice will require a different balance of ratios among contributing members of the torso, neck, and head, in order to produce the proper *appoggio*. Although the exact relationships of the individual parts of this *appoggio* mechanism vary from one voice to another, and although no specific energy level can be designated for each pitch or each amplitude level in singing, we *can* rely on the vibrato rate itself to inform us precisely when the right ratios of activity among the parts of this vocal machine are in operation. More than any other audible aspect of vocal timbre, vibrato rate is an indicator of either free or inefficient vocal production. A proper vibrato is a sign of a healthy, well-produced singing voice.

If a singer exhibits a wide, slow vibrato (wobble—or perhaps more kindly, *oscillazione*), the entire instrument tends to suffer from overweighted production. In such a case, nothing can be more beneficial than for the teacher to return to the brief vibrant onset vocalises (Chapter 1). Within the brief span of time that it takes to execute the onset, there is less potential for muscular setting, and the ear can at once be directed to the presence or absence of vibrancy in the sound, not only at its onset, but throughout its duration and at the moment of termination. (Those schools of vocal technique that find a vibrato rate of 5.0 or less to be agreeably "rich" will, of course, not express concern for slow vibrato rates.)

ELIMINATING STRAIGHT-TONE INTRUSION

The slow vibrato rate often passes over eventually into the straight tone, both in pitches of sustained duration and in rapidly occurring syllables. The singer who first produces a straight-tone onset, followed by vibrato (a favorite device of some Wagnerian and certain *Lieder* singers), does not arrive at free (efficient) muscle synergism until that moment at which vibrato makes its appearance. Vibrato, resulting from nerve impulse and coordinated muscular equilibrium, is a natural ingredient of vocal timbre unless it is purposely eliminated in order to meet the criteria of certain cultural aesthetics or stylistic considerations (often not founded on historical data).

Although it is true that the straight-tone onset may have some utility in certain literatures, its use should be infrequent. A musically refined ear grows weary of the incessant mooing of nonvibratoed pitches which occurs among some prominent and revered singers of *Lieder.* Such crooning is largely a development of the late forties and early fifties, out of which grew the burgeoning recording business, where performance is centered around the microphone, not the acoustic of the hall. Some of these singers are committed to the belief that frequent absence of vibrato shows interpretative intimacy and technical control. As the listener becomes aware of the frequency with which the straight-tone device accompanies *voce finta* timbre in circumstances where the literature clearly calls for *mezza voce* technique, the suspicion grows that either *vocal necessity* has dictated "artistic" usage of the straight tone, or that confusion regarding matters of musical style is the cause. While it is logical that vocal necessity should be incorporated into artistry in such a way as to add, rather than to detract (a lesson learned by the most accomplished artist, particularly in the declining years), to make such practices technical goals is not acceptable, no matter how famous the artist. However, the knowledgeable critic can only admire the way in which many great singers have learned to make an artistic plus of vocal necessity.

With the maturing singer who possesses a stabilized technique, it often happens that the vibrancy pattern will be perfectly regular until a sudden intervallic leap, or some ungrateful passage, presents itself, at which time a tone, or a series of them, will go straight. When straight tone intrudes, the singer's attention should immediately be drawn to the differences in timbre between the alternating vibrant and straight sounds. Correction of breath-management factors, and the elimination of laryngeal tension, will reestablish the dynamic equilibrium needed to bring in the vibrato; conversely, introducing the vibrant sound (with something around 6.5 undulations per second) will ensure the dynamic movements that must be present in all good singing.

When muscular tension locks one particular laryngeal adjustment into place, the tone will tend to go somewhat straight, as occasionally happens if the "support" is too rigid; absence of vibrato may also result from too little contact between the approximating vocal folds and the airflow.

Singers given to straight-tone practices should be directed to *consciously anticipate* a vibrant timbre. To be unaware of the presence or absence of vibrancy in the tone is to be unaware of the nature of one's vocal quality. There is little point in asking the singer devoid of vibrancy to "make the tone a little richer," to "add warmth," to "put in more overtones" (a particularly unfortunate expression), when what we actually mean is that vibrato is lacking. As has been suggested elsewhere in this work, subjective expressions tend to encourage a wide range of physical responses in a number of areas of vocalism, not necessarily the desired response. When an audible timbre characteristic presents itself as readily as does vibrancy, there is no reason why it cannot be used pedagogically. When we listen for degrees of vibrancy, we are listening for a major perceptual component of vocal timbre.

One of the best ways to approach the equalization of vibrato rate is to begin with vowel changes on one pitch, executed at slow tempos. Any straight sounds that intrude as the vowels are changed should be pointed out by the teacher and compared with those of normal vibrancy rate. The vocalises in this series must be executed in an absolutely legato fashion, without decrescendoing and crescendoing each note.

EXERCISE 14.1

[i   e   ɔ   o   u]   [u   o   ɔ   e   i]

CORRECTING THE VIBRATOLESS VOICE

Something should be said about the occasional vibratoless beginner. Thus far we have been assuming the advanced singer who occasionally falls into the error of unintentionally introducing straight-tone sounds at those points in the scale that momentarily become difficult to negotiate, or who produces straight sounds now and again as a result of slothfulness.

Voice teachers, particularly those in the academic world, sometimes must deal with students of limited vocal potential as well as with the professionally oriented singer. (Some of the greatest satisfactions in the teaching of singing come from watching the natively less-talented student develop respectable singing skills.) In the case of the occasional beginning student who seems lacking in vibrato, the important process of coordinating breath and voice can be hurried along by pointing out the essential differences in tonal quality between straight and vibrant sound. The systematized approach to coordinating breath and larynx must be the departure point with any beginning student. If vibrancy still does not emerge, some other suggestions may be helpful.

Emotional or intense speech frequently contains recognizable vibrato. For example, the fundamentalist preacher, in an impassioned prayer or sermon, may fall into an almost chant-like pattern of vibratoed speech (recall for a moment the "Oh Lord! Thou knowest" vocal quality of the radio preacher). The "old-fashioned" revival meeting, where emotions tend to run high, may produce a number of examples of speech vibrato from participants during the course of praise and prayer. Sects that practice glossolalia often concurrently employ a form of vibrato. (Interestingly, heavy oscillation often marks the singing of the emotive hymns common among such groups.) Occasionally politicians, especially when speaking in their home districts on morality or patriotism, strive to display sincerity through the addition of speech vibrato. An emotive speech is also used by the rural auctioneer at the peak of a "performance." Small children frighten each other in play as they call out "I am a ghost!" with marked vibrato. In such cases, vocal pitch and intensity often rise to a point at which singing and speaking are only minimally differentiated; we are approaching the vital recitative. Excitation forms a part of all of these spoken phenomena.

Singers who lack vibrato will sometimes discover that they do indeed recognize it and can produce it themselves in the speaking voice when they imitate a speaker heard under the kinds of conditions just described. From the spoken to the sung vibrato is an easy transition.

Although the brief onset vocalises and imitative emotional speech may be safer and more immediate modes of procedure, some teachers use other exercises that have been known to induce vibrato. The student is requested to picture some oscillating object while singing (a bouncing ball, a flickering light, for example). Because these suggestions direct attention specifically to pitch alternation rather than to a timbre concept, they are less desirable devices. They tend to induce the external epigastric vibrato.

When the brief onset vocalise or the imitation of emotional speech fail to spark an awareness of vibrancy for the beginning student, it may be best to turn to an agility vocalise consisting of a brief, quickly occurring pattern. One theory of vibrato function, it has already been noted, holds that vibrato rate is correlated with oscillations in the thoracic musculature. This is a dangerous assumption almost certain to produce a shaking torso, a negation of the *appog-*

gio, and a discernible wobble. In contrast to the shaking epigastrium, the anterolateral wall should remain firm *(ben appoggiato)*, but exhibit a supple muscle synergism that supplies the proper breath source for the glottis. This permits the appropriate nerve impulses and energy peaks of the laryngeal muscles to produce the vibrato phenomenon. This flexible, agile movement in the umbilical–epigastric area is experienced, scarcely perceptible, as a feeling of looseness. It does not resemble the externally-induced pulsation that comes from a shaking abdominal wall. Of course, a certain feeling of buoyancy and a physical and mental alertness are essential.

Short, fast exercises already encountered in the study of agility (see Chapter 3) may be used. In addition, conceiving the quick notes as rapid embellishments to a longer note may facilitate the action. This technique is sometimes described as "diaphragmatic articulation," or more accurately, anterolateral abdominal wall and diaphragmatic articulation.

EXERCISE 14.2

| [i] | [e] | [ɑ] | [ɔ] |
| [ɑ] | [i] | [e] | [o] |

CORRECTING TREMOLO ("SHAKE")

When tremolo mars the singing voice, hyperfunction is indicated, with subglottic pressure proving too intense for the normal responses at the larynx. Momentary examples of such hyperfunction can be heard in the "vibrato speeding" that sometimes accompanies dramatic operatic climaxes and releases, during which time pitch fluctuation changes; the corresponding increase in the rate of the oscillatory phases is in response to increased breath pressure and to resistance to that pressure on the part of the vocal folds. Some theories regarding the relationship between vibrato phenomena and muscle synergism may grow out of instances of hyperfunctional activity.

Shipp et al. (1983, p. 132) discuss vibrato and vocal tremor by asking, "What, then, differentiates the shaking associated with the pathological state of vocal tremor from artistic vibrato?" Shipp answers:

> Perhaps the individuals who are able to inhibit or markedly attenuate rhythmic motor impulse spillover from those

impulses travelling along the superior laryngeal nerve to the cricothyroid muscle are heard as the better singers. It may well be that the more stimulation muscles supplied by other nerves (including the recurrent laryngeal nerve) receive, the less ideal the vibrato and the more tremor-like the voice quality.

Even among singers who normally exhibit something in the nature of a 6.2 vibrato rate, the rate of tremolo may reach 8 to 10 per second, with the pitch variant becoming as wide as a whole tone. (In general, the faster the vibrancy rate, the narrower the pitch variant; in the "operatic" release, increases in both rate and width are usually audible.)

When tremolo is an isolated problem, perhaps occurring immediately before the release, or at a specific level of pitch, pointing out to the singer the rapidity of the vibrato rate in comparison with neighboring sounds may suffice to encourage relaxation of excessive intensity, removing the factor of hyperfunction. "Do you hear that the vibrato speed has increased on this pitch? Don't *assist* the vibrato!" The probable physical causes are then detailed. The singer's ear (tonal conceptual ability) thereby learns to demand uniformity of vibrato rate, and a better balance of muscular function is restored.

Even though vibrato rate is largely the result of the type of muscle synergy dictated by a specific technique, some high-strung individuals are prone to tremolo. Psychological states are to some extent responsive to an act of the will, and such persons must be reminded that their emotional motor needs to slow down during singing. The emotional pace of the phlegmatic personality may need to be accelerated, and there is a fairly frequent correlation between oscillation and a low-key personality. Physiological responses may reflect psychological states. Technical control assists in achieving psychological–physiological discipline.

The vibrato serves as a relaxing agency during phonation (Shipp, 1981, p. 70; Shipp, et al., 1983, p. 133). The physical and neurological causes of vibrato can be channeled for singing only in response to a concept of timbre. Attempting to induce vibrato through conscious physical motion is a far more cumbersome route.

Because it is the ear, not muscles, which dictates timbre concepts, it is not likely that the kind of relaxation which cures tremolo will come about in response to the general request to "relax." In the presence of tension, the admonition to "relax" is seldom useful. If a condition of hyperfunction exists in some group of muscles, relaxing them, of course, is desirable. But how does the singer know what part of the complicated muscular process should be relaxed? Indeed, as has been seen, vocal problems frequently result from *hypofunc-*

tion, not *hyperfunction,* in some part of the voice-producing instrument. In attempting to relax something, the specifics of which it is difficult to determine, the singer may actually increase the degree of hypofunction on the part of the muscles of breathing or of the muscles of laryngeal support, producing even greater instability and more tension at other points. This is because the notion of "relaxation" is inevitably associated with a decrease of whatever level of energy exists at that moment, a potentially dangerous condition to indiscriminately introduce during the act of singing.

No teacher of singing can spell out for the singer the precise muscular coordination required by the individual vocal instrument. A skillful teacher *can* determine when dynamic balance (muscle equilibrium) is lacking by analysing the vocal timbre. Only from the sound can the assessment of faulty production finally be determined. (Of course, the ear is assisted by the eye and by the singer's kinetic responses.) One of the clearest indices to the state of proper dynamic equilibrium is the vibrato rate.

If most of the singers from a vocal studio exhibit a "shake," there can be little doubt that techniques of breath management are based on false premises. If most of the singers exhibit "wobble," other muscular imbalances are dictated by the studio pedagogy. The teacher should listen to each student and make an honest assessment of what sorts of vibrancy rates characterize the studio. If most of one's singers have vibrato-related problems, it is advisable to rethink some technical principles.

Occasionally a voice will possess a vibrato rate faster than the norm, yet, through other characteristics of vocal timbre, remain appealing; however, the tremulous voice is seldom a useful instrument. Actual tremolo is frequently accompanied by shrillness and sharping, due to the lack of dynamic balance between breath energy and muscular action at the level of the larynx. Characteristics of the tremulous voice are visible tension in the throat area, high laryngeal position, tongue and jaw tensions, and rapid shaking of tongue and jaw. Fiberoptic examination of more than sixty singers (Selkin and Miller, unpublished results, 1982) reveals a corresponding shake of the epiglottis in tremulous singing. Under normal vibrato production, there is little or no oscillation in the epiglottis.

Further comment on the elimination of tremolo will be made when the pedagogical uses of straight tone are considered.

VIBRATO AND VELOCITY

Mention has already been made that some singers execute all velocity passages with basically a straight sound, a habit that can only

impair vocal quality. A different sort of pedagogical problem is demonstrated by those teachers who believe that vibrato rate and velocity must be controlled in such a manner as to "come out even" on
each rhythmic beat of the bar. In this well-publicized viewpoint it is
suggested that the singer must speed up or slow down the vibrato
rate to accommodate the rhythm of the rapid scale passage. For
example, the argument runs, if three notes per second must be sung
at a certain tempo, the vibrato rate must either slow down so as to
accommodate two cycles per note or it must speed up so that three
cycles can be devoted to each note. This is a misconception of the
role of vibrancy in velocity; although temporally dictated, vibrato
frequency *need not* exactly coincide with the written note change. If
that were the case, *no* vibrato could ever occur within the swiftly
moving pyrotechnical passages of the coloratura literature of the *bel
canto*, where the vibrant tone is at its highest degree of audibility.
This pedagogical viewpoint would seem to request change in vibratory consistency with every quickly occurring note, or even in a note
of brief duration as it appears in a slowly moving passage.

The theory of synchronizing oscillatory patterns with written
note changes is based on the false assumption that the presence of
vibrato in the human voice is perceived by the listener as off-pitch
singing; our own perceptions prove that not to be the case, because
the ear does not register pitch fluctuations of vibrato as pitch alteration but as part of vocal timbre. Vibrato and rhythmic pitch events
do not need to coincide, because vibrato is a nearly constant function in singing, resulting from the proper physiologic bases of phonation, regardless of pitch alteration or tempo. It does not matter to the
listening ear whether an oscillatory cycle is concluded before the
next written pitch change or not, unless the rate is excessively slow.
*Vibrato is part of vocal timbre and is not determined by the rhythmic
character of the musical passage.* How strange that some pedagogues
who refuse to direct the student's attention to the accomplishment
of an acceptable vibrato frequency then devote time to this *questionable* aspect of vibrato control!

PEDAGOGICAL USES OF STRAIGHT-TONE

Having been branded as something of an outlaw in what has gone
before, straight-tone deserves a bit of rehabilitation as an occasionally meritorious tool. No kind words are forthcoming with regard to
its coloristic advantages; straight-tone has imbedded itself all too
comfortably in certain vocal styles to be in need of further encour-
agement. It may even be wise for the teacher or vocal coach when

working on *Lieder* to indicate the *precise* note or notes in the score on which such coloration is allowable, making an intelligent artistic decision in advance, rather than permitting the occurrence of straight-tone by default. (Obviously, in no imaginative performance can every expressive moment be charted in advance, but if straight-tone singing becomes the singer's stock-in-trade interpretative color for most emotive occasions, some drastic temporary means are in order.)

When tremolo is a marked characteristic of a singing voice, the request for an absolutely straight sound on a phrase or two will often illustrate that varying rates of oscillation can be heard and controlled by the singer. A return to the phrase, while remembering the quality of straightness, then frequently assists in reducing the too-fast rate of the oscillatory cycle. Naturally, if the singer substitutes straight-tone for tremolo, one evil has been replaced by another, and "over-correction" has been experienced. However, when excessive subglottic pressure produces extreme tension, a request for a "straighter" sound may help to change the tonal concept so that physical pressures are reduced. The pedagogical process should be explained to the student. These suggestions do not sanction frequent straight-tone in singing. Nevertheless, in contrast to wide oscillation and tremolo, the straight-tone has limited teaching uses.

USES OF THE TRILL

Required as a musical device in certain vocal literature, the trill is seldom asked for in all vocal classifications. Despite that fact, the trill represents laryngeal freedom and should be acquired as a technical accomplishment in every voice.

It is stated repeatedly in pedagogical sources that the trill is an exaggerated form of the vibrato. Some truth resides in that assessment, inasmuch as pitch variation plays a part in both. Whereas the vibrato should be produced without any marked laryngeal movement, however, the vocal trill depends on the singer's ability to oscillate the voice box. What little information there is from earlier centuries regarding the execution of the trill is insubstantial in precise detail; some late eighteenth- and early nineteenth-century teachers recommended that two alternating pitches of a semitone or a whole tone (later progressing even to a minor third) be attempted at slow tempo, with gradual increase in speed. This approach may be profitably undertaken with some voices, especially the lighter instruments, but until that moment when pitch alternation reaches a fast temporal rate, laryngeal oscillation is not, in fact, taking place. Rather, pitch is altering without any shift in laryngeal positioning. It may be that the commencement at slow tempo is more a psychological than a physiological assist.

Equally successful in learning the trill is a direct, immediate attempt to oscillate the voice box, keeping in mind a narrow pitch fluctuation (almost always the semitone or less), removing direct concentration from specific pitch alteration to the actual oscillatory motion itself. At first, in practicing trill, a pitch level close to the center of the speech range in the male voice, and in the upper–middle or even upper voice of the female voice, may be most rewarding. Other pitches are gradually added by half-tone progression.

When trilling is first attempted, the oscillatory motion of the larynx may feel somewhat wild and uncontrolled. It is exactly therein that its advantage as a freedom-inducing device lies! Although it is not the case that "unless you can trill you cannot sing freely" (a maxim in some quarters of voice teaching), letting the larynx suddenly engage in such loose movement can free the instrument. In this respect, the trill shares some kinship with the sustained tongue-point trill, earlier encountered. Because of the size and weight of some vocal instruments, and because of corresponding registration events, the trill may be more difficult to execute in the robust voice than in the more lyric instrument. (The trill of the "nightingale" soprano is far less impressive than that of the spinto tenor.)

Much of current unearthing of *bel canto* operatic literature of the first half of the nineteenth century has brought the trill to the fore; the operatic mezzo-soprano, in particular, who lacks trill will not be able to sing that florid literature acceptably. On the other hand, bleating or shaking on a pitch is not legitimate trilling.

A cautionary word is in order. Practicing the trill should not occupy large amounts of time. Trill is not of such importance in most categories of voice that valuable hours should be spent on its acquisition. In addition, too much oscillatory action may produce undesirable results in other areas of the singing voice. Trill should be studied cautiously, and only after the basic techniques of the singing voice have been secured.

The wide variance among vibrato rates, it should be added as a final consideration, is the result of physical practices that differ from one technique to another. Obviously, some of these techniques are functionally more efficient than others, producing greater freedom in the singing voice. There is a direct correlation between clean onset, efficiently managed breath, and a vibrant tone. A too-slow or a too-rapid vibrato rate is an indication of unhealthy function.

CHAPTER 15

Coordinating Technique and Communication

A singer must operate in two worlds, occasionally separately, mostly simultaneously. It would be foolhardy to assume that an artistic temperament ensures a successful singing career, and equally faulty to hold that a perfected vocal technique guarantees success. Although early years of vocal instruction must include a great deal of technical concentration, it is not possible to become a fine singer by devoting one's early study to technical matters only, then to add "artistry." The story of the great castrato and his teacher (Farinelli and Porpora) who spent years together perfecting a small group of difficult exercises, at the conclusion of which time the teacher declared the singer a great artist, can only be apocryphal.

Artistry in singing is acquired by practice (habit) just as is technique. It matters not whether the singer is a novice or an established artist, technique and expression must be the supporting pillars of vocal art. These two levels of activity must go forward simultaneously and with equal intensity throughout the singing career.

Recognizing the need to balance technical proficiency and artistic impulse, every rehearsal or practice session should be arranged so that an even alternation exists between that which remains a challenge technically and artistically, and that which is comfortably secure. More explicitly, not only must the two pillars—technique and artistry—be kept in balance, but the most facile and the most elusive aspects of both should be part of the daily routine.

Throughout this book an attempt has been made to show that the coordination which results in skilled singing depends on (1) the source of power, (2) the vibratory action, (3) systems of resonance, and (4) the facility of articulation. Exercises have been directed toward the acquisition of precise coordinations based on a systematic approach to vocal technique. Specific functions have been considered, with vocalises designed to combine those functions into one coordinated whole.

The activities that result from this quadripartite mechanism are largely controlled by the voluntary nervous system. Kantner and West (1960, p. 53) provide a succinct summary of that coordination:

These various functions and structures are coordinated
through the activity of the voluntary nervous system—a
combination made possible by four types of activities carried on by the nervous system: (1) motor activity that provides the stimuli that cause muscles to contract; (2) sensory
reporting that gives information as to how the movements
were produced; (3) auditory monitoring that makes possible
the setting up of, and conformance to, speech standards;
and (4) the associative function that ties up the auditory
symbol with its meaning and with the motor pattern necessary to produce it.

Although written with an eye to speech, these statements apply
equally to singing.

Neurological factors largely determine coordination in singing.
The neurological effects on phonatory events are clearly stated by
van den Berg (1958, p. 231):

The innervation of the larynx is very rich. The motor supply
of the internal muscles comes from the recurrent nerves,
which also convey the proprioceptive reflexes and possibly
also the interoceptive reflexes of the lower part of the
larynx. Interoceptive reflexes of the mucous membranes of
the upper part of the larynx are conveyed by the superior
laryngeal nerve, which also contains the motor and sensory
nerves of the musculus cricothyroideus. The muscle fibers
of the musculus vocalis and the nerve fibers of the recur-
rents are of the rapid type and a great number of end
organs in the musculus vocalis suggest numerous sources of
proprioceptive reflexes. All available data indicate that the
larynx is well equipped for the tremendous task it must perform daily.

Some of the results of neurologic events in respiration and in
speech and song can be sensed while others cannot. When we establish essential coordination for singing, we cannot separate out those
aspects over which we have control from the large number that are
the result of reflex responses over which we have no conscious control. Therefore, almost all of the process of coordination that produces successful singing must be incorporated into a psychological
attitude that includes both controllable and noncontrollable events.

At this point the question might be raised, "Why then bother to
learn about the physical processes of singing if in the long run one
relies on psychological control?" The answer is obvious: When we
understand the function of the mechanism, we can train ourselves to
associate emotional and creative experiences with sensation that

results from specific kinds of physical coordination. That which functions well functions freely. We know what kinds of physical responses are engendered by which psychological concepts, and in this way we control the act of singing from both the physiological and psychological standpoints. We combine technique and art.

The violinist has to rely on a complex system of finger positions that occupy some pretrained portion of the mind at the same time that flowing line and sumptuous tone are produced on an artistic imaginative level; none of the violinist's creative music-making is possible without a technical undergirding, which remains to some extent *within* consciousness. Inasmuch as the singer's body–mind is both person and instrument, the singer must find ways to identify and objectify physical responses of that instrument in order to exercise control over its total performance.

Only systematized vocalization based on physiologically efficient function (the free voice), it has been insisted throughout this work, can provide a complete, dependable foundation for training mind and body. "Thought and muscle are schooled until instinct and reaction develop and take command. Then what was arbitrary becomes automatic" (G. Lamperti, 1931, p. 14).

Lamperti's ideal of training thought and muscle would seem to be a realizable concept when one considers the possibility of establishing habitual control over laryngeal neuromuscular activities. Wyke (1982, pp. 139–140) comments:

> [T]he laryngeal neuromuscular adjustments that take place prior to the emission of sound depend for their precision upon the acquisition and storage of an appropriate vocal control programme in the synaptic circuits of several regions of the brain—chief of which, in the majority of singers, is the right temporal lobe. The inevitable implication of this proposition, therefore, is that again (as with respiratory muscle control) it is cerebral cortical systems that the singing teacher is training in his or her pupils with the objective of producing more and more rapid and precise automatic control of the complex neuromuscular process involved in prephonatory tuning of the laryngeal musculature, and their tighter and tighter co-ordination with the developing respiratory muscle control programme.

Wyke (1982, pp. 141–142) points out that no neurological mechanisms exist to provide direct perceptual awareness of vocal-fold status during singing. It is, however, well established that "the efficiency of the reflex mechanisms involved in the control of the striated muscles anywhere in the body may be improved by repetitive practice of their operations. . . ." Wyke recalls that this is what coaches achieve with athletes.

Wyke's description of the duties of the teacher of singing are worthy of full quotation:

> Thus it is that the skilled singing teacher must aim to do two basic things simultaneously with his pupils. First, he must train the intellectual processes through which the aspiring singer acquires (against the background of his genetically endowed musical ability) increasingly efficient and elaborate cortically programmed control over his respiratory musculature and over the prephonatory tuning of his laryngeal muscles; and second, he must improve the operational efficiency of the reflexogenic systems that are responsible for the continuous intraphonatory modulation of the laryngeal musculature. In short, then, the voice teacher's global objective should be to develop the efficiency of the entire neuromuscular control system of his pupil, and not merely that of one or more specific components of that system.

Much of the coordination that exists in any activity is the result of imitating as precisely as possible the same action which previously was successful. A good serve in tennis is in imitation of previous good serves, a well-pitched ball (of several varieties of technique) is imitative of former pitches that went where the pitcher intended them to go, and the coordinated breaststroke recalls thousands of previous ones. Little conscious thought goes into many of the complex actions of everyday life as well. Based on certain physical experiences since infancy, an "imitative" routine has become second nature. Physical actions have been drilled until they become reflex actions.

Many of the technical aspects of singing can be channeled in the same "imitative" way. (In calling for imitation in the act of singing, reference here is made, of course, to one's own responses, not to those of someone else.) Technique in singing consists of establishing certain modes of procedure on which one can depend. When I do this, when I conceive of this timbre, when I sense these responses in my body, this specific sound will then result—a sound I recognize through acoustic automonitoring. "The well-trained singer develops a kind of awareness of sound which comes from factors of sensation in the vocal tract, (and) vibrations of the bones of the head, and the mouth and face. . . ." (Bunch, 1982, p. 65, paraphrasing some findings of Wyke.)

There are factors that work against the assurance of such exact results, not the least of them being performance anxiety, or poor physical condition. Even here, when the singer comes to know what to expect, what is reliable under which conditions, fewer anxieties need be present. As was early suggested with regard to range extension, one has a right to be afraid of unpredictable physical responses. But, if the body can consistently produce certain coordinated actions that can be self-monitored, it then becomes illogical to fear what the body may do. The mind is not an entity separate from an uncooperative body. Body and mind must be trained as partners.

Some teachers insist that the mind must be divorced from technical awareness during performance. If vocalism suffers solely because of performance fears, directing attention to creative matters may eliminate nervousness. On the other hand, unless the singer has ironed out the technical problems of a difficult passage, total involvement in textual and interpretative matters will not eliminate fear; the singer has a right to fear public encounter with unresolved technical problems. By eliminating sticky problems through systematically encountering them, the cause of fear is removed.

No matter what the extent of prior technical training, the singer must operate on two levels of consciousness (the two worlds mentioned at the outset of this chapter). Rather than detracting from the word and from communication, conscious technical monitoring can prove to be a stabilizing force on the creative imagination. The *craft* of singing must be placed in the background, but just as a fine actor, while actually believing the events of the dramatic situation as they unfold, is also aware of the physical and temporal factors that project the emotions to be conveyed, so must the fine singer keep some contact with the technical basis of singing while projecting musical and textual insights.

Communication in singing is dependent on those very aspects of technique that at times seem most remote from artistry. For example, vocal coloration and dynamic variation can become integrated into an expressive whole only if technical facility permits. (Let it again be noted in passing that the singer who resorts to vocal coloration and dynamic variation out of technical necessity should not be excused on the grounds of being "musical" and "sensitive," but should be assisted by the teacher to develop a dependable technique that permits *espressivo* singing as dictated by musicianly and artistic requirements.)

A major fault in performance among some singers, particularly if they study with a technique-conscious teacher (see Chapter 16), is to listen internally to the sound they produce rather than to listen with "outside" ears. A shift to "external listening" may produce remarkable improvement in the outward projection of text and music, when a technique that "internalizes" control is the problem.

A related problem of communication in singing concerns the

imaginative singer who falls into the trap of publicly wallowing in private emotion. We, the listeners, feel quite left out of it all, even uncomfortable, reduced to the role of "peeping Toms." Unless the emotional experiences and sentiments of a performer can be externalized, they have no value beyond personal therapeutic ones.

Posture itself is a major vehicle of communication. It should not be assumed that the performer will instinctively know which physical attitudes outwardly portray inner emotions. A singer has to learn almost as much about what the body can say during a performance as must be known about what vocal timbre can convey. That earmark of the beginner, extraneous movement as an attempt to communicate, should be eliminated very early in preparation for performance situations. The body must be free of rhythmic synchronization with either the impulse of beat or phrase movement, or of physical motion in dramatic works. The constant need to move about is not an indication of freedom but of slavery to rhythmic impulse.

Although it is essential for a singer to know what the body is saying during performance (the body is often most eloquent in absolute quietude), it is the face that is the chief transmitter of emotion, in partnership with musical and textual ideas. An unanimated face in singing belies all that vocal timbre and textual nuance may be communicating. Because of the close coordination of the ear and eye, we do not believe the emotion we hear in musical phrase and word if the singer's face does not register the sentiment expressed. (Although restricted in physical movement, even the artist in the recording studio feels the need to register facial emotion as completely as when on stage.) On the other hand, the mugging that sometimes goes on under the guise of singing–acting, complete with musical comedy stock gestures or the physical clichés of the television review, is perhaps even more detrimental to actual artistic communication. Self-awareness and self-esteem are not communication.

The spectrum of communicable facial expression is not unlimited. Constant facial mobility exercised in an attempt to heighten communication should be as taboo as the deadpan. The singer must learn how the face "feels" when registering the emotions called for, honestly and accurately communicating sentiment, so that specific expressive postures may be summoned up at will. The value of using the mirror cannot be overestimated. The video tape is an additional valuable resource. Both excessive physical movement and exaggerated facial mannerisms often are attempts to mask uneasiness associated with performance. Excitation of the creative imagination does not come about through physical movement and mugging, nor does such movement disguise inner disquietude.

Pavel Ivanovich Rumyantsev (Stanislavski and Rumyantsev, 1975, pp. 18–19) recalls an incident from the Stanislavski Opera Studio that deals with both communication and the control of nervousness:

"Come to the piano, Verbitski." A young, tall student with twinkling black eyes moves over to the instrument. At first glance he does not seem to be in the least nervous and very simply sings whatever Stanislavski asks for. Is he really not nervous at all? Of course he is. But we are all aware of the secret of how to hide or rather to overcome such excitement. Stanislavski himself has taught us that.

"There are two kinds of nervousness: one is creative and the other is panicky. Treasure the creative excitement and learn to overcome the panicky one. You can overcome it by means of concentration. The stronger your nervous excitement the more firmly you must attach your attention on some object and not allow yourself to be torn loose from it. If you can rivet your attention on something, anything, at the needed moment it will mean that you have learned to manage your excitement. Even a button on your jacket can save you from unnecessary and harmful nervousness. It can put you into a state of 'public solitude.'"

We have already made mention of the merit in imitating some previously experienced physical event as a device for gathering up many technical aspects of singing into one concept, one psychological attitude. We have stressed that in so doing, the singer fuses into one whole the many technical facets of singing; a single mental concept at the inception of the phrase combines them into one unified act. At the same time, in the musical realm, an equally important happening takes place: conception of the entire contour of the musical phrase in that instant in which the phrase commences. Collected into one split second of insight, by the same psychological process by which any conceptual thought can be born in an instant, the singer should sense the contour, the shape of the entire musical phrase and its literary idea, prior to the initiation of the phrase in word and tone. To do so is but to follow the procedure already established for intelligent thought and speech. Unfortunately, because of the duration factor, all too often "thought" and "expression" in singing are approached in a moment-by-moment, word-by-word, note-by-note fashion.

Even though they occur on two levels of consciousness, physical and tonal–musical–textual concepts can be fused into one experience through the simultaneous anticipation of them at the inception of the phrase. It is not enough to be aware of the possibility of such fusion. The imagination must be subjected to the schooling of this technical and artistic unity; such fusion can be practiced, and it can be mastered, as readily as any other technique of singing. The artistic temperament must be trained to think in this unified fashion without becoming fractured and splintered over the many individual factors involved in performance. "Creative thinking" cannot be reserved to the performance situation, but should be engaged any time the singer commences a phrase. (To practice without such conceptual thinking only ingrains fractural approaches to singing.)

A direct result of such conceptual coordination is the emergence of legato in singing. Conversely, a proper understanding of legato as the constantly flowing stream of uniform vocal timbre will give shape and contour to the phrase. (Without doubt, the most expressive device, the most technically efficient procedure, in singing [and the most commonly wanting ability] is the legato.) Word painting, vocal coloration, dynamic variation, rhythmic pulse, accentuation, rubato, and general nuance in good singing are only decorative details on the flowing legato structure.

No intelligent singer can conceive of a phrase shape independent of the literary concept that accompanies it. In this respect, the singer has great advantage over any other musician; the emotive character of the word, in fact, is often the determining factor in phrase shaping. Words that act as symbols cannot be intelligently sung without mental imagery. Such imagery should be so distinct, so strong, that for the singer, visualization is as perceptible as sound, during the singing act (Miller, 1968, pp. 25–26). In fact, with many imaginative artists this process of visualization is so forceful that it occurs in color. (This, too, is an artistic tool acquirable by practice.)

When this form of communication exists, the singer is neither involved in self nor in individual members of the audience. The singer visualizes the world of the song (or the role), projects it outward to the audience, which in turn looks in on and shares that world. (In stage roles, there are, of course, the additional compelling relationships with other performers and the assistance from costumes, lights, and the dramatic circumstances.) No longer, then, must it be, "Watch me, listen to me tell this story or describe this emotion," because audience and singer are participants in the mutual sharing of a world. Just as one can pick up the miniature world of the glass paperweight, shake it, hold it out for a friend to share in looking at that world, so can singer and audience look into a common world of the imagination and together find communication there.

Technique is of no value except as it makes communication possible.

CHAPTER 16

Pedagogical Attitudes

The Aesthetics of Vocal Timbre

Considerable attention has been directed in the past toward the assessment of individual musicality with regard to the ways in which the elements of music are perceived, but little study has been devoted to how one develops the aesthetic judgment to discriminate among the varieties of quality inherent in a musical sound, either instrumental or vocal. Such ability is the most essential of all musicianly skills. The reason for its neglect is perfectly clear. Aesthetic judgments lie outside the purview of science and are dependent on the peculiar genius of individual personality. There is, at least, a certain uniformity of opinion as to what constitutes the outer boundaries of beautiful, and ugly, tone.

Some singers have many of the tools required for successful singing, but lack a viable concept of beautiful vocal timbre. Fine singers have a concept of sound in the ear. This concept of timbre is the result of cultural conditioning. Techniques of singing can be identified according to cultural preferences, at least to some extent.

Physical maladjustment has not played a role, traditionally, in determining the criteria of "The Beautiful" in the Western world. We have never bound the feet to inhibit growth, mechanically stretched the neck, striated the face, or put rings through the nose (although we have permitted rings in the earlobes, at least as early as 3000 B.C., and we have removed hair from the face and body for a comparable period of time). Tattooing is an art originally imported from the South Pacific, and was at one time permitted only to sailors who had ventured so far from Western ports. Although this aesthetic may be under review because of the impact of non-Western influences, the functionally complete specimen who can engage in physical action with a physically optimal body continues to represent the artistic norm in art and action in the Western world. Vocal timbre that results from the well-formed, well-coordinated instrument, without maladjustment of any of its physical parts or functions, stands the best chance of qualifying under the artistic criteria for tonal beauty, as found in Western culture. The human body is the vocal instrument; its most freely produced sounds (the result of functionally efficient coordination) most closely adhere to the Western ideal of beauty.

More than is the case with any other musicianly ear, the singer's timbre concept must accord with the natural laws of vocal acoustics and physical freedom. There is no more logical basis on which to establish vocal aesthetics. The mind must be able to conceive a sound that results from certain muscle coordinations and emotional responses, produced by efficient use of the vocal instrument. (Other kinds of sounds can also become the ideal of the ear, unfortunately.)

How, in practice, is this tonal concept to be achieved? The task of the singing teacher is to listen carefully to the sounds the performer is making and to discover whether the singer's ear demands timbre that results from malfunction of some part of the instrument. If the tone is both free and vital, it represents a good tonal concept. Does the singer produce a sound that substitutes artificiality for natural function? Is coordination between breath and phonation inhibited by the tonal concept? Does the singer produce a variety of qualities without understanding how or why?

It is not enough that the voice teacher have an artistic ideal. The teacher must be able to diagnose in what manner free function is being violated, not only from listening to the sound and observing the student, but from weighing what is heard and seen against what is known about the physical and acoustic aspects of singing.

Sometimes it is argued that in singing, the student has no need to know what happens physiologically as long as the teacher is aware of those events and can induce better production. There are flaws in that argument. The student is not a minion, depending on but one teacher throughout a singing career (usually an undesirable condition). The student (and most singers are students even in the middle of a professional career) should be equipped to make judgments about opposing technical viewpoints that must be faced by any singer in the professional world. The ability to weigh contrasting technical notions can be achieved only if the singer has some measuring stick by which to test those opinions. (The academic habit, prevalent in educational circles these days, of examining pedagogies in a comparative fashion is a useless exercise unless it takes place within a framework of information regarding the acoustics and physiology of singing.) The student who has some understanding of how the vocal instrument functions will be in a more favorable position to select teachers with whom advanced work is to be taken. (A teacher's fabulous ear alone is not sufficient!) The "ear" of either teacher or pupil cannot be thoroughly trained unless able to recognize the presence of violations of the physical–acoustic laws of the singing voice; recognition of beautiful sound is not enough. It is essential that the "ear" of both teacher and student be trained to desire freely produced sound, recognize when it is lacking, and know how to produce it over and over again.

THE NEW STUDENT

Fortunate is the teacher who is the first to work with a singer. There are no problems with preconceived notions about terminology, no need to reassess ingrained technical habits, and best of all, there is a non-jaded response to the ideas of basic vocal technique. A singer who has studied over a period of years with a number of teachers should have a right to assume that the fundamentals of technique must by now be out of the way; when they are not, it is difficult to respond with fresh enthusiasm to yet a new look at vocal onset, breathing, agility, articulation, resonance, or registration.

Despite that, the mature singer seeks out a new teacher many times because there is "a vocal problem." Some aspect of singing is not going as well as the singer would like, and a new teacher is sought to correct the problem. That specific fault is not an isolated crack in an otherwise polished façade, easily plastered over; a "problem" in the singing voice is often an indication that the physical foundation of technique has been neglected or improperly laid.

A singer active in a performance career who seeks help from a new teacher is nonetheless often hesitant to give up the current sound (understandably!). As many wise teachers will attest, it may take weeks or months for some singers, no matter how strong the desire to improve, to be willing to accept the necessity for actual change in vocal production.

The sound I make is very much a part of me; even if it is faulty, it is mine. To let someone attempt to alter it is to allow invasion of a very central part of my person. Even though the singer may intellectually recognize that the current sound is manufactured and not the result of natural physical coordination, hesitance about changing the vocal production may still remain. Frankly discussing this frequent psychological barrier may hasten its removal so that technical work may proceed on a basis of mutual understanding.

The new student may be relatively free of an overlay of technical problems, but many students come with concepts picked up in a false, imitative way from someone else. There is always the young baritone who wants to produce a tone he believes resembles that of his favorite recording artist. He has to do things in his throat to "enrich" and "enlarge" the sound, in order to meet his tonal ideal; he wrongly assumes his model must be doing the same things to *his* throat.

Recognizing that the reworking of any singing voice is a traumatic experience for the singer (the longer he or she has been singing, the more difficult change becomes), a teacher must not be tempted to apply the battering ram in the hope of starting at once from the ground up. A progressive, systematic series of vocalises will do much to turn the singer in a new direction.

COMPENSATORY METHODS OF SINGING

An ever-present danger is to approach the alleviation of a problem by "over-correcting" it. This is a snare that even the most intuitive teacher must guard against. Many performers are left with permanent deficiencies from the over-correction of some previous fault. In this fashion can be explained many cases of nasality, driving of specific pitches, distorted diction on certain vowels (or in particular areas of the voice), or postural and physical attitudes that detract from an otherwise good performance. The singer, "compensating" for some technical problem about which at one point there was justifiable concern, then employs 150% of the suggested solution when 100% would suffice. (Most of us exaggerate the corrections we wish to make.) A singer should not continue to fight last year's technical battles if they have already been won.

Another more serious kind of compensatory teaching is the balancing out of one faulty function with another. For example, a professional performer worried that in the process of "dropping the jaw" and "yawning" (in order, it was thought, to provide space in the throat), the tone would be hollow and without projection; the antidote to this condition was to nasalize the sound in the hope of achieving better balance between "depth and focus." The singer was compensating for one faulty technical device with another, compounding unresolved functional problems. Yet, some modern vocal pedagogies are built almost entirely on compensatory solutions, considering these "discoveries" to be an improvement on the natural instrument.

Instead of adhering to laws of acoustics as they dictate resonator coupling, some teachers have devised complicated systems for ironing out the vowel series throughout the vocal scale by the use of vowel mixtures resembling the *umlaut* phonemes. Compensatory techniques of singing include systems of breath management that concentrate on the control of muscles that at best are auxiliary breathing muscles. Just as one faulty muscle action may take the place of another in pathological conditions, so some breath-management techniques alter even normal breath function and bring into play incorrect muscle activity. The complexity of the vocal instrument and the beauty of its mechanical function should discourage anyone from building a technical system for singing that replaces freedom of function with localized controls. The voice teacher should adopt the medical dictum *primum non nocere* (the first thing is not to do harm).

THE TECHNICALLY INTENSE TEACHER

A good technician in the field of vocal technique must have the ability to diagnose the causes of vocal problems and offer workable solutions in a clear fashion. The battle is not won when skills have been described and demonstrated. Above all other teachers, the teacher of singing must be persistent and tenacious. Unlike the case with other musicians, on whose very visible instruments motor skills can be superimposed through finger or arm movements, or by the measuring of intervallic distances, the singer's own body must experience the kinds of coordination that produce ideal tone.

Unquestionably, this book deals with the details of vocal technique considered from the standpoint of mechanical freedom. The need for a solid technique of singing has been its constant exposition. However, the successful teacher of singing must be much more than a mere vocal technician.

It has been pointed out that in recent decades American vocal pedagogy has become a body with two heads, one speaking with the voice of the subjective teacher, the other with the voice of the science-oriented teacher. This volume is an example of an attempt to have them speak jointly with one mouth.

There is a larger and more subtle dichotomy that includes both empirical and mechanistic teachers. There are those who contend that an understanding of the principles of technique and performance can be instilled gradually over a period of time through a kind of broadbrush approach, while another group feels compelled to work in exacting detail within highly organized pedagogies. The latter category includes a type of teacher that bears special mention, and for which the description "technically-intense" may be appropriate.

Because of the largely invisible nature of the vocal instrument, vocal technique has about it an elusive character that can lead to a preoccupation with technical matters. As a result, there is a danger of encouraging the singer to subject constantly every sound produced to some form of ongoing technical analysis. Teacher, listening for the desired quality with a technically oriented ear, fails to realize that a monstrous mechanical doll, a tone-producing machine, has been created. Well-intended technical concentration becomes an end in itself, as though the technical construction were of more importance than communication through musicianship and artistry. The technically intense pedagogue may not understand why so little success attends the recital or other public performance (aside from the reactions of other singers in the studio, who know what to look for) of a pupil who has mastered the technical precepts of the studio. All the technical details are there, but the flow of imagination and creativity are trapped in the specifics of vocal mechanics. Any teacher who takes pride in being a "voice builder" should be wary lest in constructing the technique of the singer, creativity is destroyed or obscured.

THE INTERPRETATION-ORIENTED TEACHER

Some teachers tend to avoid technical specifics, believing that general ideas will filter down into the singer's consciousness if musical and interpretative matters remain paramount. Such teaching can be of benefit if for no other reason than that the attention is turned away from the physical events of singing, permitting natural coordination a freer hand. Much of the success of the coach–accompanist (in addition to musical and stylistic advantages) results because the singer is finally free of the overly technique-conscious voice teacher. Interpretation-oriented pedagogy works well with the naturally coordinated singer (is an estimate of 1% of all who sing too high?) who already negotiates the technical demands of the voice in an admirable way.

It may be commendable, if you are a naturally coordinated animal, never to give thought to the breath ("You do not think about breath when you are not singing, so why when you sing?") or to any other aspect of singing technique. Inasmuch as singing is a physical as well as an artistic act (and part of its artistic strength lies in the degree of physical freedom displayed), the teaching of voice chiefly from the text and the music is mostly inadequate. A number of small, manageable voices are capable of putting together a pasticcio of vocal colors and expressive devices that often smacks more of gimmickry than of technical control, not because they are incapable of learning the art of coordinated singing, but because they have convinced themselves that there are no technical matters that cannot be solved through involvement in text and music.

THE TECHNIQUE-MYSTIQUE TEACHER

There is a type of teacher who approaches teaching with the confidence and zeal of the crusading prophet or prophetess. This highly committed teacher tends to give "technique" the trappings of a mystery cult. "Technique" becomes a banner that the teacher holds aloft as a bright beacon for all to see. Everything that takes place in the studio is part of technical revelation not elsewhere available. Technique-mystique teachers can seldom recommend to their departing students teachers in other cities or institutions (certainly not in their own), because no one else sufficiently understands the mysteries of "technique." The flying banner waves over a very limited geographic region! Students are held to the teacher by the belief that they are being nourished at the wellspring of technical knowledge, and that only this teacher, and no other, has the answers. (Indeed, it may even take five years rather than the usual four, or seven instead of the usual five, to perfect this mysterious technique!)

On the contrary, students should be alerted that *there are no mysteries regarding the technical aspects of singing.* The teacher who regards the technical work of singing as shrouded in mystery inadvertently admits to a lack of information on the physical and acoustic nature of the vocal instrument. Singing appears to be a kind of magical process to this person, and the technique of singing is an idiosyncratic structure built on intuition and trial and error. This explains the technique-mystique teacher's resistance to detailed information regarding the functional aspects of singing. How can one serve as priestess or priest if the mystery is taken away?

Any teacher of singing who operates under the assumption that he or she possesses unique knowledge and skill that can be imparted only to those few fortunates who are in that studio is an unintentional testimony to bigotry and professional ignorance, and very narrowly skirts the fraudulent. Student singers should be on guard against such indoctrination, however subtly it may be delivered (it usually comes down to "*our* studio versus *theirs*," in varying degrees of insinuation). Students who have been drawn and held by such parochial teachers should begin to ask why the performance world is peopled with successful singers who have not shared in this particular technical wisdom.

THE ONE-ASPECT TEACHER

Frequently, the student meets a teacher who bases everything on "breath," "resonance," "forward placement," "piano singing," "relaxation," "posture," "agility," or other single facets of the technical complex. Some successful singers will readily confess they found their breathing technique with such and such a teacher, the concept of resonance with another, and the ability to negotiate the *passaggio* with yet a third. Statements of this sort testify to the need for each teacher to have a systematized technique that covers all the technical aspects of singing. A complete technique of singing must consider the regulation of breath management (what we have earlier termed the energizing source), the accomplishment of freedom at the vibratory source (that is, at the level of the larynx), the intricate process of resonator coupling (the spatial relationships of the pharynx, the nasopharynx, the nasal passages and the mouth), and the coordination of phonetic articulation in response to language and meaning (the process of uniting motor, vibrator, and resonators).

The technical orientation of the teacher may determine the type of vocal literature assigned to students in that studio. In some studios, the agility (coloratura) factor predominates; in another, the sustained line. It is wise to check one's penchant, to be certain that undue concentration on some single aspect of literature or technique has not been elevated to the central position.

Even if a student shows lack in one specific area of vocal technique, the teacher should avoid concentrating solely on that deficiency. To do so upsets the technical balance essential to good singing. (The exercises in this manual have been collected in the hope of systematically presenting all aspects of the technique of singing.)

PEDAGOGICAL BALANCE

The ideal teacher of singing most probably will remain an ideal. Voice teachers deal with a centuries-old art in which a limited number of persons have excelled where others have failed, regardless of methodology. It is not easy to assess the impact of the voice teacher on the successful artist. A final accounting sheet on the result of pedagogical efforts in professional singing careers might not prove to be as favorable as the voice teaching profession might wish. It cannot be doubted that some voice teachers are more successful than others, however, regardless of actual teaching aptitude. There must be reasons.

Can the singing teacher be directed to certain axioms regarding pedagogical balance that may assure some positive impact on the singing profession? Three important principles may be cited:

1. *Stability*, resulting from the possession of a body of factual information, which is constant.
2. *Growth*, the ability to incorporate new concepts and information (after weighing them against fact), and a willingness to change.
3. *Artistic imagination* and *musicianship*.

Vocalism is replete with fadism. At least once a year, it would seem, a new revolutionary approach to the technique of singing appears (generally a slightly refurbished version of something from the forties, long since rejected). The teacher of singing must possess a repository of factual information against which new ideas can be measured. The instructor who is informed on the mechanics of vocalism is unlikely to embrace some false claim for miraculous technical aids. If the teacher is to offer the student an enduring technical basis for singing, there must be a stable core of factual material, a willingness to look at emerging information, and a solid concept of artistry, together with precise musicianship.

There is a breed of singing teacher that assembles a set of pedagogical expressions, a group of vocalises, and a swatch of repertory that goes on, year after year, without alteration. New information is unwelcome. Such persons assume that they have always known how to teach, or that they carry on the tradition of one of their famous teachers, or that they can deliver to every singer the same technique that they "gave" to the successful pupil who now sings at the Metropolitan Opera House. Teachers who claim to teach exactly the things they taught 25 years ago have slipped into a state of moribundity. Conversely, teachers who change techniques several times in the course of a few years lack a stabilized concept of either tone or physical function in singing.

There will be little danger of falling into the errors of compensatory teaching, of becoming technically too intense, of relying solely on interpretation and style to solve vocal problems, of becoming the technique-mystique figure, or of stressing but one part of the complex technique of singing, if stability and willingness to respond to new ideas are kept in balance. To maintain this balance, we must know the heritage of the vocal art, know what is currently going on in fields related to singing, and be informed on the literature of vocal pedagogy. (How is it possible for an expert in any field, including the teacher of singing, not to know the literature of that field?) Musical intelligence, stylistic knowledge, and the ability to articulate concepts are, of course, prerequisites for all musician–teachers. To attempt to rely solely on one's own experience as performer and teacher is as foolhardy as it would be for the researcher or practitioner in any other discipline. No one of us has it all.

TEACHING ONESELF

"I taught myself how to sing" is a claim occasionally heard from some professional singer of stature. The statement should surprise no one, because all singers must be their own teachers. Learning to sing involves unification of the musicianly ear, the controlled body, and the creative intelligence, an act of artistic integration that cannot be superimposed on the singer from the outside. In this sense, no teacher teaches any singer how to sing. One of the most serious perils for the student of singing lies in the expectation that a fine teacher will build a technique for the pupil. The singer must have trust in the ear of the teacher and in the school of technique being presented, but neither of these positive factors is sufficient. Only the *singer* can put together physical and artistic information in such a fashion that it can be personally experienced again and again (that is, be given technical expression). The work of the teacher can only be to point the way (an essential service).

If the advanced singer continues to need the controlling hand of the teacher in technical matters, following some few years of study, the teacher has not done a proper job. Good teaching produces independent singers, capable of trusting their own ears and their own bodies. All professional singers must eventually become their own daily teachers, although they should never dispense with an occasional outside ear. If anyone else knows the singer's voice better than the mature singer, the technical foundation of that voice is incomplete.

Intelligent singers will take a representative group of vocalises built on the categories presented in this book and give themselves a voice lesson every day. Any time the mouth is opened for singing, the ear and the intelligence should be involved in a process of monitoring, the most basic form of teaching. After the singer has become aware of the beauty of the functionally free voice, the *singer* is the best teacher of that instrument!

During the formative years (usually passed in the conservatory, the school of music, the graduate school), when technique is being formed and performance attitudes established, the singer should be encouraged toward independence with regard to the psychological preparation for public performance. Teacher's insistence on "warming up" the singer immediately before a performance builds a vocal and psychological dependency that is unhealthy. Regardless of whatever good intent may prompt such procedures, the voice teacher actually is fostering the notion of personal indispensability. It may be an unconscious device for drawing the student more closely to the teacher.

Some few professional singers must always stop off at teacher's studio before a performance, or even take the singing teacher along on tour; such singers are not known for their dependability in performance. Few singers can enjoy such a luxury, in any event. The voice teacher who can devote such amounts of time to one singer can scarcely undertake other professional commitments that should mark the successful teacher.

Most professionally active singers discover that the demands of travel, rehearsal, score preparation, and performance leave little opportunity for regularly scheduled voice lessons. For the most part, a loose arrangement for an occasional "check-up" with a reliable teacher is the only formal voice study managed by the busy artist. If the singer possesses a solid technique, the arrangement is fine. Instruction continues—most of it self-instruction.

It would be disastrous for the young singer (under age 25 is a safe boundary for that designation) to take at face value the claim of several established singers—that they have taught themselves to sing—and to attempt to do likewise. Most of such claims inadvertently support the fact that only the singer can integrate the essential information and skill that produce a firm technique. In the case of a broader claim than that, skepticism is very much in order. It is a matter of public record that several professional singers who have stated in interviews that they are self-taught have actually studied with recognized teachers or have been in attendance at major (and not so major) schools of music for long periods of time.

The professional singer who states that everything that previously had been learned from voice teachers had to be put aside, and that "I've now worked out my own technique," is giving naive expression to what every successful singer and every successful teacher of singing knows. Only singers can integrate their own voices. However, it can be safely asserted that almost no successful singer has acquired technical facility without the help of a good voice teacher somewhere along the way.

In an age where it is very much in vogue for the civil engineer to be an authority on Chinese cooking, for the parish priest to know the batting averages of major league players over the past three decades, and for the popular TV personality to be acquainted with the most minute details of the career of "The Desert Fox," it is not uncommon for the professional singer to seek some new and interesting personality dimension to present to the public. (If the singer can't think of one, the agency will.) Thus we have the "I just fell into singing more or less by accident" motif, with psychology, ballet, "pre-med" or "pre-law" (the latter two academic programs general enough to go unquestioned) presented as the major field of study. Indeed, if the number of professional singers who gave up careers as "concert violinist" and "concert pianist" were tabulated, one would tremble for the artists who dominate those fields, had the singers not opted for their current performance medium.

A close look will reveal that, while almost any professional singer may have profited from a wide spread of intellectual and artistic interests, the technique of singing has been seriously studied for a number of years. The public image of some contemporary singers should not confuse the young singer; learning to sing is a demanding discipline, and no one should pretend that it is not, nor is there any reason to apologize for pursuing it.

In similar vein, some professional singers intrigued by the self-made image, which is so coveted in our culture, have a problem admitting the debt they owe to someone else (that someone else is often an early teacher whose name is not nationally or internationally known). On the other hand, some singers are collectors of prominent teachers, "studying" a little with anyone whose name will add prestige, particularly if the teacher has a pupil, or several, currently in the public eye.

Hesitant to admit the need for continued technical work, some singers euphemistically report that they are "coaching" with some well-known teacher of singing. Frequently, the teacher who was largely responsible for the emergence of the singer's career is then relegated to an "early-training-took-place-with" category, if mentioned at all.

Perhaps most saddening of all is the prominent professional singer who develops obvious vocal problems but is unwilling to face them, because of belief in the copy of advertising writers, which places the singer at the pinnacle of the profession; if you are the embodiment of *bel canto,* you cannot very well admit to a developing *passaggio* problem unless you are a very objective person. Too proud to seek help from a voice teacher, many an artist has had to accept a truncated career unnecessarily (or the termination of the career is the result of the singer trying to find a teacher with "tricks" that will save the voice). Just as voice teachers who feel there is nothing more to be learned from outside sources seriously narrow their capabilities for teaching, so the professional singer who feels there is nothing to be learned from anyone else will not long maintain a successful career. Teach yourself, but do not make the mistake of believing you are entirely self-sufficient.

CHAPTER 17

Healthy Singing

Musicians who play stringed instruments may have bad days when weather is unkindly humid, brass players grow restless keeping the mouthpiece warm during some seemingly interminable wait in the symphonic literature, and the making and conditioning of reeds must not be without its own special set of annoyances. Transporting a harp, a double bass, or a tuba requires a fair amount of advance planning; the pianist must either put up with the varying condition of instruments from hall to hall or cart around a private instrument.

The musician who is a singer has an instrument that does not have to be tuned in public, needs no carrying case, requires no early shipment, cannot easily be sat on or dropped, and is in no danger of being stolen. Advantages beyond those points are somewhat negligible. The singer cannot purchase a finely constructed instrument that 200 years of aging and playing have mellowed, nor can the singer keep "trading up," eventually becoming the possessor of a fine Cremona product. Major reparations on the structure, and actual rebuilding, are not possible with the vocal instrument. Furthermore, heat, cold, precipitation, digestion, toothache, bad back, cocktail party, hernia, nosebleed, domestic quarrel, and especially respiratory ailments, may be totally incapacitating. In addition to threading through these pitfalls, prior to the third decade of life the singer is seldom established as a full-fledged professional performer; then, rarely does a public listen without at least some nostalgia for what used to be, after the sixth decade (and more probably after the fifth) of the life span of the vocal instrument.

It is difficult to determine where the instrument of the singer leaves off and where the instrument case begins. In any event, the singing instrument is dependent on the condition of its carrying case. The indulgent smiles, raised eyebrows, and numerous anecdotes about vain singers (especially sopranos and tenors) who wrap themselves up in scarves, remove themselves from drafts, and in general treat the body as something fragile, would quickly change to sympathetic understanding were other musicians similarly united physically to their instruments. Even on vacation, singers take the instrument along and know that whatever they do will contribute to

218

its condition. Little wonder that the singer seems never to forget the physical status of the instrument.

Most of the measures taken by singers to remain healthy are of dubious value, even psychologically. The number of throat lozenges consumed by singers is incredible and has very little effect on bettering the voice, inasmuch as lozenges reach the esophagus, not the larynx, after contributing considerably to dental caries. The gallons of tea, with honey or lemon, or even both, poured forth from the ubiquitous flask in the green room, if taken all together, must surely produce an eighth sea, while the antihistamine tablets and vitamin pills dropped into the stomachs of singers, if placed one on top of the other, would create a towering monument to hypochondria. Nasal sprays, gargles, sinus masks, lotions, and neck salves, together with pre-performance diet fads (an egg in a jigger of cognac, a can of pineapple juice, a head of lettuce, a serving of beefsteak tartar, are a few of the perennials), further attest to the plight of the musician whose instrument depends on top-flight condition of the physical mass in which it is lodged.

The poor singer, when faced with an upcoming performance and an oncoming cold, can hardly be blamed for searching for some magic potion that will restore lost facility. It is a terrible feeling to know that what one can normally do so well must be attempted without the full cooperation of the carefully trained and well-prepared instrument, and to be aware that audiences and critics make no allowances.

There are singers who even under optimal physical conditions are caught in a web of psychological encumbrances; the greater the accumulation of these circumstances "essential" for singing well, the less probability that they can all be fulfilled. Thus, the singer with the fewest performance fetishes is psychologically the healthiest, regardless of physical condition.

Many times there is nothing to be done during periods of incapacitation except to fall in with one's fate. Particularly, however, in the case of the singer, preventive medicine is the best medicine. (Several sources that contain information regarding the health of the singer are heartily recommended: Friedrich Brodnitz's *Keep Your Voice Healthy* (1953), Norman Punt's *The Singer's and Actor's Throat* (1979), and a series of articles by Van Lawrence on the care of the singing voice, "LaryngoSCOPE," *The NATS Bulletin*, beginning with Jan/Feb, 1981.) Are there ways of living sanely, without constant apprehension about physical condition, which the intelligent, stable singer can adopt?

CONDITIONING FOR PERFORMANCE READINESS

It has been a recurring theme throughout this book that if a singer will follow a specific regimen of daily vocalization touching all aspects of physical function as they are found in singing, general vocal health will inevitably result. Such a routine avoids the vocal strain that otherwise comes from long rehearsal periods and from series of performances of works that may not be grateful for a voice but must nevertheless be undertaken. No singer should expect sudden bursts of vocal endurance without a continuing discipline. For this vocal conditioning, the singer must take responsibility, and it is often hard to make oneself do it.

Within the singer's voluntary control over vocal condition is the avoidance of certain habits which, when indulged, will most assuredly take a toll (Ballantyne, 1961, pp. 541–557). Although the Surgeon General has sufficiently warned of the hazards of smoking, it is not only the long-range specter of emphysema, cancer of the lung, tongue, trachea, or larynx that should frighten off the singer, but the more immediate, day-by-day effects of trauma on the delicate membrane that lines the vocal tract (including the bands themselves). The heat from smoke inhalation, and its desiccating action, causes irritation; the membrane secretes in an attempt to compensate for the condition of dryness, setting up the throat-clearing syndrome. Furthermore, the lung deteriorates in cigarette smoking. An unsigned article in the *British Medical Journal* (1975, pp. 273–274) makes the following statement:

> Most people who smoke cigarettes concede the risk of future lung cancer. Nevertheless, few seem aware of the steadily accumulating evidence which suggests that cigarettes also speed development of persistent and disabling dyspnea [labored respiration] by damaging lung function in a way resembling aging of lungs.

There is little point in citing the one or two international artists who smoke two packs a day and still manage to perform (perhaps even they do not escape some audible results). Nor does "laying off" for a few days before an important performance repair the damage, because the membrane cannot so quickly recover its lost elasticity. Any singer already addicted to tobacco should undertake whatever tremendous act of the will is required to break the habit. A young singer may well be burning up future engagements with the first cigarette lighted. While smoking has perils for everyone, the singer has the most compelling reasons for avoiding smoke inhalation.

Singers should be aggressive in requesting that smoke inhalation not be forced on them. Temporary irritation to the nose and throat can be serious enough to cause the singer discomfort. (The extent of permanent damage to the respiratory mechanism from smoke inhaled by nonsmokers has not yet been conclusively determined.) No singer should be subjected to that kind of potential danger through polite indulgence of those who blow smoke into the atmosphere around them.

The deleterious effects of alcohol on body tissue have been documented many times and need not be repeated here. Studies on the effects of alcohol on phonation show loss of both perception and coordination (Trojan and Kryssin-Exner, 1968, pp. 217–238). It is presumed that drunkenness is not a live issue for the seriously committed singer, although alcoholism has terminated several major careers. The singer who imbibes the evening before a performance day will almost certainly pay for it with less than optimum vocal condition. To put alcohol into the system on a performance day is unthinkable. The combination of cigarette smoke (including that of other people), alcohol, and animated conversation carried on above the noise generated by a room full of people, spells sure vocal suicide.

PERFORMANCE-DAY ROUTINE

Singers should never compete with the strident voices of extroverted friends under any circumstances, especially on a performance day. The same caution regarding speech at high dynamic levels should be exercised when riding in cars, subways, airplanes, buses, and railway coaches (they still exist in Europe). An hour's ride from the airport to the rehearsal hall while talking above the motor noise in an attempt to satisfy the curiosity of the music enthusiast who picks up the singer for the local opera or symphony society, is not conducive to maintaining good vocal condition. A simple explanation that talking is to be avoided on rehearsal and performance days is generally all that is needed to remove this hazard.

On a performance day, or a general rehearsal day, no singer should be tempted into long conversations, either in person or on the telephone, with spouse, hosts, local friends, newspaper or television interviewers, accompanist, or colleagues. A major role or a recital makes physical demands that ought to be taken fully into account. It is foolish to throw away long hours of vocal conditioning simply in order to respond to the good intentions of persons who themselves do not have to stand on the stage before thousands of people, totally dependent on vocal-fold function.

Even established singers find themselves in situations where a conductor will insist on run-throughs on the morning of performance days (generally for the conductor's benefit, not yours); it is difficult for the singer to resist. Not all conductors are cognizant of what can reasonably be expected of singers. Sometimes contractual agreements (especially recording contracts) even with professional orchestras of international repute require "rehearse and perform" sessions. The conductor's "Just mark it, I don't want full voice," is not very helpful. Most singers feel the need of a warm-up for any kind of vocal activity. "Marking" (indicating rather than using *voce piena*) can sometimes be more injurious than singing full voice, particularly in orchestral rehearsals in an unfamiliar hall, with chorus and orchestra singing and playing at full volume.

The technique of "marking" must be learned by every singer. It should not involve the singing of most portions of the role an octave lower (although some isolated phrase may best be handled that way), nor should support of the voice be removed. Some pitches may be raised or lowered an octave (*punktiert*), and only entrances sung at audible level. Yet an ill singer who "marks" a rehearsal must do so cautiously.

Unfortunately, it is the fledgling artist, least equipped to deal with such "rehearse–perform" situations, who is often forced into them through the ignorance of minor-league conductors, or by knowledgeable major-league conductors who have little concern for artistic welfare other than their own. The established artist may be able to ensure that such unreasonable demands will not be made. It takes a great deal of courage for a young artist facing a battery of orchestral, choral, and solo participants (and other professional pressures) to only move the lips during rehearsal, or to maintain silence when rehearsal demands are excessive. Always to be remembered is that "getting through the rehearsal" is not the reason why one came!

One of the potentially most disastrous situations for the established artist is the "open dress rehearsal" to which "guild members," "the women's auxiliary," and dignitaries and critics are invited. Supposedly a rehearsal, it is actually a performance on the basis of which many judgments are made. The singer may very well need to protect a limping instrument, conserving energy and sound for the premier. More than one critique has been written following the open rehearsal, and the premier performance has been diminished by the rigors of that rehearsal. Many professional singers view the practice as a managerial trick for squeezing out an extra performance.

A major mistake is to allow the entire performance day to pass without any vocal activity whatsoever. Sometimes a singer is uncertain of the exact state of vocal condition, particularly after a long plane flight, a time change, and a restless night not spent in one's own bed (some singers never get over the problem of trying to sleep in strange cities). Spending the entire performance day "resting" the voice, not really knowing what kind of vocal response may be present, is both nerve-racking and nonconducive to good vocal condition. To throw the laryngeal mechanism into strenuous activity suddenly about one or two hours before concert time, after a day of total silence, is not sensible procedure.

There is a time-honored routine of the international school for performance days, observed by many singers whose careers have become legendary. Maestro Luigi Ricci, who certainly had first-hand acquaintance with as large a number of major careers as has any teacher of this century, followed tradition in admonishing his "coachees" to sleep well, but to be up in the morning before it is too far gone (both on regular and performance days), to eat breakfast because of the benefits of chewing and swallowing to the wake-up process of the voice (if only hard rolls and caffelatte), to wait a bit for breakfast to settle, and then to begin the daily vocalization routine. Having run through some selected vocalises from the several facets of vocal technique (with brief resting periods of several minutes between), the singer will have experienced proper muscular action in all areas of the instrument. The morning process of vocalization need not occupy more than half an hour. The voice will be conditioned for the rest of the day. On performance days, no further singing takes place until an hour or so prior to concert time, when a brief run-through of selected vocalises is sufficient warm-up for the evening ahead. The singer who demands a total run-through of the role immediately before the performance shows musical and vocal insecurity. For recital, 10 minutes beforehand, spent checking tempi and entrances with one's accompanist, may also be in order.

Several artists of international standing refuse to use the voice at all on performance day, or even the previous day. This seems a somewhat exaggerated procedure for protecting the vocal instrument. However, the period of silence (broken, of course, by the necessary communications of any day) and rest might include a mental read-through of the role or of the music to be performed, with creative thinking about what is to be done with it in performance. A good book, a catnap or two, an easy walk, should pass the time agreeably. Some singers attend movies or watch television (perhaps as a total distraction from artistic thought). For others, it is disturbing to occupy the mind with the trite emotional events of the screen on the day when one wants to communicate emotions of a more profound nature. Sleep, close to the hour of performance, is very definitely *not* recommended. It would seem self-evident that the singer should arrive early at the theater or hall to become accustomed to the environment of the building. Late arrival may spell disaster, because there is no time to become accustomed to the hall ambience and to compose oneself.

Many people are acquainted with the practices of the Metropolitan Opera baritone who vigorously swims for an hour on the day of performance, with the basso who insists on playing nine holes of golf on a performance day, with the successful tenor who indulges in emotionally strenuous activity prior to each performance, or with the soprano who sunbathes all day or who goes on a shopping spree. Most of us, however, need to husband our physical and mental energies.

WHEN *NOT* TO SING

No singer can afford the luxury of performing only when in perfect physical condition. Recall the comment of the famous Russian bass who said that if he were to sing only when in fine fettle he would perform no more than twice a year. It is sometimes by the narrowest margin that a professional singer decides cancellation is necessary. Given the structure of concert and opera schedules, pressures from agencies, and one's own artistic standards, cancellation is never a light-hearted decision. Decisions to cancel in the opera house have to be made in time to find replacements. Sometimes the decision to go ahead with a performance is the wrong decision; another artist will be called in to finish remaining acts, because the singer misjudged vocal condition that morning (a relatively frequent happening, it would seem).

When physical irritation is not located directly in the larynx, the singer can sometimes turn in a performance that shows no evidence of trouble, by the sheer weight of technical know-how, without causing harm to the voice. However, as soon as laryngeal function itself is impaired through marked edema (swelling) in the vocal folds, the singer should remain silent. (Shots of cortisone during intermission, so that the singer can go on, are shunned by most singers. Medical opinion appears divided on its use.) Conditions of edema are most often accompanied by slight hoarseness or raspiness, the speaking voice feels higher than usual, and vocal quality sounds thicker and less than clean. Through the techniques of exact vocal-fold approximation, learned through the disciplining that takes place in the onset vocalise, a singer may still be able to produce decent vocal sound despite incipient edema, or during its less-developed stages. However, if strenuous singing is continued, additional swelling will occur, with results that can be detrimental to the voice.

Damage can be done by performing when vocal condition is less than ideal. A series of such experiences can produce serious disturbances. Compensatory actions called upon may be difficult to rechannel. Laryngologists are frequently officially or semi-officially attached to European opera houses (and increasingly in America), and are accustomed to viewing singers' vocal bands with some degree of regularity. Often, they prefer to examine the ailing singer the morning following performance, because the results of the evening's vocal activity will best be judged at that point.

The experienced singer's own understanding of the vocal instrument is the only reliable indicator of when to sing under difficulty. The laryngologist may see and hear favorable signs for phonation in speaking, but the more complicated requirements of the singing role are not for the medical specialist alone to decide. When recovery from a disabling upper respiratory ailment is nearly complete, the quick adjustments needed for easy registration of the voice or for successful negotiation of the range extremes may not yet be fully operative. An artist may be able to make one scheduled performance when vocal condition is not optimum, while canceling another wherein the demands of range, tessitura, weight, or length of the role are beyond the still limping instrument's capabilities. The singer's judgment, based on experience and reinforced by a knowledge of vocal condition, should always be accepted in borderline cases.

The ideal situation would be for the singer to sing only when the voice is in good condition. Few performers are in that position, regardless of fame or fee. Sometimes "out-of-voice" periods seem to go on interminably because of insufficient opportunity for physical recuperation. The singer should have the courage to say "no" to performance commitments, no matter how important, if the vocal instrument runs the risk of injury. Someone else's disappointment or anger, the loss of probable re-engagement, and financial hardship should all be seen in the perspective of an entire career. If the singer goes ahead with a performance in which vocal damage of long consequence occurs, gratitude on the part of persons who hire singers will not extend to the future employment of a sick voice. In most cases, heavy responsibilities should not be undertaken by singers who are not in reasonably good vocal condition.

WHAT TO SING

Equally difficult for the artist is the decision as to what roles, and in what combinations, can be successfully undertaken over the course of a season. The maturing young soprano who could very successfully sing Donna Anna in the production at a major midwestern school of music as a graduate student may have to learn that as a professional she should not take on that role at the same time she is required to sing several other heavy roles. Stamina in singing, as in athletics, is built through involvement, but determining what is excessive is not always easy.

Beyond the problem of the cumulative effect of specific roles performed within brief periods of time is the problem of outright miscasting. The artist, one would assume, should be able to trust the judgment of voice teachers, conductors, and general managers. When it comes to role assignments, it is exactly in that area that incompetence even in positions of authority seems most prevalent. This situation has been sagely commented on by one critic of the operatic scene (Hume, 1977, pp. G–5):

> These questions, however, should not really come up. If the people in charge of opera theaters knew their business as they should, they would not want to cast mezzo-sopranos as Selika in Meyerbeer's "L'Africaine" for the best of all reasons: because it would not sound the way Meyerbeer intended it to. Lyric sopranos would not be given heavy dramatic roles, and exquisite tenors, who often need to be saved from themselves, would not be permitted to sing roles where vocal demands quickly rob their voices of the velvet cushion they need to keep on singing for years.

The same source concludes:

> There is a serious shortage of really fine operatic voices these days. It is compounded by teachers who do not know how to teach, singers who refuse to admit that there is anything they cannot sing and opera directors who think every soprano can sing every soprano role, every tenor take on the entire tenor repertoire, every baritone launch into the whole baritone list. If the situation is not altered, the present problems of casting Aida, Trovatore and Turandot will quickly multiply.

In European opera houses (where many Americans still find their livelihood), singers have some protection against the problem of miscasting, and of too many public performances, yet most persons under permanent contract find themselves involved in major roles several times per week, which is almost always too much. Union contracts demand protective clauses against miscasting and too frequent public performance, but many singers succumb to management's financial inducements. In Italy, the deplorable practice of signing up promising young singers to long-range contracts that included a modest living subsistence rather than a per-performance fee sounded the death knell for a number of beautiful young Italian voices.

Of course, the international artist, firmly established, is in a favorable position with regard to the selection of roles and the frequency of performances. Yet a look at some of the schedules of major artists attests to the durability of the human voice and to good technical grounding (or at least to human grit!). Theater and concert managements seldom play any responsible role in the artist's development. The success of the immediate season and the planning of the next, the political necessity to please the conducting staff, the stage directors, the board, the *Stadtrat* or whatever governing body, is paramount. There is little indication that this situation will change so long as general directorships are in the hands of nonmusicians. Seldom do former singers manage opera houses these days, as they not infrequently did at one glorious period in operatic history.

The wide disparity of vocal skill exhibited within a single performance in international houses attests to the indisputable fact that casting often has little to do with informed judgment about the art of singing. The modern opera-goer may be subjected to fabulous vocalism from the Octavian, off-pitch wobbling from the Marschallin, ferocious non-pitch barking from the Ochs, and exquisite phrasing from the Sophie. (Repeated attendance proves that it is not "off-night" variances here and there that produce such uneven performances.) One must either conclude that *Intendanten* and conductors know less about vocalism than ought to be the case, that they are impelled by non-artistic considerations (such as public response to an advertised and recognizable product, without regard to current vocal merit), or that magnanimity rules in retaining the artist with diminishing vocal ability.

Guidelines for the young artist who must decide which roles to accept are not easy to formulate for general observance, but it should be perfectly clear in the case of the individual instrument. It is nothing short of scandalous that sound advice is not available from every house management. The young professional is fortunate if the teacher is experienced, knows what a role entails, and has concern for the resources of the voice. No singer should be encouraged to sing a role that is out of *Fach*. The singer does well to investigate what was considered appropriate material at various phases of the careers of other artists in that *Fach* in former decades. (For example, at what age did Gigli first sing Radames?)

THE TEACHER–PERFORMER

Not to be forgotten in this consideration of the healthy performer is the teacher–performer who has to use the vocal instrument to teach a full schedule, fly out, or drive long distances, for a week or week-end of rehearsal and performances, deliver in on-campus opera pro-ductions, oratorio and recital appearances, present master classes here and there, and still show up for committee duties. ("Have you published anything recently?" "When do you plan to finish your DMA?") Increasingly, a large share of musical life in America takes place on the college and university campus. Resident faculty mem-bers are active performers as well as dedicated teachers. It is unfor-tunate that academe has not given more thought to flexible solutions to accommodate the teacher–performer. State legislatures (imbued with the 40-hour-week mentality) and boards of regents (trustees) are seldom able to determine the importance of performance contri-butions by faculty artists, looking instead at teaching credits and enrollment figures. Some administrators (may their tribe increase!) understand the phenomenal feat of such combination careers and try to mitigate circumstances whenever possible. (In general, the more vision in such matters, the stronger the school of music that administrator heads.)

Any activity that involves phonation for long periods of time will eventually tire the vocal instrument. Teaching singing is no excep-tion. Whereas piano and violin professors may talk all day without tiring their instruments, the teacher of singing must constantly use the instrument during teaching (even if not a single note is modeled). Habitual ways of using the speaking voice may well determine the continued vocal health of the singing teacher. Singers (especially those who teach) should learn to "support" the speaking voice with as much skill as they do the singing voice, being certain that pitch level is neither too low nor too high, and that amplitude is at a level to permit ease of production. (The controversial doctrine of "optimal pitch" is not here the question.) Harm can be done to the speaking voice by attempting to spare it or protect it through low, breathy, unenergized speech (a cultural development within the past decade or so, patterned after the intimacy and "sincerity" of the talk-show participant). Well-projected, resonant, supported speech will be much less tiring on the vocal mechanism.

As a teacher of singing, keeping one's own singing voice in good condition cannot be put off to the end of the long workday, when energies are depleted. Before beginning the teaching day, with its potential problems, the performer–teacher's own daily regimen of vocalization should take place. That early practice hour is difficult to find, yet if the voice teacher wants to continue an active performance career, it must somehow be found. Destructive to the voice is the need to demonstrate for the student when one's own instrument is not properly warmed up. Further, the speaking voice itself will be in much better shape for the constant use it must go through during the day if proper vocalization has taken place prior to the first lesson. One's success as a teacher has some relationship to the caliber of vocal sound one is capable of making.

THE QUESTION OF COMPLETE VOCAL REST

What should the professional singer do when an extended period of vocal weariness rears its ugly head? It is pointless to say that with perfect vocal technique such problems should not occur; the most perfect vocal technique in the world cannot surmount some of the demands of the current professional performance world. If possible, simply taking time out for a week or ten days of moderate voice rest usually works miracles.

There is a divergence of medical opinion today regarding "vocal rest." It is quite true that inactivity encourages sluggish muscle coordination, and that daily use of the whole vocal instrument is necessary to general vocal health for the singer. However, when the singer has limped along, pulling off performance after performance under undesirable physical conditions, total vocal rest for a brief period of time may be best. (So is a rare vacation from it all!)

Complete vocal rest should be used only after all other means of restoring vocal vitality have failed. Complete voice rest must forego all action that involves vocal-fold approximation. A legal pad and a box of sharp pencils replaces the vocalis muscle, and total silence should be religiously observed. Whispering as a substitute for full phonation should be avoided at all costs; the emission of breath over slack vocal cords, often at stage-whisper level (the posture of the inter-cartilaginous whispering triangle), is perhaps more detrimental to the welfare of the voice than is hoarse speech.

Two or three days of total vocal rest may do wonders. If neces-

230 The Structure of Singing

sary, go away for the weekend. If improvement is not shown following a few days of return to moderate voice use, then the most drastic treatment of all should begin: 10 days (even 2 weeks) of total silence. Repeatedly, such a prescription has proved to be more beneficial to the truly weary vocal instrument than all the therapeutic exercises, inhalations, medications, massages, and heat treatments taken together.

Of course, if bad vocal habits have been the cause of weariness, all the vocal rest (along with the steam and the cortisone) will be of no avail when one resumes faulty phonation. However, even a technically secure singer may have had to face a heavy upper-respiratory infection and to keep on meeting professional commitments, thereby tiring the instrument. In such a case, total vocal rest may be the only appropriate measure and may save months of "limping." On return to voice use, the singer should begin modest vocalizing. Without doubt, muscle tonus will not be at normal functioning level. By gradually increasing initial, brief periods of vocalization, the singer should be able to recuperate within a few weeks. (Let it be clear that total vocal rest is a drastic step. *It should be discussed with a laryngologist.* If your laryngologist is unalterably opposed to any period of total vocal rest, seek a second or third opinion.)

THE QUESTION OF MEDICATION

Women who follow singing careers may feel that pregnancy is a condition to avoid. At least one major conductor was known to tell female singers to avoid becoming pregnant so that he might use them the following season.

At conferences that deal with the care of the professional voice, the effect of the contraceptive pill on the voice is inevitably raised in any period devoted to questions from the floor. It is a burning issue with many singers, and most persons associated with the opera house have heard of cases where the singer on the pill lost a major third from her range, or developed laryngeal problems. Doctors are not in agreement about the extent of risk involved in taking the pill. It is possible that the phase of the menstrual cycle partly determines the effect of the pill on the larynx. There is also the strong probability that some oral contraceptives are less harmful than others. *The best advice is for the female singer to consult her laryngologist before beginning with this medication.*

The reliance on antihistamines by singers has already been mentioned. Perhaps less well known is the drying effect of these drugs. Lawrence (1981a, p. 25) has this to say:

Antihistamines are all "drier-outers," and probably won't hurt if one's nose is pouring hot water and one's eyes are streaming. (Who's going to think of singing then?) But again, one wants rich, slick, supple, well-lubricated vocal folds to sing well, and the antihistamines won't help accomplish that."

Lawrence (1981c, pp. 24–25) also warns of the possible drying effect of large doses of vitamin C combined with antihistamine tablets. In addition, aspirin, Lawrence says, may promote capillary fragility in the larynx. *The best advice is to check with your doctor, and do not self-medicate.*

DRY THROAT

Singers sometimes complain about throat dryness during performance. Can anything be done about this common condition? First of all, the singer should recognize that dry throat accompanies situations of anxiety. During singing, dryness is largely a side effect of performance nerves. The better prepared, technically and musically, the lower the incidence of dryness. Biting the blade of the tongue (gently!) and taking that last backstage sip of water give some momentary relief. Most important, however, is the psychology of performance attitudes. Regard the audience as people who are in need of your services; accept the responsibility that you are there in front of them to share some musical and artistic insights.

Many singers discover that throat dryness diminishes considerably when little or no salt is taken in food near performance. Deliberately drinking more water during the course of performance days (or in general) may somewhat alleviate the tendency toward dry throat during singing.

Chewing gum and sucking lozenges seldom assist in providing more than a temporary saliva flow, followed by an even greater sense of dryness. Chewing and swallowing a section or two of citrus fruit between entrances or groups may be a somewhat better idea. Above all, the cultivation of a happy and positive performance environment will do much to eliminate "dry throat."

"CLEARING" THE THROAT

In the interest of vocal health, all attempts to "clear" the throat must be avoided by the singer. This is particularly the case at those inevitable times of vocal disability. Most singers tend to be extremely healthy, probably freer of colds and respiratory ailments than many people. When such ailments do strike, they are more urgent with the singer. The urge to clear the throat in instances when a cold has struck is caused chiefly by the very condition of edema which "throat clearing" will only serve to exacerbate. When the throat is "cleared," we require an action from the vocal folds that only irritates them further and causes an increase in the secretion of mucus. Often, the best means of clearing mucus from the folds is to sing it off. The execution of rapid arpeggios, glissando, rapid onset, or trilling, is almost always more productive than is "clearing" the throat, if indeed there is something there to clear away. Unfortunately, the singer cannot follow that suggestion while sitting on stage waiting for a vocal entrance. At such moments, swallowing may be helpful. (One of the chief pedagogical uses of fiberoptic observation is for the singer to see what the vocal folds must undergo in "throat clearing.") Don't "clear" the throat!

Coughing should not be used by the singer as a means of clearing the vocal tract when superficial mucus is lodged somewhere in trachea, larynx, or pharynx (that is, voluntary coughing). Both coughing and "throat clearing" are to be avoided as much as possible in the interest of vocal health.

FIGHTING THE COUGH

The cough is a necessary evil at certain stages of an upper respiratory infection. However, a lingering, irritating cough can very quickly impair the usefulness of the hardiest vocal instrument. Singers suffering from cough after the worst of the respiratory infection is over should not allow a self-perpetuating cough to go on; the forced action of the vocal folds during coughing is detrimental to the membrane. Medical advice should be sought; singers should not just let a cough "wear itself out." Preparations that suppress the impulse to cough (used only at the correct phase of the cold) and expectorants that assist in clearing the air passages can often prove of value to the singer. According to Gold (1953, p. 90):

> A simple upper respiratory infection often presents cough as the dominant symptom. Through severe blasts and long volleys the cough produces sufficient irritation to sustain itself through a chain reaction long after the primary condition is gone. This is the kind in which prolonging the interval between volleys by a centrally acting cough medicine or reducing the number and severity in blasts in each volley by

an expectorant produces the extraordinary spectacle of a cough of long duration "cured" by a few doses of cough medicine.

Singers should also avoid hurried eating, or the inhalation of foreign material, which may cause coughing (powdered sugar and nuts are notoriously bad). A coughing spell can be as harmful as yelling for the same period of time.

CHEWING

Is there a practical exercise the singer can use when tension and strain caused by excessive performance have taken their toll, or when temporary physical condition interferes with optimal vocal production?

For several decades, some speech therapists and laryngologists have expressed interest in the relationship between chewing and speech. Chewing, under certain circumstances, may improve voice by finding an association between primitive vocal sound and speech. (It does not, therefore, follow that as singers we must attempt to rediscover the primitive noises that resemble the chattering of the rhesus monkey, or that we should imitate "pre-speech" sounds as some few modern vocal pedagogues would have us do.)

Emil Froeschels (1952, p. 427), who pioneered in the therapeutic use of chewing, remarked that "The chewing method is not a 'relaxation' method, but a means of bringing forth the still-present original association of voice and speech." However, a distinct sense of vocal relaxation is often experienced by singers who call on this association through chewing–speaking exercises. Froeschels explains his discovery as follows:

> Since one can chew food and talk at the same time, and since the nerves, the muscles, and even the center in the anterior central convolution are the same, the chewing and speaking (articulation movements) must be the same. Since I came to this conclusion (1934) several X-ray films have proved it to be correct. If the patient is taught to think of chewing while speaking, there is no overcontraction of the muscles concerned in speech (and voice).

Froeschels suggests the use of "ham-ham-ham" as the kind of syllable appropriate, and further advises that "Experience shows that it is best to practice twenty times a day, each time for a few seconds only, but always with the guiding idea of the real chewing while they are thinking of what they are saying."

Brodnitz (1971, pp. 97–99) makes these comments about the chewing method:

> By using the motions of chewing for voice production, we transfer the undisturbed muscular teamwork of chewing to the motion of voiced speech by appealing to an inborn automatic function. In doing this, we not only reduce hyperfunctional tension of the resonator but also improve, at the same time, vocal cord function, including the adjustment of pitch to a more natural level. . . . The training of voices by the chewing method is a conditioning process that makes use of a primitive animalistic function that happens to be, in many respects, a twin function of the use of the resonating cavities in the production of the voice. . . .

Vocal fatigue in the singing voice does not necessarily stem from conditions present in the speaking voice, yet initial muscle hyperfunction is usually the source of both. If you have undergone a hectic performance week as a professional singer, perhaps having sung more than one role that came close to taxing your physical, vocal, and emotional endurance (a set of circumstances to avoid), or if you have had to use your voice excessively in rehearsals or in teaching, try the following practical exercise, which is an adaptation for singers from a number of therapeutical sources such as Weiss and Beebe (1950), Froeschels (1952, p. 427), Hollingsworth (1939, pp. 385–386) and Brodnitz (1971, pp. 98–99).

EXERCISE 17.1

FIND A COMFORTABLE POSITION IN YOUR FAVORITE CHAIR, BUT WITH HEAD AND NECK IN UPRIGHT THOUGH RELAXED POSITION. (STANDING DOES NOT DETRACT FROM THE VALUE OF THE EXERCISE, IF YOU ARE COMFORTABLE.) IMAGINE CHEWING TWO LARGE PIECES OF STEAK (TWO LARGE WADS OF BUBBLE GUM WILL ALSO DO), ONE ON EITHER SIDE OF THE MOUTH. BE INELEGANT ABOUT IT, CHEWING WITH THE MOUTH OPEN, AND MUTTERING "MUM-MUM-MUM" AT NORMAL SPEECH LEVEL. DON'T HANG THE JAW OR ENGAGE IT IN EXCESSIVELY PERPENDICULAR MOVEMENTS, BECAUSE YOU NEVER DO THAT EITHER IN CHEWING OR IN SPEAKING. CHEW A FEW SECONDS AND THEN STOP. BE DELIBERATE ABOUT THE CHEWING–MUTTERING PROCESS. AFTER A FEW SERIES OF THESE ACTIONS, REST. IN A FEW MINUTES ADD SEVERAL SYLLABLES, SUCH AS A LINE OF SONG TEXT, STILL CHEWING VIGOROUSLY WITH CONSIDERABLE MOBILITY OF LIPS, CHEEKS, AND JAWS. SPEND VERY BRIEF PERIODS OF TIME IN THIS MANNER AT SEVERAL INTERVALS THROUGHOUT THE DAY.

You may very well experience a remarkable sense of relaxation of the throat and neck musculature; it has been established (Hollingsworth, 1939, p. 386) that muscular tension in the laryngeal region decreases during chewing. It should also be kept in view that "real functional trouble with the voice always begins with hyperfunction" (Froeschels, 1943, p. 127). (No claim is made that the author's adaptation of the techniques described in the aforementioned sources has been endorsed by those sources. Empirical evidence supports the exercise, however.)

The exercise is no answer to permanent habits of poor vocal production that result from overcontraction of the muscles of phonation, but it may prove helpful in achieving muscle relaxation when the singer is less than fit and still has to perform. Because chewing and swallowing are primitive functions, they are among the last conscious responses to resist final debility. Calling on this reserve of instinct may be helpful, on occasion, for the singer. However, repeated swallowing should be avoided, because the act of swallowing involves muscles that close the throat. The gum-chewing chorister and amateur singer may have a point. Yet the constant need to counteract "dryness" by chewing and swallowing attests to a lack of technical ease in singing.

Actual, as opposed to imaginary, chewing is periodically used by professional singers. A number of noted singers munch away between entrances or between acts, using small quantities of food, thereby relaxing the vocal mechanism through chewing while at the same time clearing the throat through occasional swallowing. Noticing two apples in a colleague's dressing room one evening, the great (a lesser adjective is surely inappropriate) Jussi Bjoerling commented, "So! You too are an apple eater between the acts!" He went on to say that he found a piece of apple just right for a little chewing and swallowing after an act of hard singing. He preferred apples to oranges, which he found to be too acidic. He related that a world-renowned conductor once came into his dressing room to discuss a musical point, saw several apples on Bjoerling's makeup desk, and asked, "Mr. Bjoerling, why do you have these apples I always see sitting about in your dressing room?" Bjoerling reported that his reply was, "Maestro, I *eat* them!"

SINGERS AND THE LARYNGOLOGIST

In whatever community the singer lives, an appointment should be made early with the nearest otolaryngologist at a time when there is no physical problem with the singing voice. Teachers of singing, especially those associated with colleges and universities having a resident laryngologist in the health service unit (any school offering a voice major degree should be so provided), should arrange for all major students to be briefly examined early in their study so that any future upper respiratory illnesses can be diagnosed against conditions of good health.

The relationship between the singer and the laryngologist is second only to that between singer and teacher. The laryngologist who is unaccustomed to dealing with singers may at times be mystified as to why patients have presented themselves. A singer should be able to see the "throat doctor" without fear of embarrassment. Slight irritation in the throat may cause a crisis for the singer. Nothing is more discouraging than to have the laryngologist say, "Don't be such a baby; you have only a small amount of redness there." A good singer needs a good laryngologist who understands the singer personality. Most singers do not foolishly run to the clinic each time they have an upper respiratory ailment. However, when performance anxieties are compounded by physical problems, the laryngologist should play a major role in performance psychology.

The laryngologist and the voice teacher should cooperate in dealing with the ill voice. No teacher of singing should take on medical responsibilities, nor should any laryngologist teach singing. (Even the laryngologist who has studied singing and has had some success as an amateur singer should hesitate to offer specific advice about singing techniques; voice teachers ought not to dispense medical prescriptions.)

WEIGHT AND THE SINGING VOICE

What is the ideal weight for the singer? Is it true, as has often been stated in interviews given by prominent overweight artists, that additional avoirdupois is needed in order to project the voice in the opera house, or to "improve resonance" (as if padding contributed to resonance). Certainly not! The ideal weight for singing is the ideal weight for any vital activity. Most singers who are obese got that way because the responsibility of a major career is a heavy burden. Eating is one of the ways the psyche is kind to itself, making up physically for all the mental pain that accompanies artistic discipline. Fat singers are notoriously short-winded, just as fat baseball players have a problem with running bases. The heaving chest of the out-of-breath, overweight singer at the conclusion of a dramatic aria is neither pleasant to watch nor healthful for the artist. The oft-repeated story of the famous diva who lost weight and acquired a wobble as a result is incorrect; the tendency to oscillate in the top voice was always there, simply becoming more marked with the passage of years. Waistline had nothing to do with it.

The conventions of the lyric theater have undergone some

improvement in recent decades with regard to the personal discipline demanded of singing artists. If one chooses to ply the trade of the
theater, one should be willing to accept the physical discipline that
goes with it. There is no more reason to accept an obese Romeo in
opera than in drama. Sound simply is not everything, either in the
lyric theater or on the concert stage.

Young singers who want careers on the operatic stage should
consider weight loss to be as essential to building a career as other
parts of career preparation. The few persons who have made modern major careers regardless of the handicap of obesity should not
serve to mislead aspiring singers into believing that being overweight
does not matter. It is *almost* impossible to be successful in today's
theater if one is obese, just as it is impossible for a male singer who is
five feet tall to have an operatic career. It may not be fair, but it is a
fact of the real world. Character roles then are the only possible
routes open.

DIET AND THE SINGER

We have already briefly mentioned in another context some per-
formance-day diet fads among singers. Whatever the value of "natural" foods, roughage diets, vegetarian diets, yogurt, or steak and lettuce, the best habitual diet of the singer is the diet that best equips
for general living. There is no specific food or drink that produces
some uniquely favorable condition within the larynx, despite prevalent singer superstitions. (Pity the poor soprano who must sing with
the tenor who chews garlic cloves to put "ring" in his voice!) Whatever is nourishing and avoids gastric disturbance is an appropriate
diet for the singer. A high-protein diet is always advisable for heightened physical activity, while high salt content in the diet may cause
thirst and throat dryness, as it does in any athletic event. Singers
need moist vocal folds (Lawrence, 1981, p. 25) and should develop
the habit of high liquid consumption, partly because of the loss of
liquid through perspiring in costume, under heavy lights, in demanding roles.

Eating habits of singers are frequently based on the national
habits with which they have grown up. Some singers take a late noon
meal and do not eat until after the performance (a common American practice because most Americans have become accustomed to
an early dinner hour, which often occurs too close to performance
time). Many Italian and French singers eat lightly several hours
before performance time, then more heartily afterward (partly
because they are usually accustomed to a late dinner hour), while
Germans, who are prone to use techniques of *Bauchaussenstütze*

(distended abdominal "support"), often eat heartily before performance (which takes place earlier in the German than in the Italian theater), so that there will be something to push against while singing. Whatever the technique of breath management, it is clear that a full stomach inhibits proper diaphragmatic descent, yet some reserve of energy must be present for the active physical work of singing. A nourishing, unsalted, modest meal, several hours before curtain time, seems sensible.

PHYSICAL EXERCISE AND SINGING

It has already been suggested that quietude might be advisable for the artist on a performance day. What about physical activity during the course of each training day? (Any nonperformance day is a training day for the serious singer, except for an occasional holiday break or for periods of illness.) Singers are quite familiar with the colleague (generally an aggressive baritone or dramatic mezzo) who is convinced that muscles make the singer: weight lifting, isometrics, handball, squash, perhaps tennis and swimming, and today, especially jogging, are thought to develop the body for the physical events of singing. Such activities are fine if they ensure excellent, general physical condition and if they are not strenuously carried out past the age when physical exercise should be cut back.

Even in the prime years, it is questionable that muscular development, including those muscles directly related to singing, need attain special dimensions for singing. Physical activities that produce flexibility and suppleness for light movement are best for the singer. Running outdoors in cold weather causes respiratory problems in some singers and should be avoided by them. In general, the singer should probably spend more time in the practice room and less time working out in the gymnasium or running in the park.

LONGEVITY AND THE VOICE

What can a singer do that will ensure vocal longevity? Longevity in singing is difficult to predict. One would like to think that a fine vocal technique would be the answer to that question. Then one recalls the ancient tenor who always sang out of the corner of his mouth and who pushed his voice to what seemed the ultimate limit, but who nevertheless continued to sing publicly until after age 70, while a much-admired "technician" was finished at 40. What can it mean? It means that in singing, as in all of life, control is not always in our hands.

There are certain aspects of aging in the vocal mechanism that can be mitigated. There is no way we can directly control the process of gradual ossification of cartilage (which begins the day we are born; studies indicate that certain kinds of flexibility in laryngeal cartilage have already largely disappeared by the thirtieth year of life), but constant exercising of the "voice machine" may retard the process of aging, delaying at least some of the ravages of time. Just as the body of Martha Graham at age 70 bore little relationship to the normal grandmotherly body of that age, the singer's larynx need not mirror that of the normal "non-athletic" speech mechanism. The aging singer who has the incentive to get up in the morning and sing through the regimen of vocal technique, along the lines indicated in this book, will certainly continue to sing longer than if no serious attempt is made to keep the instrument flexible and in performance condition.

Even in cases where singers, caught up by problems of teaching or career, have allowed the daily regimen to lapse, the body will respond by recovering forgotten skills, if once again recalled to them. No one can be guaranteed that at age 67 he or she will possess the same relative degree of singing skill demonstrated by Gigli or Schipa (and if recordings are reliable, by De Luca) at that age, but there is absolute assurance that if one keeps the voice going, daily, it will reward one, whereas inactivity will produce nothing but silence.

THE OPTIMISTIC PERFORMER

There are those who would transfer the art of singing out of the physical world into the realm of the mind. Mental attitude, we are told, determines everything in singing. A number of the pages of this book have been devoted to describing the physiological and acoustical processes that produce the optimum vocal timbre and control the technical aspects of singing; these processes supply the means through which artistic communication can be presented. However, no matter what the technical orientation or level of skill, a pessimistic singer is not a successful singer; mental attitude can make or break a career. The singer who has acquired free physical responses, who has digested the poem, the dramatic situation, and the musical idiom, and who feels compelled to express personal reactions through the amalgamation of body, word, and imagination, should enter confidently into the act of performance, believing in its rightness.

Laryngeal Structure and Function

The complex human respiratory–phonatory mechanism evolved from the need to protect the upper air passages of the respiratory system during the essential exchange of metabolic gas—a biological function. Phonation arose as a secondary, specialized activity, as the result of certain gains and losses accompanying physiological changes within the vocal tract. According to Negus (1949, p. 194), the human larynx, as a result of the process of evolution, is uniquely suited to the demands of speech and song:

> There is no doubt that a simple larynx, such as that of the cat tribe, would be sufficient for the needs of Man in mere speech; his more highly evolved organ, with its secondary valvular fold (usually called the vocal cord or vocal fold), is of advantage for purposes of song because of its greater flexibility and is of value in allowing modulation of the speaking voice.
>
> The vocal tones of Man are of a more mellow quality than those of a Gibbon or a Chimpanzee, because the vocal cords have less sharp edges; this change to a less efficient type of valve is consequent upon the abandonment of a purely arboreal existence, as the complete valvular closure of Lemurs, Monkeys and Apes is not required.

Although humans are ill-suited to an arboreal existence and are at a distinct disadvantage in running when pitted against the antelope and the horse (partly because humans cannot open the glottis as widely), the relative shortness of the human arytenoid cartilages and the length of the human vocal folds (not to mention the atrophied condition of the human epiglottis) give humans certain advantages in phonation. Negus (1949, p. 194) offers comfort for any apparent loss to humans through the evolutionary process by remarking that the relatively slow intake of extra air so necessary for rapid running and climbing now lacking in humans is compensated for by the superior intelligence that results in general predominance. It would appear to be a fair trade-off.

Zemlin (1981, p. 127) suggests that as primates, we view the principal nonbiological function of the larynx to be sound production. He modifies the viewpoint that sound production is not biological, reminding:

> Because speech is an integral part of human behavior, however, the notion that it is nonbiological may be open to criticism. It is largely through speech that we are able to communicate with others and to

make known our wants and needs. Indeed, speech is so much a part
of human behavior, it might well be considered a "second order"
biological function. Regardless of the stand one may take, there is
no debating that the larynx functions as a sound generator only
when it is not fulfilling the vital biological functions. . . .

Complementing the earlier views of Negus, Zemlin continues:

The human larynx is especially well-equipped for sound production.
The vocal folds are long, smoothly rounded bands of muscle tissue
which may be lengthened and shortened, tensed and relaxed, and
abducted and adducted. In addition, there is good evidence that the
tension of the vocal folds may be varied segmentally as well as
grossly. Compared with less well-developed animals, the human
arytenoid cartilages are quite small with respect to the total length
of the valvular mechanism. This means that the muscular, vibrating
portion of the vocal fold is quite long and well suited for sound
production.

Singing is an extension of the nonbiological function (or the "second
order" function) of the larynx. At least a rudimentary understanding of the
physiology of the larynx is essential in determining functional efficiency in
singing. Kenyon (1922, p. 428) has suggested that the physiological larynx
should be defined as the entire mechanism on which vocal fold movement
depends. Not only is the laryngeal box suspended, but the box is movable
only as part of the total mechanism that moves the hyoid bone; this mechanism includes the base of the tongue, the floor of the mouth, and the lower
jaw.

The structure and function of the larynx provide a logical starting point
for even a brief examination of the mechanics of the instrument of voicing.

CARTILAGINOUS STRUCTURE OF THE LARYNX

The larynx is situated at the top of the trachea, occupying a somewhat central position in the respiratory tract that extends from the nose and lips to
the bronchioles in the lungs (see Figure 2.1). The cartilaginous framework of
the larynx is made up of a total of nine cartilages: three single (unpaired)
cartilages, and three paired cartilages of lesser dimension, all connected by
ligaments and membranes. The cartilages are subject to movement by a
number of muscles (see Figures A1.1 and A1.2).

The Single or Unpaired Laryngeal Cartilages

The shield-shaped *thyroid cartilage* is the largest of the laryngeal cartilages,
often quite prominent in males. The laryngeal prominence or "Adam's apple"
(pomum Adami) is formed by the laminae of the thyroid cartilage (see Figure A1.1a), which join in front and diverge like the covers of a slightly

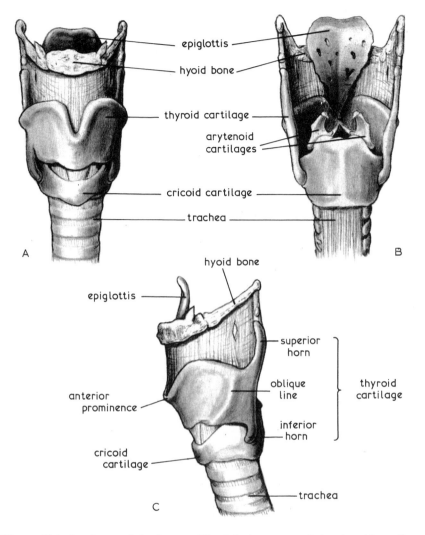

Figure A1.1. Cartilages of the larynx. (The inferior cornu of the thyroid cartilage articulates with the cricoid cartilage. This synovial joint permits a forward or backward rocking movement.) (From Meribeth Bunch, *Dynamics of the Singing Voice*, 1982. New York: Springer-Verlag. By permission.)

opened book. At the back (posteriorly) of the thyroid cartilage are located, on each side, an upper and a lower horn (see Figures A1.1 and A1.2); each upper horn (superior cornu) is attached to the hyoid bone; the lower horn (inferior cornu) extends downward posteriorly over the side of the cricoid cartilage, articulating with the cricoid by means of a facet on the surface of the tip of each horn (see Figures A1.1c and A1.2c).

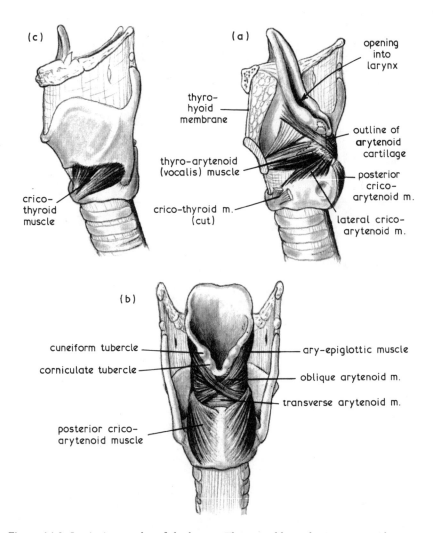

Figure A1.2. Intrinsic muscles of the larynx. The paired lateral cricoarytenoids (a) are attached to the lateral and superior portions of the cricoid cartilage, and the tips of the vocal processes of the arytenoid cartilages. The interarytenoid muscle (b) is attached to the posterior surface of both arytenoid cartilages. The cricothyroid muscle (c) is paired and attached to the anterior portion of the cricoid cartilage and the inferior horn and inner and outer edges of the lower border of the thyroid cartilage. The paired thyroarytenoid (a) muscle consists of two parts: the internal thyroarytenoid or vocalis, which forms the body of the vocal fold, and the external thyroarytenoid, which is lateral to the vocal fold and the vestibular fold; often some of its fibers are found in the vestibular fold. The posterior cricoarytenoid (b) is paired, and attached to the posterior portion of the cricoid lamina and the posterior surface of the muscular process of each arytenoid. (From Meribeth Bunch, *Dynamics of the Singing Voice*, 1982. New York: Springer-Verlag. By permission.)

Located at the top of the trachea, the *cricoid cartilage,* the lowest of the three single unpaired cartilages of the larynx, has a shape suggesting a signet ring with the seal portion located posteriorly and the arch anteriorly; it forms the lower part of the front and side walls of the larynx and much of its posterior wall (see Figures A1.1 and A1.2). On each side of the arch, small oval facets provide articulation with the lower horn (inferior cornu) of the thyroid cartilage. Shallow depressions mark the origin of the posterior cricoarytenoid muscles. The cricoid cartilage is attached anteriorly and laterally to the cricothyroid muscles (see Figures A1.1 and A1.2) and posteriorly to the inferior constrictor of the pharynx.

A third single cartilage, the *epiglottis* (see Figures A1.1a,b,c), has frequently been described as having the shape of a bicycle seat, or a leaf, with the broad end swinging upward and hanging free; the narrow inferior portion of the epiglottis is attached to the thyroid cartilage by ligaments, and to the arytenoid cartilages by the aryepiglottic folds.

The Paired Laryngeal Cartilages

Of the three sets of paired cartilages of the larynx, the *arytenoids,* to which are attached the vocal ligaments and the internal muscles of the larynx (see Figures 1.1 and A1.1), are the most important. Each arytenoid cartilage is pyramidal in shape, with three surfaces, a base, and an apex (see Figures A1.1a and A1.1b). The base of each arytenoid cartilage is concave, presenting a smooth surface for articulation with the cricoid cartilage, and each of these paired arytenoid cartilages is located on top of the posterior laminae of the cricoid cartilage. Projecting laterally, the rounded muscular processes afford insertion for the posterior cricoarytenoid muscles in back (see Figure A1.2a) and to the lateral cricoarytenoid muscles in front (see Figure A1.2a). The horizontal transverse arytenoid is a single muscle that extends from one arytenoid cartilage to the other and covers the posterior border of each arytenoid cartilage. The oblique arytenoid muscle pair crisscrosses the transverse arytenoid muscle from the base of one arytenoid cartilage to the apex of the opposite arytenoid cartilage in an X-like fashion (see Figure A1.2b). These muscles, the single horizontal transverse, and the oblique pair, are sometimes described as two parts of the same muscle—the arytenoid muscle. The pointed vocal processes of the arytenoid cartilages project forward, providing attachment for the vocal ligaments (see Figures 1.1 and A1.2a).

Through its backward and medial curvature, the apex of each arytenoid cartilage articulates with a very small conical elastic cartilage, the *corniculate cartilage of Santorini.*

The *cuneiform cartilages of Wrisberg* are two small paired elastic cartilages that support the aryepiglottic fold. Vennard (1967, p. 53) gives a colorful description of their function: "Stiffening these [aryepiglottic] folds, like whalebone in the collar of a woman's dress, are the cartilages of Wrisberg."

In addition to these three cartilage pairs, *triticeal cartilages* (small grain-like, cartilaginous lumps) are located in ligaments that suspend the thyroid cartilage from the hyoid bone. Vennard (1967, p. 53) points out that the cuneiform cartilages of Wrisberg and the triticeal cartilages are vestigial in humans.

LIGAMENTS AND MEMBRANES OF THE LARYNX

The laryngeal cartilages are joined to adjacent structures by a number of ligamentous membranes.

A broad sheet of membrane, the *hyothyroid membrane* (also called the *thyrohyoid membrane*) (see Figures 4.8 and 4.9) arises along the superior border of the thyroid cartilage and attaches to the superior horns of the thyroid cartilage; the hyothyroid membrane connects to the posterior surface of the hyoid bone and to the greater horns *(superior cornua)* of the hyoid bone (see Figure A1.3). The thicker middle portion of the membrane is known as the *middle hyothyroid ligament* (also *median thyrohyoid ligament*). The posterior borders of the hyothyroid membrane connect the tips of the superior horns of the thyroid cartilage to the lower ends of the horns of the hyoid bone, and are termed *lateral hyothyroid ligaments*. The triticeal cartilages are imbedded in these ligaments.

The *cricotracheal ligament* connects the inferior border of the cricoid cartilage with the first tracheal ring.

The large elastic membrane of the larynx (covered on its inner surface by mucous membrane) consists of a nearly continuous broad sheet of tissue that contains elastic fibers. This membrane has been variously described anatomically, but generally as two separate membranes or elastic ligaments. The upper, less well-defined part of this broad membrane is sometimes designated as the *quadrangular membrane*, terminology that describes its shape (see Figure A1.3). The lower anterior portion of the membrane is well defined, consisting of paired lateral sections that form the *conus elasticus* (in some literature called the *cricovocal membrane*). The conus elasticus connects the thyroid, the cricoid, and the arytenoid cartilages. Zemlin (1981, pp. 143–144) says:

> A frontal section through a larynx . . . reveals the cavity below the vocal folds to be funnel- or cone-shaped. This explains the term *conus elasticus*. . . . It is actually a connective tissue lining of the larynx. Although it is a continuous sheet of membrane which connects the thyroid, cricoid, and arytenoid cartilages with one another, it is commonly divided (for descriptive purposes) into an *anterior* or *medial cricothyroid ligament* and two *lateral cricothyroid membranes*. Together they constitute the conus elasticus, which extends from the superior border of the arch and lamina of the cricoid cartilage to the upper limit of the true vocal folds. . . .

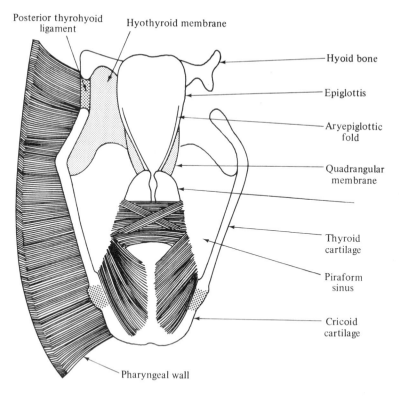

Figure A1.3. Posterior view of the larynx in two levels of dissection. (From *Normal Aspects of Speech, Hearing, and Language*, ed. by Fred. D. Minifie, Thomas J. Hixon, and Frederick Williams, 1973. Englewood Cliffs, NJ: Prentice-Hall, Inc. By permission.)

Appelman (1967, pp. 47–48) succinctly details the structure and function of the conus elasticus and the cricothyroid membrane:

> The conus is slit along its upper edge, and the upper borders of the slit form the vocal ligament. . . . The posterior and superior portion of the slits are attached to the base of the vocal process of each arytenoid. The arytenoids in their gliding articulations open and close the slit (the glottis). The anterior portion of the cone forms the cricothyroid membrane. The conus elasticus is covered with muscle and tissue, which are loosely attached to it. As the thyroarytenoid muscle contracts the conus becomes firm. . . .

Several additional ligaments should be mentioned, at least in passing, as forming part of the complex laryngeal mechanism:

- The *thyroepiglottic ligaments* connect the epiglottis and the thyroid cartilage.

- The *hyoepiglottic ligament* is an unpaired ligament that connects the epiglottis to the superior border of the hyoid bone.
- The *medial cricothyroid ligament* connects the cricoid and thyroid cartilages.
- The *posterior* and *lateral ceratocricoid ligament* pairs connect the cricoid and thyroid cartilages.
- The *cricoarytenoid ligaments* serve as a connecting link between the arytenoid and the cricoid cartilages.
- The *corniculate pharyngeal ligaments* connect the corniculate cartilages to the cricoid cartilage at the pharyngeal wall.
- The *aryepiglottic folds* extend from the epiglottis to the apexes of the arytenoids, and they form the lateral boundaries of the vestibule of the larynx.

THE INTERIOR OF THE LARYNX

The laryngeal cavity is divided into three compartments by two pairs of folds that extend from front to back on each side: the false cords (the vestibular folds) above, and the true vocal folds below (see Figure A1.4). The superior compartment of the laryngeal cavity is known as the *vestibule of the larynx,* and extends from the pharyngeal opening of the larynx *(aditus laryngis)* to the vestibular folds. This aperture is bounded anteriorly by the upper part of the epiglottis, posteriorly by mucous membrane that stretches between the arytenoids, and laterally by the aryepiglottic folds (see Figure A1.5). The *pyriform* (also *piriform*) sinus is a deep depression lateral to the aditus laryngis (see Figures A1.3, and A1.4), the upper aperture of the larynx that leads to the pharynx. The middle compartment of the cavity of the larynx consists of the laryngeal ventricles. The *rima glottidis* is the rim formed by the true vocal folds (see Figure A1.5). The space between the ligamentous portions of the rima glottidis is known as the *glottis vocalis;* the space between the cartilaginous portions, between the arytenoid cartilages, is the *glottis respiratoria.* (The *glottis,* of course, is the space between the true vocal folds.)

MUSCLES OF THE LARYNX AND THEIR FUNCTION

Muscle function is described by indicating points of muscle origin and muscle insertion. (A muscle has its origin in the relatively fixed framework of the body; the opposite end of the muscle inserts in the bone or cartilage which it moves.) The intrinsic laryngeal muscles have both their origin and their insertion within the larynx, except for the cricothyroids, which may be considered both intrinsic and extrinsic laryngeal muscles (Zenker, 1964b, p. 20).

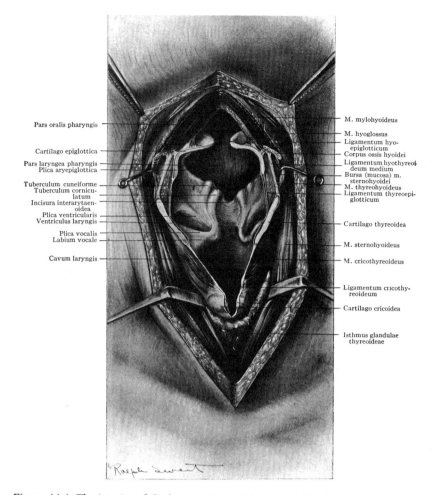

Pars oralis pharyngis

Cartilago epiglottica

Pars laryngea pharyngis
Plica aryepiglottica

Tuberculum cuneiforme
Tuberculum cornicu-
latum
Incisura interarytaen-
oidea
Plica ventricularis
Ventriculus laryngis

Plica vocalis
Labium vocale

Cavum laryngis

M. mylohyoideus

M. hyoglossus
Ligamentum hyo-
epiglotticum
Corpus ossis hyoidei
Ligamentum hyothyreoi-
deum medium
Bursa (mucosa) m.
sternohyoidei
M. thyreohyoideus
Ligamentum thyreoepi-
glotticum

Cartilago thyreoidea

M. sternohyoideus

M. cricothyreoideus

Ligamentum cricothy-
reoideum

Cartilago cricoidea

Isthmus glandulae
thyreoideae

Figure A1.4. The interior of the larynx. (From C. Latimer Callander, *Surgical Anatomy*, 1948, 2d ed. Philadelphia: W. B. Saunders Company. By permission.)

The extrinsic muscles have at least one attachment outside the larynx; they offer the larynx structural support and often help fix it in position.

Extrinsic Muscles

Suprahyoid Muscles (Laryngeal Elevators). The suprahyoid muscles raise the larynx.

The *digastric muscle* has its origin in two locations: the posterior belly from the temporal bone at the mastoid notch; the anterior belly from the fossa of the mandible (see Figure A1.6). Both parts of this paired muscle are

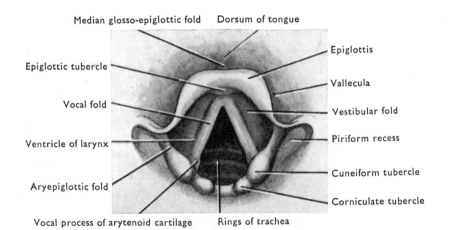

Median glosso-epiglottic fold   Dorsum of tongue

Epiglottic tubercle

Vocal fold

Ventricle of larynx

Aryepiglottic fold

Vocal process of arytenoid cartilage   Rings of trachea

Epiglottis

Vallecula

Vestibular fold

Piriform recess

Cuneiform tubercle

Corniculate tubercle

Figure A1.5. Laryngoscopic view of the cavity of the larynx during moderate inspiration. The rima glottidis is widely open. (From *Cunningham's Manual of Practical Anatomy*, 13th ed., Vol. 3, ed. by G. J. Romanes, 1967. London: Oxford University Press. By permission.)

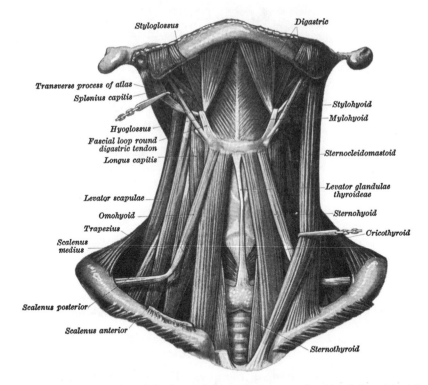

Styloglossus

Digastric

Transverse process of atlas

Splenius capitis

Hyoglossus

Fascial loop round digastric tendon

Longus capitis

Levator scapulae

Omohyoid

Trapezius

Scalenus medius

Scalenus posterior

Scalenus anterior

Stylohyoid

Mylohyoid

Sternocleidomastoid

Levator glandulae thyroideae

Sternohyoid

Cricothyroid

Sternothyroid

Figure A1.6. The muscles of the front of the neck. On the right side of the subject the sternocleidomastoid muscle has been removed. In this subject, the origin of the scalenus medius extended up to the transverse process of the atlas. (From *Gray's Anatomy*, 36th ed., ed. by Peter L. Williams and Roger Warwick, 1980. Edinburgh: Churchill Livingstone. By permission.)

inserted into an intermediate tendon, which in turn is attached by a fibrous loop to the hyoid bone. The digastric muscle raises the hyoid bone as well as the base of the tongue, and steadies the hyoid bone. If the hyoid bone is in a fixed position, the digastric assists in depressing the mandible.

The *stylohyoid muscle* has its origin at the posterior border of the styloid process of the temporal bone (see Figures 4.8, and A1.6). The stylohyoid is inserted at the junction of the hyoid bone with the greater cornu, immediately above the omohyoid muscle. Both the hyoid bone and the base of the tongue are elevated by the stylohyoid muscle.

The *mylohyoid muscle* takes its origin along the mylohyoid line, which extends from the mandibular symphysis to the last molar. This muscle is inserted into the median raphé from the chin to the hyoid bone; posterior fibers are attached to the body of the hyoid bone (see Figure 4.9). When the hyoid bone is fixed, the mylohyoid depresses the mandible; the mylohyoid muscle elevates the hyoid bone and the base of the tongue, and raises the floor of the mouth.

The *geniohyoid muscle* originates at the lower genial tubercle on the back of the mandibular symphysis, insertion occurring at the anterior surface of the body of the hyoid bone (see Figures 4.7, 4.8, and 4.9). The geniohyoid elevates the hyoid bone and the tongue.

Two additional muscles act as supplementary laryngeal elevators, when called on, although they are intrinsic tongue muscles. The *genioglossus muscle* (see Figure 4.8) arises from the symphysis of the mandible, above the geniohyoid. The lower fibers of the genioglossus are inserted into the hyoid bone, middle fibers are inserted along the inferior surface of the tongue, and insertion of superior fibers occurs at the tip of the tongue. In contraction, the genioglossus muscle raises the hyoid bone and moves it forward, or it lifts both the hyoid and the larynx, or it draws the tongue downward to the hyoid bone. The middle fibers of the genioglossus also protrude the tongue.

The *hyoglossus muscle* has its origin in the sides and body of the greater horn of the hyoid bone. The hyoglossus inserts into the sides and the back of the tongue, and interlaces with fibers of the *styloglossus* and the *longitudinalis inferior* muscle of the tongue. The *hyoglossus* muscle draws down the sides of the tongue; together with the genioglossus, the hyoglossus depresses the tongue (see Figures 4.8, 4.9, and A1.6).

Infrahyoid Muscles (Laryngeal Depressors). The infrahyoid muscles lower the larynx.

The *sternohyoid muscle* (see Figure A1.6) takes its origin from the posterior surface of the manubrium of the sternum, from the posterior of the sternoclavicular ligament, and from the medial end of the clavicle. This muscle inserts into the lower border of the hyoid bone, and depresses the larynx and the hyoid bone; when the hyoid bone is in a fixed position, the sternohyoid muscle assists in raising the sternum.

The *sternothyroid muscle* arises from the posterior surface of the manubrium of the sternum and from the edge of the first costal cartilage. The

muscle inserts along the oblique line of the thyroid lamina and lowers the
larynx by pulling the thyroid cartilage downward. The sternothyroid tilts the
thyroid cartilage down and forward, thereby enlarging the pharynx (see
Figure A1.6).

The *omohyoid muscle* has an inferior and a superior belly, the first arising from the upper border of the scapula and the suprascapular ligament,
the second extending upward from a tendon under the sternocleidomastoid
muscles. These bellies insert into the inferior border of the body of the hyoid
bone. In contracting, the omohyoid muscle depresses the hyoid bone. The
hyoid bone is steadied by the omohyoid. The omohyoid can retract and
depress the larynx (see Figure A1.6).

The *thyrohyoid muscle* appears to be an extension of the sternothyroid,
originating from the posterior surfaces of the oblique line of the laminae of the
thyroid cartilage. The thyrohyoid has its insertion in the lower border of the
hyoid bone, and in the greater horn. When the thyroid cartilage is fixed, the
thyrohyoid depresses the hyoid bone and the larynx. When the hyoid bone is
fixed, the thyrohyoid muscle elevates the thyroid cartilage.

Intrinsic Muscles

Laryngeal muscles function as abductors (openers), adductors (closers), tensors, and relaxers of the vocal folds. The arytenoids are separated by the
abductor muscles at inspiration, and the abductors are opposed by the
adductors, which close the glottis for phonatory function and for protection.
The vocal folds are tightened and elongated by the glottal tensors. The tensor muscles are opposed by the relaxers, which shorten the vocal folds.

The *thyroarytenoid muscle* (see Figure A1.2a) is a complex paired muscle of two parts: the *thyromuscularis* (also *external thyroarytenoid*) and the
thyrovocalis (also *internal thyroarytenoid,* or simply *vocalis*). The *thyromuscularis* is bound by and attaches to the lamina of the thyroid cartilage. Its
fibers have their origin in the lower half of the thyroid cartilage at the angle,
and are inserted into the anterolateral surface and the muscular processes
of the arytenoid cartilages.

The *internal thyroarytenoid (vocalis)* has its origin in the posterior surface of the angle of the thyroid cartilage and inserts into the vocal processes
and the lateral surfaces of the arytenoids. The *vocalis* muscle (see Figure A1.2a) forms the medial portion of the complex paired thyroarytenoid
muscle, and provides the main mass of each vocal fold. Vocalis muscle fibers adjoin the vocal ligaments and attach to the inferior and lateral surfaces
of the vocal ligaments. Appelman (1967, p. 46) states:

> Some of the fibers of the vocalis muscle are short and do not extend
> to the vocal process of each arytenoid cartilage. The fibers, attached
> to the vocal ligament and conus elasticus . . . perform the refined
> tasks of controlling the conformation of the vocal fold in its various
> states of thickness and thinness during changes in pitch.

Appelman (1967, p. 57) further describes possible actions of the thyro-arytenoid muscles:

1. Relax and shorten the vocal ligament by drawing the arytenoids towards the thyroid cartilage for the singing of low pitches.
2. Draw the vocal processes of the arytenoids downward and inward, approximating the vocal folds.
3. Pull the vocal folds apart by their lateral contraction.
4. Become stabilized throughout their active length and, thereby, aid in raising the pitch of the phonated sound.
5. Vary both the length and the thickness of the vibrating segment.
6. Render a portion of the vocal fold tense while the remainder is relaxed.

The Muscles of Adduction

The muscles of adduction bring the vocal folds together.

The *transverse arytenoid* is a single muscle that assists in closing the glottis by approximating the arytenoid cartilages. Fibers of the transverse arytenoid muscle have their origin in the lateral and posterior surface of an arytenoid cartilage and insert into corresponding surfaces of the opposite arytenoid (see Figures 1.1 and A1.2b).

The paired *oblique arytenoid* muscle assists in closing the glottis by approximating the arytenoid cartilages (see Figure 1.1). Each of these muscles originates in the posterior surface of the muscular process of an arytenoid and inserts into the apex of the opposite muscular process (see Figure A1.2b).

The *lateral cricoarytenoid* muscles approximate the vocal processes by rotating the arytenoid cartilages inward. Arising from the upper lateral part of the cricoid cartilage, this fan-shaped muscle inserts on the muscular process of each arytenoid (see Figure A1.2a,b). Zemlin (1981, pp. 163–164) states:

> The lateral cricoarytenoid muscle is an important glottal adductor that may also function as a glottal relaxor . . . both functions are important for voice production. It is a slightly fan-shaped muscle, located deep to the thyroid cartilage in the anterolateral wall of the larynx. The medial surface of this muscle lies in direct contact with the conus elasticus, and . . . from an anatomical standpoint it really seems to be an extension of the muscle mass which makes up the vocal fold (cricothyroarytenoid).

The *posterior cricoarytenoid* (also *dorsal cricoarytenoid,* or simply—especially among teachers of singing who use functional language—*posticus*)

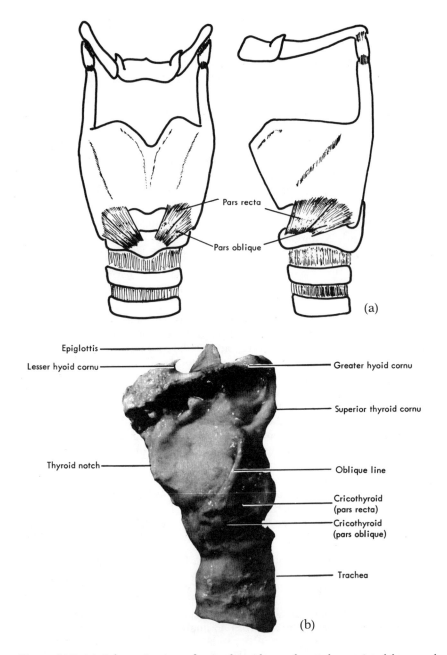

Figure A1.7. (a) Schematic view of cricothyroid muscles and associated laryngeal structures; (b) photograph of cricothyroid and associated laryngeal structures. (From W. R. Zemlin, *Speech and Hearing Science*, 2d ed., 1981. Englewood, NJ: Prentice-Hall, Inc. By permission.)

has its origin on the posterior surface of the cricoid cartilage; its fibers insert into the muscular process of the arytenoid cartilage (see Figure A1.2b). The superior fibers of the posterior cricoarytenoid rotate the arytenoids, so that the vocal processes are pulled apart and the glottis opened.

The Muscles of Elongation

The *cricothyroid* muscle (see Figure A1.2c) elongates and tenses the vocal folds. The cricothyroid consists of two parts: the *pars recta* and the *pars obliqua* (see Figure A1.7). These muscles have a common origin in the lateral surfaces of the cricoid cartilage. The lower, oblique fibers insert into the anterior margin of each lower horn (inferior cornu) of the thyroid cartilage, the upper pars recta fibers insert into the inferior border of each lamina of the thyroid cartilage. The contraction of the cricothyroid muscle causes the thyroid cartilage to tip forward at its articulation with the cricoid cartilage, thus stretching and lengthening the vocal ligament that extends from the angle of the thyroid cartilage to the arytenoid cartilage (see Figure A1.8).

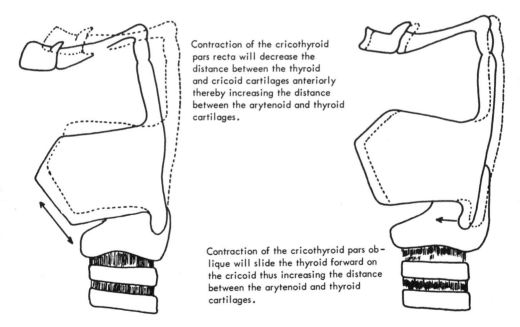

Contraction of the cricothyroid pars recta will decrease the distance between the thyroid and cricoid cartilages anteriorly thereby increasing the distance between the arytenoid and thyroid cartilages.

Contraction of the cricothyroid pars oblique will slide the thyroid forward on the cricoid thus increasing the distance between the arytenoid and thyroid cartilages.

Figure A1.8. Means by which the cricothyroid may function to tense the vocal folds. (From W. R. Zemlin, *Speech and Hearing Science*, 2d. ed., 1981. Englewood Cliffs, NJ: Prentice-Hall, Inc. By permission.)

SUMMARY OF INTRINSIC LARYNGEAL ACTION

The vocalis muscles are largely responsible for determining the degree of vocal fold tension and approximation in phonation. Although the arytenoids move the folds to the median position, the vocalis muscles finally dictate the shape of the glottis during phonation. The glottal opening is shaped in response to the adduction actions of the lateral cricoarytenoids and the transverse and oblique arytenoids, to the abducting action of the posterior cricoarytenoids, and to the stretching actions (longitudinal pull) of the cricothyroids.

However, the mechanics of muscle motion do not alone explain the intricate, subtle coordination required for singing. The state of laryngeal tissue and its response to air movement are major factors in laryngeal action. The vocal folds are made up of soft tissue which consists of mucous membrane, submucosal layer, the elastic vocal ligament, and the vocalis muscle (Titze, 1981a, p. 245).

Hirano (1977, p. 20) suggests that the vocal folds be considered as a tripartite structure: (1) body; (2) cover; and (3) a transitional layer between the body and the cover layers (see Figure A1.9).

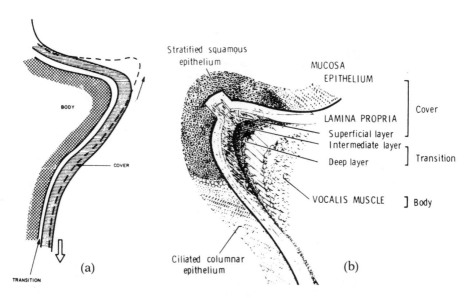

Figure A1.9. (a) Schematic cross-section of vocal fold showing body, transition, and cover. The dashed line and upper arrow show the kind of sliding motion that is postulated to occur between cover and body. The possibility of a vertical force on the cover is indicated by the arrow at the bottom. (b) A frontal section of a human vocal fold at the midpoint of the membranous portion, schematically presented. (From *Vocal Fold Physiology*, ed. by Kenneth N. Stevens and Minoru Hirano, 1981. Tokyo: Tokyo University Press. By permission.)

These tissues of the vocal folds have elastic properties that may be passive or active. Titze (1981g, pp. 30–31) presents a clear description of the importance of the elastic properties of the vocal folds:

> Vocal fold length ... governs the effective stiffness of the ligamental and membranous layers of the vocal folds. As the folds are shortened, the passive layers become more lax. But the length is in turn controlled by the active tissues, i.e., the intrinsic laryngeal muscles. Their effective stiffness has a more complicated relationship with length. A contracted (shortened) muscle may actually be stiffer than the same muscle in its uncontracted state. Furthermore, if the muscle has an antagonist, large changes in effective stiffness may result with no change in length at all in the so-called isometric condition.

Titze goes on to say that a great deal of flexibility in fundamental frequency control is possible because the tissue may be passive or active:

> Consider the case where the cricothyroid muscle contracts and the vocalis is not active. The vocal folds will lengthen, the effective stiffness of all the vocal fold tissue layers will increase, and the fundamental frequency will increase. ... Next consider the case where the vocalis muscle contracts and the cricothyroid muscle remains inactive. The length will decrease, resulting in a decrease in the stiffness of the cover. But the stiffness of the body of the folds may in fact increase.

It is the differential control that is exercised over the various muscle groups, rather than a uniformity of action among them, which permits the singer to arrive at the fine dynamic muscle balances needed for rapid changes in range, dynamics, velocity, sostenuto, and vocal coloration. That such muscle coordination is possible in singing may be due to the fact that "the vocalis muscle and cricothyroid muscle are innervated separately, the former by the recurrent laryngeal nerve and the latter by the superior laryngeal nerve" (Titze, 1981g, pp. 30–31). On the other hand, both of these nerves are branches of the vagus nerve, and it is probably difficult to determine how significant this separate innervation may actually be.

Efficient phonation is largely dependent, then, on balanced interaction among the intrinsic laryngeal muscles and vocal-fold tissues in response to the demands of pitch, volume, and phonetic timbres, and to the application of appropriate subglottic pressure and airflow.

Sound waves that we hear are, of course, caused by vibrating resonator chambers, the result of air being set in motion by sharp taps. Ladefoged (1962a, pp. 88–89) explains that sound production occurs in the larynx as a result of air from the lungs passing between the vocal folds that have been approximated, setting up the sharp taps:

> The taps that set the air in the mouth and throat in vibration are due to the action of the vocal cords on the air which is being forced out of the lungs. The air in the lungs is compressed due to the action

of the respiratory muscles. When the vocal cords, which are actually small folds of muscle and cartilage in the larynx, are together, pressure is built up beneath them. If this pressure is big enough, the vocal cords may be forced apart and the lung air released. This sudden release of air under pressure acts like a sharp tap on the air in the vocal tract, which is accordingly set vibrating.

Waveforms are generated. "Each of these damped waves is produced by the vibrations of air in the vocal tract, which recur every time there is a pulse from the vocal cords" (Ladefoged, 1962a, p. 90). The number of vocal fold vibrations and puffs of air per second determines the fundamental frequency of the sound (for example, A_4=440 Hz).

Sound production is the result of the muscle activity just described and the filtering processes of the resonating chambers.

The Structure and Mechanics of the Breath Apparatus

THE THORACIC CAGE

The bony cage of the thorax is composed of sternum, ribs, and vertebrae (see Figure A2.1). The chief organs of respiration are housed and protected within the thoracic cage. The cage is somewhat cone-shaped, with the large end of the cone situated inferiorly.

Because the thorax is lightly covered in front and on the sides by relatively flat muscles, its topography makes it one of the areas of the body most easily subjected to surface observation. Certainly the physical action of the thorax during singing can be better viewed than can that of the laryngeal area, and can provide information to the voice teacher.

THE REGION OF THE STERNUM

The sternum (breastbone) lies in the upper middle of the thoracic cage and acts like the hub of a wheel in its structural relationship to the costae (ribs). The upper seven pairs of ribs are true or sternal ribs, in that they attach in front to the sternum. All twelve pairs complete the cage in back (see Figures A2.1 and A2.2). Each rib is bony, and, in the case of the upper seven pairs, is attached to the sternum by a short section of cartilage. These costal cartilages form the sternocostal joints.

What singing teachers often call the false ribs, the eighth, ninth, and tenth pairs, are merged with the sternum through the cartilage of the seventh pair, without being directly joined to the sternum (see Figures A2.1 and A2.2.) This rib convergence defines a triangular area just below the sternum that is of interest to many singers and teachers of singing. An additional two pairs of ribs, the eleventh and twelfth (often erroneously termed "floating ribs") are shorter and are not joined to the sternum. They are attached posteriorly to the spinal vertebrae (see Figure A2.2).

If one raises the sternum, the entire region of the thorax is influenced by that action. Alternately, if the sternum is dropped, the relationship of the ribs to the organs of respiration housed within the thorax changes. The positioning of the sternum, therefore, occupies a place of prime importance in systems of breath management in vocal instruction.

Because of the relationship of the sternocleidomastoid muscles to the supportive structure of the larynx (the sternocleidomastoid muscles do not, of course, directly affect the action of extrinsic laryngeal muscles), and

259

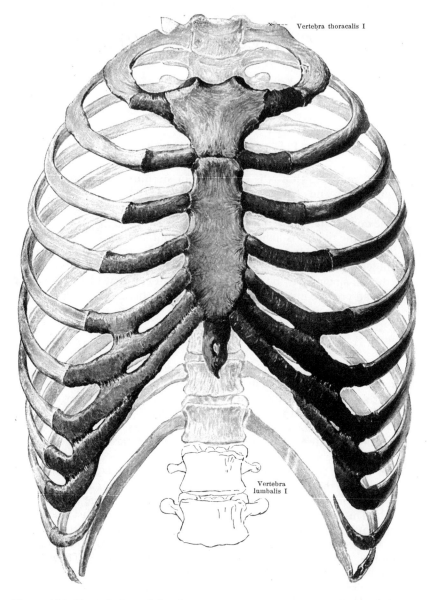

Figure A2.1. Frontal view of the thoracic cage. (From Werner Spalteholz, *Handatlas der Anatomie des Menschen*, 13th ed., Vol. 2, 1932. Leipzig: S. Hirzel-Verlag.)

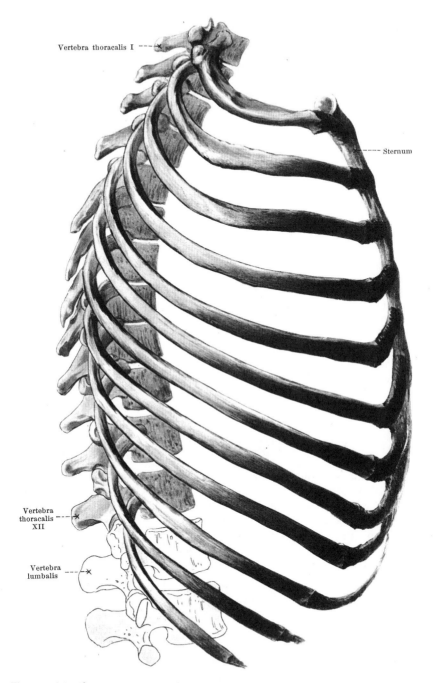

Figure A2.2. Thorax (sternum, ribs, vertebrae) from the right side. (From Werner Spalteholz, *Handatlas der Anatomie des Menschen*, 13th ed., Vol. 2, 1932. Leipzig: S. Hirzel-Verlag.)

because of the relation of the skeletal frame to the sternum and to sternal posture (either high or low), the sternocleidomastoid muscles can, to some degree, be considered supportive of the phonatory mechanism (see Figure A1.6). They play a role in the highly important external frame support of the singing instrument. Even the well-positioned sternum can be considered, to some extent, structurally supportive of the phonatory mechanism.

Significantly, in some techniques of singing sternal elevation is relatively high, while in other techniques a lowered sternum (producing radically different muscle relationships within the thorax and around the larynx) is considered desirable. The most favorable of these relationships can be determined only after a more complete examination of activity in the costal region is considered.

THE INTERCOSTAL MUSCLES

These muscles are divided into two groups: internal and external (see Figures 2.2 and 2.3). Opinion regarding actions of the intercostals is by no means unanimous. Several views are maintained: (1) both the internal and external intercostals are active in elevating the ribs: (2) the external intercostals elevate the ribs, and the internal intercostals depress the ribs; and (3) the intercartilaginous parts of the internals join with the externals in inspiration and both provide the elastic supports that prohibit the bulging out or the drawing inward of the intercostal spaces (*Gray's Anatomy*, 1980, p. 547). Campbell and Newsom Davis (1970a, pp. 170–171) suggest the most acceptable theory to be that the external intercostals and the intercartilaginous intercostals raise the ribs; the interosseus internal intercostals depress the ribs.

THE DIAPHRAGM

Many techniques of singing attempt conscious control over the diaphragm. Teachers of singing who urge diaphragmatic control may only be using such terminology loosely to indicate other possible muscular controls around the diaphragmatic region. The diaphragm is incapable of providing sensation regarding its precise movements or its exact position within the torso. It may play a completely different role in breath management from that assigned it by some teachers. Wyke (1974, p. 297) maintains that

> Contrary to the views of many professional teachers of singing . . . *the diaphragm is relaxed during the whole of the phonatory process associated with singing . . . except during each interphrase inspiration*, and therefore makes no contribution to the so-called "support of the voice." [Emphasis added]

Luchsinger and Arnold (1965, p. 149) express a similar viewpoint:

> The diaphragm is inactive during expiration, be it silent or phonic. Since it lacks proprioceptive sensation, the movements of the dia-

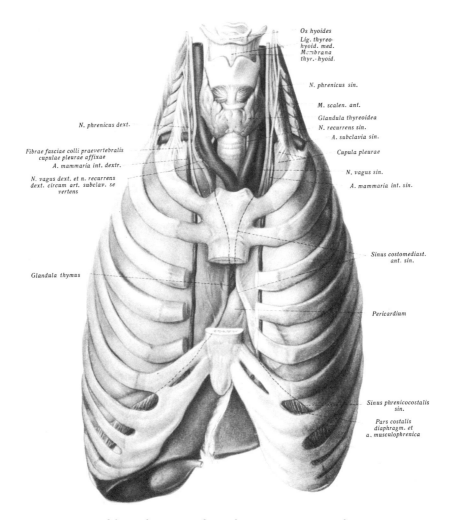

Figure A2.3. Hyoid bone, larynx, trachea, rib cage, sternum (partly cut away), peri-cardium. (From O. Schultze, *Topographische Anatomie*, 4th ed., ed. by Wilhelm Lubosch, 1935. Munich: J. F. Lehmanns Verlag. By permission, Springer-Verlag.)

phragm cannot be felt. Since it is extended horizontally between the lungs and intestines, the diaphragm cannot be seen from the out-side. What may be observed by external inspection is the action of the abdominal muscles. . . . It is nonsense when some naive voice teacher proudly taps his inflated chest, proclaiming, "Look at my diaphragm."

In a detailed study of the physiology of breathing, Bouhuys (1977, pp. 271–272) discusses the results of electromyographic (EMG) studies of the breath cycle, with attention to the relationship between the diaphragm and other muscle groups both in speech and in singing. Bouhuy's study is quoted here at some length because of its considerable significance for the interpretation of conflicting pedagogical viewpoints about the role of the diaphragm in singing:

> During speech, EMG recordings indicate inspiratory muscle activity (external intercostal muscles) at high lung volumes. As lung volume decreases, inspiratory muscle activity decreases, while that of the expiratory muscles (internal intercostals) increases. Even though considerable inspiratory force is required to produce soft tones at high lung volumes, EMG recordings suggest that the strongest inspiratory muscle, the diaphragm, does not contribute to this force. The diaphragm remains electrically silent, while the external intercostal muscles show marked EMG activity.... Fortunately, since the mechanical interaction between the intrapleural and intra-abdominal pressures regulates the position of the diaphragm, contraction of the diaphragm is not needed to regulate subglottic pressure.... The elasticity of the external abdominal wall provides the primary support for the viscera. The diaphragm is subject to an upward pull exerted by the negative intrapleural pressure. Hence, lung elastic recoil tends to pull the diaphragm and the abdominal viscera upward. This tendency is counteracted by the weight of the abdominal viscera, an opposing force which is greater the larger the hydrostatic pressure gradient, a pressure exerted uniformly and perpendicularly to all surfaces in the abdominal cavity. Hence, the opposing force increases with elevation of the diaphragm. A person who begins to sing a soft tone near TLC [total lung capacity] expands the rib cage by contracting inspiratory muscles and relaxing the abdominal muscles. Although the negative intrapleural pressure pulls the diaphragm upward, this force is checked by the weight of the abdominal contents, which tends to pull it downward. In this way, the weight of the abdominal viscera replaces active contraction of the diaphragm with a passive inspiratory force and makes possible the production of soft sung tones at high lung volumes while the diaphragm remains relaxed. Analysis of intra-abdominal (intragastric) and intrapleural pressures suggested that this maneuver required an elevated rib cage and relaxed abdominal muscles. Direct movements of rib cage and abdominal wall displacements during singing have confirmed this conclusion.

Spinal anesthesia may inhibit movement of the rib and abdominal muscles, yet the patient can breathe and exercise control over respiration through compensatory means. It would appear that some independence of diaphragm positioning is possible. However, excercises for "singing with the diaphragm," or for "supporting the voice with the diaphragm" are techniques for training the entire thoracic, diaphragmatic, abdominal complex. Watson and Hixon (1985, p. 120) comment that

> The singing folklore is rich in misconceptions concerning the transform between body biomechanics and artistic performance.... The

myth of singing from the diaphragm, for example, has persisted for about as long as has the history of vocal performance. . . . [M]yths are alive in even highly trained singers, one consequence being that subjects who sing in relatively similar manners can come to conceptualize their performances in dramatically different ways.

Until various methods of breath management for singing have been separately investigated by researchers, the question of how much direct control over the diaphragm can be achieved by the singer may remain unanswered. Radiographic research undertaken by Miller and Bianco (1985) tends to confirm that diaphragmatic movement during singing varies from one breath-management technique to another. Diaphragmatic ascent is considerably slower (and therefore more desirable) during the expiratory phases of the breath cycle when the *appoggio* technique is used.

The dome-shaped muscle called the diaphragm is a musculomembranous structure that divides the thoracic cavity from the abdominal cavity (*Gray's Anatomy*, 1980, pp. 549–550; see Figure A2.4.) The thoracic surface of the diaphragm forms the floor of the chest cavity and is in contact with the pleurae (membranes that surround the lungs) and the pericardium (the conical sac that encloses the heart and the root of the great blood vessels) (see Figure A2.3). The abdominal surface of the diaphragm is covered in part by the peritoneum (the membrane that lines the cavity of the abdomen). On inspiration, the diaphragm presses on the abdominal viscera through a downward and forward movement (see Figure A2.3). The abdomen, in response to that action, swells outward. When the limit of this descent is accomplished, the abdominal viscera serve as a fixated part for the central tendon, from which the ribs are elevated by muscle fibers. *Gray's Anatomy* (1980, p. 550) observes: "The central tendon, applied to the abdominal viscera, thus becomes a fixed point for the action of the diaphragm, the effect of which is to elevate the lower ribs and through them to push forward the body of the sternum and the upper ribs." The cone-shaped curve moves downward in this fashion, causing the lungs to expand. Luchsinger and Arnold (1964, p. 4) report that during subsequent relaxation, "The diaphragm reverts to its dome-shaped form, pushed upward by the contents of the abdominal cavity. The lungs are also pushed upward, expelling the air content as they are compressed." This mechanical action involves simultaneous movement in both abdomen and chest, serving to alter chest cavity volume and, subsequently, the volume of the lungs, all being the inevitable result of chest wall activity (see Figure A2.5). This movement is partially observable externally; if a singer places the hands at the bottom of the rib cage, the lateral outward movement of the lower ribs can be felt. This costal movement, although less complete and less obvious, also occurs with the upper ribs. The possibility of expansion, both at the flanks and at the level of the upper ribs, has proved a fertile field for various systems of rib action within several vocal pedagogies.

Such possibilities of flank and rib movement have also given rise to theories of essential differences in the breath management during singing for

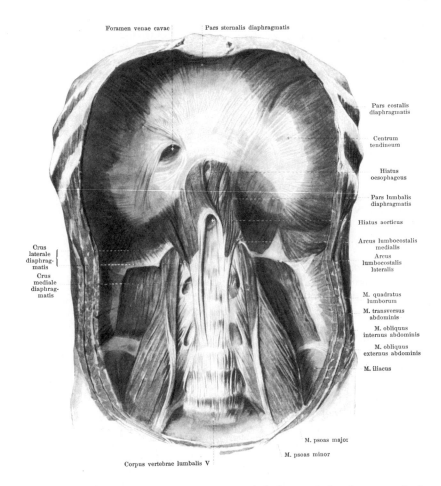

Figure A2.4. The diaphragm. (From Werner Spalteholz, *Handatlas der Anatomie des Menschen*, 13th ed., Vol. 2, 1932. Leipzig: S. Hirzel-Verlag.)

men and women, generally with exaggerated conclusions. Obviously, the conditions of pregnancy alter relationships within the musculature of the abdomen, and will affect the extent of diaphragmatic descent and rib expansion during the breath cycle; there will be greater reliance during pregnancy on lateral expansion. Although there are potential differences based on such sexually related physical functions, it is by no means the case that all females mystically develop an advance preference for upper pectoral respiration as opposed to predominantly abdominal respiration in the male. Yet that assumption continues to prevail, perhaps dating back to the period of tight lacing for the female singer, a subject that caught the attention of a number of singing teachers at the turn of the century (Browne and Behnke, 1884a, pp. 121–122).

It is true that some female singers are given to high-chest breathing, but the objective teacher of singing can attest to the large percentage of males who also are high-chest breathers. There would appear to be a correlation between upper pectoral respiration and livelihoods that involve limited physical exertion, regardless of the sex of the singer. When not engaged in effortful activity, most persons habitually breathe shallowly, regardless of their sex. Rather than to search for physiological reasons based on gender, one might better look to the cultural patterns that have historically been parceled out to the two sexes. It is highly doubtful that structural differences between the sexes produce greatly contrasting methods of breath management *in singing.*

THE LUNGS AND THE PLEURAE

The pleurae are two closed, independent sacs, each of which encloses an organ of respiration, a lung (see Figures A2.5 and A2.6). Each pleural cavity

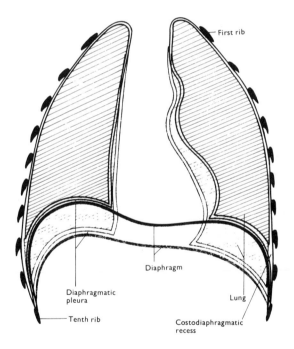

Figure A2.5. An outline drawing to show the change in shape of the thoracic contents resulting from contraction of the diaphragm alone. With diaphragmatic contraction, the lungs and mediastinal structures are elongated, and the lungs expand to fill the space vacated by the mediastinal structures and to enter the costodiaphragmatic recesses of the pleura. The movements which the ribs undergo in inspiration are not shown. (From *Cunningham's Manual of Practical Anatomy*, 14th ed., edited by G. J. Romanes, Vol. 2, 1977. Oxford: Oxford University Press. By permission.)

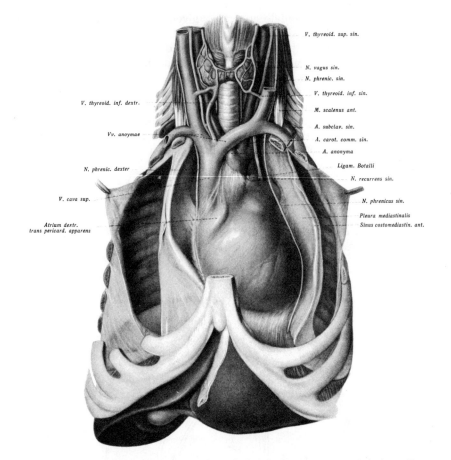

V. thyreoid. sup. sin.

N. vagus sin.
N. phrenic. sin.

V. thyreoid. inf. sin.

M. scalenus ant.

A. subclav. sin.

A. carot. comm. sin.

A. anonyma

Ligam. Botalli

N. recurrens sin.

N. phrenicus sin.

Pleura mediastinalis
Sinus costomediastin. ant.

V. thyreoid. inf. dextr.

Vv. anoymae

N. phrenic. dexter

V. cava sup.

Atrium dextr.
trans pericard. apparens

Figure A2.6. Interior view of the neck and the thorax. (From O. Schultze, *Topo-graphische Anatomie*, 4th ed., edited by Wilhelm Lubosch, 1935. Munich: J. F. Leh-manns Verlag. By permission Springer-Verlag.)

consists of two layers of serous membrane with a small amount of fluid between. Pressures within the pleural cavities contribute to the mechanics of breathing (Callander, 1948, pp. 241–243).

Each lung is attached to the middle mediastinum by its root (see Figure A2.6), but possesses considerable elasticity, and is capable of movement; an elastic property is characteristic of tissues of the lung and thorax (Comroe et al., 1968, p. 163):

> Like springs, these tissues must be stretched during inspiration by an external force (muscular effort); when the external force is removed, the tissues recoil to their resting position. . . . The greater the muscular force applied, the more the springs are stretched and the greater the volume change on inspiration.

The lung adapts itself to the wall of the chest cavity. Although the lungs are the most important organs of respiration, their movement is dependent on the action of the musculature around them. Lung volume is governed by the total action of the thoracic cage in which the lungs are housed.

The bronchi, right and left, arise from the bottom of the trachea, dividing repeatedly, with ramifications becoming thinner and smaller (see Figures 2.1, A2.7, and A2.8). Comroe and associates (1968, p. 162) describe the reaction of the tracheobronchial system during inspiration:

> If air is to flow into the alveoli [the smallest air cavities or cells in the lung] the alveolar pressure must be less than atmospheric during inspiration. Active contraction of the inspiratory muscles enlarges the thorax and further lowers intrathoracic pressure (normally subatmospheric, because the elastic lung tends to recoil inward, away from the thoracic cage). The decrease in intrathoracic pressure enlarges the alveoli, expands the alveolar gas and lowers the total alveolar gas pressure to less than atmospheric so that air flows into the alveoli.

The frequency and the depth of breathing for phonation are determined by the breath-energy requirements of the phrase. The respiratory muscles respond to this demand, and the healthy lung complies.

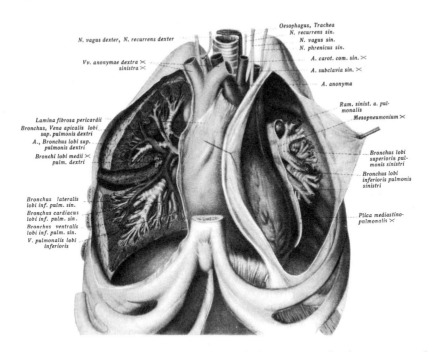

Figure A2.7. Organs of the thorax. (From O. Schultze, *Topographische Anatomie*, 4th ed., edited by Wilhelm Lubosch, 1935. Munich: J. F. Lehmanns Verlag. By permission, Springer-Verlag.)

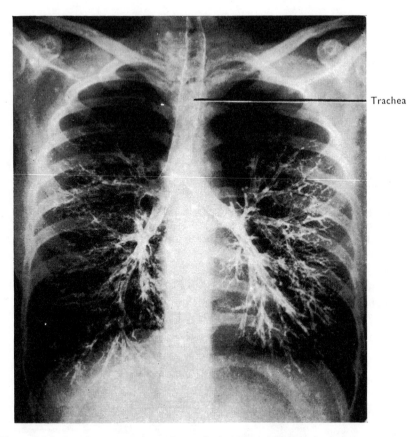

Trachea

Figure A2.8. An anteroposterior radiograph (bronchogram). The trachea and bronchi are outlined by the introduction of X-ray-opaque material. (From *Cunningham's Manual of Practical Anatomy*, 13th ed., edited by G. Romanes, Vol. 2, 1967. Oxford: Oxford University Press. By permission.)

MUSCLES OF THE NECK

Isolating individual parts of the respiratory–speech mechanism is a necessary but artificial device, a convenient way of looking at the functional cooperation that exists among them. Although neither the external muscles of the neck nor those muscles of the upper costal region that relate to the shoulder are usually included among the direct participants in the mechanics of phonation or of breath management, they contribute externally in a structural way to both activities. (They also play a compensatory functional role in clavicular breathing.)

The neck offers a connecting passage not only for the respiratory–phonatory mechanism, which extends from trunk to head, but for other muscular structures as well. The most visible of the neck muscles is the sternocleidomastoid pair, which provides essential postural support between head and torso. A sharp turn of the head to the side clearly reveals this strong paired muscle (see Figure A1.6). The name of the muscle (often truncated to sterno-mastoid) describes its location. It runs from the mastoidal area behind the ear down to the medial end of the clavicle, and to the sternum. The larynx and its related muscles are for the most part lodged between these two supportive muscular pillars.

A momentary digression will permit a quick look at the general anatomy of the neck region and help place the musculature of the neck in relation to other systems. In some necks with clearly defined muscular contours, a landmark is the thyroid gland, which lies against the laminae of the thyroid cartilage and the pharyngeal walls (see Figures A2.3 and A2.6). The thyroid gland is mentioned here because any change in the perception of its definition on the external surface of the throat during singing may be an indication of general throat tension.

If the throat were to be cut just across the thyrohyoid space, then the anterior jugular vein, the superior laryngeal nerve, the superior thyroid artery, the omohyoid, the thyrohyoid membrane, and the inferior constrictor muscles would all experience division. Were the front of the throat cut just above the hyoid bone, the anterior jugular vein, the mylohyoid, the hyo-glossal, the genioglossal, the geniohyoid, the lingual vessels, the hyoglossal nerves, and the external maxillary vessels would be severed (Callander, 1948, pp. 47; 178) (see Figure A2.9). Teachers of singing, however, must restrict themselves to surface observation of this complex structure.

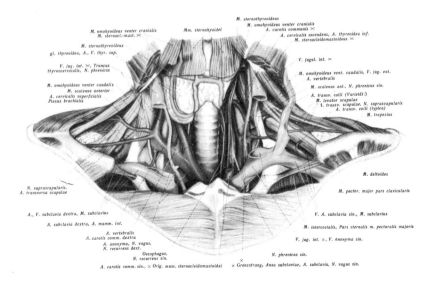

Figure A2.9. A dissection of the anterior of the neck. (From O. Schultze, *Topographische Anatomie*, 4th ed., ed. by Wilhelm Lubosch, 1935. Munich: J. F. Lehmanns Verlag. By permission, Springer-Verlag.)

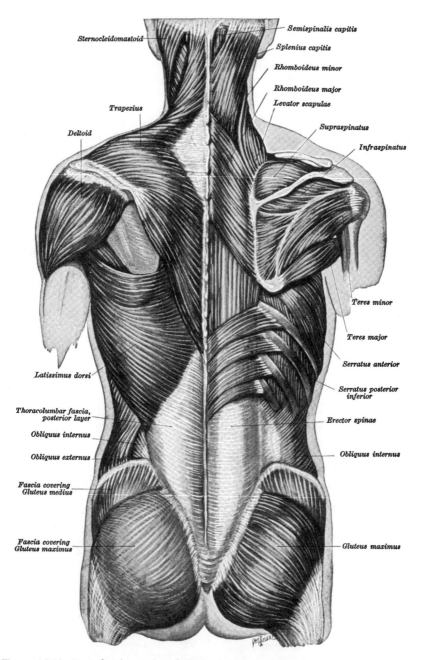

Figure A2.10. Superficial muscles of the back of the neck and trunk. On the left only the skin, superficial and deep fasciae have been removed. On the right, the sternocleidomastoid, trapezius, latissimus dorsi, deltoid, and obliquus externus abdominis have been dissected away. (From *Gray's Anatomy*, 36th ed., ed. by Peter L. Williams and Roger Warwick, 1980. Edinburgh: Churchill Livingstone. By permission.)

MUSCLES OF THE UPPER TORSO

Running down the back of the neck, a muscle pair called the *levator scapulae* (see Figure A2.10) arises from the upper angle of the scapula (the shoulder blade); as its name implies, levator scapulae pulls up the scapula. The major and minor *rhomboid* muscles (see Figure A2.10) arise from the upper spine and are inserted into the scapula. The *supraspinatus*, the *infraspinatus*, the *teres major*, and the *teres minor* (see Figure A2.10) are muscles that have to do chiefly with shoulder and arm movements. The *trapezius*, the *deltoid*, and the *latissimus dorsi* muscles (see Figure A2.10) form a powerful enveloping layer over this portion of the torso. The edge of the trapezius muscle can often be traced at the sides of the neck as it prominently crosses to the rear from the base of the skull to the shoulder and spine (see Figure A2.10).

Other muscles of the upper torso that sometimes figure in singing techniques are the *pectoralis major*, the *pectoralis minor*, and the *serratus anterior* muscles (see Figures A2.10 and A2.11). When we look at the surface of the chest, it is understandable why the muscles of the pectoral area appear important in breathing. They respond visibly to actions of the lungs and the rib cage. But it should be recalled that these muscles that cover so much of the upper costal region are largely associated with the shoulder girdle and its related musculature (*Gray's Anatomy*, 1980, pp. 567–568).

The pectoralis minor and the serratus anterior offer assistance in lifting the upper ribs (second through fifth) if the shoulders are firmly set. The subclavius, which originates on the lower surface of the clavicle and attaches to the first rib, provides elevation of that rib if the clavicle remains fixed.

From its appearance, the serratus anterior (see Figures A2.10, A2.11, A2.12, and A2.13) might be thought important in breath management in singing. Boxers rely on the serratus anterior for help in delivering a knockout, and the muscle is sometimes popularly called "the boxer's muscle." But for those moments of great impact in the dramatic vocal literature, the singer cannot look to the serratus anterior for assistance.

Even though the pectoralis major, the pectoralis minor, the serratus anterior, and the subclavius relate to the walls of the chest anteriorly and laterally, they serve during singing chiefly as postural muscles. Some teachers assign the postural muscles major importance in controlling expiration, but according to Campbell et al. (1970, p. 181): "[O]f all the muscles which are generally thought to act as accessory muscles of inspiration, only the scaleni and the sternomastoids show significant respiratory activity in man."

The large triangular trapezius muscle (muscle fibers of which converge toward the clavicle, the acromion, and the spine of the scapula) covers the upper part of the back (see Figure A2.10). The trapezius steadies the scapula, thereby determining the position of the shoulder. Together with the latissimus dorsi (see Figures A2.10 and A2.12), the trapezius is often thought to be of importance in controlling the breath cycle during singing. Certainly, as a

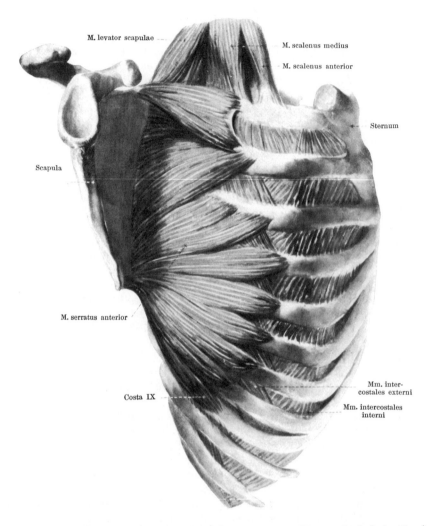

Figure A2.11. Muscles of the right side of the torso. (From Werner Spalteholz, *Hand-atlas der Anatomie des Menschen*, Vol. 2, 1932. Leipzig: S. Hirzel-Verlag.)

postural muscle the trapezius is significant, but its role as an accessory muscle of inspiration cannot be major.

The latissimus dorsi extends outward from under the arms and spreads widely across the back. Evidence that it plays a major role in breath control is limited. Because the latissimus dorsi contains fibers that arise from the lower three or four ribs, the muscle can help elevate those ribs when the humerus is in a fixed position, thus facilitating inspiration. Contraction of the latissimus dorsi as a whole compresses the lower thorax and assists expiration (Campbell et al., 1970, p. 187) (see Figures A2.10 and A2.13).

Antagonists of the trapezius and the serratus anterior muscles are the levator scapulae and the major and minor rhomboid muscles (see Figure A2.10); these are vertebroscapular muscles that rotate the scapula, but they play no important role in breathing.

When considering methods for breath management ("support") in singing, it should be kept in mind that—of dorsal and other accessory respiratory muscles (see Figure A2.10) including the anterior, medius, and posterior scaleni, the sternomastoids, the subclavius, the serratus posterior, superior, and inferior, the quadratus lumborum, and the sacrospinalis group—only the scaleni and the sternomastoids contribute significantly to respiration.

MUSCLES OF THE ANTEROLATERAL ABDOMINAL WALL

The movements of the intercostal muscles and diaphragm have been considered at some length. Other contributors to breath management in singing must now be examined.

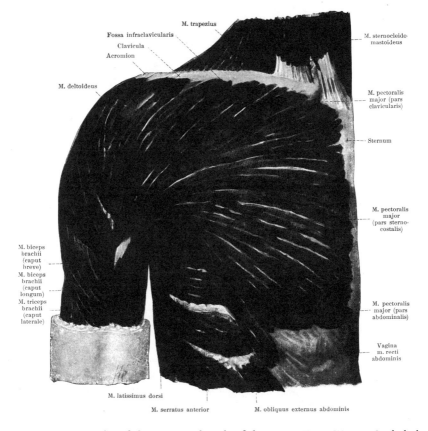

Figure A2.12. Muscles of the upper right side of the torso. (From Werner Spalteholz, *Handatlas der Anatomie des Menschen*, Vol. 2, 1932. Leipzig: S. Hirzel-Verlag.)

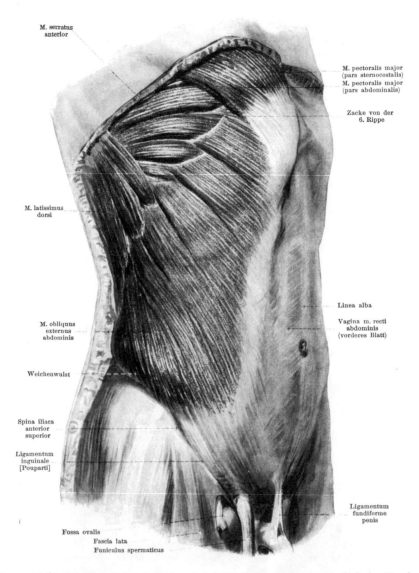

M. serratus
anterior

M. pectoralis major
(pars sternocostalis)
M. pectoralis major
(pars abdominalis)

Zacke von der
6. Rippe

M. latissimus
dorsi

Linea alba

Vagina m. recti
abdominis
(vorderes Blatt)

M. obliquus
externus
abdominis

Weichenwulst

Spina iliaca
anterior
superior

Ligamentum
inguinale
[Pouparti]

Ligamentum
fundiforme
penis

Fossa ovalis
Fascia lata
Funiculus spermaticus

Figure A2.13. Muscles of the thorax and abdomen. (From Werner Spalteholz, *Hand-atlas der Anatomie des Menschen*, 13th ed, Vol. 2, 1932, Leipzig: S. Hirzel-Verlag.)

In considering the surface musculature of the front of the body, it is useful to divide the area below the sternum into nine chief regions, created by two vertical and two horizontal lines (see Figure 1.3). These areas are composed of three anterior segments, the epigastric, the umbilical, and the pubic (also hypogastric), and of three corresponding lateral pairs, the hypochondriac, the lateral (also lumbar), and the inguinal (also iliac).

The contents of the abdominal cavity are protected by the broad flat muscles of the abdomen (see Figures 2.4, 2.12, and 2.13). These muscles exert pressure on the abdominal viscera and help maintain the proper position of the internal organs of the abdomen. Movements of the abdominal muscles can be initiated by the respiratory organs and the muscles of the chest that control respiration. The abdominal muscles respond to the elastic recoil of the lungs and the chest cavity by pushing up the diaphragm. The flexor abdominal muscles also assist in maintaining the lower thorax and pelvis in antagonism to the spinal muscles. Additional lower-trunk strength is present in the anterolateral area because the large flat abdominal muscles cross each other in a mutually supportive fashion in this bone-free area, which is without skeletal support. The *external oblique* (see Figures 2.2 and A2.13) is the most superficial of the flat muscles of the abdomen, its fibers originating in the ninth, tenth, and eleventh ribs, and descending downward and forward in an oblique manner, as indicated by its name. Astraquillo and associates (1977, p. 504) found that, in singing,

> The most active of the muscles of the abdomen is the external oblique. This muscle characteristically shows contraction immediately before the production of sound and in a phasic quality toward the end of articulation, especially in staccato vocalises. When sustained voice was produced there was also sustained contraction.

At a deeper level than the external oblique, the *internal oblique* muscle inserts its uppermost fibers into the lower ribs and into the rib cartilages. The internal oblique muscle lies beneath the external oblique, and is thinner and not as bulky as the external muscle (see Figure 2.2).

Yet more deeply placed is the *transversus abdominis* muscle (see Figure 2.2), an important abdominal constrictor. The internal oblique, external oblique, and the transversus muscles form the anterior rectus sheath (see Figures 2.2, 2.3, and 2.4). The *rectus abdominis* (see Figures 2.3 and 2.4) is attached superiorly to the fifth, sixth, and seventh costal cartilages, and inferiorly to the pelvis.

If the abdominal musculature is well developed, as it should be with any singer, one can readily locate the linia alba (see Figure 2.4) by surface observation. This line extends perpendicularly from the sternum to the pubic region, and is divided into an upper and lower region by the umbilicus. If the surface musculature is clearly defined, the rectus muscles form observable bands on either side of this line. The liniae transversae, tendinous intersections, produce depressions that plainly mark off the segments of the rectus abdominis in the muscular individual.

Complex interrelationships of the muscles of the abdominal wall are reflected externally. Teachers of singing often have the singer place hands on the abdomen to experience muscular movement. According to Astraquillo and associates (1977, p. 512),

> What the singer "feels" when he puts his hands on his upper abdomen is the slow contraction of the abdominal muscles. . . . These

muscles, like those of inhalation, are paired. They are (1) the external oblique, fibers coursing downward; (2) the internal oblique, fibers coursing upward; (3) the rectus abdominis, which extends vertically at the anterior or forward wall of the abdomen; and (4) the transversus abdominis, with fibers coursing horizontally across the anterior wall of the abdomen.

There is, it should be noted, no universal agreement as to what form of abdominal muscle activity is best for singing. Indeed, widely disseminated techniques of singing have been based on assumed muscle relationships that are patently absurd. Some brief comment about such pedagogical systems may help in understanding proper coordination of the muscles of the antero-lateral abdominal wall.

SYSTEMS OF BREATH CONTROL

Breath control in singing is concerned with delaying both the collapse of the ribs and the reversion of the diaphragm to its dome-shaped posture. Put another way, the musculature of *inspiration* offers continued resistance to the collapsing breath mechanism. Some teaching methods assert that this resistance can best be accomplished by pushing downward and outward on the abdominal viscera, much as in difficult defecation. One can readily find a number of singing manuals with drawings of outward and downward pressure against the wall (including the hypogastric area), which supposedly will produce better management of the breath. Such action is commonly termed "belly breathing." A related technique promotes squeezing the anal sphincter ("squeeze the dime") and tilting the pelvis. Other teachers falsely assume that by drawing the abdominal wall inward, the upward surge of the diaphragm can be delayed, resulting in a "fixated diaphragm." Yet another pedagogy advocates "spreading" the muscles in the upper or middle back, actions involving muscles that are not essential to the mechanics of breathing. These approaches illustrate confusion about the physiology of breathing. At times they are imaginatively combined, and may call on disjunct anatomical information (Miller, 1977, pp. 21–44).

When control of breath emission is given over almost entirely to the muscles of the flank and lower abdomen, the chest tends to collapse because the ribs are not able to maintain sufficient distention in the presence of mis-placed abdominal pressures. When the pectoral musculature is assigned the task of controlling the breath, the lack of abdominal muscle interaction with the diaphragm results in the diaphragm's rapid ascent. Any system of breath management that permits the sternum to lower will invite collapse of the thoracic cage. Sternum and rib cage elevation are closely wedded to abdom-inal action. Bishop (1968, p. 199) states: "In their respiratory capacity, the rib cage and the abdominal wall may be considered a functional unit acting synergistically to empty the lungs."

Studies of lung volume are concerned with vital capacity, tidal breath, complemental breath, supplemental breath, and residual breath. Some definitions are in order: (1) vital capacity: the maximum breath inhaled following forced inspiration, comprising the total of complemental, tidal, and supplemental breath, being roughly some 3700 cc., or about 7 to 8 pints; (2) tidal breath: the amount of air exchanged during a cycle of quiet breathing; (3) complemental breath: additional air inhaled beyond quiet breathing; (4) supplemental breath: air that can be exhaled beyond that exhaled during quiet breathing; (5) residual breath (or volume): air that remains in the lungs following expiration; air that cannot voluntarily be discharged.

The mechanical problems involved in combining respiratory and phonatory control are described in some detail by Sears and Newsom Davis (1968, p. 184):

> In phonation the production of a note at constant pitch and intensity requires a constant airflow through the glottis, and this can be achieved for up to 90% of the vital capacity. Yet over this range the driving force for the airflow, the subglottal pressure, is influenced profoundly by the changing, combined elastic recoil force of the lungs and chest wall. . . . These recoil forces assist expiratory airflow at high lung volumes and actually oppose it at low lung volumes. The relaxation pressure is zero with respect to atmospheric pressure at the mechanical mid-point of the system when the individual recoil forces of the lungs and chest wall exert pressures on the pleural cavity. . . . Thus, for a constant subglottal pressure to be generated at different lung volumes, these passive forces must be controlled by an appropriately graded activation of inspiratory and expiratory muscles. In order to achieve the demand for a constant airflow, the central nervous system has to take into account not only the magnitude of the load provided by the phonating larynx . . . but also the changing value of the internal load as lung volume diminishes.

Vocal-fold approximation and subglottic pressure unite in a nonstatic relationship dictated by pitch, power, and phoneme.

The Physiology of the Vocal Tract Resonator System

The upper vocal tract is the articulatory mechanism for speech and singing. The movements of the tongue, lips, palate, cheeks, and mandible alter the dimensions of the resonator tract. These movements in turn are partly determined by the face and neck muscles. The bones of the facial skeleton, together with the mandible, provide structure for the muscles of the face.

The zygomatic bones supply the framework for the upper part of the face. These bones are highly visible at the cheeks. The maxillae are large bones that form the upper jaw, provide a roof for the mouth, and give form to the nasal cavities. The horseshoe-shaped mandible is the largest bone of the face. The tongue is attached to the mandible, and the lower teeth are rooted in the mandible.

Muscles of the face (see Figures A3.1 and A3.2) that respond to articulatory gestures are the following:

- The *levator anguli oris*, which elevates the angles of the mouth;
- the *zygomaticus major*, which draws the angles of the mouth upward and backward, as in laughter;
- the *risorius*, which retracts the angles of the mouth, as in smiling;
- the *depressor labii inferioris*, which draws down the lower lip, laterally, as in an ironic expression;
- the *depressor anguli oris*, which lowers the angles of the mouth as in weeping;
- the *mentalis*, which protrudes and raises the lower lip, as in petulance;
- the *buccinator*, which assists chewing, pushes food onto the teeth, and which alters the shape of the cheeks;
- the *orbicularis oris*, which compresses, contracts, and protrudes the lips, and which is responsible for many facial expressions;
- the *temporalis*, which raises and retracts the mandible, and clenches the teeth;
- the *masseter*, which raises the mandible and clenches the teeth;
- the *pterygoideus medialis*, which elevates the mandible, and provides rotary motion in chewing;
- the *pterygoideus lateralis*, which protrudes the mandible, and provides rotary motion in chewing;
- the *platysma*, which depresses the mandible and lips, and tenses the skin of the neck, as in a grimace.

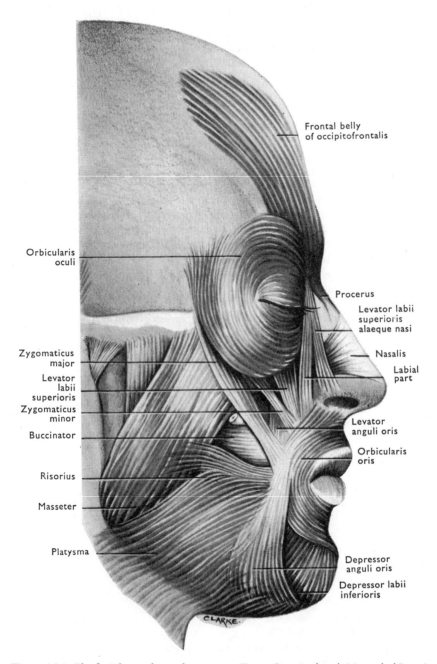

Figure A3.1. The facial muscles and masseter. (From *Cunningham's Manual of Practical Anatomy*, 13th ed., Vol. 3, ed. by G. J. Romanes, 1967. London: Oxford University Press. By permission.)

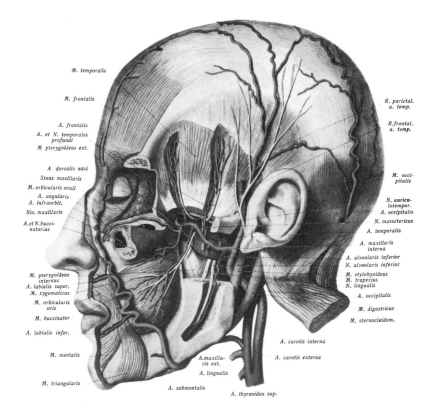

Figure A3.2. Some details of the face and head. (From O. Schultze, *Topographische Anatomie*, 4th ed., ed. by Wilhelm Lubosch, 1935. Munich: J. F. Lehmanns Verlag. By permission, Springer-Verlag.)

The mouth is the most adjustable of the vocal tract cavities, because of the mobility of the lips, the tongue, and the lower jaw.

In the articulation of certain sounds, the nasal cavities (see Figures 4.1 and 4.4) are joined with the mouth and the pharynx as part of the resonator tube. Divided into halves by the nasal septum, the nasal cavities consist of the vestibule, the olfactory region, and the respiratory region. The nares (nostrils) have an anterior opening, and communicate with the pharynx; the nasal apertures widen posteriorly as they meet the nasopharynx.

The paranasal sinuses include the frontal, ethmoidal, sphenoidal, and maxillary sinuses (see Figures A3.3 and A3.4). However, they play a negligible role in resonance, either in speech or in singing.

The mouth and the pharynx (buccopharyngeal resonator) are connected by the *oropharyngeal isthmus* (see Figure A3.5). The *oropharynx* extends from the velum downward to the top of the epiglottis. Two sets of paired arches, the palatoglossal and the palatopharyngeal arches (see Figures 4.1

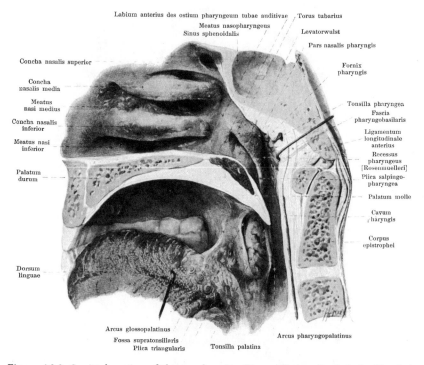

Labium anterius des ostium pharyngeum tubae auditivae Torus tubarius
Meatus nasopharyngeus
Sinus sphenoidalis   Levatorwulst
Pars nasalis pharyngis
Concha nasalis superior
Fornix
pharyngis
Concha
nasalis media
Meatus
nasi medius   Tonsilla pharyngea
Fascia
pharyngobasilaris
Concha nasalis
inferior   Ligamentum
longitudinale
Meatus nasi   anterius
inferior   Recessus
pharyngeus
[Rosenmuelleri]
Palatum   Plica salpingo-
durum   pharyngea

Palatum molle

Cavum
pharyngis

Corpus
epistrophei

Dorsum
linguae

Arcus glossopalatinus
Fossa supratonsillaris   Arcus pharyngopalatinus
Plica triangularis   Tonsilla palatina

Figure A3.3. Sagittal section of the nasal cavity. (From Werner Spalteholz, *Handatlas der Anatomie des Menschen*, 13th ed., Vol. 2, 1933. Leipzig: S. Hirzel-Verlag.)

and A3.3) are located on either side of the oropharyngeal isthmus. Tonsils lie between each palatoglossal–palatopharyngeal pair. The *palatopharyngeus* muscles are attached to the uvula and to the pharyngeal wall; the *palatoglossus* (also *glossopalatinus*) muscles are attached to the uvula and to the tongue. The *levator palatini* muscles elevate the velum; the *tensor veli palatini* muscles tighten the velum, or flatten out the velar arch; and the *musculus uvulae* muscles pull the uvula upward and backward (see Figures 4.7, 4.8, and 4.9).

The *nasopharynx* lies behind the nose, immediately above the level of the velum, and connects with the nasal cavities. The *laryngopharynx* extends from the apex of the epiglottis to the base of the cricoid cartilage.

The walls of the pharynx are formed by three large constrictor muscles (see Figures 4.7, 4.8, and 4.9), which are active in deglutition (swallowing) and alter the shape of the laryngopharynx. The *constrictor pharyngis inferior* is divided into the *cricopharyngeus* muscle and the *thyropharyngeus*. *Constrictor pharyngis medius* is divided into the *chondropharyngeus* muscle and the *ceratopharyngeus* muscle. The *constrictor pharyngis superior* is divided into four parts: the *pterygopharyngeus* muscle, which is attached to the lamina of the pterygoideus process; the *buccopharyngeus*, which is joined to the buccinator; the *mylopharyngeus*, which is attached to the mandible; and the *glossopharyngeus*, which is attached to the floor of the tongue. Briefly stated, the walls of the pharynx are made up of muscles and fibrous tissue.

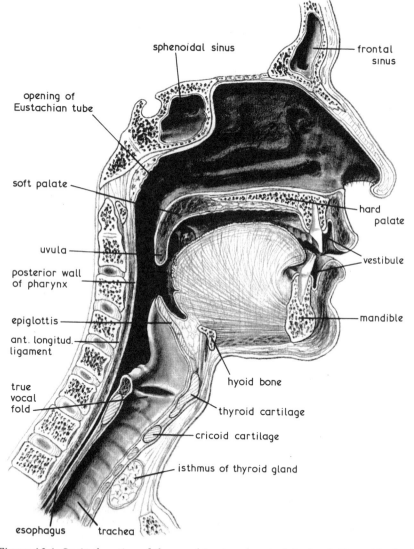

Figure A3.4. Sagittal section of the vocal tract and part of the head. (From Meribeth Bunch, *Dynamics of the Singing Voice*, 1982. Vienna: Springer-Verlag. By permission.)

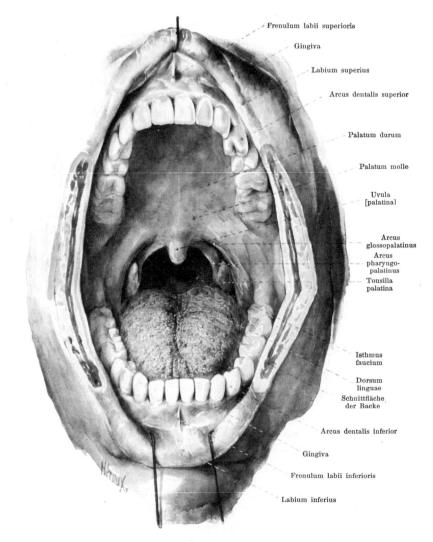

Figure A3.5. The cavity of the mouth. (From Werner Spalteholz, *Handatlas der Anatomie des Menschen,* 13th ed., Vol. 3, 1933. Leipzig: S. Hirzel-Verlag.)

APPENDIX 4

The Physical Factors of Vocal Registration

Nadoleczny, in a chapter on vocal registers in *Untersuchungen über den Kunstgesang* (1923, pp. 32–46), presents a summary of viewpoints and terminology from the period of Tosi onward. Although even the existence of registers has at times been in dispute, a vocal register may be briefly defined as a series of consecutive voice tones of equal timbre, which can be distinguished from adjoining series.

Early in the history of singing, performers perceived that certain notes in the scale could be grouped as to timbre and as to resonance sensations. The trained singer learns to go from one register to another without disrupting the unity of the scale, and thus confounds the study of registers in the professional voice. Committees of auditors in perceptual studies may find it difficult to detect any register demarcations, or perceive only those exhibited in the extremes of range, when they deal with well-trained subjects. Regardless of excellent technique that "hides" the events of registration, almost all professional singers are convinced that register phenomena do indeed exist. Much of their technical work has been devoted to scale equalization.

Luchsinger and Arnold (1965, pp. 96–97) report: "In the untrained singer, certain disturbances occur. At specific points in the frequency range a marked reaction of the resonators of the larynx may be heard in a changed intensity of timbre of the tones. These points are known as *register passages* or transitions."

CRICOTHYROID ACTION IN REGISTRATION

Although the shape of the glottis is ultimately determined by action of the internal laryngeal muscles, the cricothyroid muscles serve as external muscles of pitch adjustment (Zenker, 1964b, pp. 24–27). The cricothyroids (see Figure A1.1c) spread outward and backward from their anterior position on the cricoid cartilage, to become attached to the laminae of the thyroid cartilage and to the inferior horns of the thyroid cartilage. The cricothyroid muscles pull the thyroid cartilage forward and downward from its resting position on the cricoid cartilage (see Figure A4.1d). When the cricothyroids contract, the vocal folds are stretched and adjusted to the paramedian position.

287

(The arrows show the direction of movement of the arytenoid cartilages)

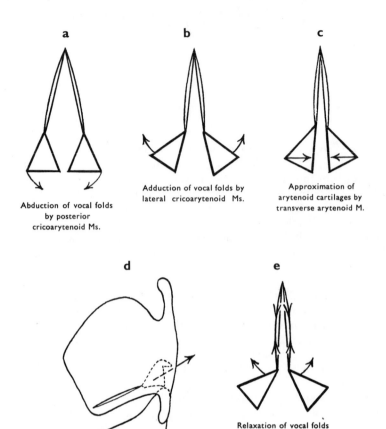

Figure A4.1. A series of diagrams to show several positions of the vocal folds and cartilages. (From Sir Solly Zuckerman, *A New System of Anatomy*, 1961. London: Oxford University Press. By permission.)

Moore (1964, p. 144) describes the interaction of cricothyroid muscles with internal laryngeal muscles:

When the vocal cords are approximated as in phonation, their elongation decreases their effective mass, increases their elasticity, and alters their contour; shortening the folds reverses the process. However, if shortening is prevented by action of the cricothyroid muscles, thereby stabilizing the attachments of the vocal folds, contraction of the muscles within the folds increases the elasticity, changes the contour of the supplementary, oblique muscle fibres attached to the conus elasticus, and reduces the effective mass.

The vocal ligaments (edges of the vocal folds) are comprised of fibers of an elastic character, and of collagenous fibers that are attached to the vocalis muscles. When the vocal ligaments are stretched by means of the cricothyroid muscles, they elongate up to the point where the collagenous fibers cannot yield any further because they have been fully stretched. At this point, longitudinal tension can be increased, but not length. In order to arrive at the highest pitches, the vocalis muscles must relax, while the lateral thyroarytenoids should contract (van den Berg, 1964, p. 97).

Van den Berg (1968b, pp. 22–23) provides a precise description of the physical causes of register variation:

> Variations in this register [chest] are primarily brought about by variations in the internal tensions in the body of the vocal folds, i.e., by variations of the contracting forces in the vocalis muscle. These forces need some compensatory forces, however, and thus other muscles are also involved in chest voice to some extent. In the phonatory position, contraction of the vocalis muscles abducts the glottis and this requires a compensatory medial compression. Furthermore, contraction of the vocalis muscles tends to shorten the glottis and to tilt the thyroid cartilage. With shortening beyond a critical value, this requires a compensatory contraction of the cricothyroid muscles, which increases the length of the vocal folds. This increase is limited, however, and length is only slightly increased beyond the resting length or not at all. Therefore, the longitudinal tension in the vocal ligaments remains negligible compared with the longitudinal tensions in the vocalis muscles. The vibrational patterns, large amplitudes and long closure of the glottis during the cycle, are thus primarily determined by the body of the vocal folds and not by their margins.

Regarding the *middle* and *upper* registers, van den Berg (1968b, p. 23) continues:

> The longitudinal forces in the vocal ligaments are no longer negligible compared with those in the vocalis muscles, but are of the same order of magnitude. To achieve this, the contraction of the vocalis muscles must be submaximal, because these muscles are antagonistic to the cricothyroid muscles which passively stretch the vocal folds and thus the vocal ligaments. This adjustment requires a somewhat stronger contraction of the interarytenoid muscles and a medial compression beyond a minimal value, otherwise the glottis becomes too wide, and the vocal folds cannot be thrown into vibration by the air. In this register, the vibratory patterns, intermediate amplitudes, and short closure of the glottis during the cycle, are determined by the body of the vocal folds and by their margins. The adjustment and the patterns have a mixed character.

Although muscle adjustment is gradual, certain laryngeal muscle coordinations must at some point in the ascending scale be superseded by others. Luchsinger and Arnold (1965, p. 97) state that vocal-fold vibrations follow different patterns in different registers. During the production of low pitches, the folds appear rounded, full, and relaxed; in high pitches they are sharp-edged, thin, and taut. The partner–opponent relationship between the thyroarytenoids and the cricothyroids is of increased importance in registration action during singing. In rising pitch, the stretching force of the cricothyroids cannot be resisted by the thyroarytenoids to the same degree as in low or middle pitch without strenuous muscle conflict ensuing—a sorry condition for ease in singing. This viewpoint is further supported by van den Berg (1968c, pp. 132–134):

> When the subject sings an ascending or a descending scale with no appreciable transition in sound quality, he needs to change gradually from one type of adjustment to the other. That means that the antagonistic active tensions in the vocalis muscles and the passive tensions in the vocal ligaments, together with the adduction of the glottis and the value of the flow of air, need to balance smoothly and gradually.

Van den Berg points out that some pitches that lie in a region where overlapping of function may occur can be sung in several ways.

Predominating thyroarytenoid contraction is described by Briess (1964, p. 259) as "the full vibration" function of the folds, producing a "robust" character of voice; a "delicate" character of voice is characterized by predominating cricothyroid function, Briess says. At the identical pitch, varying ratios of thyroarytenoid or cricothyroid function may occur. Voice teachers who recognize registration events in singing designate Briess's "robust" quality as chest voice. Robust quality is appropriate to the low range of the singing voice; the thyroarytenoids are shortened and thickened. The amplitude of vibration is greater in low register because the glottis opens widely, and there is a full vibratory sweep of the folds away from the paramedian position. The cricothyroid muscles do not offer very great antagonism to the thyroarytenoid muscles in this range, and therefore there is limited resistance to the airstream (Vennard, 1967, pp. 66–67).

As pitch rises, the folds elongate. With the ascent of pitch from low to middle voice, the relationship between the thyroarytenoid muscles and the cricothyroid muscles changes in favor of Briess's more "delicate" ratio. If the folds remain too thick, an increase in breath pressure is required for phonation. If this thickness remains during further progression up the scale into upper-middle voice, there will arrive a point at which the degree of muscle tension and breath pressure can no longer be maintained without a sudden alteration of this adjustment. Unless some gradual reduction of muscular antagonism has previously been made, the voice will either "break" or squeeze off. Smooth entrance into middle and upper voice requires flexible balance of the laryngeal muscles, vibrating vocal-fold mass, subglottic pressure, and air flow rate.

EXTERNAL FRAME FUNCTION

Factors not directly related to internal laryngeal function play a role in determining events of vocal registration. The external structure surrounding the larynx and connecting the neck to the head and to the torso can be directed toward pitch change. Because the cricothyroid joint is not at a fixed position, the thyroid and cricoid cartilages have several possibilities of movement in relation to the spine and to each other (Sonninen, 1968, p. 80). Sonninen, in a study of the effects of external frame musculature on pitch control (1968, pp. 68–89), describes an external mechanism consisting of simultaneous contraction of the sternohyoid muscles and of the thyromandibular muscles (which attach to the thyroid cartilage, to the hyoid bone, and to the jaw); these muscles can pull the thyroid cartilage in a forward direction. In addition, "The cricopharyngeal muscles act in a dorso–cranial direction and thus shorten the vocal folds. This occurs only, however, when the larynx is in a low position and when there is no anterior pull on the thyroid cartilage." This effect becomes weaker as the larynx is raised (Sonninen, 1968, p. 80).

Other factors that may act on the mechanisms of pitch are the position of the ventricular (false) folds, the position of the epiglottis (Zenker, 1964b, p. 28), the extent of esophageal opening, and the degree of tracheal bending (Sonninen, 1968, p. 75). The supportive muscles of the neck structure contribute to the character of vocal timbre (Zenker and Zenker, 1960, pp. 32–33). (The exact nature of external frame function as contributor to vocal registration should receive further study.)

Individual anatomical structure and orientation in vocal technique probably determine specific external frame contributions to registration practices.

DAMPING

Damping is an acoustical term that describes the process by which energy is lost in a vibrating system through decrease in amplitude. As considered here, damping refers to a specific registration phenomenon in which there occurs a decrease or cessation in the amplitude of vocal fold vibration as a result of pressure exerted on the fold during rapid vibration at high pitch. In addition to vocal-fold elongation and corresponding reduction in mass, damping is a method for pitch adjustment.

Briess (1964, p. 268) describes what occurs in phonation during conditions of extreme hyperfunction of the cricothyroid muscles without proper counterpull of muscle antagonists. Damping action begins at the posterior ends of the folds, with forceful approximation; as pitch rises, the portion of the area that is damped becomes greater, progressing anteriorly; air pressure increases with increase in damping. Briess states that such undesirable phonation often is to be found in screaming children and in female singers with abusive singing techniques. "In such instances, the vocal cords are damped over almost their entire length, with the exception of a small orifice anteriorly. Sound can be produced only under excessive air pressure" (Briess, 1964, p. 268).

Excessive damping is to be avoided. However, progressive damping appears essential in ascending pitch in the uppermost range of the singing voice; some pitches in the flageolet voice (see Chapter 10) are not physiologically possible unless the folds are heavily damped.

SUMMARY OF PHYSICAL ASPECTS OF REGISTRATION

Vocal registers appear to be determined by actions of the intrinsic muscles of the larynx, by actions of the cricothyroid muscles in altering relationships between the laryngeal muscles and the laryngeal cartilages, by actions of certain neck muscles that function as an external frame to the laryngeal musculature, by subglottic pressure and breath flow rate, possibly by the extent of tracheal pull, by coupling between the larynx and the resonators above the larynx, and, at least in some voices, by the degree of vocal fold damping.

Questions important to vocal pedagogy can be posed. Where do register events most commonly occur in a particular category of voice? At what point should the heavier mechanical production give way to a lighter mechanical action? How are registers mixed? How best can the voice be trained to produce a unified scale without audible registration demarcations?

Answers to these questions differ remarkably among pedagogies (Miller, 1977, pp. 99–136). The effectiveness of vocalises in Chapters 10 and 11 can best be determined in light of what is understood about the physiology of vocal registration.

Influences of Various Voiced and Unvoiced Consonants on Resonator Adjustment

The articulatory system coordinates and modifies actions initiated by the respiratory–phonatory mechanism. Consonantal maneuvers bring about changes in the configuration of the resonator tube. Any consonantal phoneme can be identified as a member of one or more family groups, yet the possible overlapping of articulatory modifiers of vocal sound complicates stringent codification of each variant.

Consonants may be grouped according to the extent of airflow during phonation (Klatt et al., 1968, pp. 46–51). Not surprisingly, airflow rates are similar in the nasal continuants [m] and [n], and in vowel sounds. The consonants [r] and [l] use a slightly lower rate of airflow than do the nasals and vowels, but not significantly so. The phoneme [h] has a high rate of airflow.

Consonants [v], [z], and [ð] are voiced throughout their durations, with a higher degree of laryngeal resistance to airflow than is found in the voiceless fricatives. Because of glottal involvement, voiced fricatives have a lower airflow rate than do the voiceless fricatives [f], [s], and [θ], but a higher rate of flow than vowels.

In the case of consonants [b], [d], and [g], the singer often is aware of the stoppage of air and its subsequent sudden release. This burst of air, a result of the sudden release of mouth pressure, can be significant in locating articulatory sensation for the singer.

Consonants [p], [t], and [k] indicate a fast burst release with a somewhat slower return to airflow characteristics of the subsequent vowel. In producing this set of consonants, airflow rate is high, similar to that found in the phoneme [h]; according to Klatt et al. (1968, p. 48), during the interval of aspiration, the vocal folds gradually begin to approximate, and vibration is observable just shortly before the flow levels off to a relatively steady rate. When a consonant of this type occurs at the close of a syllable, it has a somewhat smaller peak in airflow rate, and shorter durations of high airflow, probably because the vowel that follows can be produced with lower subglottic pressure (Isshiki and Ringel, 1964, p. 241).

Isshiki and Ringel (1964, p. 241) established that the flow rate during a sustained phonation depends on (1) expiratory effort; and (2) degree of resistance within the vocal tract. Ladefoged (1962a, pp. 248–249) reports similar conclusions, as does Schutte (1980, p. 163). Flow rate is greater for voice-

293

less consonants than for voiced because it is essential for the glottis to close in voicing and to be abducted in unvoiced consonants.

Regarding intra-vocal tract pressure, the pressure for a voiceless consonant is greater than that for its voiced counterpart, which partially explains the high airflow rate during voiceless consonant production (Isshiki and Ringel, 1964, p. 243):

> The volume of the cavity behind the points of vocal tract closure in which pressure mounts up is composed of the supra- and sub-glottal cavities during the production of voiceless consonants. In the case of the production of the voiced consonant the cavity behind the closure consists of the supra-glottal cavity. This difference in the size of the cavity ("capacity of condenser," after Fant) may also contribute to the difference in flow rate between the voiced and voiceless consonants. It also appears logical to assume that the air supply from the lungs through the glottis is greater, due to the lack of glottal resistance, during the period of explosion of a voiceless stop consonant than during similar period of a voiced consonant. This factor also influences the flow pattern of the various stop consonants.

In all probability, the speed and degree of release of these points of stricture, suggest Isshiki and Ringel, is inversely related to airflow rate. Some consonantal characteristics related to airflow rate and to stricture points have direct influence on resonator adjustments for singing, and on that account serve teaching purposes.

Several teams of researchers have concluded that the intranasal sound pressure for nasal consonants is markedly high and that the pressure for preceding waves of [r] or voiced consonant syllables is considerably more pronounced in the *nasal* cavity than in the front of the mouth (Hirano et al., 1966, p. 378). Hirano, Takeuchi, and Hiroto remark that internal pressure decreases with the elevation of the soft palate, and that there would appear to be some discrepancy between the low velum (a cause of nasalization) and the high level of intranasal pressure:

> Here it is suggested that differences in intranasal pressure in pronouncing vowels are mainly due to factors other than an elevation of the soft palate. . . . [I]ntranasal sound pressure varies according to different vowels because of differences in internal impedance of the vowel tract for vowels.

(Impedance is an acoustic term that refers to the ratio of the pressure to the volume displacement at a given surface in the medium that transmits sound.) The same source concludes:

> The present experiments revealed a pronouncedly high intranasal sound pressure for the preceding R/sound and voiced consonant syllables. This suggests that a nasopharyngeal closure fails to reach its maximum when the preceding wave is uttered. During this period of speech sound production the vocal tract is obstructed at

the articulatory region, e.g., the lips for labial sounds, the alveola for dental sounds and the palate for palatal sounds. Therefore, it is understood that energy is chiefly released through the nasal cavity, resulting in high intranasal sound pressure.

The coupling of the front vowel [i] with the nasal continuants is common practice in teaching resonance balancing in singing, combining the sensations of the open throat *(gola aperta)* and good resonance balance *(impostazione).*

Böhme et al. (1966, p. 9) conducted a series of investigations on actions of the levator and tensor veli palatini on the velum. The activity of those muscles was summarized as follows: "Our investigation shows that a prephonatory phase varying in length occurs in both muscles. Among the vowels it is [i] which shows the greatest activity of the tensor veli palatini. In general a complex functioning of Mm. levator and tensor palatini in vowel production can be demonstrated from our investigations." The coupling of nasal continuant and high formant vowel, such as [i] or [e], so typical of the Italian School, is an important procedure in inducing laryngeal as well as vocal tract action favorable for vocal timbre in singing.

Although even slight nasality is produced by coupling the nasal resonator to the oral and pharyngeal cavities, considerable evidence indicates that vocal-fold activity during nasality differs somewhat from non-nasal activity. The recent technique of flexible fiberoptic examination of the larynx (fiberoptic nasopharyngolaryngoscopy) (Silberman et al., 1976, pp. 640–646), which permits the vocal folds to be observed during nearly optimal conditions for singing, supports the assumption that certain laryngeal configurations appear to accompany nasality. A brief survey of literature sources dealing with possible laryngeal contribution to nasality is offered by Zemlin (1981, pp. 224–225). Thus the considerable controversy over whether vocal timbre, which is perceived by some singers and listeners as being marked by "nasal resonance" but free of "nasality," may also depend on laryngeal configuration as well as on internal vocal tract impedance.

Reporting on analog studies of nasalization of vowels (as opposed to events that take place in the nasal continuants themselves), House and Stevens (1956, p. 230) conclude that coupling the nasal cavity to the vocal tract results (in all probability) in the following:

1. a differential reduction in the amplitude of the first formant of various vowels, with a concomitant increase in formant bandwidth and an upward shift in the center frequency of the formant;
2. a reduction in the over-all level of the vowel;
3. various "secondary" effects on the spectrum (notably the introduction of an anti-resonance, the elimination of the third formant and irregularities in upper formants, as well as the possible introduction of additional spectral peaks);
4. the perception of "nasality" when the major effects on the acoustic output reach appropriate magnitudes.

Other reports confirm the effect of even slight nasalization on formant relationships, a matter of vital importance in the teaching of singing. According to Fant (1964, p. 232):

> The effect of a slight nasalization (velopharyngeal coupling area on the order of 60mm^2) as in normal speech in segments close to nasal consonants is primarily the reduction of the first formant level versus other formants. There also appear extra formants and spectral minima. The split of the first formant into two peaks is a typical effect.

Fant mentions two other matters that may help explain the voice teacher's nearly universal urge to couple nasal continuants with other phonemes as vocalization patterns for resonance adjustment:

1. The assimilated nasality on both sides of a nasal consonant in connected speech affects a larger part of the speech before the nasal consonant than after the nasal consonant. Even unvoiced stops and fricatives may be affected to some extent without serious effects on speech quality as judged by trained listeners.

2. The effect of an extremely large degree of nasalization, in which the velum may approach the back of the tongue and the velopharyngeal coupling area is of the order of 250 mm, is a shift down in the frequency of the first formant and a relative decrease of the levels of the second and third formants. An additional closing of the nostrils causes an increase in the relative level of the first formant (low-frequency resonance).

Fant (1964, pp. 223–233), in discussing the degree of nasalization in non-nasalized sounds, adds: "A relatively prominent second harmonic, presumably originating from the glottal source, can be apparent in nasalized as well as non-nasalized parts of the utterance." The several contributive factors to nasality and to "nasal resonance" (a timbre perception that is for most schooled listeners not the same as nasality) in singing require additional investigation.

International Phonetic Alphabet (IPA) Symbols

The most logical phonetic system is one, developed over several decades, which enjoys universal acceptance. Although not perfect in comparing sounds from one language to another, the International Phonetic Alphabet (IPA) symbols accurately identify the sounds of speech. The system is indispensable in the vocal studio.

The most frequently encountered IPA symbols are presented here in a correlative fashion, with model words in English, German, Italian, and French.

A CONCISE CORRELATIVE PRONUNCIATION GUIDE

The close vowel sound in non-English languages is in general much closer than sounds in American speech. Both close and open vowels in the Romance and Germanic languages are "higher" than in American English, including so-called "Standard American Speech." When singing English, most singers introduce closer vowel sounds than would be used in spoken English. The same considerations, however, apply to singing foreign language sounds.

Words that serve as pronunciation keys are indicated in the following list, using symbols of the International Phonetic Alphabet. No attention has been given to vowel duration, which is a distinguishing characteristic of vowel sounds in several languages. Although the IPA symbols show correlation between English, French, Italian, and German sounds, such correlation is by no means absolute.

IPA SYMBOLS FOR VOWELS, SEMI-VOWELS, AND FRENCH VOWEL SOUNDS

IPA Symbols	English	German	Italian	French
		Vowels		
[i]	keen	Liebe	prima	lis
[ɪ]	thin	ich		
[e]	chaos	Leben	pena	été, crier
[ɛ]	bet	Bett, Gäste,	tempo	êtes, père neige
[æ]	bat			
[a]	task (American)			parle
[ɑ]	father	Stadt	camera	ras, âge
[ɒ]	hot (British)			
[ɔ]	soft, all	Sonne	morto	somme, joli, votre
[o]	note	Sohn	non	beaux, pauvre, gros
[ʊ]	nook	Mutter		
[u]	gnu, fool	Mut	uso	ou
[ʌ]	up			
[ə]	(schwa) ahead	getan		demain
[y]	(approximates [i] plus [u]) müde			une,
[ʏ]	(approximates [ɪ] plus [ʊ]) Glück			
[ø]	(approximates [e] plus [o]) schön			peu,
[œ]	(approximates [ɛ] plus [ɔ]) Köpfe			heure,

Semi-Vowels (Glides) and Diphthongs

[j]	yes		ja		piú, pieno		lion, pied
[w]	wish				uomo, guida		moins
[ɑɪ]	nice	[ae]	Mai, Ei	[ai]	mai		
[ɑʊ]	house	[ao]	Haus	[au]	aura		
[eɪ]	way			[ei]	dovei		
[ɔɪ]	boy	[ɔø]	Häuser, Kreuz	[ɔi]	vuoi		
[oʊ]	so						

Vowel Sounds Peculiar to the French Language

[ã]				temps
[ɛ̃]				faim, vin,
[õ]				nom, long
[œ̃]				parfum jeun

INTERNATIONAL PHONETIC ALPHABET SYMBOLS FOR CONSONANT SOUNDS

Pairs of consonants, one voiced and the other unvoiced, are executed with similar tongue and lip positions.

	Voiceless	Classification by Formation		Voiced
[p]	pope	bilabial	[b]	bob
[t]	tote	lingua-alveolar	[d]	dead
[k]	coke	velar	[g]	glug
[f]	fife	labiodental	[v]	valve
[θ]	think	linguadental	[ð]	the
[s]	cease	dental	[z]	zones
[ʃ]	Sh!	lingua-alveolar	[ʒ]	vision
[ç]	ich (German)	palatal		
[x]	ach (German)	velar	[ʁ]	Paris (French)
[h]	ha-ha! (aspirate)	glottal	[ʔ]	uh-oh! (stroked glottal)
[tʃ]	chase	lingua-alveolar	[dʒ]	judgment
[ts]	tsetse	linguadental	[dz]	adds

As just indicated, the pairs are as follows:

[p]–[b]
[t]–[d]
[k]–[g]
[f]–[v]
[θ]–[ð]
[s]–[z]
[ʃ]–[ʒ]
[ç]–

([ç] *is generally believed to be without a voiced counterpart*)

[x]–[ʁ]
[h]–[ʔ]
[tʃ]–[dʒ]
[ts]–[dz]

NASAL CONSONANTS

[m]	ma	bilabial nasal
[n]	no	alveolar nasal
[ŋ]	song	velar nasal
[ɲ]	ogni (Italian), onion (English), agneau (French)	palatal nasal
[ɱ]	conforto (Italian)	nasal labio-dental

OTHER VOICED CONSONANTS

[ʎ]	fo<u>gli</u>a (Italian)
[l]	lu<u>ll</u>
[ɹ]	<u>r</u>a<u>r</u>e (retroflex r, sometimes referred to as midwestern r)
[r]	ve<u>r</u>y (single tap r, as in British speech)
[r̄]*	ca<u>rr</u>o (Italian); G<u>r</u>und (German) (alveolar trill)

---

*The symbol [r̄] is used in this work, and in many phonetic sources, to represent the alveolar rolled r, because the IPA symbol for the trilled r [r], is used indiscriminately in many American sources.

Glossary of Nonmusical Terms

abdomen: that part of the body (excepting the back) that lies between the pelvis and the thorax; the cavity of this part of the torso, lined by the peritoneum, enclosed by the walls of the body, the diaphragm, and containing the viscera.

abduction: action by which a part is drawn away from the median line (as in the opening of the glottis).

acoustics: the science of sound, including its production, transmission, and effects; the sum of the qualities (such as reverberation) of an enclosure that determines the degree of distinctness of sound generated within it.

acromion: the lateral, triangular projection of the scapula that forms the point of the shoulder, articulating with the clavicle.

adduction: to draw toward a median axis (as in the closure of the glottis).

aditus: a passage for entrance (as in the aditus laryngis).

adrenaline: a hormone naturally secreted by the medulla of the suprarenal glands, which generally acts as stimulant.

aerodynamics: pertaining to the force of gases in motion, to the force acting on bodies moving through gases, and to the forces involved when gases pass over bodies.

ala (alae):   wing-like process or structure, as of the thyroid cartilage.

alveolar: speech sound produced with the apex of the tongue touching the upper alveolar ridge.

alveolus (alveoli):   an air cell of the lungs.

anterolateral: in front and to the side.

apex: the tip, point, or angular summit (as the apex of the tongue).

aponeurosis: thick and dense deep fasciae that connect muscle to bone; a flat tendon may be called an aponeurosis (as in central tendon of the diaphragm).

approximate: to come near to, to approach (as in vocal-fold approximation).

articulate: to join.

articulators: the tongue, the lips, the teeth, the soft palate and the hard palate, which modify the acoustic properties of the vocal tract.

aryepiglottic: muscles that form the sides of the collar of the larynx, extending from the arytenoids to the sides of the epiglottis.

arytenoid muscles: the transverse arytenoid and the oblique arytenoid muscles.

arytenoids: paired cartilages to which the vocal folds are attached.

atmospheric pressure: pressure exerted by the atmosphere in every direction, approximately 15 pounds per square inch (at sea level).

301

Bernoulli principle: air in motion has less pressure or density than when immobile, producing suction; if flow is constantly maintained, air will speed up at a constricted area, with a decrease in pressure occurring at that point.

bilabial: consonants formed with the aid of both lips (as in [p], [b], and [m]).

bilateral: having two sides.

bronchiole: a minute bronchial tube.

bronchogram: an x-ray picture of the lungs and bronchi.

bronchus (bronchi): a subdivision of the trachea formed by a bifurcation of the trachea.

buccal cavity: cavity of the mouth; oral cavity.

buccinator: thin, broad muscle forming the wall of the cheek.

buccopharyngeal resonator: the resonator system formed by the mouth and the pharynx.

cartilage: nonvascular connecting tissue that is more flexible than bone.

caudal: situated in or near the tail; posterior.

central tendon: large tendon of the diaphragm; diaphragmatic aponeurosis.

collagenous: pertaining to collagen, the chief constituent of the gelatinlike protein found in connective tissue.

collar of the larynx: the vestibule of the larynx; a muscular ring composed of the aryepiglottic folds, the epiglottis, and the arytenoids.

commissure: a joint, seam, or closure; an interstice, cleft, or juncture; a place where parts of the body meet.

complemental air: air which can be inhaled in addition to that taken in during quiet breathing (also known as *inspiratory reserve* air).

constrictor muscles: one of three pairs of muscles (superior, middle, and inferior) which form the pharyngeal walls.

continuant: a speech sound that may be prolonged during one breath (as in nasal continuant).

contraction: the shortening and thickening of a mŭscle fiber (or of the entire muscle) when activated.

conus elasticus: a cone-shaped structure of elastic tissue attached below the upper border of the cricoid cartilage, in front of the thyroid cartilage, and behind the arytenoid cartilages; it includes the vocal and cricothyroid ligaments and is also called the cricovocal membrane.

corniculate: having horns or small horn-like processes.

cornu (cornua): horn-shaped laryngeal cartilages.

cortex: the outer or superior part of an organ.

costal: pertaining to a rib or costa.

cricoarytenoids: muscles which rotate the arytenoid cartilages on the cricoid cartilage.

cricothyroids: four muscles which attach to the front of the cricoid cartilage and which pull down on the thyroid cartilage.

cricovocal membrane: *see* conus elasticus.

crus (crura): tendinous attachment of the diaphragm to lumbar vertebrae, forming the sides of the aortic opening.

cuneiform cartilage: wedge-shaped pair of cartilages lying in the aryepiglottic folds, known as the "cartilages of Wrisberg."

damping: diminution in amplitude of successive oscillations or waves.

diaphragm: organ composed of muscles and sinews, the partition between the chest cavity and the abdominal cavity (separates the respiratory and digestive systems).

digastric: having two bellies; applied chiefly to muscles that are fleshy at each end with a tendon in the middle.

digitation: a finger-like process (as of the ribs).

dorsal: directed toward the back.

dorsum: the upper side or part of an appendage (as in the dorsum of the tongue—the upper side behind the tip).

dysphonia: impaired voicing.

ectomorphic: of light body build.

edema: abnormal accumulation of fluid in the tissues; swelling (as of the vocal folds).

EGG: *see* electroglottography.

electrode: either terminal of an electric source; a plate through which electrical current is sent through a body structure.

electroglottography (EGG): process for measuring changes in electrical impedance (resistance) between two electrodes placed on opposite sides of the larynx, creating a wave-form on a visual display.

electromyography (EMG): a process for recording electrical energy generated by activated muscles.

EMG: *see* electromyography.

epiglottis: one of the three single cartilages of the larynx, located between the root of the tongue and the entrance to the larynx.

epithelium: a cellular tissue that covers free surfaces, tubes, or cavities of the body, enclosing and protecting.

exhalation (expiration): that part of the breath cycle during which breath is emitted.

expiratory reserve volume: the amount of air which can be exhaled from the lungs beyond that exhaled in quiet respiration.

extensors: muscles which extend or straighten a part (as opposed to flexors).

external oblique muscle: the fibers of the external oblique run downward (in general), and they form layers of the lateral walls of the abdomen; it fuses with the internal oblique to form the linea alba.

extrinsic: external.

fascia (fasciae): a sheet or layer of connective tissue that covers, sheathes, supports or binds together internal parts or structures of the body; separates muscle bundles from each other.

fauces: narrow passage from mouth to the pharynx, situated between the velum and the base of the tongue; the space surrounded by the soft palate, the palatine arches, and the base of the tongue; also termed the isthmus of the fauces; the pillars of the fauces are two folds on either side, between which lie the tonsils.

fiber: of a thread-like character; elongated strands of connective nerve or muscle tissue.

fissure: a narrow opening between parts.

flexor: a muscle that bends a part or limb (as opposed to extensor).

formant: partials of a vocal tone that determine the characteristic quality of a vowel; partial tones originated by action of the breath on the resonance chambers that have regions of prominent energy distribution.

fossa (fossae): a pit, cavity, or depression (as in nasal fossae, or as in the zygomatic fossa).

frequency: number of vibrations or cycles per second; the greater the number of vibrations per second, the higher the pitch.

fricative: a speech sound (voiced or unvoiced) caused by friction as air passes through a narrow aperture (as in [f], [v], [s], [z], etc.)

genioglossus: pair of fan-shaped muscles with fibers that radiate from the chin; these fibers insert on the hyoid bone, attach to the sides of the pharynx, and insert into the tongue.

geniohyoid: pair of slender muscles that arise from the mandible and insert on the hyoid bone.

glottis: the space between the vocal folds.

harmonic: an overtone or upper partial; vibration frequency that is an integral multiple of the vibration rate produced by the fundamental frequency.

hyoid bone: U-shaped bone situated at the base of the tongue and above the larynx.

hyothyroid: connecting the thyroid cartilage of the larynx and the hyoid bone, as the thyrohyoid muscle and the thyrohyoid ligaments.

hyperfunction: use of the phonatory (or any) mechanism, or some part of it, with excessive tension.

hypofunction: insufficient activity in the phonatory (or any) mechanism, or some part of it.

hypogastrium: the lowest of three median areas into which the abdomen is divided by imaginary planes.

Hz: unit of measurement of cycles per second (as in 440 Hz); named for the physicist Gustav Hertz.

ilium: the upper part of the hipbone.

inguinal: referring to the groin region.

inhalation (inspiration): that part of the breath cycle during which breath enters the lungs.

innervation: the distribution of nerves in or to a part or organ.

insertion: that part of a muscle which is attached to the bone it moves.

inspiratory reserve volume: quantity of air that can be inhaled beyond what is taken in during quiet breathing.

intercostal: short external and internal muscles between the ribs.

internal oblique: abdominal muscles whose fibers run upward (in general); they form layers of the lateral walls of the abdomen, and fuse with the external oblique to form the linea alba.

intrapulmonary: within the lungs.

intrinsic: on the inside; within (as the intrinsic muscles of the larynx).

isometric contraction: contraction of a muscle against a strong resistance, which permits the muscle to shorten very little.

jugular: pertaining to the throat, neck, or jugular vein.

labial: pertaining to the lips.

labiodental: a speech sound formed with the lower lip and the upper teeth (as in [f] and [v]).

lamina (laminae): a thin plate or sheet (as in the cricoid cartilage).

laryngoscope: a device for examination of the larynx.

latissimus dorsi: the broadest back muscle; flat, superficial muscle of the lower back.

levator: muscle that raises or elevates (as in levator scapula, levator veli palatini).

ligament: a tough band of tissue that connects the articular extremities of bones.

linea alba: a median, tendinous line that separates the right and left sides of the abdominal musculature.

lingua: tongue.

lumbar: of or near the loins.

mandible: the lower jaw.

manubrium: the upper portion of the sternum (breastbone).

masseter: a large muscle that raises the mandible and assists in mastication.

mastication: chewing.

maxilla (maxillae): the upper jaw, left or right.

maxillary: refers to the upper jaw.

maxillary sinus: air cavity of the maxillary bone.

medial: toward the middle.

mediastinum: space in the chest between the pleural sacs of the lungs; contains the heart and all the viscera of the chest except the lungs.

medulla (medullae): the deep or inner substance of an organ or part (as in the medulla oblongata).

membrane: thin layer of tissue that covers, separates, binds, or lines cavities or members of the body.

membranous: characterized or formed by membrane (as in the membranous portion of the vocal fold).

msec./millisecond: the 1000th part of a second.

mucosa: mucous membrane.

mucous membrane: membrane which lines passages and cavities of the body that communicate with the exterior (as in the respiratory tract).

muscular process: a marked process or projection to which a muscle is attached (as in the sideward projections of the arytenoid cartilages).

mylohyoid: paired muscle attached to the inside edge of the mandible (lower jaw) and to the hyoid bone, and forming the floor of the mouth.

myoelastic: the property of elasticity in muscles.

myoelastic-aerodynamic theory of voice production: vocal fold vibration is the result of muscular tension and breath pressure.

naris (nares): nostril.

neural: of or pertaining to nerves or the nervous system.

neuron: a nerve cell.

node: a knotty swelling.

nodule: a lump formed by an aggregate of cells (as on the vocal fold).

occlusion: closure (as in glottal occlusion).

omohyoid: muscle that arises from the upper border of the scapula and inserts into the body of the hyoid.

orifice: an opening of relatively small size—often a passage between two parts.

oropharyngeal isthmus: the passage from the mouth to the pharynx; that part of the juncture of mouth and pharynx which is visible when looking into the mouth.

oscillation: moving backward and forward; vibration; pitch fluctuation; in singing, generally refers to a wobble—pitch variant that is too wide and too slow.

osseous: bony.

ossify: to turn into bone (as with cartilage, in aging).

overtone: one of the upper harmonic partials that together with the fundamental make up a complex musical tone; these are integral multiples of the fundamental frequency.

palate: roof of the mouth.

palatoglossus: two muscles which extend from the soft palate to the side of the tongue.

palatopharyngeus: two muscles which extend from the soft palate into the pharyngeal wall. Fibers join the salpingopharyngeus and reach as far as the thyroid cartilage.

palatosalpingeus: the tensor veli palatini muscle.

paranasal sinus: sinus near the nose: ethmoid, frontal, maxillary, and sphenoid; all exhibit tiny apertures into the nasal cavities.

pars: a part.

pars obliqua: four muscles attach to the anterior of the cricoid cartilage: two of these, the pars obliqua, are located at the sides of the cartilage and have diagonal fibers that pull the thyroid cartilage down and also pull it forward.

pars recta: four muscles attach to the anterior of the cricoid cartilage: two of these, the pars recta, are located in front and have vertical fibers that pull directly on the thyroid cartilage.

partial: a component of a complex tone.

pectoral: pertains to the chest.

pelvic fascia: fascia lining the cavity of the pelvis.

pelvis: the cavity of the pelvis; the bony structure of the lower trunk.

pericardium: the conical sac of serous membrane enclosing the heart and the roots of the great blood vessels.

perichondrium: the membrane formed of fibrous connective tissue investing the surface of cartilage, except at joints.

period: interval of time required for an oscillating body to complete one vibratory cycle.

peritoneum: serous membrane that lines the abdominal cavity.

phonation: the process of voicing; sound produced by the vocal folds.

phoneme: variant of a speech sound.

phrenic nerve: a nerve of each side of the body, arising from the fourth cervical nerve and passing through the thorax downward to the diaphragm; it is distributed chiefly over the lower surface of the diaphragm.

piriform sinus: *see* pyriform sinus.

platysma: broad, thin muscle layer on either side of the neck under the superficial fascia.

pleura (pleurae): serous membrane that lines each half of the thorax; the cavity of the pleura contains serous fluid which renders the respiratory motions frictionless.

pleura costalis: delicate serous membrane that adheres to the pericardium, to the side of the thorax, and to the upper surface of the diaphragm.

pleura pulmonalis: the pulmonary layer, closely adherent to the lung, where it is continuous with the pleura costalis.

plosive: a speech sound that is a complete stop, closure, and release of air by either the articulators or the glottis (as in some forms of [p, b, t, d, k, g]).

pomum Adami: laryngeal prominence; Adam's apple.

posticus: posterior cricoarytenoid muscle.

process: prominence of bone or cartilage (as in the vocal process).

proprioceptive: designating stimuli produced within the organism by its own tension or movement, as in muscle sense.

pyriform sinus: the space between the laryngeal collar and the alae of the thyroid cartilage.

quadrangular: having four angles or sides.

radiography: photograph made by roentgen (X) rays (named for physicist Wilhelm Conrad Röntgen).

ramus: the posterior, vertical part of the jaw that articulates with the skull.

raphé: the seam-like union of two lateral halves of an organ (as of the tongue), having a ridge or furrow.

rectus: any of several straight muscles (as the rectus abdominis and the pars rectus).

rectus abdominis: a long, flat muscle located on either side of the linea alba, extending the whole length of the front of the abdomen; it arises from the pubic crest and inserts into the cartilages of the 5th, 6th, and 7th ribs; its upper three fourths is enclosed in the rectus sheath formed by the aponeuroses of the external and internal oblique muscles ventrally, and the internal oblique and transversus abdominis dorsally.

recurrent nerve: branch of the vagus nerve that supplies all laryngeal muscles, except the cricothyroid muscle.

residual breath: breath that remains in the lung after the strongest possible (forced) expiration.

respiration: the breath cycle; the exchange of internal and external gases.

respiratory passage: the nostrils, the nasal cavities, the pharyngeal cavities, the oral cavity, the larynx, the trachea, and the bronchial tubes.

rhomboideus: a muscle under the trapezius which joins the scapulae to the spine.

rima: aperture (as in rima glottidis).

rima glottidis: the opening between the true vocal folds.

risorius: a narrow band of muscle fibers arising from the fascia over the masseter muscle, inserted into tissue at the corners of the mouth; a muscle of the cheek.

scalenus: three deep muscles (scalenus anterior, scalenus medius, scalenus posterior) on each side of the neck, extending from the transverse processes of two or more cervical vertebrae to the first or second rib; accessory muscles of respiration.

scapula: the shoulder blade.

septum: a division between two cavities (as the septum of the nose).

serous fluid: thin, watery fluid found in cavities of the body.

serous membrane: thin membranes (as in the peritoneum, pericardium, and the pleurae) that form a sac, lining a cavity or the organs in it.

serratus: muscles that arise from the ribs or vertebrae.

sheath: connective tissue covering an elongated organ or parts (as in abdominal sheath).

sibilant: characterized by a hissing sound (as in [s] and [z]).

sinus: a cavity, recess, depression (as in the sinus of Morgagni or the paranasal sinuses).

spectrogram: diagram of a spectrum.

spectrograph: apparatus for photographing the spectrum; photograph or picture of a spectrum.

spectrum analyzer: a device that displays the relative amplitudes of all the overtones of the voice in a phonation; vowel definition is shown as spectral peaks, and the singer's formant is displayed as a region of strong acoustic energy.

sphenoidal sinus: one of two irregular cavities (of the sphenoid bone) that communicate with the nasal cavities.

sphincter: a ring-like muscle around an orifice, which is capable of inducing closure.

squamous epithelium: stratified epithelium which in its outer layers consists of small scalelike cells.

sternocleidomastoid: a thick, superficial muscle on each side of the neck, arising from the sternum and the clavicle and inserting into the mastoid bone.

sternohyoid: pertains to the sternum and the hyoid (as in the muscle that extends from the medial part of the clavicle and the first segment of the sternum to the hyoid bone).

sternothyroid: pertains to sternum and thyroid (as in sternothyroid muscle).

striated muscle: fibers bound together in bundles and enclosed in a sheath of protective tissue.

styloglossus: a muscle connecting the styloid process and the tongue.

stylohyoid: pertaining to the styloid process and hyoid bone; the stylohyoid muscle.

styloid process: a long, slender process found on the lower side of the temporal bone.

subclavius: a small muscle extending from the first rib to the undersurface of the clavicle.

subglottic: below the glottis.

superficial: on or near the surface.

superior: upper.

supplemental air: air that can be expelled forcibly beyond what is exhaled during quiet breathing (also known as *reserve air*).

supraglottic: above the glottis.

suprahyoid: above the hyoid bone.

suprahyoid muscles: geniohyoid, stylohyoid, mylohyoid, and digastric muscles.

symphysis: point of union of two structures (as in the two halves of the lower jaw).

synapse: the area in which impulses are communicated between neurons (the synapse is the selective element of the nervous system; it determines whether a nervous impulse will pass through it to the next neuron).

synergy: the working together of two or more muscles (or groups) or organs.

synovia: a transparent, viscid lubricating fluid secreted by the synovial membranes of articulations, bursae, and tendon sheaths.

synovial: of or pertaining to synovia; secreting synovia.

tendon: a band of dense, fibrous connective tissue that provides attachment of muscle to bone.

tensor: a muscle that tenses (as in tensor veli palatini).

thorax: that part of the torso which houses the organs of breathing, situated between the neck and the abdomen, supported by the ribs, the costal cartilages, and the sternum.

thyroid cartilage: the largest single cartilage of the larynx.

thyroarytenoid muscle: one of the two muscles arising below the thyroidal notch and inserted into each arytenoid.

thyroepiglottic fibers: fibers of the thyroarytenoid that connect the thyroid cartilage and the epiglottis.

thyrohyoid: *see* hyothyroid.

thyromuscularis: external thyroarytenoid muscle.

thyrovocalis: the internal division of the thyroarytenoid, also known as the vocalis muscle.

tidal air: air exchanged during quiet normal breathing (same as tidal volume).

trachea: the windpipe; the main tubular system by which air passes to and from the lungs.

transverse: in a crosswise direction (as in transverse abdominis, or transverse arytenoid).

transverse abdominis: deep abdominal muscle that works synergistically with other abdominal muscles in breath management; lies just beneath the oblique abdominal muscles.

transverse arytenoid: a single muscle located horizontally between the two arytenoid cartilages, underneath the oblique arytenoid muscles.

trapezius: large, flat, triangular superficial muscle on each side of the upper back.

umbilicus: the navel.

uvula: fleshy pendant lobe located in middle of the posterior part of the soft palate.

velum: a membranous partition; the muscular portion of the soft palate.

ventral: in humans, situated anteriorly.

ventricle: a small cavity or pouch (as in the ventricles of Morgagni—the laryngeal sinuses).

vestibule: the part of the larynx above the false vocal folds.

vestigial: refers to some part of the body which was more fully developed in an earlier stage, and that may now serve no purpose.

viscera (viscerae): the soft internal organs of the body, especially those of the trunk, such as the intestines.

vital capacity: maximum amount of air that can be expired after maximum inspiration.

vocal folds: vocal cords, vocal bands; the lower part of the thyroarytenoid muscles; the true vocal cords.

vocalis muscle: the internal thyroarytenoid.

voiced: sound produced by vocal folds that have been set in motion by airflow.

xiphoid process: the lowest division of the sternum.

zygomatic arch: the arch of the bone that extends along the front and side of the skull, formed by the union of the zygomatic process of the temporal bone with the zygomatic bone.

zygomatic bone: a bone of the side of the face, below the eyes.

zygomatic muscle: a slender band of muscle on either side of the face, which arises from the zygomatic bone, and which inserts into the orbicularis oris and the skin at the corners of the mouth.

Glossary of Vocal Terms

attack (*attacco, Einsatz*): onset of voicing.

aggiustamento: vowel modification in singing; a technique for achieving an even scale throughout the registers of the singing voice.

appoggio: the establishment of dynamic balance between the inspiratory, phonatory, and resonatory systems in singing.

Bauchaussenstütze: distended abdominal "support," frequently encountered in some Nordic schools.

bel canto: "beautiful singing"; a term now frequently applied to early solo vocal literature and singing style prior to the middle of the nineteenth century; often narrowly restricted to the vocal writing (and performance practices) of Rossini, Bellini, Donizetti, and their contemporaries.

breath management: a learned technique of breath control for singing which permits efficient handling of the breath cycle.

cabaletta: the second major portion of the opera scena form (which generally consists of the cavatina, a bridging recitative, and the subsequent cabaletta); usually a florid and dramatic contrast to the preceding cantilena.

cantabile: in singing style.

cantilena: a graceful flowing melody in "singing" style.

chest voice: descriptive term for sensations experienced in lower range where "heavy mechanism" is allowed to predominate.

chiaroscuro tone: the "dark–light" tone which characterizes well-balanced resonance in the singing voice.

colpo di glottide (also *colpo della glottide*): the vocal onset which results when airflow commences over occluded vocal folds.

copertura: the technique of singing with *voce chiusa* timbre as opposed to *voce aperta* (also, *voce bianca*) timbre.

coup de glotte: the onset of singing tone that results when airflow commences over the occluded vocal folds, resulting in a click-like sound.

cover: a term often used as a description of laryngeal events coupled with excessive vowel modification that produce darkened vocal timbre; an exact definition is not possible because of the variations in meaning.

Deckung: "cover."

Fach: a term universally used to designate vocal category; type of singing voice.

fioriture: ornaments, cadenzas, and florid passages.

flageolet voice: a register of the female voice often extending more than a perfect fifth beyond the normal pitches of the head voice, the result of extreme vocal fold damping.

311

Glottisschlag: stroke of the glottis.

heavy mechanism: a term sometimes used to describe the predominant action of the vocalis muscle; chest voice.

imposto (*impostazione della voce*):   placement of the voice.
Intendant: general manager of an opera theater.

Knacklaut: a glottal attack.

light mechanism: a term sometimes used to describe the predominant action of the vocal ligament as opposed to the predominant action of the vocalis muscle; head voice.
lotta vocale (also *lutta vocale*, and *lutte vocale*):   the vocal contest or struggle.

marking: an international term for the technique of sparing the voice in rehearsal.
mask sensations: vibratory sensation in the zygomatic and nasal regions of the face, through bone conduction.
melisma (melismatic):   several notes to a single syllable (florid singing).

oscillation (wobble):   in vocal pedagogy, generally refers to a pitch variant of the vibrato phenomenon that is too slow and too wide.

passaggio: vocal register pivotal point (as in *primo passaggio, secondo passaggio*).
placement of the voice: a subjective term denoting vibratory sensations during singing.

register: a series of consecutive voice tones of equal (or similar) timbre, which can be distinguished from adjoining series of tones.

Schnarrbass: a register in the male voice that lies below the normal pitches used in speech or song.
sostenuto: the sustaining of the singing voice.
Sprengeinsatz: the heavy glottal stroke as a technique for vocal attack.
straight tone: tone devoid of vibrato, in which the relaxant principle that produces vibrato is not permitted to function.
Strohbass: *see* Schnarrbass.

tremolo: in vocal pedagogy the term properly refers to a vibrato rate that is too fast and too narrow (in opposition to the wobble or oscillation).
trill: a pitch variant of a semitone or more in width, produced by an intended oscillation of the voice box.

vibrato: a phenomenon of the schooled singing voice; a pitch variant produced as a result of neurological impulses that occur when proper coordination exists between the breath mechanism and the phonatory mechanism; a natural result of the dynamic balancing of airflow and vocal-fold approximation.

vocal fry: considered by some as a register of the male voice; it resembles a "frying" sound; considered by others to be a prolonged, inefficient vocal onset.

voce aperta: open, unskillful singing.

voce chiara: clearly produced vocal timbre.

voce chiusa: well-balanced resonance in the singing voice; avoidance of *voce aperta.*

voce coperta: timbre that is equalized in the upper ranges through proper *aggiustamento* of the vowel so as to avoid shrill or blatant timbre.

voce finta: feigned voice; a timbre in the male voice that avoids the *voce piena* timbre associated with the "well-supported" voice.

voce mista: a descriptive term that refers to the vocal timbre in the *zona intermedia* (*zona di passaggio*) where elements of *voce di testa* greatly modify action of the "heavy mechanism."

voce di petto: vocal timbre produced largely by the vocalis activity of the vocal folds; the "heavy mechanism."

voce piena: "full" voice as opposed to *voce finta* and falsetto; the term does not refer solely to dynamic level, but rather to timbre as well.

voce di testa: the "head voice" of the classic schools; there is a marked diminution of "chest voice" activity in this range.

wobble: undesirable oscillation of the singing voice.

zona di passaggio: that area of the voice wherein a number of tones can be sung by varying register principles; middle voice.

Bibliography

ARTICLES

ACKERMAN, ELLA LAURETTA (1935). "Action of the velum palatinum on the velar sounds [k] and [g]." *Vox*, Heft 1:6; 2:9.

AGOSTONI, EMILIO (1961). "A graphical analysis of thoracoabdominal mechanics during the breathing cycle." *Journal of Applied Physiology* 15: 349–353.

———(1962). "Diaphragm activity and thoraco-abdominal mechanics during positive-pressure breathing." *Journal of Applied Physiology* 17: 215–220.

———(1963). "Diaphragm activity in breath holding: factors related to onset." *Journal of Applied Physiology* 18: 30–36.

———(1970a). "Dynamics." *The Respiratory Muscles*, ed. by E. J. M. Campbell, E. Agostoni, and J. Newsom Davis, 2d ed. London: Lloyd-Luke [Medical Books], 80–113.

———(1970b). "Kinematics." *The Respiratory Muscles,* ed. by E. J. M. Campbell, E. Agostoni, and J. Newsom Davis, 2d ed. London: Lloyd-Luke [Medical Books], 23–47.

AGOSTONI, EMILIO; MOGNONI, P.; TORRI, G.; AND SARACINO, F. (1965). "Relation between changes of rib cage circumference and lung volume." *Journal of Applied Physiology* 20: 1179–1186.

———(1965). "Static features of the passive rib cage and abdomen–diaphragm." *Journal of Applied Physiology* 20: 1187–1189.

ÅGREN, KARIN, AND SUNDBERG, JOHAN (1978). "An acoustic comparison of alto and tenor voices." *Journal of Research in Singing* 2, 1: 26–33.

AIKEN, R. C. C.; ZEALLEY, A. K.; AND ROSENTHAL, S. V. (1970). "Some psychological and physiological considerations of breathlessness." *Breathing: Hering–Breuer Centenary Symposium (Ciba Foundation)*, ed. by Ruth Porter. London: J. & A. Churchill, 253–264.

ALBANESE, LICIA (1944). "How much of singing can be taught?" *The Etude* July, 62: 387.

ALBERTI, HELEN (1947). "Facts concerning the art of bel canto or the basis of bel canto." *The NATS Bulletin* 4, 2: 4–6.

ALEXANDER, A. B. (1971a). "The medical care of singers and actors in different European countries." *Folia Phoniatrica* 23: 323.

———(1971b) "Aspects of symmetry in male and female laryngeal function." *Folia Phoniatrica* 23: 232.

ALLEN, ELIZABETH (1981). "An integration of research in singing." *Transcripts of the Ninth Symposium: Care of the Professional Voice*, Part I, ed. by V. Lawrence. New York: The Voice Foundation, 66–71.

ALLEN, G. D. (1970). "Temporal structures in speech production." *Journal of the Acoustical Society of America* 47: 58.

AMERMAN, J. D.; DANILOFF, R. G.; AND MOLL, K. L. (1970). "Lip and jaw coartic-

315

ulation for the phoneme [æ]. *Journal of the Acoustical Society of America* 13: 147–161.

ANDREW, B. L. (1953). "The respiratory displacement of the larynx: a study of the innervation of accessory respiratory muscles." *Journal of Psychology* 130: 474–487.

APPELMAN, D. RALPH (1959). "Science of resonance." *Music Journal* 17, 3: 44–45.

———(1968). "Whither vocal pedagogy?" *The NATS Bulletin* 24, 4: 17–21; 34–35; 56.

ARKEBAUER, H.; HIXON, T. J.; AND HARDY, J. C. (1967). "Peak intraoral air pressure during speech." *Journal of Speech and Hearing Research* 10: 196–208.

ARMSTRONG, B. W., AND SMITH, D. J. (1955). "Function of certain neck muscles during the expiratory cycle." *American Journal of Physiology* 182: 599–600.

ARMSTRONG, WILLIAM G. (1944). "The art of classifying voices." *The Etude* February, 62: 87.

———(1944). "Weak low tones." *The Etude* October, 62: 56–57.

———(1945). "The use of the palato-pharyngeal muscles in singing." *The Etude* February, 63: 75.

ARNOLD, G. E. (1957). "Morphology and physiology of the speech organs." *Manual of Phonetics*, ed. by Louise Kaiser. Amsterdam: North-Holland Publishing, 31–64.

———(1961). "Physiology and pathology of the cricothyroid muscle." *Laryngoscope* 71: 687–753.

ASHBY, M. G. (1983). "Effects of variation in larynx height." *Speech, Hearing and Language: Work in Progress 1983*, ed. by V. Hazan and A. J. Fourcin, U. C. L., No. 1. London: University College, 31–39.

ASSMAN, PETER F.; NEAREY, TERRANCE M.; AND HOGAN, JOHN (1982). "Vowel identification: orthographic, perceptual and acoustic aspects." *Journal of the Acoustical Society of America* 71: 975–989.

ASTRAQUILLO, CORBELITA J.; BLATT, IRVING M.; HOPPEL, LEO; AND MARTINEZ, ROBERT (1977). "Investigation of the relationship between abdominal muscular discipline and the art of singing: an electromyographic study." *American Academy of Ophthalmology and Otolaryngology*, 498–519.

AUERSWALD, ADRIENNE (1968). "How singers *think* they sing." *Sound Production in Man: Annals of the New York Academy of Sciences*, ed. by Arend Bouhuys. New York: New York Academy of Sciences, 230–246.

BAER, HERMANUS (1972). "Establishing a correct basic technique for singing." *The NATS Bulletin* 28, 4: 12–14.

BAER, THOMAS; BELL-BERTI, FREDERICKA; AND RUBIN, PHILIP (1979). "Articulation and voice quality." *Transcripts of the Seventh Symposium: Care of the Professional Voice*, Part I, ed. by V. Lawrence. New York: The Voice Foundation, 48–53.

BAKEN, R. J., AND CAVALLO, S. A. (1981). "Prephonatory chest wall posturing." *Folia Phoniatrica* 33: 193–203.

BAKER, GEORGE (1965). "Singers and teachers." *Opera* 16: 473–478.

BALLANTYNE, JOHN (1961). "Occupational disorders of the larynx." *Scott-Brown's Diseases of the Ear, Nose and Throat*, Vol. IV, *The Throat*, 3d ed. London: Butterworth, 541–557.

BARNEY, H. L.; DUNN, H. K.; AND HILL, MURRAY (1957a). "Speech analysis."

Manual of Phonetics, ed. by Louise Kaiser. Amsterdam: North-Holland Publishing, 180–201.

———(1957b). "Speech synthesis." *Manual of Phonetics,* ed. by Louise Kaiser. Amsterdam: North-Holland Publishing, 203–212.

BARTHOLOMEW, W. T. (1934). "A physical definition of 'good voice quality' in the male voice." *Journal of the Acoustical Society of America* 23, 6: 25–33.

BASTIAN, ROBERT (1984). "Hoarseness in singers." *The NATS Bulletin* 40, 3: 26–27.

BEARD, CHARLES (1980). "Recognition of chest, head, and falsetto isoparametric tones." *The NATS Bulletin* 37, 1: 8–14.

BEHNKE, EMIL (1883). "Names of the registers." *The Voice* 5, 12: 187.

BELL-BERTI, FREDERICKA (1975). "Control of pharyngeal cavity size for English voiced and voiceless stops." *Journal of the Acoustical Society of America* 57, 2: 456–461.

BELL-BERTI, FREDERICKA, AND HARRIS, KATHERINE S. (1982). "Temporal patterns of coarticulation: lip rounding." *Journal of the Acoustical Society of America* 71, 2: 449–454.

BENNETT, GERALD (1981). "Singing synthesis in electronic music." *Research Aspects on Singing,* ed. by J. Sundberg. Stockholm: The Royal Swedish Academy of Music, 34–50.

BERCI, G.; FLEMING, W. B.; DUNLOP, E. E.; MADIGAN, J. P.; CAMPBELL, J. J.; KONT, L. A. (1967). "New endoscopic technique for examination and cinematography of the nasopharynx." *Cancer* 20: 2013–2019.

BERGOFSKY, E. H. (1964). "Relative contribution of the rib cage and the diaphragm to ventilation in man." *Journal of Applied Physiology* 19: 698–706.

BISHOP, BEVERLY (1968). "Neural regulation of abdominal muscle contractions." *Sound Production in Man: Annals of the New York Academy of Sciences,* ed. by Arend Bouhuys. New York: New York Academy of Sciences, 191–200.

BJOERLING, JUSSI (1950). "Your vocal problem." *The Etude* June, 68: 21.

BJORK, L. (1961). "Velopharyngeal function in connected speech." *Acta Radiologica* (supplement): 202, 1–94.

BJØRKLUND, ADOLPH (1961). "Analyses of soprano voices." *Journal of the Acoustical Society of America* 33: 575–582.

BJÖRN, E.; LINDBLOM, F.; LUBKEN, J. F., AND PAULI, STEFAN (1977). "An acoustic-perceptual method for the qualitative evaluation of hypernasality." *Journal of Speech and Hearing Research* 60: 486.

BLACK, J. W. (1939). "The effects of the consonant on the vowel." *Journal of the Acoustical Society of America* 9: 203–205.

———(1958). "The pressure component in the production of consonants." *Journal of Speech and Hearing Disorders* 15:206–210.

BLANTON, P. L., AND BRIGGS, N. L. (1969). "Eighteen hundred years of controversy: the paranasal sinuses." *American Journal of Anatomy* 124: 135–148.

BLOOM, S. W. (1969). "Cancer of the nasopharynx: a study of ninety cases." *Journal of Mt. Sinai Hospital* 36: 277–293.

BLOOMER, HARLAN H. (1953). "Observations on palatopharyngeal movements in speech and deglutition." *Journal of Speech and Hearing Disorders* 18: 230–246.

BOË, LOUIS-JEAN, AND RAKOTOFIRLINGA, HIPPOLYTE (1975). "A statistical analysis of laryngeal frequency; its relationship to intensity level and duration." *Language and Speech* 18: 1–13.

BÖHME, G.; ŠRAM, F.; AND KALVODOVÁ, B. (1966). "Elektromyographische Untersuchungen über das Verhalten der Mm. levator und tensor palatini bei der Atmung und bei Phonation von Vokalen." *Folia Phoniatrica* 18: 9.

BOLLEW,, JOSEPH A. (1952). "Breathing and breath control in singing." *The Etude* February, 70: 22.

———(1953). "Attack and emission in singing." *The Etude* February, 71: 14.

———(1954a). "Is the falsetto false?" *The Etude* July, 72: 14.

———(1954b). "What price vocal longevity?" *The Etude* April, 72: 17.

———(1956). "Diction in singing." *The Etude* May–June, 74: 14.

BOND, Z. B. (1976). "Identification of vowels excerpted from /1/ and /r/ contexts." *Journal of the Acoustical Society of America* 60: 906–910.

BOONE, DANIEL (1980). "Vocal hygiene: the optimal use of the larynx." *Journal of Research in Singing* 4, 1: 35–43.

BORCHERS, ORVILLE J. (1951). "The phenomenon of vocal tone quality." *The NATS Bulletin* 8, 2: 15.

BORI, LUCREZIA (1947). "Technical proficiency in singing." *The Etude* June, 65: 324.

BOSMA, J. F. (1961). "Comparative physiology of the pharynx." *Congenital Physiology of the Face and Associated Structures,* ed. by S. Pruzansky. Springfield, IL: Charles C Thomas.

BOSMA, J. F.; SHEETS, B.; AND SHELTON, B. (1960). "Tongue, hyoid and larynx displacement in swallowing and phonation." *Journal of Applied Physiology* 15: 283.

BOUHUYS, AREND; PROCTOR, D. F.; AND MEAD, J. (1966). "Kinetic aspects of singing." *Journal of Applied Physiology* 21: 483–496.

BOUHUYS, AREND; PROCTOR, D. F.; MEAD, J.; AND STEVENS, K. H. (1968). "Pressure-flow events during singing." *Sound Production in Man: Annals of the New York Academy of Sciences.* New York: New York Academy of Sciences, 165–176.

BRACKETT, I. P. (1948). "The vibration of the vocal folds at selected frequencies." *Annals of Otology, Rhinology and Laryngology* 57: 556.

BRAVENDER, PAUL E. (1980). "The effect of cheerleading on the female singing voice." *The NATS Bulletin* 37, 2: 9–13.

BREUER, J. (1868). "Self-steering of respiration through the *nervus vagus.*" *Breathing: Hering–Breuer Centenary Symposium,* ed. by Ruth Porter; transl. by Elizabeth Ullmann. London: J. & A. Churchill, 365–394.

BREWER, DAVID W.; BRIESS, F. BERTRAM; AND FAABORG-ANDERSEN, KNUD (1960). "Phonation: clinical testing versus electromyography." *Annals of Otology, Rhinology and Laryngology* 69: 781.

BRIESS, BERTRAM (1964). "Voice diagnosis and therapy." *Research Potentials in Voice Physiology,* ed. by David W. Brewer. Syracuse, NY: State University of New York, 259–295.

BRITISH MEDICAL JOURNAL (1975). "Smoking and Aging." 5991: 273–274.

BROAD, DAVID J. (1973). "Phonation." *Normal Aspects of Speech, Hearing and Language,* ed. by Fred D. Minifie, Thomas J. Hixon, and Frederick Williams. Englewood Cliffs, NJ: Prentice-Hall, 127–167.

BRODNITZ, FRIEDRICH S. (1954). "Voice problems of the actor and singer." *Journal of Speech and Hearing Disorders* 19: 322–326.

———(1957). "The singing teacher and the laryngologist." *The NATS Bulletin* 13, 3: 2–3; 15.

———(1971a). "Hormones and the human voice." *The NATS Bulletin* 37, 2: 16–18.

———(1975). "The age of the castrato voice." *Journal of Speech and Hearing Disorders* 19: 322–326.

———(1984). "On change of voice." *The NATS Bulletin* 40, 2: 24–26.

BRODY, VIOLA A., AND WESTERMAN, KENNETH (1951). "An emergent concept of the singing art." *The NATS Bulletin* 8, 2: 7; 22–24.

BROWN, OREN (1953). "Principles of voice therapy as applied to teaching." *The NATS Bulletin* 9, 5: 16; 21.

———(1958). "Causes of voice strain in singing." *The NATS Bulletin* 15, 2; 20–21; 30.

———(1978). "Voice examination of the professional." *The NATS Bulletin* 34, 4: 14–15.

BROWN, W. S., JR., AND HOLLIEN, HARRY (1982). "Effect of menstruation on fundamental frequency." *Transcripts of the Tenth Symposium: Care of the Professional Voice*, Part I, ed. by V. Lawrence. New York: The Voice Foundation, 94–101.

BROWNE, LENNOX, AND BEHNKE, EMIL (1884a). "The dangers of tight-lacing: vocalists warned against impeding respiration by wearing close-fitting, unyielding stays." *The Voice* 6, 8: 121–122.

———(1884b). "Photographing the vocal organs." *The Voice* 6, 1: cover pages.

———(1884c). "The registers of the human voice." *The Voice* 6, 3: 42–44.

BRUCE, R. A.; LOVEJOY, F. W., JR.; PEARSON, R.; YU, P. N. G.; BROTHERS, B. G.; AND VELASQUEZ, T. (1949). "Normal respiratory and circulatory pathways of adaptation in exercise." *Journal of Clinical Investigation* 28: 1423.

BULLARD, EDITH (1947). "Breathing in relation to vocal expression." *The Etude* February, 65: 75.

BUNCH, MERIBETH (1976). "A cephalometric study of structures of the head and neck during sustained phonation of covered and open qualities." *Folia Phoniatrica* 28: 321–328.

———(1977). A survey of the research on covered and open voice qualities." *The NATS Bulletin* 33, 3: 11–18.

BUNCH, M., AND SONNINEN, AATTO (1977). "Some further observations on covered and open voice qualities." *The NATS Bulletin* 34, 1: 26–30; 33.

BURGIN, JOHN. (1978). "Contributions to vocal pedagogy, 1972–1975." *The NATS Bulletin* 34, 3: 13–22.

CALNAN, J. S. (1953). "Movements of the soft palate." *British Journal of Plastic Surgery* 5: 286.

CAMPBELL,, E. J. MORAN (1955). "The role of the scalene and sternomastoid muscles in breathing in normal subjects: an electromyographic study." *Journal of Anatomy* 89: 373–386.

———(1968). "The respiratory muscles." *Sound Production in Man: Annals of the New York Academy of Sciences*. New York: New York Academy of Sciences, 135–140.

———(1970). "Accessory muscles." *The Respiratory Muscles*, ed. by E. J. Moran Campbell, E. Agostoni, and J. Newsom Davis. London: Lloyd-Luke [Medical Books], 181–193.

CAMPBELL, E. J. MORAN, AND GREEN, J. H. (1955). "The behaviour of the abdominal muscles and the intra-abdominal pressure during quiet breathing and increased ventilation: a study in man." *Journal of Physiology* 127: 423–426.

CAMPBELL, E. J. MORAN, AND NEWSOM DAVIS, J. (1970a). "The intercostal muscles and other muscles of the rib cage." *The Respiratory Muscles*, ed. by E. J. Moran Campbell, E. Agostoni, and J. Newsom Davis. London: Lloyd-Luke [Medical Books], 161–180.

———(1970b). "Muscles of the larynx and thyroid cartilage." *The Respiratory Muscles*, ed. by E. J. Moran Campbell, E. Agostoni, and J. Newsom Davis. London: Lloyd-Luke [Medical Books], 194–198.

———(1970c). "Respiratory Sensation." *The Respiratory Muscles*, ed. by E. J. Moran Campbell, E. Agostoni, and J. Newsom Davis. London: Lloyd-Luke [Medical Books], 291–306.

CAPPIANI, LUISA (1883). "Vocal culture dependent more upon a musical ear and the right use of the voice than upon a naturally fine voice." *The Voice* 5: 191–192.

CARHART, PAUL W., AND KENYON, JOHN S. (1961). "A guide to pronunciation." *Webster's New International Dictionary of the English Language*, 2d ed., unabridged. Springfield, MA: G. & C. Merriam, xxii–lxxx.

CARROLL, CHRISTINA (1974). "Longevity of vocal careers." *Folia Phoniatrica* 26: 293–294.

CASSELMAN, EUGENE (1950). "The secret of bel canto." *The Etude* September, 68: 20–22.

———(1951). "The singer's breath" (Part I). *The Etude* October, 68: 22.

———(1951). "The singer's breath" (Part II). *The Etude* November, 68: 20–23.

CATELL, McKEEN; LANSDOWNE, FRANCES S.; MUSCHENHEIM, CARL; GOLD, HARRY; GUION, CONNIE M.; LOVELESS, MARY; LEVINE, MILTON I.; AND MODELL, WALTER (1953). "Conference on therapy, treatment of cough." *The American Journal of Medicine* 14: 87–98.

CATFORD, J. C. (1968). "The articulatory possibilities of man." *Manual of Phonetics*, ed. by Bertil Malmberg. Amsterdam: North-Holland Publishing, 309–333.

CAVAGNA, GIOVANNI A., AND MARGARIA, RODOLFO (1965). "An analysis of the mechanics of phonation." *Journal of Applied Physiology* 20: 301.

———(1968). "Airflow rates and efficiency changes during phonation." *Sound Production in Man: Annals of the New York Academy of Sciences*, ed. by Arend Bouhuys. New York: New York Academy of Sciences, 152–164.

CAVALLO, STEPHEN A., AND BACON, R. J. (1983). "The laryngeal component of prephonatory chest wall posturing." *Transcripts of the Eleventh Symposium: Care of the Professional Voice*, Part I, ed. by V. Lawrence. New York: The Voice Foundation, 37–45.

CLEVELAND, THOMAS (1977). "Acoustic properties of voice timbre types and their influence on voice classification." *The Journal of the Acoustical Society of America* 61:1622–1629.

CLIPPINGER, D. A. (1920). "The eye and ear in voice teaching." *The Etude* January, 38: 51–52.

COFFIN, BERTON (1964). "The singer's diction." *The NATS Bulletin* 20, 3: 10; 19.

———(1974). "The instrumental resonance of the singing voice." *The NATS Bulletin* 31, 2: 26–33, 39.

———(1975). "The relationship of the breath, phonation and resonance in singing." *The NATS Bulletin* 31, 3: 37–44.

———(1976). "Articulation for opera, oratorio and recital." *The NATS Bulletin* 32, 3:26–39; 37–41.

COKER, C. H., AND UMEDA, N. (1975). "The importance of spectral detail in initial–final contrasts of voiced stops." *Journal of Phonetics* 3: 63–68.

COLE, R. A., AND SCOTT, B. (1974a). "Phantom in the phoneme: invariant cues for stop consonants." *Perception and Psychology* 15: 101–107.

———(1974b). "Toward a theory of speech perception." *Psychological Review* 81: 348–374.

COLEMAN, ROBERT F. (1981). "Acoustic and perceptual factors in vibrato." *Transcripts of the Eighth Symposium: Care of the Professional Voice*, ed. by V. Lawrence and B. Weinberg. New York: The Voice Foundation, 36–38.

———(1982). "Vocal adaptation to performance sites." *Transcripts of the Tenth Symposium: Care of the Professional Voice*, Part II, ed. by V. Lawrence. New York: The Voice Foundation, 110–114.

COLLINS, JOHN C. (1969a). "Singing, a comparative analysis." Part I. *The NATS Bulletin*, 25, 3: 32–37, 58.

———(1969b). "Singing, a comparative analysis." Part II. *The NATS Bulletin*, 25, 4: 12–19; 32–33.

COLTON, RAY H. (1972). "The source spectrum in the modal and falsetto registers." *Folia Phoniatrica* 24: 331–334.

———(1973). "Some acoustic parameters related to the perception of modal-falsetto voice quality." *Folia Phoniatrica* 25: 302–311.

COLTON, RAY H., AND ESTILL, JO (1976). "Perceptual differentiation of voice modes." *Report to the Fifth Symposium: Care of the Professional Voice.* New York: The Voice Foundation.

CONDAX, I. D.; ACSON, V.; MIKI, C. C.; AND SAKODA, K. K. (1976). "A technique for monitoring velic action by means of a photo-electric nasal probe: application to French." *Journal of Phonetics* 4: 178–181.

CONLEY, EUGENE (1950). "How to build a voice." *The Etude* March, 68: 14.

CONLEY, EUGENE T. (1967). "An X-ray study of the larynx position of good and poor speakers." *The NATS Bulletin* 24, 1: 4–5.

CONNER, NADINE (1945). "Mental projection in singing." *The Etude* May, 63: 249.

COOPER, F. S. (1950). "Spectrum analysis." *Journal of the Acoustical Society of America* 22: 761–762.

COOPER MORTON (1970). "Vocal suicide in singers." *The NATS Bulletin* 26, 3: 7–10; 31.

———(1982). "The tired speaking voice and the negative effect on the singing voice." *The NATS Bulletin* 39, 2: 11–14.

COOPER, WILLIAM E. (1974). "Selective adaptation for acoustic cues of voicing in initial stops." *Journal of Phonetics* 2: 303–343.

CORSO, J. F. (1963). "Bone conducted thresholds for sonic and ultrasonic frequencies." *Journal of the Acoustical Society of America* 35: 1738–1743.

CRONIN, P. H. (1884). "How shall we breathe?" *The Voice* 6, 4: 8.

CRUL, THOM A. M. (1981). "The phoneme discrimination test: a valid diagnostic test?" *Congress Proceedings and Abstracts of the IXth Congress of the Union of European Phoniatricians*, ed. by H. K. Schutte. Groningen: Centrale Reproductiendienst Vrije Universiteit, 38–59.

CRYSTAL, DAVID (1983). "Psycholinguistics." XIXth International Congress of Logopedics and Phoniatrics. *Folia Phoniatrica* 35: 1–12.

CURRY, ROBERT (1938). "The physiology of the contralto voice." *Archives néerlandaises de phonétique expérimentale.* 15: 73–79.

_____(1959). "The mechanism for breathing for voice." *Quarterly Journal of Experimental Physiology* 44: 139.

CUTTING, JAMES E., AND DAY, RUTH S. (1975). "The perception of stop-liquid clusters in phonological fusion." *Journal of Phonetics* 3: 99–113.

DANILOFF, RAYMOND D. (1973). "Normal articulation processes." *Normal Aspects of Speech, Hearing and Language*, ed. by Fred D. Minifie, Thomas J. Hixon, and Frederick Williams. Englewood Cliffs, NJ: Prentice-Hall, 169–209.

_____(1981). "Supraglottal aspects of voicing." *Transcripts of the Ninth Symposium: Care of the Professional Voice*, Part II, ed. by V. Lawrence. New York: The Voice Foundation, 38–44.

DEATHERAGE, B. H.; DAVIS, J.; AND ELDREDGE, D. H. (1957). "Physiological evidence for the masking of low frequencies by high." *Journal of the Acoustical Society of America* 29: 132–137.

DE BIDOLI, EMI (1947). "Old methods of voice teaching versus new ones." *The NATS Bulletin* 3, 4: 3.

DELATTRE, PIERRE (1958). "Vocal color and voice quality: an acoustic articulatory comparison." *The NATS Bulletin* 15, 1: 4–7.

DE LOS ANGELES, VICTORIA (1957). "Singing must be natural." *The Etude* March, 75: 13.

DE LUCA, GIUSEPPE (1946). "Singing at Sixty-Nine." *The Etude* August, 64: 435.

_____(1950). "Good singing takes time." *The Etude* November, 68: 435.

DEUTSCH, J. A., AND CLARKSON, J. K. (1959). "The nature of the vibrato and control loop in singing." *Nature* 183: 167–168.

DEYOUNG, RICHARD (1953). "Some practical aspects of educational psychology." *The NATS Bulletin* 9, 3: 7–8; 17.

DICKENSON, JEAN (1944). "Make haste slowly." *The Etude* March, 62: 136.

DICKSON, D. R., AND DICKSON, W. M. (1972). "Velopharyngeal anatomy." *Journal of Speech and Hearing Research* 15:372.

DMITRIEV, L. B.; CHERNOV, B. P.; AND MASLOV, V. T. (1983). "Function of the voice mechanism in double-vowel Touvinian singing." *Folia Phoniatrica* 35: 193–197.

DMITRIEV, L. B., AND KISELEVA, A. (1979). "Relationship between the formant structure of different types of singing voices and the dimensions of the supraglottic cavities." *Folia Phoniatrica* 31: 238–241.

DOMINGO, PLACIDO (1982). Interview by Jerome Hines in *Great Singers on Great Singing.* New York: Doubleday, 99–108.

DONALD, K. W. (1953). "The definition and assessment of respiratory function." *British Medical Journal* 4807: 415.

DONALDSON, ROBERT P. (1973). "The practice and pedagogy of vocal legato." *The NATS Bulletin* 29, 4: 12–21.

DOOB, DOROTHY (1958). "Rhinolalia." *Twentieth Century Speech and Voice Correction*, ed. by Emil Froeschels. New York: Philosophical Library, pp. 152–165.

DOSCHER, BARBARA M. (1975). "The beginning voice class." *The NATS Bulletin* 32, 1: 31–33; 45.

DOW, SABRINA H. (1883). "Articulation in singing." *The Voice* 5, 7: 145–147.

DRAPER, M. H.; LADEFOGED, PETER; AND WHITTERIDGE, D. (1959). "Respiratory muscles in speech." *Journal of Speech and Hearing Research* 2: 16–27.

DUBOIS, A.B.; BRODY, A. W.; LEWIS, D. H.; AND BURGESS, F. (1956). "Oscillation mechanics of lungs and chest in man." *Journal of Applied Physiology* 16: 29–30.

DUNN, H. K. (1950). "The calculation of vowel resonances, and an electrical vocal tract." *Journal of the Acoustical Society of America* 22: 740.

DWYER, EDWARD J. (1967). "Concepts of breathing for singing." *The NATS Bulletin* 14, 1: 40–43.

EDWIN, ROBERT (1982). "Voice and speech dynamics in the total personality." *The NATS Bulletin* 38, 3: 38–42.

EKSTROM, E. ROSS (1960). "Control of singing intensity as related to singer experience." *The NATS Bulletin* 17, 2: 8–12.

ESTILL, JO (1983). "The control of voice quality." *Transcripts of the Eleventh Symposium: Care of the Professional Voice*, Part II, ed. by V. Lawrence. New York: The Voice Foundation, 152–169.

FAABORG-ANDERSEN, KNUD (1957). "Electromyographic investigation of intrinsic laryngeal muscles in humans." *Acta Physiologica Scandinavica* (supplement) 41: 140.

_____(1964). "Electromyography of the laryngeal muscles in man." *Research Potentials in Voice Physiology*, ed. by David W. Brewer. Syracuse, NY: State University of New York, 105–123.

FAABORG-ANDERSEN, KNUD, AND SONNINEN, AATTO A. (1958). "The function of the extrinsic laryngeal muscles at different pitch levels." *Acta Otolaryngologica* 49: 47.

FANT, GUNNAR (1962). "Descriptive analysis of the acoustic aspects of speech." *Logos* 5: 3–17.

_____(1964). "Phonetics and speech research." *Research Potentials in Voice Physiology*, ed. by David W. Brewer. Syracuse, NY: State University of New York, 199–239.

_____(1968). "Analysis and synthesis of speech processes." *Manual of Phonetics*, ed. by Bertil Malmberg. Amsterdam: North-Holland Publishing, 173–277.

FANT, GUNNAR; FENTOFT, K.; LILJENCRANTS, J.; LINDBLOM, B.; AND MARTONY, J. (1963). "Formant amplitude measurements." *Journal of the Acoustical Society of America* 35: 1753.

FIELDS, VICTOR A. (1970). "Review of the literature on vocal registers." *The NATS Bulletin* 26, 3: 37–39; 53.

_____(1972a). "Art versus science in singing: a basic approach for the teacher." Part I. *The NATS Bulletin* 29, 1: 26; 29.

_____(1972b). "How mind governs voice: a basic approach in the teaching of singing." Part II. *The NATS Bulletin* 29, 2: 2–10; 29.

_____(1973). "Prerequisites in freeing the voice: a basic approach in the teaching of singing." Part III. *The NATS Bulletin* 29, 3: 16–21; 25; 41.

FILLENZ, MARIANNE, AND WOODS, R. I. (1970). "Sensory innervations of the airways." *Breathing: Hering–Breuer Centenary Symposium*, ed. by Ruth Porter. London: J. & A. Churchill, 101–109.

FINK B. R.; BASEK, M; AND EPANCHIN, V. (1956). "The mechanism of opening the human larynx." *Laryngoscope* 66: 410.

FISCHER-JØRGENSEN, ELI (1954). "Acoustic analysis of stop consonants." *Miscellanea Phonetica* 2: 42–59.

FLANAGAN, J. L. (1958). "Some properties of the glottal sound source." *Journal of Speech and Hearing Research* 1: 99–116.

FLANK, M. (1964). "Über die unterschiedliche Grösse der Morganischen Ventrikel bei Sängern." *Folia Phoniatrica* 16: 67–74.

FLETCHER, HARVEY (1934). "Loudness, pitch, and timbre of musical tones and their relationship to the intensity, frequency, and the overtone structure." *Journal of the Acoustical Society of America* 6: 59–69.

FLETCHER, S. G. (1959). "Growth and development of the mouth and the pharynx: a review of normal growth patterns and a method of cephalometric evaluation applied to individuals having hypernasal voice." *Logo* 2: 71.

FLOYD, W. F.; NEGUS, V. E.; AND NEIL, E. (1956). "Observations on the mechanism of phonation." *Laryngoscope* 66: 410.

FOOTE, BRUCE (1963). "New horizons in the teaching of voice pedagogy." *The NATS Bulletin* 19, 3: 22–23; 26–27.

FOX, WILLIAM H. (1950). "Some psychological principles involved in the teaching of singing." *The NATS Bulletin* 7, 1: 8–9.

FRANKSTEIN, S. I. (1970). "Neural control of respiration." *Breathing: Hering–Breuer Centenary Symposium*, ed. by Ruth Porter. London: J. & A. Churchill, 53–76.

FREEDMAN, L. M. (1955). "The role of the cricothyroid muscles in tension of the vocal cords." *Archives of Otolaryngology* 62: 347.

FRITZELL, BJÖRN (1963). "An electromyographic study of the movements of the soft palate." *Folia Phoniatrica* 15: 307–311.

———(1969). "The velopharyngeal muscles in speech: an electromyographic and cineradiographic study." *Acta Oto-laryngologica* (supplement) 250: 1–81.

———(1979). "Electromyography in the study of velopharyngeal function—a review." *Folia Phoniatrica* 31: 93–102.

———(1981). "Singing and the health of the voice." *Research Aspects in Singing*, ed. by J. Sundberg. Stockholm: The Royal Swedish Academy of Music, 92–108.

FROESCHELS, EMIL (1940). "Psychology of the laryngeal functions." *Archives of Otolaryngology* 32: 1030–1044.

———(1943). "Hygiene of the voice." *Archives of Otolaryngology* 38: 122–130.

———(1944). "Uvula and tonsils." *Archives of Otolaryngology* 50: 216.

———(1952). "Chewing method as therapy." *Archives of Otolaryngology* 56: 427.

———(1954). "Phonetics—old and new." *Folia Phoniatrica* 6: 101–110.

———(1957a). "Nose and nasality." *Archives of Otolaryngology* 66: 629–633.

———(1957b). "The question of the origin of the vibrations of the vocal cords." *Archives of Otolaryngology* 66: 512.

FROESCHELS, EMIL, AND SITTIG, ELLY (1948). "Anatomy and physiology." *Twentieth Century Speech and Voice Correction*, ed. by Emil Froeschels. New York: Philosophical Library, pp. 2–34.

FROMMHOLD, W., AND HOPPE, G. (1965). "Tomographische Studien zur Funktion des menschlichen Kehlkopfes (I Mitteilung: Unterschiede in der Stimmlippenmechanik)." *Folia Phoniatrica* 17: 81–89.

———(1966). "Tomographische Studien zur Funktion des menschlichen Kehlkopfes (III Mitteilung: Haltungsänderung des knockernen Rahmens der äusseren Kehlkopfmuskeln [Halswirbelsäule])." *Folia Phoniatrica* 18: 81–90.

FRY, D. B. (1957). "Speech and language." *Journal of Laryngology and Otolaryngology* 7: 434.

FRY, D. B., AND MANÉN, LUCIE (1957). "Basis for acoustical study of singing." *Journal of the Acoustical Society of America* 29: 690–692.

FUCHS, VIKTOR (1950). "On a high note." *The Etude* February, 69: 13.

———(1951). "The 'covered' tone—what is it?" *The Etude* December, 69: 19.

_____(1965). "The microphone and head resonance." *The NATS Bulletin* 22, 2: 12–13; 35.

FUJIMURA, OSAMU (1961). "Analysis of nasal consonants." *Journal of the Acoustical Society of America* 33: 589–596.

_____(1961). "Bilabial stop and nasal consonants: a motion picture study and its acoustical implications." *Journal of Speech and Hearing Research* 4: 223–247.

FUJIMURA, OSAMU, AND LINDQVIST, J. (1971). "Sweep-tone measurements of the vocal tract." *Journal of the Acoustical Society of America* 49: 541–558.

FURSTENBERG, A. C. (1958). "Evidence of laryngeal participation in emotional expression: its relation to hysterical aphonia." *Annals of Otology, Rhinology and Laryngology* 67: 516.

GARCIA, MANUEL (1854–1855). "Observations on the human voice." *Proceedings of the Royal Society* (London): 399–410.

GARDINI, NELLI (1947). "Voice foundation." *The NATS Bulletin* 4, 1: 4.

GARLINGHOUSE, BURTON (1951). "Rhythm and relaxation in breathing." *The NATS Bulletin* 7, 4: 2; 5; 7.

_____(1955). "The musical approach." *The NATS Bulletin* 12, 1: 5–6.

_____(1970). "Dialogue on vocal pedagogy." *The NATS Bulletin* 26, 3: 25; 30–31.

GARSON, J. Z. (1950). "Acute laryngo–tracheo–bronchitis." *British Medical Journal* 1: 578.

GEDDA, NICOLAI (1982). Interviewed by Jerome Hines in *Great Singers on Great Singing.* New York: Doubleday, 118–125.

GERARD, R. W., AND TAYLOR, R. E. (1953). "Muscle and nerve—physiologic orientation." *The American Journal of Medicine* 15: 83–91.

GERRY, ARTHUR (1948). "The importance of technique." *The NATS Bulletin* 5, 1: 6.

GILES, HENRY W. (1883). "How to cultivate the voice." *The Voice* 5: 129.

GILLILAND, DALE V. (1955). "Beliefs and knowledge in the teaching of singing." *The NATS Bulletin* 12, 1: 7–8.

_____(1965). "Fundamental precepts for voice educators." *The NATS Bulletin* 21, 3: 11–12.

GOLD, HARRY (1953). "Treatment of cough: conference on therapy." *The American Journal of Medicine* 14: 90.

GOULD, HERBERT (1949). "Phonation." *The NATS Bulletin* 5, 5: 6–7.

GOULD, WILBUR J. (1971). "The effect of respiratory and postural mechanisms upon the action of the vocal cords." *Folia Phoniatrica* 23: 211–224.

_____(1977). "The effect of voice training on lung volumes in singers and the possible relationship to the damping factor of Pressman." *Journal of Research in Singing* 1, 1: 3–15.

_____(1981). "The pulmonary–laryngeal system." *Vocal Fold Physiology,* ed. by K. N. Stevens and M. Hirano. Tokyo: University of Tokyo Press, 23–29.

GOULD, WILBUR J., AND OKAMURA, HIROSHI (1971). "Respiratory training of the singer." *Folia Phoniatrica* 26: 255–262.

GREENBERGER, DAVID (1884). "The nerves of the vocal organs." *The Voice* 6: 11–12.

GRIESMAN, B. L. (1943). "Mechanism of phonation demonstrated by planigraphy of the larynx." *Archives of Otolaryngology* 38: 17–26.

GRIMBY, G.; BUNN, J.; AND MEAD, J. (1967). "Relative contribution of rib cage and abdomen to ventilation during exercise." *Journal of Applied Physiology* 24: 159–166.

HAGERTY, R. F.; HILL, M. J.; PETIT, H. S.; AND KANE, J. J. (1958a). "Posterior pharyngeal wall movement in normals." *Journal of Speech and Hearing Research* 1: 203.

_____(1958b). "Soft palate movement in normals." *Journal of Speech and Hearing Research* 1: 325–330.

HALLE, M.; HUGHES, G. W.; AND RADLEY, J. P. A. (1957). "Acoustic properties of stop consonants." *Journal of the Acoustical Society of America* 29: 107–116.

HAMILTON, W. J., AND HARRISON, B. J. (1971a). "Anatomy of the larynx and tracheobronchial tree." *Scott-Brown's Diseases of the Ear, Nose and Throat,* ed. by John Ballantyne and John Groves. Vol. 1, 3d ed. London: Butterworth, 123–146.

_____(1971b). "Anatomy of the nose, nasal cavity and paranasal sinuses." *Scott-Brown's Diseases of the Ear, Nose and Throat,* ed. by John Ballantyne and John Groves, Vol. 1, 3d ed. London: Butterworth, 147–170.

HAMLET, SANDRA L. (1971). "Phonation during glottal stops." *Journal of the Acoustical Society of America* 49: 132.

_____(1978). "Interpretation of ultrasonic signals in terms of phase difference of vocal-fold vibration." *Journal of the Acoustical Society of America* 48: 51–90.

HAMLET, SANDRA L., AND PALMER, J. M. (1974). "Investigation of laryngeal trills using the transmission of ultrasound through the larynx." *Folia Phoniatrica* 26: 363–377.

HARDWICKE, H. J. (1883). "The human voice in singing and speaking." *The Voice* 5: 73–74.

HARDY, LEE (1958). "The physiology of breathing." *The NATS Bulletin* 15, 2: 12–14.

HARRELL, MACK (1949). "Strictly American vocal problems." *The Etude* August, 67: 479.

HARRINGTON, R. (1944). "Study of the mechanism of velopharyngeal closure." *Journal of Speech Disorders* 9: 325–345.

HARRIS, K. S. (1963). "Behavior of the tongue in the production of some alveolar consonants." *Journal of the Acoustical Society of America* 35: 784.

HARTLIEB, K. (1952). "Wie sang Caruso?" *Folia Phoniatrica* 4: 53.

HATTORI, S.; YAMAMOTO, K.; AND FUJIMURA, O. (1958). "Nasalization of vowels in relation to nasals." *Journal of the Acoustical Society of America* 30: 267–274.

HEINZ, J. M., AND STEVENS, K. N. (1961). "On the properties of voiceless fricative consonants." *Journal of the Acoustical Society of America* 33: 589–596.

HERING, EWALD (1868). "Self-steering of respiration through the *nervus vagus.*" Transl. by Elizabeth Ullmann. *Breathing: Hering–Breuer Centenary Symposium,* ed. by Ruth Porter, 1970. London: J. & A. Churchill, 359–364.

HERXHEIMER, H. (1949). "Some observations on the coordination of diaphragmatic and rib movements in respiration." *Thorax* 4: 65–72.

HICKS, P., AND TROUP, G. J. (1980). "Source spectrum in professional singing." *Folia Phoniatrica* 32: 23–28.

HILL, A. V. (1949). "Is relaxation an active process?" *Proceedings of the R Society of London* 136: 428.

HIRANO, MINORU (1974). "Morphological structure of the vocal cord as vibrator and its variations." *Folia Phoniatrica* 26: 89–94.

———(1977). "Structures and vibratory behavior of the vocal folds." *Dynamic Aspects of Speech Production,* ed. by M. Sawashima and F. S. Cooper. Tokyo: University of Tokyo Press, 13–27.

HIRANO, M.; KOIKE, Y.: AND VON LEDEN, HANS (1968). "Maximum phonation time and air usage during phonation." *Folia Phoniatrica* 20: 185–201.

HIRANO, M.; KURITA, S.; AND KAKASHIMA, T. (1981). "The structure of the vocal folds." *Vocal Fold Physiology,* ed. by K. N. Stevens and M. Hirano. Tokyo: University of Tokyo Press, 33–43.

HIRANO, M., AND OHALA, J. (1969). "Use of hooked-wire electrodes for electromyography of the intrinsic laryngeal muscles." *Journal of Speech and Hearing Research* 12: 362–372.

HIRANO, M.; OHALA, J.; AND VENNARD, W. (1969). "The function of laryngeal muscles in regulating fundamental frequency and intensity of phonation." *Journal of Speech and Hearing Research* 12: 616–628.

HIRANO, M.; TAKEUCHI, Y.; AND HIROTO, I. (1966). "Intranasal sound pressures during the utterance of speech sounds." *Folia Phoniatrica* 18: 369–378.

HIRANO, M.; VENNARD, W.; AND OHALA, J. (1970). "Regulation of register, pitch and intensity of voice: an electromyographic investigation of intrinsic laryngeal muscles." *Folia Phoniatrica* 22: 1–20.

HISEY, PHILIP D. (1970). "Scientific versus empirical methods of teaching voice." *The NATS Bulletin* 27, 2: 14–17; 44.

———(1971). "Head quality versus nasality: a review of some pertinent literature." *The NATS Bulletin* 28, 2: 4–15; 18.

HIXON, THOMAS J. (1973). "Respiratory function in speech." *Normal Aspects of Speech, Hearing, and Language,* ed. by Fred D. Minifie, Thomas J. Hixon, and Frederick Williams. Englewood Cliffs, NJ: Prentice-Hall, 73–125.

HIXON, THOMAS J., AND HOFFMAN, CYNTHIA (1979). "Chest wall shape in singing." *Transcripts of the Seventh Symposium: Care of the Professional Voice,* Part I, ed. by V. Lawrence. New York: The Voice Foundation, 9–10.

HIXON, THOMAS J.; LANGHANS, JOSEPH J.; AND SMITHERAN, JUDITH R. (1982). "Laryngeal airway resistance during singing." *Transcripts of the Tenth Symposium: Care of the Professional Voice,* Part I, ed. by V. Lawrence. New York: The Voice Foundation, 60–65.

HIXON, THOMAS J.; MEAD, J.; AND GOLDMAN, M. (1976). "Dynamics of the chest wall during speech production: function of the thorax, rib cage, diaphragm and abdomen." *Journal of Speech and Hearing Research* 19: 297–356.

HOLBROOK, ANTHONY, AND FAIRBANKS, GRANT (1962). "Diphthong formants and their movements." *Journal of Speech and Hearing Research* 5: 38–58.

HOLLIEN, H. (1960). "Vocal pitch variation related to changes in vocal fold length." *Journal of Speech and Hearing Research* 3: 150–156.

———(1962). "Vocal fold thickness and fundamental frequency of phonation." *Journal of Speech and Hearing Research* 54: 227–243.

———(1974). "On vocal registers." *Journal of Phonetics* 2: 125–143.

HOLLIEN, H.; BROWN, W. S., JR.; AND HOLLIEN, K. (1971). "Vocal fold length associated with modal, falsetto and varying intensity phonation." *Folia Phoniatrica* 23: 62.

.; AND MOORE, P. (1968). "Stroboscopic laminagraphy ...*ta Oto-Laryngologica* 65: 209–215.

...RTIS, J. F. (1960). "A laminagraphic study of vocal pitch." *...eech and Hearing Research* 3: 353–363.

...ievation and tilting of the vocal folds as a function of vocal *...olia Phoniatrica* 14: 23–36.

...; DEW, D.; AND PHILLIPS, P. (1971). "Phonational frequency ranges ...ults." *Journal of Speech and Hearing Research* 14: 755–765.

...N, H., AND KEISTER, ELWOOD (1978). "Pilot data on frequency production abilities of singers and non-singers." *Journal of Research in Singing* 2, 1: 15–23.

_____(1980). "The varying characteristics of the singer's formant." *Transcripts of the Seventh Symposium: Care of the Professional Voice*, Part I, ed. by V. Lawrence. New York: The Voice Foundation, 40–43.

HOLLIEN, H., AND MOORE, PAUL (1960). "Measurements of the vocal folds during changes in pitch." *Journal of Speech and Hearing Research* 3: 157–165.

_____(1960). "Some laryngeal correlates of vocal pitch." *Journal of Speech and Hearing Research* 3: 52–58.

HOLLINGSWORTH, H. L. (1939). "Chewing as a technique of relaxation." *Science* 90: 385–387.

HONDA, KIYOSHI, AND BAER, THOMAS (1982). "External frame function, pitch control, and vowel production." *Transcripts of the Tenth Symposium: Care of the Professional Voice*, Part I, ed. by V. Lawrence. New York: The Voice Foundation, 66–73.

HOPPE G., AND FROMMHOLD, W. (1965). "Tomographische Studien zur Funktion des menschlichen Kehlkopfes (II Mitteilung: Bewegung des Zungenbeines." *Folia Phoniatrica* 17: 161–171.

HORNE, MARILYN (1982). Interviewed by Jerome Hines in *Great Singers on Great Singing*. New York: Doubleday, 134–143.

HOSHIKO, M. (1960). "Sequence of action of breathing muscles during speech." *Journal of Speech and Hearing Research* 3: 291–297.

HOUSE, ARTHUR S. (1957). "Analog studies of nasal consonants." *Journal of Speech and Hearing Disorders* 22: 191–204.

_____(1959). "A note on optimal vocal frequency." *Journal of Speech and Hearing Disorders* 24: 55–60.

HOUSE, ARTHUR S., AND FAIRBANKS, GRANT (1953). "The influence of consonant environment upon the secondary acoustical characteristics of vowels." *Journal of the Acoustical Society of America* 25: 105–113.

HOUSE, ARTHUR S., AND STEVENS, E. L. (1956). "Analog studies of the nasalization of vowels." *Journal of Speech and Hearing Disorders* 22, 2: 218–231.

HOWARD, JOHN (1883). "The false vocal cords." *The Voice* 5, 4: 6–7.

_____(1884). "The secret of the peculiar singing quality of famous vocalists." *The Voice* 6, 11: 138–140.

_____(1884). "Vocal facts and errors; or 'Voice, Song and Speech' reviewed." *The Voice* 6, 8: 59–60.

HOWIE, JOHN, AND DELATTRE, PIERRE (1962). "An experimental study of the effect of pitch on the intelligibility of vowels." *The NATS Bulletin* 18, 4: 6–9.

HUME, PAUL (1977). "Game plan for disaster: the right singer in the wrong role." *The Washington Post* 13 February, G–5.

HUSSON, RAOUL (1956). "A new look at phonation." *The NATS Bulletin* 13, 2: 12–13.

_____(1957). "The classification of human voices." *The NATS Bulletin* 13, 4: 6–11.

_____(1957). "Special physiology in singing with power." *The NATS Bulletin* 14, 1: 12–15.

_____(1960). "The pharyngo-buccal cavity and its phonatory physiology." *The NATS Bulletin* 16, 3: 4–11.

_____(1962). "How the acoustics of a hall affect the singer and the speaker." *The NATS Bulletin* 18, 3: 8–13; 17.

ILLINGWORTH, C. R. (1882). "Mechanism of the voice." *The Voice* 3, 8: 5.

ISSHIKI, NOBUHIKO (1964). "Regulatory mechanism of voice intensity variation." *Journal of Speech and Hearing Research* 7: 17–29.

_____(1965). "Vocal intensity and air flow rate." *Folia Phoniatrica* 17: 92–104.

ISSHIKI, NOBUHIKO, AND RINGEL, ROBERT (1964). "Air flow during the production of selected consonants." *Journal of Speech and Hearing Research* 7: 233–244.

JACKSON, CHEVALIER (1940). "Myasthenia laryngis: observations on the larynx as an air-column instrument." *Archives of Otolaryngology* 32: 434–463.

JAGEL, FREDERICK (1947). "Developing the tenor voice." *The Etude* August, 65: 444.

JAMES, DAVID (1983). "Intonation problems at the level of the larynx." *The NATS Bulletin* 39, 4: 14–16.

JERITZA, MARIA (1947). "The singer faces the world!" *The Etude* April, 65: 185.

JOOS, MARTIN (1948). "Acoustic phonetics." *Language* (supplement) 24: 1–136.

KAHANE, JOEL (1978). "A morphological study of the human prepubertal and pubertal larynx." *American Journal of Anatomy* 115: 11–20.

_____(1981) "Age-related histological changes in the human male and female laryngeal cartilages: biological and functional implications." *Transcripts of the Ninth Symposium: Care of the Professional Voice*, Part I, ed. by V. Lawrence. New York: The Voice Foundation, 11–20.

KAISER, LOUISE (1934). "Some properties of speech muscles and the influence thereof on language." *Archives néerlandaises de phonétique expérimentale* 10: 121–133.

KARNELL, MICHAEL P., AND WILLIS, CLYDE R. (1982). "The effect of vowel context on consonantal interoral air." *Folia Phoniatrica* 34: 1–8.

KEENE, M. F. L. (1961). "Muscle spindles in human laryngeal muscles." *Journal of Anatomy* 95: 25–29.

KELEMEN, G. (1958). "Physiology of phonation in primates." *Logos* 1: 32.

KELLÝ, JUSTIN (1982). "Relaxation in singing and voice training." *The NATS Bulletin* 38, 1: 16–18.

KELMAN, A. W. (1981). "Vibratory patterns of the vocal folds." *Folia Phoniatrica* 33: 73–99.

KELSEY, FRANKLYN (1948). "The riddle of the voice." *Music and Letters* 29: 238.

_____(1949). "What is singing?" *Music and Letters* 30: 216–230.

KENT, R. D., AND MURRAY, A. D. (1982). "Acoustic features of infant vocalic utterances at 3, 6, and 9 months." *Journal of the Acoustical Society of America* 72: 353–365.

KENYON, ELMER L. (1922) "Significance of the extrinsic musculature of the larynx." *Journal of the American Medical Association* 79: 428–431.

———(1928). "Action and control of the peripheral organs of speech: psychologic principles, and a scientific basis for methods of training." *Journal of the American Medical Assocation* 91: 1341–1346.

KHANNA, SHYAN M.; TONNDORF, JUERGEN; AND QUELLER, JUDITH E. (1976). "Mechanical parameters of hearing by bone conduction." *Journal of the Acoustical Society of America* 60: 139.

KIESEL, DENNIS L. (1980). "The effect of music on the auditory systems of the musician and listener." *The NATS Bulletin* 37, 3: 21–23.

KIPNIS, ALEXANDER (1951). "The art of mezza-voce singing." *The Etude* January, 69: 20.

KIRCHNER, J. A., AND SUZUKI, M. (1968). "Laryngeal reflexes and voice production." *Sound Production in Man: Annals of the New York Academy of Sciences*, ed. by A. Bouhuys. New York: New York Academy of Sciences, 98–109.

KITCHEN, J. M. W. (1884). "Ventriloquism." *The Voice* 6, 9: 35.

KITZING, PETER (1982). "Photo- and electroglottographical recording of the laryngeal vibratory pattern during different registers." *Folia Phoniatrica* 34: 234–241.

KITZING, PETER; CARLBORG, BJÖRN; AND LÖFQUIST, ANDERS (1982). "Aerodynamic and glottographic studies of the laryngeal vibratory cycle." *Folia Phoniatrica* 34: 116–144.

KITZING, PETER, AND SONESSON, B. (1974). "A photoglottographical study of the female vocal folds during phonation." *Folia Phoniatrica* 26: 138–149.

KLATT, DENNIS H. (1973). "Interaction between two factors that influence vowel duration." *Journal of the Acoustical Society of America* 54: 1102.

KLATT, DENNIS H.; STEVENS, K. N.; AND MEAD, J. (1968). "Studies of articulatory activity and airflow during speech." *Sound Production in Man: Annals of the New York Academy of Sciences*, ed. by A. Bouhuys. New York: New York Academy of Sciences, 42–55.

KLEIN, MAX (1950a). "How Jean de Reszke taught singing" (Part I). *The Etude* October, 68: 14.

———(1950b). "How Jean de Reszke taught singing" (Part II). *The Etude* November, 68: 21.

KLEIN, W.; PLOMP, R.; AND POLS, L. (1970) "Vowel spectra, vowel spaces, and vowel identification." *Journal of the Acoustical Society of America* 48: 999–1009.

KOENIG, W. F.; DUNN, H. K.; AND LACEY, L. Y. (1946). "The sound spectrograph." *Journal of the Acoustical Society of America* 17: 19–49.

———(1948). "The sound spectrum." *Journal of the Acoustical Society of America* 18: 1–89.

KOENIG, W. F., AND VON LEDEN, HANS (1961). "The peripheral nerves of the human larynx." *Archives of Otolaryngology* 74: 153.

KOFLER, LEO (1884). "Cultivation of the voice: which is the proper time—can it ever be too early or too late in life to begin it?" *The Voice* 6, 2: 33–34.

KOIKE, Y. (1981). "Sub- and supraglottal pressure variation during phonation." *Vocal Fold Physiology*, ed. by K. N. Stevens and M. Hirano. Tokyo: University of Tokyo Press, 181–191.

KONNO, K., AND MEAD, J. (1967). "Measurement of the separate volume changes of rib cage and abdomen during breathing." *Journal of Applied Physiology* 24: 407–422.

———(1969). "Static volume-pressure characteristics of the rib cage and abdomen." *Journal of Applied Physiology* 24: 544–548.

KONRAD, H. R., AND RATTENBORG, C. C. (1969). "Combined action of the laryngeal muscles." *Acta Oto-Laryngologica Scandinavica* 67: 646–649.

KOUTSTAAL, CORNELIS W. (1971) "Acoustic differentiation of musical and a-musical voice production." *The NATS Bulletin* 28, 4: 18–20.

KOYAMA, T. (1971). "Mechanics of voice production: II. Regulation of pitch." *Laryngoscope* 81: 47–65.

KOYAMA, T., AND HARVEY, J. E. (1972). "Mechanics of voice production: III. Efficiency of voice production." *Laryngoscope* 82: 210–217.

KUHN, G. (1975). "On the front cavity resonance and its possible role in speech perception." *Journal of the Acoustical Society of America* 58: 428–433.

KUHN, GEORGE F., AND GUERNSEY, RICHARD M. (1983). "Sound pressure distribution about the human head and torso." *Journal of the Acoustical Society of America* 73: 95–105.

LABELLE, J. L. (1973). "Judgments of vocal roughness related to rate and extent of vibrato." *Folia Phoniatrica* 25: 196–202.

LACZKOWSKA, M. (1961). "Concerning the function of the velum." *Folia Phoniatrica* 13: 107–111.

LADEFOGED, PETER (1962a). "Sub-glottal activity during speech." *Proceedings of the Fourth International Congress of Phonetic Sciences.* The Hague: Mouton, 247–265.

———(1968). "Linguistic aspects of respiratory phenomena." *Sound Production in Man: Annals of the New York Academy of Sciences,* ed. by A. Bouhuys. New York: New York Academy of Sciences, 141–151.

LADEFOGED, PETER, AND BROADBENT, D. E. (1957). "Information conveyed by vowels." *Journal of the Acoustical Society of America* 29: 98.

LADEFOGED, PETER; DRAPER, M.; AND WHITTERIDGE, D. (1958). "Syllables and stress." *Miscellanea Phonetica* 3: 1–15.

LADEFOGED, PETER; HARSHMAN, RICHARD; GOLDSTEIN, LOUIS; AND RICE, LOYD (1979). "Generating vocal tract shapes from formant frequencies." *Journal of the Acoustical Society of America* 64, 4: 1027–1035.

LADEFOGED, PETER, AND MCKINNEY, N. P. (1963). "Loudness, sound pressure, and subglottal pressure in speech." *Journal of the Acoustical Society of America* 35: 454–460.

LAFON, JEAN-CLAUDE (1968). "Auditory basis of phonetics." *Manual of Phonetics,* ed. by B. Malmberg. Amsterdam: North-Holland Publishing, 76–104.

LANDEAU, MICHEL (1963). "Voice classification." Transl. by Harold T. Luckstone. *The NATS Bulletin* 20, 1: 4–7; 31.

LANDEAU, MICHEL, AND ZUILI, H. (1963). "Vocal emission and tomograms of the larynx." *The NATS Bulletin* 19, 3: 6–11.

LARGE, JOHN (1968). "An acoustical study of isoparametric tones in the female chest and middle registers in singing." *The NATS Bulletin* 25, 2: 12–15.

———(1969). "A method for the selection of samples for acoustical and perceptual studies of voice registers." *The NATS Bulletin* 25, 3: 40–42.

———(1972). "Towards an integrated physiologic–acoustic theory of vocal registers." *The NATS Bulletin* 28, 3: 18.

———(1973). "Acoustic study of register equalization in singing." *Folia Phoniatrica* 25: 39–61.

———(1974). "Acoustic–perceptual evaluation of register equalization." *The NATS Bulletin* 31, 1: 20–27; 40–41.

_____(1978). "Vocal abuse and misuse." *The NATS Bulletin* 34, 3: 23–37.

_____(1984). "The German *Fach* system." *The Journal for Research in Singing* 7, 2: 45–53.

LARGE, JOHN; BAIRD, EDWARD; AND JENKINS, TIMOTHY (1981). "Studies of the male high voice mechanisms: preliminary report and definition of the term 'register'." *Journal of Research in Singing* 4, 1: 26.

LARGE, JOHN, AND IWATA, SHIGENOBU (1971). "Aerodynamic study of vibrato and voluntary straight-tone pairs in singing." *Folia Phoniatrica* 23: 50–65.

_____(1976). "The significance of air flow modulations in vocal vibrato." *The NATS Bulletin* 32, 3: 42–46.

LARGE, JOHN; IWATA, S.; AND VON LEDEN, HANS (1970). "The primary female register transition in singing." *Folia Phoniatrica* 22: 385–396.

_____(1972). "The male operatic head register versus falsetto." *Folia Phoniatrica* 24: 19–29.

LARGE, JOHN, AND MURRAY, THOMAS (1978a). "Studies of the Marchesi model for female registration." *Journal of Research in Singing* 1, 1: 14.

_____(1978b). "Studies of extended vocal techniques: safety." *The NATS Bulletin* 34, 4: 30–33.

LARGE, JOHN, AND ROTHMAN, HOWARD (1980). "Electrical analogs of the vocal system: application to singing." *Journal of Research in Singing* 3, 1: 1.

LARGE, JOHN, AND SHIPP, THOMAS (1969). "The effect of certain parameters on the perception of vocal registers." *The NATS Bulletin* 26, 1: 12–15.

LAWRENCE, VAN (1981a). "Handy household hints: To sing or not to sing." *The NATS Bulletin* 37, 3; 23–25.

_____(1981b). "U.R.I.s" *The NATS Bulletin* 37, 4: 41–42.

_____(1981c). "Vitamin C." *The NATS Bulletin* 37, 5: 24–25.

_____(1981d). "What about cortisone?" *The NATS Bulletin* 38, 1: 28–29.

_____(1981e). "Nodules and other things that go bump in the night." *The NATS Bulletin* 38, 2: 27; 30.

_____(1982a). "Cigareets and whiskey and wild, wild women." *The NATS Bulletin* 38, 3: 27; 32.

_____(1982b). "Singers and surgery (part I: surgery in general)." *The NATS Bulletin* 38, 4: 22–23.

_____(1982c). "Singers and surgery (part II: vocal tract surgery)." *The NATS Bulletin* 38, 5: 20–21.

_____(1982d). "Post-nasal drip." *The NATS Bulletin* 39, 1: 27–28.

_____(1982e). "Glue in the gizzard: phlegm." *The NATS Bulletin* 39, 2: 24–25.

_____(1983a). "When all else fails, read the instructions." *The NATS Bulletin* 39, 3: 16–18.

_____(1983b). "Do buzzards roost in your mouth at night?" *The NATS Bulletin* 39, 4: 19–20; 42.

_____(1983c) "Nose drops." *The NATS Bulletin* 39, 5: 26–27.

_____(1984a). "Will knowing how my voice works make me sing better?" *The NATS Bulletin* 40, 4: 24–25; 31.

_____(1984b). "Is allergy often a problem for the singer who comes into the laryngology office?" *The NATS Bulletin* 40, 5: 20–21; 27.

LEBRUN, YVAN (1983). "Cerebral dominance for language." *Folia Phoniatrica* 35: 13–39.

LEHISTE, ILSE, AND PETERSON, GORDON E. (1961). "Transitions, glides and diphthongs." *Journal of the Acoustical Society of America* 33: 268–277.

LERMAN, J., AND DUFFY, R. (1970). "Recognition of falsetto voice quality." *Folia Phoniatrica* 22: 21–27.

LESTER, JOHN L. (1951). "The key to coordination." *The NATS Bulletin* 8, 2: 4; 25.

———(1957). "Breathing related to phonation." *The NATS Bulletin* 14, 2: 26–27; 29.

LEWIS, D. (1936). "Vocal resonance." *Journal of the Acoustical Society of America* 8: 91–99.

LIEBERMAN, PHILIP (1968). "Vocal cord motion in man." *Sound Production in Man: Annals of the New York Academy of Sciences*, ed. by A. Bouhuys. New York: New York Academy of Sciences, 28–41.

LIGHTFOOT, C. (1950). "Effects of common cold on speech." *Archives of Otolaryngology* 51: 500.

LINDBLOM, BJØRN E. F.; LUBKER, JAMES F.; AND STEFAN, PAULI (1977). "An acoustic–perceptual method for the quantitative evaluation of hypernasality." *Journal of Speech and Hearing Research* 20: 485–496.

LINDBLOM, BJØRN E. F., AND SUNDBERG, JOHAN (1971). "Acoustical consequences of lip, tongue, jaw and larynx movements." *Journal of the Acoustical Society of America* 50: 1166–1179.

———(1972). "Observations on tongue contour length in spoken and sung vowels. *Speech Transmission Laboratory Quarterly Progress and Status Report* 4: 1–5.

LINCKE, C. E. (1973). "A study of pitch characteristics of female voices and their relationship to vocal effectiveness." *Folia Phoniatrica* 25: 173–185.

LINTZ, L. B., AND SHERMAN, D. (1961). "Phonetic elements and perception of nasality." *Journal of Speech and Hearing Research* 4: 381–396.

LÖBL, KARL (1977). "Trotz Feuer keine Wärme." *Kurier* (Vienna) 26 June, 1977, 9.

LONDON, GEORGE (1953). "Don't look for short cuts." *The Etude* May, 71: 18.

LONDON, S. J. (1965a). "Vox humana: theme and variations" (Part I). *The NATS Bulletin* 21, 4: 10–11.

———(1965b). "Vox humana: theme and variations:" (Part II). *The NATS Bulletin* 22, 1: 34–37.

LUBKER, JAMES (1975). "Transglottal airflow during stop consonant production." *Journal of the Acoustical Society of America* 53: 212.

LUCHSINGER, RICHARD (1951). "Schalldruck und Geschwindigkeitregistrierung der Atemkraft beim Singen." *Folia Phoniatrica* 3: 25–51.

———(1953). "Physiologie der Stimme." *Folia Phoniatrica* 5: 58.

———(1963). "Phonetics and pathology." *Manual of Phonetics*, ed. by B. Malmberg. Amsterdam: North-Holland Publishing, 502–532.

LUCHSINGER, RICHARD, AND FAABORG-ANDERSEN, KNUD (1966). "Phonetische und elektromyographische Registrierungen beim Tonhalten." *Folia Phoniatrica* 18: 91–97.

LUCHSINGER, RICHARD, AND PFISTER, K. (1961). "Die Messung der Stimmlippenverlängerung beim Steigern des Tonhöhe." *Folia Phoniatrica* 13: 1.

LUKKEN, ALBERT (1945). "A plea for simplicity in singing." *The NATS Bulletin* 1, 4: 3–4.

LUNN, CHARLES (1883). "Voice training of the future." *The Voice* 5, 5: 38–39.

LYNCH, CHRISTOPHER (1947). "The secret of singing." *The Etude* February, 65: 69.

MACK, MOLLY (1982). "Voicing-dependent vowel duration in English and French: monolingual and bilingual production." *Journal of the Acoustical Society of America* 71: 173–178.

MACNEILAGE, P. F. (1963). "Electromyographic and acoustic study of the production of certain final clusters." *Journal of the Acoustical Society of America* 35: 461–463.

———(1973). "The motor patterns of speech production." *Journal of the Acoustical Society of America* 35: 779.

MacNeilage, P. F., and Scholes, George N. (1964). "An electromyographic study of the tongue during vowel production." *Journal of Speech and Hearing Research* 7: 209–232.

Mallett, Lloyd (1963). "Some vocal training ideas re-explored." *The NATS Bulletin* 20, 1: 8–11.

Manchester, Arthur (1920). "Vocal concepts—tonal and physical." *The Etude* February, 38: 124–126.

Martensson, A. (1968). "The functional organization of the intrinsic laryngeal muscles." *Sound Production in Man: Annals of the New York Academy of Sciences,* ed by. A. Bouhuys. New York: New York Academy of Sciences, 91–97.

Martin, Anna Y. (1960). "The physiological and psychological concomitants of stage fright." *The NATS Bulletin* 17, 2: 18–23.

Mason, R. M., and Zemlin, W. R. (1966). "The phenomenon of vocal vibrato." *The NATS Bulletin* 22, 3: 12–17; 37.

Maximov, I, and Moskov, S. (1981). "Acute vocal deterioration in connection with vocal practices at high professional level." *Congress Proceedings and Abstracts of the IXth Congress of the Union of European Phoniatricians,* ed. by H. K. Schutte. Groningen: Centrale Reproductiendienst Vrije Universiteit, 201–209.

Mayer, Martin (1971). "Marilyn Horne becomes a prima donna." *The New York Times Magazine* 17 January, Section 6, 14–15; 42–47.

McClintock, Carol (1976). "Caccini's trillo: a re-examination." *The NATS Bulletin* 33, 1: 38–41; 43.

McGinnis, C. S.; Elnick, M.; and Kraichman, M. (1951). "A study of the vowel formants of well-known male operatic singers." *Journal of the Acoustical Society of America* 23: 440–446.

McGlone, R. E. (1966). "An investigation of air flow and subglottal air pressure related to fundamental frequency of phonation." *Folia Phoniatrica* 18: 313–322.

McGlone, R. E., and Brown, W. S., Jr. (1969). "Identification of the 'shift' between registers." *Journal of the Acoustical Society of America* 46: 1033–1036.

McGlone, R. E., and Manning, Walter H. (1979). "Role of the second formant in pitch perception of whispered and voiced vowels." *Folia Phoniatrica* 31: 974.

McLean, Cameron (1951). "Causes for confusion in the teaching of singing." *The NATS Bulletin* 7, 6: 15.

Mead, Jere (1960). "Control of respiratory frequency." *Journal of Applied Physiology* 15: 325–336.

Mead, Jere; Bouhuys, Arend; and Proctor, Donald F. (1968). "Mechanisms generating subglottic pressure. *Sound Production in Man: Annals of the New York Academy of Sciences,* ed. by A. Bouhuys. New York: The New York Academy of Sciences, 177–181.

Merrill, Robert (1947). "Requisites for the young singer." *The Etude* June, 65: 13.

———(1955). "The singer's development." *The Etude* January, 73: 19.

MERTON, P. A. (1970). "The sense of effort." *Breathing: Hering–Breuer Centenary Symposium*, ed. by Ruth Porter. London: J. & A. Churchill, 207–211.

METFESSEL, MILTON (1932). "The vibrato in artistic voices." *University of Iowa Studies in the Psychology of Music.* Vol. I: 14.

MICHEL, JOHN, AND GRASHEL, JOHN (1980). "Vocal vibrato as a function of frequency and intensity." *Transcripts of the Ninth Symposium: Care of the Professional Voice*, Part I, ed. by V. Lawrence. New York: The Voice Foundation, 45–48.

MICHEL, R. (1954). "Die Bedeutung des Musculus sternothyreoideus für die Rahmenmodulation der menschlichen Stimme." *Folia Phoniatrica* 6: 65–100.

MICHINSON, A. G. H., AND YOFFEY, J. M. (1947). "Respiratory displacement of larynx, hyoid bone and tongue." *Journal of Anatomy* 81: 118–129.

_____(1948). "Changes in the vocal folds in humming low and high notes; a radiographic study." *Journal of Anatomy* 82: 88.

MILLER, MAURICE, AND ALLEN, ELIZABETH L. (1978). "Auditory hygiene for the voice teacher and his students." *The NATS Bulletin* 34, 3: 39–41.

MILLER, RICHARD (1966a). "Legato in singing, part I: diction in relation to the vocal legato." *The NATS Bulletin* 22, 3: 10–11; 21.

_____(1966b). "Legato in singing, part II: vibrato in relation to vocal legato." *The NATS Bulletin* 22, 4: 11; 18–21.

_____(1968). "The sense of immediacy in singing." *The American Music Teacher* 17, 3: 25–26; 37.

_____(1979). "A brief consideration of some registration practices in national schools of singing." *Journal of Research in Singing*, 2, 1: 2–4.

_____(1981). "Supraglottal considerations and vocal pedagogy." *Transcripts of the Ninth Symposium: Care of the Professional Voice*, Part II, ed. by V. Lawrence. New York: The Voice Foundation, 55–63.

MILLER, RICHARD, AND BIANCO, ERKKI (1985). "Three approaches to breath management in singing." *Transcripts of the Fourteenth Symposium: Care of the Professional Voice*, ed. by V. Lawrence. New York: The Voice Foundation.

MILLER, RICHARD, AND SCHUTTE, HARM K. (1981). "The effect of tongue position on spectra in singing." *The NATS Bulletin* 37, 3: 26–27; 34.

_____(1983). "Spectral analysis of several categories of timbre in a professional male (tenor) voice." *Journal of Research in Singing* 7, 1: 6–10.

MILLER, RICHARD L. (1959). "The nature of the vocal cord wave." *Journal of the Acoustical Society of America* 31: 667–677.

MILLS, J. N. (1950). "The nature of the limitation of inspiratory and expiratory efforts." *Journal of Physiology* 111: 376–381.

MILNES, SHERRILL (1982). Interviewed by Jerome Hines in *Great Singers on Great Singing.* New York: Doubleday, 173–181.

MINIFIE, FRED D. (1973). "Speech acoustics." *Normal Aspects of Speech, Hearing, and Language*, ed. by Fred D. Minifie, Thomas J. Hixon, and Frederick Williams. Englewood Cliffs, NJ: Prentice-Hall, 235–284.

MOLL, K. L. (1962). "Velopharyngeal closure on vowels." *Journal of Speech and Hearing Research* 5: 30–37.

MOLL, K. L., AND DANILOFF, R. G. (1971). "An investigation of the timing of velar movements during speech." *Journal of the Acoustical Society of America* 50: 678–684.

MOLLENHAUER, FREDERICK (1884). "Americans endowed with superior natural voices." *The Voice* 6, 10: 29.

MOLLER, KARLIND T.; PATH, MICHAEL; AND WERTH, LARRY J. (1973). "The modification of velar movement." *Journal of Speech and Hearing Disorders* 38: 323–334.

MONSON, PATRICIA; VOLLERTSEN, C.; AND HUFNAGLE, J. (1981). "The relationship between selected physiologic respiratory parameters and singing ability." *Journal of Research in Singing* 3, 2: 1–13.

MONSON, PATRICIA, AND ZEMLIN, WILLARD (1984). "Quantitative study of whisper." *Folia Phoniatrica* 36: 53–65.

MOORE, PAUL (1938). "Motion picture studies of the vocal cords and vocal attack." *Journal of Speech Disorders* 3: 235–238.

_____(1964). "The larynx and voice: the function of the pathological larynx." *Research Potentials in Voice Physiology*, ed. by D. W. Brewer. Syracuse, NY: State University of New York, 143–145.

MOORE, PAUL, AND VON LEDEN, HANS (1958). "Dynamic variations of the vibratory pattern in the normal larynx." *Folia Phoniatrica* 10: 205–238.

MOORE, PAUL; WHITE, F. D.; AND VON LEDEN, HANS (1962). "Ultra high speed photography in laryngeal physiology." *Journal of Speech and Hearing Disorders* 27: 165.

MULLIGAN, C. (1883). "The falsetto voice." *The Voice* 5, 7: 88.

MURRAY, SIDNEY (1968). "Scientific pedagogy one hundred years before Garcia." *The NATS Bulletin* 25, 2: 29–30.

MURRY, THOMAS, AND BROWN, W. S., JR. (1979). "Aerodynamic interactions associated with voiced-voiceless stop consonants." *Folia Phoniatrica* 31: 82–88.

MURTAUGH, J. A., AND CAMPBELL, E. J. MORAN (1961). "The respiratory function of the larynx." *Laryngoscope* 61: 581–590.

MYER, EDMUND J. (1883). "Form and action in the singing voice." *The Voice* 5, 11: 172–173.

NAGEL, JULIE; HIMLE, D.; AND PAPSDORF, J. (1980). "Coping with performance anxiety." *The NATS Bulletin* 37, 4: 26–27; 31–33.

NAIMARK, A., AND CHERNIACK, R. M. (1950). "Compliance of the respiratory system and its components in health and obesity." *Journal of Applied Physiology* 111: 376–381.

NAKAMURA, FUMIO (1964). "Hearing and speech." *Research Potentials in Voice Physiology*, ed. by D. W. Brewer. Syracuse, NY: State University of New York, 299–308.

NAKAMURA, FUMIO; UYEDA, Y.; AND SONODA, Y. (1958). "Electromyographic study on respiratory movement of the intrinsic laryngeal muscles." *Laryngoscope* 68: 109.

NATHAN, P. W. (1963). "The descending respiratory pathway in man." *Journal of Neurological and Neurosurgical Psychiatry* 26: 487–499.

National Association of Teachers of Singing (1948). "Fundamental requirements for teachers of singing; supplementary report of the advisory committee on vocal education." *The NATS Bulletin* 5, 1: 1–2; 7–8.

NAUNTON, RALPH N. (1963). "The measurement of hearing by bone conduction." *Modern Developments in Audiology*, ed. by James Jerger. New York: Academic Press, 1–29.

NEGUS, SIR VICTOR E. (1957). "Voice." *Encyclopedia Britannica*, ed. by Walter Yust, Vol. 23. London: William Benton, 233–236.

NELSON, HOWARD D., AND TIFFANY, WILLIAM R. (1968). "The intelligibility of song." *The NATS Bulletin* 25, 4: 22–28.

NEWTON, GEORGE (1950). "On imaginative singing." *The NATS Bulletin* 7, 2: 5; 8.

_____(1954). "Articulation—a summary." *The NATS Bulletin* 11, 3: 8.

_____(1972). "Random notes for a study of interpretation." *The NATS Bulletin* 28, 4: 22–27.

NILSSON, BIRGIT (1982). Interviewed by Jerome Hines in *Great Singers on Great Singing.* New York: Doubleday, 193–201.

NIMII, SEIJI; BELL-BERTI, FREDERICKA; AND HARRIS, KATHERINE S. (1982). "Dynamic aspects of velopharyngeal closure." *Folia Phoniatrica* 34: 246–257.

ONCLEY, PAUL B. (1951a). "What acoustics means to the teacher of singing." *The NATS Bulletin* 8, 1: 8–9; 23.

_____(1951b). "Higher formants in the human voice." *Journal of the Acoustical Society of America* 24: 175.

_____(1953). "Acoustics of the singing voice." *Journal of the Acoustical Society of America* 26: 932.

ONDRACKOVA, JANA (1961). "The movement of the tongue and the soft palate in the singing of vowels." *Folia Phoniatrica* 13: 99–106.

_____(1972). "Vocal cord activity." *Folia Phoniatrica* 24: 405–419.

OTIS, A. B.; FENN, W. O.; AND RAHN, H. (1950). "Mechanics of breathing in man." *Journal of Applied Physiology* 2: 592–607.

PAHN, J. (1966). "Zur Entwicklung und Behandlung funktioneller Singstimmerkrankungen." *Folia Phoniatrica* 18: 117–130.

PAREMETER, C. E., AND TRAVENO, S. N. (1932). "Vowel position as shown by X-ray." *Quarterly Journal of Speech* 18: 351–369.

PAWŁOWSKI, ZYGMUNT, AND ZOŁTOWSKI, MAREK (1982). "Fundamental aspects of aeroacoustics in singing." *Archives of Acoustics* 7, 3–4; 207–224.

PAWŁUCZYK, ROMUALD; KRASKA, ZBIGNIEW; AND PAWŁOWSKI, ZYGMUNT (1982). "Holistic investigations of skin vibrations," *Applied Optics* 21, 5: 759–765.

PAYNE, W. H. (1884). "Some applications of psychology to the art of teaching." *The Voice* 6, 10: 122–124.

PEERCE, JAN (1982). Interviewed by Jerome Hines in *Great Singers on Great Singing.* New York: Doubleday, 207–224.

PELSKY, BORIS LASTOTCHKINE (n.d.) "La structure de quelques voyelles chantées." *Archives néerlandaises de phonétique expérimentale* 17: 123–124.

PERKINS, WILLIAM; SAWYER, GRANVILLE; AND HARRISON, PEGGY (1958). "Research on vocal efficiency." *The NATS Bulletin* 15, 2: 4–7.

PETERSON, GORDON E. (1951). "The phonetic value of vowels." *Language* 27: 541–553.

_____(1959). "Vowel formant measurements." *Journal of Speech and Hearing Research* 2: 173–183.

_____(1968a). "Articulation." *Manual of Phonetics,* ed. by B. Malmberg. Amsterdam: North-Holland Publishing, 156–165.

_____(1968b). "Breath stream dynamics." *Manual of Phonetics,* ed. by B. Malmberg. Amsterdam: North-Holland Publishing, 130–148.

_____(1968c). "Laryngeal vibrations." *Manual of Phonetics,* ed. by B. Malmberg. Amsterdam: North-Holland Publishing, 149–155.

PETERSON, GORDON E., AND SHOUP, J. E. (1966a). "The elements of an acoustic phonetic theory." *Journal of Speech and Hearing Research* 9: 68–99.

_____(1966b). "A physiological theory of phonetics." *Journal of Speech and Hearing Research* 9: 5–67.

PETERSON, SALLY J. (1973). "Velopharyngeal function: some important differences." *Journal of Speech and Hearing Disorders* 38: 89–97.

PETIT, J. M.; MILI-EMILI, G.; AND DEHLEZ, L. (1960). "Role of the diaphragm in conscious normal man: an electromyographic study." *Journal of Applied Physiology* 15: 1101–1106.

PFAU, EVA-MARIE (1982). "Ein Verfahren der Stimmfunktionstherapie: Summen im Kopfregister." *Folia Phoniatrica* 34: 289–295.

PLISHKA, PAUL (1982). Interviewed by Jerome Hines in *Great Singers on Great Singing*. New York: Doubleday, 240–249.

PLUM, FRED (1970). "Neurological integration of behavioural and metabolic control of breathing." *Breathing: Hering–Breuer Centenary Symposium,* ed. by Ruth Porter. London: J. & A. Churchill, 159–174.

PORTER, SAMUEL (1884). "Vowel Formation." *The Voice* 6, 12: 191.

POTTER, RALPH K.; AND PETERSON, GORDON E. (1948). "The representation of vowels and their movements." *Journal of the Acoustical Society of America* 20: 528–535.

PRESSMAN, JOEL J. (1942). "Physiology of the vocal cords in phonation and respiration." *Archives of Otolaryngology* 35: 355.

_____(1954). "Sphincters of the larynx." *Archives of Otolaryngology* 59: 32.

PRESSMAN, JOEL J., AND KELEMEN, G. (1955). "Physiology of the larynx." *Physiological Review* 35: 506–554.

PROCTOR, DONALD F. (1968). "The physiologic basis of voice training." *Sound Production in Man: Annals of the New York Academy of Sciences,* ed. by A. Bouhuys. New York: New York Academy of Sciences, 208–228.

_____(1980a). "Breath, the power source for the voice." *The NATS Bulletin* 37, 2: 26–30.

PUNT, NORMAN A. (1973). "Management of ear, nose, throat disabilities of singers." *Proceedings of the Royal Society of Medicine* 66: 1075.

_____(1974). "Lubrication of the vocal mechanism." *Folia Phoniatrica* 26: 287–288.

RAKOWSKI, ANDRZEJ (1979). "The magic number two: seven examples of binary apposition in pitch theory." *The Humanities Association Review* 30, 1/2: 24–25.

READ, DONALD, AND OSBORNE, CLIFFORD (1981). "The three variables, the break and registration." *The NATS Bulletin* 37, 5: 19–20.

REES, M. (1958a). "Harshness and glottal attack." *Journal of Speech and Hearing Research* 1: 344.

_____(1958b). "Some variables affecting perceived loudness." *Journal of Speech and Hearing Research* 1: 155.

RESCH, RITA (1974). "George Bernard Shaw's criticism of singers and singing." *The NATS Bulletin* 31, 2: 2; 4–10.

RINGEL, HARVEY (1947). "Vowel vanish—a vocal deterrent." *The NATS Bulletin* 4, 1: 3–6.

_____(1948). "Consonantal deterrence." *The NATS Bulletin* 5, 2: 8; 11.

ROBBINS, SAMUEL D. (1948). "Dyslalia." *Twentieth Century Speech and Voice Correction,* ed. by Emil Froeschels. New York: Philosophical Library, 118–141.

ROGERS, FRANCIS (1944a). "What is bel canto anyhow?" (Part I). *The Etude* March, 62: 147.

_____(1944b). "What is bel canto anyhow?" (Part II). *The Etude* April, 62: 207.

_____(1944c). "What is bel canto anyhow?" (Part III). *The Etude* May, 62: 267.

ROMAN, STELLA (1949). "The Italian and German approaches to singing." *Music Journal* 7: 22.

ROSE, ARNOLD (1955). "The Italian method, and the English singer." *Musical Times* 96: 637–638.

ROSS, WILLIAM E. (1945). "Voice teaching." *The NATS Bulletin* 2, 1: 3.

_____(1955). "The high-voice mechanism." *The NATS Bulletin* 12, 4: 14–15.

ROTHENBERG, MARTIN (1968). "The breath stream dynamics of simple-released-plosive production." *Bibliotheca Phonetica* 6. Basel: S. Karger, 1–117.

_____(1972). "The glottal velocity waveform during loose and tight voiced glottal adjustments." *Proceedings of the Seventh International Congress of Phonetic Sciences*, ed. by A. Rigault and R. Charbonneau. The Hague: Mouton, 380–388.

_____(1977). "Measurements of airflow in speech." *Journal of Speech and Hearing Research* 20: 155–176.

_____(1981a). "Acoustic interaction between the glottal source and the vocal tract." *Vocal Fold Physiology*, ed. K. N. Stevens and M. Hirano. Tokyo: University of Tokyo, 305–323.

_____(1981b). "Some relations between glottal air flow and vocal fold contact area." *The American Speech–Language–Hearing Association*, Report 11: 88–96.

_____(1981c). "The voice source in singing." *Research Aspects of Singing*, ed. by Johan Sundberg. Stockholm: The Royal Swedish Academy of Music, 15–33.

_____(1982). "Interpolating subglottic pressure from oral pressure." *Journal of Speech and Hearing Disorders* 47, 1: 119–120.

ROTHENBERG, MARTIN, AND MAHSHIE, J. (n.d.). "Induced transglottal pressure variations during voicing." Paper presented at the 94th meeting of the Acoustical Society of America, Miami Beach, Florida.

ROTHENBERG, MARTIN, AND MOLITOR, RICHARD D. (1979). "Encoding voice fundamental frequency into vibrotactile frequency." *Journal of the Acoustical Society of America* 66: 1029–1038.

RUBIN, HENRY J. (1960). "The neurochronaxic theory of voice production—a refutation." *Archives of Otolaryngology* 71: 913–921.

_____(1963). "Experimental studies on vocal pitch and intensity in phonation." *Laryngoscope* 73: 973–1075.

_____(1966). "Role of the laryngologist in management of dysfunctions of the singing voice." *The NATS Bulletin* 22, 4: 22–27.

_____(1967). "Vocal intensity, subglottic pressure and air flow in relationship to singers." *Folia Phoniatrica* 19: 393.

RUBIN, HENRY J., AND HIRT, CHARLES C. (1960). "The falsetto: a high speed cinematographic study." *Laryngoscope* 70: 1305–1324.

RUBIN, HENRY J.; LeCOVER, C.; AND VENNARD, W. (1967). "Vocal intensity, subglottic pressure and air flow relationships in singers." *Folia Phoniatrica* 19: 393–414.

RUSHMORE, ROBERT (1967a). "The singing voice: indisposed." *Opera News* 31, 22: 29–30.

_____(1967b). "The singing voice: the ages of man." *Opera News* 31, 23: 26–28.

_____(1967c). "The singing voice: national types." *Opera News* 31, 24: 22–25.

RUSSO, VINCENT, AND LARGE, JOHN (1978). "Psychoacoustic study of the bel canto model for register equalization: male chest and falsetto." *Journal of Research in Singing* 2, 1: 1–25.

RUTH, WILHELM (1963). "The registers of the singing voice." *The NATS Bulletin* 19, 4: 2–5.

———(1966). "The cause of individual differences in the sensation of head resonance in singing." *The NATS Bulletin* 23, 1: 20–21; 50.

SATALOFF, R. T. (1981). "Professional singers: the science and art of clinical care." *American Journal of Otology* 2, 3: 251–266.

———(1983). "Physical examination of the professional singer; special aspects." *Transcripts of the Eleventh Symposium: Care of the Professional Voice,* Part I, ed. by V. Lawrence. New York: The Voice Foundation, pp. 216–222.

SAWASHIMA, M., AND HIROSE, H. (1981). "Abduction–adduction at the glottis in speech and voice production." *Vocal Fold Physiology,* ed. by K. N. Stevens, and M. Hirano. Tokyo: University of Tokyo Press, 329–346.

SCHARF, DONALD (1971). "Perceptual parameters of consonant sounds." *Language and Speech* 14: 169–177.

SCHIFF, MAURICE, AND GOULD, WILBUR J. (1978). "Hormones and their influence on the performer's voice." *Transcripts of the Seventh Symposium: Care of the Professional Voice,* Part III, ed. by V. Lawrence. New York: The Voice Foundation, 43–48.

SCHLAWSON, W. (1968). "Vowel quality and musical timbre as functions of spectrum envelopes and fundamental frequency." *Journal of the Acoustical Society of America* 43: 87.

SCHLOSSHAUER, BURKHARD (1964). "Vocal cord vibrations in voice disorders." *Research Potentials in Voice Physiology,* ed. by David W. Brewer. Syracuse, NY: State University of New York, 173–184.

SCHOEN, M. (1922). "The pitch factor in artistic singing." *Psychological Monograph* 31: 230.

SCHOENHARD, CAROL, AND HOLLIEN, HARRY (1982). "A perceptual study of registration in female singers." *The NATS Bulletin* 39, 1: 3.

SCHONBERG, HAROLD C. (1982). "A bravo for opera's black voices." *The New York Times Magazine,* 17 January, Section 6, 24–27; 80–82; 90–91.

SCHUBERT, EARL D. (1983). "On hearing your own performance." *Transcripts of the Eleventh Symposium: Care of the Professional Voice,* Part I, ed. by V. Lawrence. New York: The Voice Foundation, 161–185.

SCHULTZ-COULON, H.-J., AND BATTMER, R. D. (1981). "Die Quantitatif Bewertung des Sängervibratos." *Folia Phoniatrica* 33: 1–14.

SCHUTTE, HARM K., AND VAN DEN BERG, JW. (1981). "The efficiency of voice production." *Congress Proceedings and Abstracts of the IXth Congress of the Union of European Phoniatricians,* ed. by Harm K. Schutte. Groningen: Centrale Reproductiendienst Vrije Universiteit, 148–156.

SCHUTTE, HARM K., AND HOEKSEMA, P. E. (1981). "Effect of voice therapy measured by comparing vocal efficiency values." *Congress Proceedings and Abstracts of the IXth Congress of the Union of European Phoniatricians,* ed. by Harm K. Schutte. Groningen: Centrale Reproductiendienst Vrije Universiteit, 157–165.

SCOTT, ANTHONY (1968). "A study of the components of the singing tone utilizing the audio spectrum analyzer." *The NATS Bulletin* 24, 4: 40–41.

———(1974). "Acoustical peculiarities of head tone and falsetto." *The NATS Bulletin* 30, 4: 32–35.

SEABURY, DEBORAH (1978). "The singers' world: voice teachers" (Part I). *Opera News* 43: 40–47.

———(1978). "The singers' world: voice teachers" (Part II). *Opera News* 43: 15–23.

SEARS, T., AND NEWSOM DAVIS, J. (1968). "The control of respiratory muscles during voluntary breathing." *Sound Production in Man: Annals of the New York Academy of Sciences,* ed. by A. Bouhuys. New York: New York Academy of Sciences, 183–190.

SEASHORE, CARL E. (1932). "The hearing of pitch and intensity of vibrato." *University of Iowa Studies in the Psychology of Music* 1: 213.

———(1936). "Psychology of the vibrato in voice and instrument." *University of Iowa Studies in the Psychology of Music* 3: 7.

SELKIN, STUART, AND MILLER, RICHARD (1982). Unpublished audio-visual tapes of fiberoptic examination of 60 singers. Oberlin Conservatory of Music, Oberlin, Ohio.

SHARNOVA, SONIA (1947). "Diction." *The NATS Bulletin* 3, 6: 4.

———(1949). "Breath control—foundation of singing and acting technique." *The NATS Bulletin* 7, 1: 6.

SHIPP, THOMAS (1977). "Vertical laryngeal position in singing." *Journal of Research in Singing* 1, 1: 16–24.

———(1981). Cited as participant in panel discussion, "Supraglottal aspects of singing." *Transcripts of the Ninth Symposium: Care of the Professional Voice.* Part II, ed. by V. Lawrence. New York: The Voice Foundation, 70.

———(1982). "Variability in vibrato rate: extent and regularity." *Transcripts of the Ninth Symposium: Care of the Professional Voice.* Part I, ed. by V. Lawrence. New York: The Voice Foundation, 44–48.

———(1984). "Effects of vocal frequency and effort on vertical laryngeal position." *Journal of Research in Singing* 7, 2: 1–5.

SHIPP, THOMAS, AND IZDEBSKI, K. (1975). "Vocal frequency and vertical larynx positioning by singers and non-singers." *Journal of the Acoustical Society of America* 58: 1104–1106.

———(1976). "Elements of frequency and amplitude modulation in the trained and pathological voice." *Journal of the Acoustical Society of America* 66 (supplement 1): 56.

SHIPP, THOMAS; LEANDERSON, ROLF; AND HAGLUND, STIG (1983). "Contribution of the cricothyroid muscle to vocal vibrato." *Transcripts of the Eleventh Symposium: Care of the Professional Voice.* Part I, ed. by V. Lawrence. New York: The Voice Foundation, 131–133.

SIEPE, CESARE (1952). "Forget about your throat." *The Etude* June, 70: 26.

———(1956). "Caring for the voice." *The Etude* January, 74: 14.

SILBERMAN, H. D.; WILF, H.; AND TUCKER, J. A. (1976). "Flexible fiberoptic nasopharyngolaryngoscope." *Annals of Otology, Rhinology, and Laryngology* 85, 5: 640–646.

SIMMONS, OTIS D. (1965). "Neurophysiology and muscular function of the vocal mechanism: implications for singers and teachers of singing." *The NATS Bulletin* 22, 1: 22–23; 33.

———(1969). "A conceptual approach to singing." *The NATS Bulletin* 26, 1: 15–18.

SLIS, I. H. (1970). "Articulatory measurements on voiced, voiceless and nasal consonants." *Phonetics* 21: 193–210.

SLOME, D. (1971). "Physiology of the mouth, pharynx and oesophagus." *Scott-*

Brown's Diseases of the Ear, Nose and Throat, ed. by John Ballantyne and John Groves, Vol. I, 3d ed. London: Butterworth, 235–302.

SMALL, ARNOLD M. (1973). "Acoustics." *Normal Aspects of Speech, Hearing, and Language,* ed. by Fred D. Minifie, Thomas J. Hixon, and Frederick Williams. Englewood Cliffs, NJ: Prentice-Hall, 343–420.

SMITH, ETHEL (1970). "An electromyographic investigation of the relationship between abdominal muscular effort and the rate of vocal vibrato." *The NATS Bulletin* 26, 4: 2; 4; 6; 8–17.

SMITH, MICHAEL (1972). "The effect of straight-tone feedback on the vibrato." *The NATS Bulletin* 28, 4: 28–32.

SMITH, S. (1954). "Remarks on the physiology of the vibrations of the vocal cords." *Folia Phoniatrica* 6: 166.

SMOLOVER, RAYMOND (1983). "Vocal behavior analysis and modification under conditions of expiratory and inspiratory phonation." *Journal of Research in Singing* 7, 1: 11–37.

SOKOLOWSKY, R. (1931). "Dunkel-und Hellfärbung der Stimme." *Handbuch der normalen und pathologischen Physiologie,* Vol. 15. Berlin: Julius Springer-Verlag.

SONDHI, MAN MOHAN, AND RESNICK, J. R. (1983). "The inverse problem for the vocal tract: numerical methods, acoustical experiments, and speech synthesis." *Journal of the Acoustical Society of America* 73: 985–1002.

SONESSON, BERTIL (1960). "On the anatomy and vibratory pattern of the human vocal folds." *Acta Oto-laryngologica* (supplement 156).

SONNINEN, AATTO A. (1954). "Is the length of the vocal cords the same at all different levels of singing?" *Acta Oto-laryngologica* (supplement 118), 219.

——(1956). "The role of the external laryngeal muscles in length-adjustment of the vocal cords in singing." *Acta Oto-laryngologica* (supplement 130), 1–102.

——(1968). "The external frame function in the control of pitch in the human voice." *Sound Production in Man: Annals of the New York Academy of Sciences,* ed. by A. Bouhuys. New York: New York Academy of Sciences, 68–90.

SONNINEN, AATTO A.; DAMSTE, P. H.; JOL, J.; AND FORKENS, J. (1972). "On vocal strain." *Folia Phoniatrica* 24: 321–336.

SORON, H. I.; MICHAELS, H. B.; AND LIEBERMAN, P. (1967). "Some observations of laryngeal phenomena derived from high speed motion pictures." *Journal of the Acoustical Society of America* 41: 1614.

STANLEY, DOUGLAS (1934). "All great voices have one characteristic in common." *The Etude* April, 52: 254–255.

STEBER, ELEANOR (1946). "Prepare for good luck." *The Etude* July, 64: 64.

STETSON, R. H. (1931). "The breathing movements in singing." *Archives Néerlandaises de phonétique expérimentale,* 115–164. Reprinted in *Contributions of Voice Research to Singing,* ed. by John Large. Houston, TX: College Hill Press, 1980, 5–47.

STEVENS, KENNETH, AND BLUMSTEIN, S. E. (1978). "Invariant cues for place of articulation in stop consonants." *Journal of the Acoustical Society of America* 65: 1358.

STEVENS, KENNETH, AND HOUSE, A. S. (1955). "Development of a quantitative description of vowel articulation." *Journal of the Acoustical Society of America* 27: 487–493.

——(1963). "Perturbation of vowel articulation by consonantal context: an acoustical study." *Journal of Speech and Hearing Research* 6: 111–128.

STEVENS, RISE (1947). "Make the right start!" *The Etude* May, 65: 245.

STIGNANI, EBE (1949). "The elements of bel canto." *The Etude* June, 67: 350.

STRENGER, FALKE (1968). "Radiographic, palatographic and labiographic methods in phonetics." *Manual of Phonetics*, ed. by Bertil Malmberg. Amsterdam: North-Holland Publishing, 334–364.

STRONGIN, LILLIAN (1965). "What is bel canto?" *The NATS Bulletin* 22, 2: 14–15; 35.

STRUVE, HANS WERNER (1974). "Determination of the instant of glottal closure from the speech wave." *Journal of the Acoustical Society of America* 56: 1625–1629.

SUNDBERG, JOHAN (1968). "Formant frequencies of a bass singer." *Speech Transmission Laboratory Quarterly Progress and Status Report* 1: 1–16.

———(1973). "The source spectrum in professional singing." *Folia Phoniatrica* 25: 71–90.

———(1974). "Articulatory interpretation of the 'Singing Formant.'" *Journal of the Acoustical Society of America* 55: 838–844.

———(1975). "Formant technique in a professional female singer." *Acustica* 32, 2: 89–96.

———(1977a). "The acoustics of the singing voice." *Scientific American* 236, 3: 82–91.

———(1977b). "Studies of the soprano voice." *Journal of Research in Singing* 1, 1: 25–35.

———(1981). "The voice as a sound generator." *Research Aspects in Singing*, ed. by J. Sundberg. Stockholm: the Royal Swedish Academy of Music, 6–14.

———(1983). "Chest wall vibrations in singers." *Journal of Speech and Hearing*, 26, 3: 329–340.

SUNDBERG, JOHAN, AND GAUFFIN, J. (1983). "Amplitude of the voice source fundamental and the intelligibility of super pitch vowels." *Journal of Research in Singing* 7, 1: 1–5.

SUNDBERG, JOHAN, AND NORDSTROM, P. E. (1983). "Raised and lowered larynx: the effect on vowel formant frequencies." *Journal of Research in Singing* 6, 2: 7–15.

SWING, DOLF (1973). "Teaching the professional Broadway voice." *The NATS Bulletin* 29, 3: 38–41.

TAFF, MERLE E. (1965). "An acoustic study of vowel modification and register transition in the male singing voice." *The NATS Bulletin* 22, 2: 5–11; 35.

TAKAGI, Y.; IRWIN, J. V.; AND BOSMA, J. F. (1966). "Effect of electrical stimulation of the pharyngeal wall on respiratory action." *Journal of Applied Physiology* 21: 454–462.

TARNEAUD, J. (1958). "Psychological and clinical study of the pneumophonic synergy." *The NATS Bulletin*, 14, 3: 12–15.

TARNÓCZY, THOMAS A. (1948). "Resonance data concerning nasals, laterals and trills." *Word* 4: 71–77.

———(1951). "The opening time and open quotient of the vocal folds during phonation." *Journal of the Acoustical Society of America* 23: 42.

TAYLOR, A. (1960). "The contribution of the intercostal muscles to the effort of respiration in man." *Journal of Physiology* 151: 390–402.

TAYLOR, ROBERT M. (1955). "Acoustics as an aid to ease of singing." *The NATS Bulletin* 12, 2: 19–20.

———(1958). "Acoustics for the Singer." *Emporia State Research Studies* 6: 5–35.

TEBALDI, RENATA (1957). "Good vocal habits." *The Etude* May–June, 75: 13.

TEYTE, MAGGIE (1946). "A philosophy of vocal study." *The Etude* January, 64: 5.

THEBOM, BLANCHE (1948). "Conquering tensions." *The Etude* July, 66: 411.

THIBAULT, CONRAD (1946). "The secret of song speech." *The Etude* December, 64: 669.

THOMAS, JOHN CHARLES (1943). "Color in singing." *The Etude* November, 61: 701.

TIFFIN, JOSEPH (1932). "The role of pitch and intensity in the vocal vibrato of students and artists." *University of Iowa Studies in the Psychology of Music* 1: 134.

TIMCKE, R.; VON LEDEN, HANS; AND MOORE, PAUL (1958). "Laryngeal vibrations: measurements of the glottic wave. Part I: the normal vibratory cycle." *Archives of Otolaryngology* 68: 1–19.

———(1959). "Laryngeal vibrations: measurements of the glottic wave. Part II: physiologic vibrations." *Archives of Otolaryngology* 69: 434–444.

TITZE, INGO (1976). "On the mechanics of vocal-fold vibration." *Journal of the Acoustical Society of America* 60: 1366–1380.

———(1979a). "A physiological interpretation of vocal registers." *Journal of the Acoustical Society of America* 66 (supplement), 56.

———(1979b). "A theoretical study of the effects of various laryngeal configurations on the acoustics of phonation." *Journal of the Acoustical Society of America* 66: 60–70.

———(1980). "Fundamental frequency scaling and voice classification." *The NATS Bulletin* 37, 1: 18–22.

———(1981a). "Biomechanic and distributed-mass models of vocal fold vibration." *Vocal Fold Physiology*, ed. by K. N. Stevens and M. Hirano, Tokyo: University of Tokyo Press, 245–270.

———(1981b). "How can the vocal mechanism be tuned for maximum acoustic output power?" *The NATS Bulletin* 37, 4: 45.

———(1981c). "Is there a scientific explanation for tone focus and tone placement?" *The NATS Bulletin* 37, 5: 26.

———(1981d). "What physical factors are involved in the relationship between vocal pitch and breath support?" *The NATS Bulletin* 37, 3: 37.

———(1981e). "Properties of the vocal folds, and how important are they?" *The NATS Bulletin* 38, 1: 30.

———(1981f). "Shattering crystal goblets; the ultimate vocal prowess." *The NATS Bulletin* 38, 2: 32.

———(1981g). "What determines the elastic properties of the vocal folds and how important are they?" *The NATS Bulletin* 38, 1: 30–31.

———(1982a). "Why is the verbal message less intelligible in singing than in speech?" *The NATS Bulletin* 38, 3: 37.

———(1982b). "Sensory Feedback in Voice Production." *The NATS Bulletin* 38, 4: 32.

———(1982c). "Some thoughts on source–system interdependence." *The NATS Bulletin* 38, 5: 27.

———(1982d). "Random acoustic factors in voice production." *The NATS Bulletin* 39, 1: 30.

———(1982e). "Some thoughts on airflow in singing." *The NATS Bulletin* 39, 2: 32.

———(1983a). "Vocal fatigue." *The NATS Bulletin* 39, 3: 22.

———(1983b). "Vocal registers." *The NATS Bulletin* 39, 4: 21.

——(1983c). "Instrumentation for voice analysis." *The NATS Bulletin* 39, 5: 29.

——(1983d). "Some additional thoughts on vocal fatigue" (Part I). *The NATS Bulletin* 40, 1: 26.

TITZE, INGO, AND STRONG, W. J. (1972). "Simulated vocal cord motions in speech and singing." *Journal of the Acoustical Society of America* 52: 123–124.

——(1975). "Normal modes in vocal cord tissues." *Journal of the Acoustical Society of America* 57: 736–744.

TOUREL, JENNIE (1943). "A basis for good singing." *The Etude* March, 61: 154.

TRAUBEL, HELEN (1943). "Make haste slowly." *The Etude* January, 61: 154.

TREASH, LEONARD (1947). "The importance of vowel sounds and their modification in producing good tone." *The NATS Bulletin* 4, 1: 3–6.

TREMBLE, G. E. (1950). "Mechanics of the nose, with special reference to nasopharyngeal discharge." *Archives of Otolaryngology* 51: 205.

TRENDELENBURG, F. (1935). "On the physics of speech sounds." *Journal of the Acoustical Society of America* 7: 142.

TRIPLETT, W. M. (1967). "An investigation concerning vocal sounds of high pitches." *The NATS Bulletin* 23, 3: 6–8; 50.

TROJAN, FELIX (1953). "Psychodiagnostik der Sprechstimme." *Folia Phoniatrica* 5: 216.

TROJAN, FELIX, AND KRYSSIN-EXNER, K. (1968). "The decay of articulation under the influence of alcohol and paraldehyde." *Folia Phoniatrica* 20: 217–238.

TROUP, GORDON, AND CLINCH, P. G. (1982a). "The physics of the singing voice." *Physics Reports* 74, 5: 381–401.

——(1982b). "Some problems common to singers and reed wind instrument players." *The NATS Bulletin* 38, 4: 18, 21–23.

TRUBY, H. M. (1962). "Contribution of the pharyngeal cavity to vowel resonances and in general." *Journal of the Acoustical Society of America* 34: 1978.

TUBBS, FRANK R. (1884). "Attack of tone." *The Voice* 6, 8: 104.

TUCKER, RICHARD (1954). "The first step is honesty." *The Etude* November, 72: 13.

TUOMI, SEPPO, AND FISHER, JAMES (1979). "Characteristics of simulated sexy voice." *Folia Phoniatrica* 31: 242–249.

ULLMANN, ELIZABETH (1970). "About Hering and Breuer." *Breathing: Hering-Breuer Centenary Symposium*, ed. by Ruth Porter. London: J. & A. Churchill, 3–15.

VAN DEINSE, J. B. (1981). "Registers." *Folia Phoniatrica* 33: 37–50.

——; FRATEUR, LUCIE; AND KEIZER, J. (1974). "Problems of the singing voice." *Folia Phoniatrica* 26: 428–434.

VAN DEN BERG, JANWILLEM (1955a). "Calculations on a model of the vocal tract for the vowel /i/ (meat) and on the larynx." *Journal of the Acoustical Society of America* 27: 332–337.

——(1955b). "On the role of the laryngeal ventricle in voice production." *Folia Phoniatrica* 7: 57.

——(1956). "Direct and indirect determination of the mean subglottic pressure." *Folia Phoniatrica* 8: 1–24.

——(1957). "On the air resistance and the Bernoulli effect of the human larynx." *Journal of the Acoustical Society of America* 29: 626–31.

_____(1958). "Myoelastic—aerodynamic theory of voice production." *Journal of Speech and Hearing Research* 1: 227–244.

_____(1960). "Vocal ligaments versus registers." *Current Problems in Phoniatrics and Logopedics* 1: 19–34. Reprinted 1963, *The NATS Bulletin* 20, 2: 16–21; 31.

_____(1962). "Modern research in experimental phoniatrics." *Folia Phoniatrica* 14: 8.

_____(1964). "Some physical aspects of voice production." *Research Potentials in Voice Physiology*, ed. by David W. Brewer. Syracuse, NY: State University of New York, 63–101.

_____(1968a). "Mechanism of the larynx and the laryngeal vibrations." *Manual of Phonetics*, ed. by Bertil Malmberg. Amsterdam: North-Holland Publishing, 278–308.

_____(1968b). "Sound production in isolated human larynges." *Sound Production in Man: Annals of the New York Academy of Sciences*, ed. by A. Bouhuys. New York: New York Academy of Sciences, 18–27.

_____(1968c). "Register problems." *Sound Production in Man: Annals of the New York Academy of Sciences*, ed. by A. Bouhuys. New York: New York Academy of Sciences, 129–134.

_____(1968d). Discussion remarks. *Sound Production in Man: Annals of the New York Academy of Sciences*, ed. by A. Bouhuys. New York: New York Academy of Sciences, 140.

VAN DEN BERG, JANWILLEM, AND VENNARD, WILLIAM (1959). "Toward an objective vocabulary for voice pedagogy." *The NATS Bulletin* 15, 6: 10–15.

VARNAY, ASTRID (1952). "Hear yourself as others hear you." *The Etude* May 19, 70: 10.

VENNARD, WILLIAM (1955). "Three ways to sing softly." *The NATS Bulletin* 11, 3: 5; 14.

_____(1956). "Pitch difficulties." *The NATS Bulletin* 12, 4: 4–5.

_____(1957). "Some implications of the Husson research." *The NATS Bulletin* 13, 3: 4–5; 26–27; 32.

_____(1959). "Some implications of the Sonninen research." *The NATS Bulletin* 15, 4: 8–13.

_____(1961). "The Bernoulli effect in singing." *The NATS Bulletin* 17, 3: 8–11.

_____(1962). "Building correct singing habits." *Voice and Speech Disorders*, ed. by Nathaniel M. Levin, Springfield, IL: Charles C Thomas.

_____(1964). "An experiment to evaluate the importance of nasal resonance." *Folia Phoniatrica* 16: 146–153.

VENNARD, WILLIAM, AND HIRANO, MINORU (1971). "Varieties of voice production." *The NATS Bulletin* 27, 3: 26–32.

VENNARD, WILLIAM; HIRANO, MINORU; AND FRITZELL, BJÖRN (1971). "The extrinsic laryngeal muscles." *The NATS Bulletin* 27, 4: 22–30.

VENNARD, WILLIAM; HIRANO, MINORU; AND OHALA, JOHN (1970). "Laryngeal synergy in singing." *The NATS Bulletin* 27, 1: 16–21.

_____(1971). "Chest, head, and falsetto." *The NATS Bulletin* 27, 2: 30–37.

VENNARD, WILLIAM, AND IRWIN, JAMES W. (1966). "Speech and song compared in sonagrams." *The NATS Bulletin* 23, 2: 18–23.

VENNARD, WILLIAM, AND ISSHIKI, NOBUHIKO (1964). "Coup de glotte." *The NATS Bulletin* 20, 3: 15–18.

VENNARD, WILLIAM, AND VON LEDEN, HANS (1967). "The importance of intensity modulation in the perception of a trill." *Folia Phoniatrica* 19: 19–26.

VON BÉKÉSY, GEORG (1948). "Vibration of the head in a sound field and its role in hearing by bone conduction." *Journal of the Acoustical Society of America* 20: 749–760.

———(1949). "The structure of the middle ear and the hearing of one's own voice by bone conduction." *Journal of the Acoustical Society of America* 21: 217–323.

VON COBLENZER, H., AND MUHAR, F. (1965). "Die Phonationsatmung." *Wiener klinische Wochenschrift* 48: 945–953.

VON ESSEN, O. (1961). "Die phonetische Dokumentation der Nasalität und des offenen Näselns." *Folia Phoniatrica* 13: 32.

VON LEDEN, HANS (1961). "The mechanism of phonation." *Archives of Otolaryngology* 74: 660–676.

———(1968). "Objective measures of laryngeal function and phonation." *Sound Production in Man: Annals of the New York Academy of Sciences,* ed. by A. Bouhuys. New York: New York Academy of Sciences, 56–67.

———(1969). "The larynx and the voice." *Archives of Otolaryngology* 89: 550–551.

VON VOGELSANGER, T. G. (1954). "Experimental Prüfung der Stimmleistung beim Singen." *Folia Phoniatrica* 6: 193.

VRBANICH, LAV (1960). "On the teaching of voice." *The NATS Bulletin* 17, 1: 4–6; 8–9.

WADE, O. L. (1954). "Movements of the thoracic cage and diaphragm in respiration." *Journal of Physiology* 124: 193–212.

WADSWORTH, STEPHEN (1976). "Bonynge on bel canto: interpreting the early 19th century." *Opera News* 40: 18–22.

WAENGLER, HANS-HEINRICH (1968). "Some remarks and observations on the function of the soft palate." *The NATS Bulletin* 25, 1: 24–25; 30–32.

WALSCHE, WALTER HALE (1883). "Dramatic singing physiologically estimated." *The Voice* 5, 3: 24–25.

WARD, DIXON, AND BURNS, EDWARD (1978). "Singing without auditory feedback." *Journal of Research in Singing* 2, 1: 24–44.

WARNER, EDGAR S. (1884). "Science or empiricism in voice culture?" *The Voice* 6, 10: 144.

WARREN, D. W., AND HALL, D. J. (1973). "Glottal activity and intravocal pressure during stop consonant productions." *Folia Phoniatrica* 25: 122–129.

WARREN, LEONARD (1949). "How to build confidence." *The Etude* March, 67: 149.

WATERS, CRYSTAL (1949). "Is there a break in your voice?" *The Etude* April, 67: 221.

———(1953). "Steps to artistic vocal success." *The Etude* March, 71: 11.

———(1954). "How to sing more fluently." *The Etude* August, 72: 17.

WATSON, PETER J., AND HIXON, THOMAS J. (1985). "Respiratory kinematics in classical (opera) singers." *Journal of Speech and Hearing Research* 28: 104–122.

WEEDE, ROBERT (1947). "Intelligent care of the singing voice." *The Etude* December, 65: 679.

WEISS, DESO A. (1950). "The pubertal change of the human voice." *Folia Phoniatrica* 2: 126–159.

———(1959). "Discussion of the neurochronaxic theory (Husson)." *Archives of Otolaryngology* 70: 607–618.

WELITSCH, LJUBA (1950). "Breathing is everything." *The Etude* October, 68, 18.

WENDAHL, R. W.; MOORE, G. P.; AND HOLLIEN, HARRY (1963). "Comments on vocal fry." *Folia Phoniatrica* 15: 251–255.

WERRENRATH, REINALD (1951). "Singing can be simple." *The Etude* February, 69: 16.

WESTERMAN, KENNETH N. (1948). "Resonation." *The NATS Bulletin* 5, 5: 2; 8.

_____(1950). "The framework for developing the coordinated muscle actions of singing." *The NATS Bulletin* 6, 5: 2; 7.

_____(1953). "The physiology of vibrato." *The NATS Bulletin* 9, 3: 14–18.

WHILLIS, J. A. (1930). "A note on the muscles of the palate and the superior constrictor." *Journal of Anatomy* 65: 92–95.

WHITLOCK, WELDON (1966). "Practical use of bel canto." *The NATS Bulletin* 22, 4: 28–29; 43–44.

_____(1968). "The problem of the passaggio." *The NATS Bulletin* 24, 3: 10–13.

WIENER, P. S. (1967). "Auditory discrimination and articulation." *Journal of Speech and Hearing Disorders* 32: 19–28.

WILCOX, JOHN C. (1944). "About tone placing." *The Etude* June, 62: 327.

WILDER, CAROL (1979). "Vocal Aging." *Transcripts of the Seventh Symposium: Care of the Professional Voice,* Part II, ed. by V. Lawrence. New York: The Voice Foundation, 51–59.

WILLIAMS, A. F. (1951). "The nerve supply of the laryngeal muscles." *Journal of Laryngology and Otology* 65: 343.

WILLIAMSON, JOHN FINLEY (1951a). "Correct breathing for singers" (Part I). *The Etude* February, 69: 18.

_____(1951b). "Correct breathing for singers" (Part II). *The Etude* March, 69: 22.

_____(1951c). "Good singing requires good diction." *The Etude* September, 69: 23.

_____(1951d). "The importance of vowel coloring." *The Etude* October, 69: 23.

WILSON, JAMES E. (1977). "Variations of the laryngo–pharynx in singing." *The NATS Bulletin* 33, 2: 22–24; 31.

WINCKEL, F. (1952). "Elektroakustische Untersuchungen an der menschlichen Stimme." *Folia Phoniatrica* 4: 93–113.

_____(1971). "How to measure the effectiveness of stage singers' voices." *Folia Phoniatrica* 23: 228–233.

_____(1976). "Measurements of the acoustic effectiveness and quality of trained singers' voices." *The NATS Bulletin* 33, 1: 44.

WOLF, S., AND SETT, W. (1965). "Quantitative studies on the singing voice." *Journal of the Acoustical Society of America* 6: 255–266.

WOLFF, H. C. (1940). "Die Sprachmelodie in alten Opernrezitativ." *Archiv für Sprach-und Stimmphysiologie und Sprach-und Stimmheilkunde* 4: 30.

WOLLMANN, A. M. (1953). "Empirical method versus the scientific." *The NATS Bulletin* 9, 4: 20.

WOOLDRIDGE, WARREN B. (1956). "Is there nasal resonance?" *The NATS Bulletin* 13, 1: 28–29.

WORMHOUDT, PEARL (1984). "Some thoughts on the psychology of singing and teaching of singing." *The NATS Bulletin* 40, 5: 28–31.

WYKE, B. D. (1974). "Laryngeal neuromuscular control systems in singing: a review of current concepts." *Folia Phoniatrica* 26, 1: 295–306.

_____(1979). "Neurological aspects of phonatory control systems in the larynx: a review of current concepts." *Transcripts of the Eighth Sympo-*

sium: Care of the Professional Voice, Part II, ed. V. Lawrence. New York: The Voice Foundation, 42–53.

———(1982). "Neurological aspects of singing." *Tiefenstruktur der Musik: Festschrift Fritz Winckel zum 75. Geburtstag*, ed. by C. Dahlhaus and Manfred Krause. Berlin. Technische Universität der Künste, 129–156.

YANAGIHARA, NAOKU; KOIKE, YASUO; AND VON LEDEN, HANS (1966). "Phonation and respiration." *Folia Phoniatrica* 18: 323–340.

YORK, WYNN (1959). "Stress and vowel values." *The NATS Bulletin* 16, 1: 10–12.

———(1963). "The use of imagery in posture training." *The NATS Bulletin* 19, 4: 6, 27, 34.

ZEMLIN, W. R.; MASON, ROBERT M.; AND HOLSTEAD, LISA (1972). "Notes on the mechanics of vocal vibrato." *The NATS Bulletin* 28, 2: 22–26.

ZENATTI, ARLETTE (1970). "Le Développement génétique de la perception musicale." *Monographies françaises de psychologie*, ed. by Pierre Oléron, Vol. 17. Paris: Centre national de la recherche scientifique.

ZENKER, WOLFGANG (1958a). "Über Bindesgewebstrukturen des Kehlkopfes und seines Aufhängesystems und deren funktionelle Bedeutung für den Kehlkopfraum." (Part I). *Monatsschrift für Ohrenheilkunde und Laryngo-Rhinologie* 5, 92: 269–307.

———(1958b). "Über Bindesgewebstrukturen des Kehlkopfes und seines Aufhängesystems und deren funktionelle Bedeutung für den Kehlkopfraum." (Part II). *Monatsschrift fur Ohrenheilkunde und Laryngo-Rhinologie* 6, 92: 349–383.

———(1964a). "Vocal muscle fibers and their motor end-plates." *Research Potentials in Voice Physiology*, ed. by D. Brewer. Syracuse, New York: State University of New York, 7–19.

———(1964b). "Questions regarding the function of external laryngeal muscles." *Research Potentials in Voice Physiology*, ed. by D. Brewer. Syracuse, New York: State University of New York, 20–40.

———(1966). "Zur Frage der Endigung von Muskelfasern am Bindegewebsapparat des menschlichen Stimmbandes." *Acta Anatomica* 64: 198–213.

ZENKER, WOLFGANG, AND GLANINGER, J. (1959). "Die Stärke des Trachealzuges beim lebenden Menschen und seine Bedeutung für die Kehlkopfmechanik." *Zeitschrift fur Biologie* III: 143–164.

ZENKER, WOLFGANG, AND ZENKER, ADOLF (1960). "Über die Regelung der Stimmlippenspannung durch von aussen eingreifende Mechanismen." *Folia Phoniatrica* (separatum) 12, 1: 1–36.

ZIMMERMAN, R. (1938). "Die Messung der Stimmlippenlänge bei Sängern und Sängerinnen." *Archiv für Sprach-und Stimmheilkunde* 2: 103.

ZOCCHE, G. P.; FRITTS, H. W., JR.; AND COURNAND, A. (1960). "Fraction of maximum breathing capacity available for prolonged hyperventilation." *Journal of Applied Physiology* 15: 1073–1074.

ZWITMAN, DANIEL H.; GYEPES, MICHAEL T.; AND SAMPLE, FREDERICK (1973). "The submentovertical projection in the radiographic analysis of velopharyngeal dynamics." *Journal of Speech and Hearing Disorders* 38: 473–477.

ZWITMAN, DANIEL, AND WARD, PAUL H. (1974). "Variations in velopharyngeal closure assessed by endoscopy." *Journal of Speech and Hearing Disorders* 39: 366–372.

BOOKS

ADAMS, FREDERIC A. (1849). *The Singer's Manual: for Teachers, Pupils and Private Students.* New York: John Wiley.

ADLER, KURT (1967). *Phonetics and Diction in Singing.* Minneapolis: The University of Minnesota Press.

AIKIN, W. A. (1910). *The Voice: An Introduction to Practical Phonology.* Reprint 1951. London: Longmans Green.

AKIN, JOHNNYE (1958). *And So We Speak: Voice and Articulation.* Englewood Cliffs, NJ: Prentice-Hall.

ANDERSON, V. A. (1942). *Training the Speaking Voice.* New York: Oxford University Press.

ANSALDO, LEA, AND BASSETTI, ELDES (1977). *La voce dell'attore e la voce del cantante.* Genoa: Sabatelli Editore.

APPELMAN, D. RALPH (1967). *The Science of Vocal Pedagogy.* Reprint 1974. Bloomington, IN: Indiana University Press.

ARMHOLD, ADELHEID (1963). *Singing.* Cape Town: Tafelburg-Uitgeuers.

ARMIN, GEORG (1931). *Die Technik der Breitspannung: in Beitrag über die horizontal-vertikalen Spannkräfte beim Aufbau der Stimme nach dem "Stauprinzip."* Berlin: Verlag der Gesellschaft für Stimmkultur Berlin-Wilmersdorf.

_____(n.d.) *Von der Urkraft der Stimme,* 3d ed. Lippstadt: Kistner & Siegel.

ARNOLD, GOTTFRIED EDUARD (1948). *Die traumatischen und konstitutionellen Störungen der Stimme und Sprache.* Vienna: Urban & Schwarzenberg.

ARONSON, A. E. (1980). *Clinical Voice Disorders: An Interdisciplinary Approach.* New York: Brian C. Decker.

BACH, ALBERTO B. (1886). *The Art of Singing.* Reprint 1944. New York: I. B. Fischer.

BACHNER, LOUIS (1940). *Dynamic Singing.* London: Dobson.

BAGLEY, SILVIA R. (1955). *Viewpoint for Singers.* Denver: World Press.

BAIRSTOWE, EDWARD C., AND GREENE, HARRY PLUNKET (1945). *Singing Learned from Speech.* London: Macmillan.

BAKER, FREDERICK CLARK (1901). *How We Hear: A Treatise on Sound.* Boston: Oliver Ditson.

BAKER, GEORGE (1963). *The Common Sense of Singing.* London: Pergamon Press.

BALK, WESLEY (1973). *The Complete Singer–Actor.* Minneapolis: University of Minnesota Press.

BALLANTYNE, JOHN, AND GROVES, JOHN, eds. (1971). *Scott-Brown's Diseases of the Ear, Nose and Throat,* 3d ed., 4 vols. London: Butterworth.

BALLENGER, H. C. (1947). *A Manual of Otology, Rhinology and Laryngology,* 3rd ed. Philadelphia: Lea and Febiger.

BANKS, LOUIS (1941). *Voice Culture.* Philadelphia: Elkan-Vogel.

BARLOW, W. (1973). *The Alexander Technique.* New York: Alfred A. Knopf.

BARRAUD, A.; ESCHER, E.; HANHARD, E.; LUCHSINGER, R.; MONTANDO, A.; NAGER, F. R.; OPPIKER, E.; RÜEDI, L.; AND TALLIENS, J. P. (1953). *Hals–Nasen–Ohrenheilkunde.* Basel: S. Karger.

BARTHOLOMEW, WILMER T. (1942). *Acoustics of Music.* New York: Prentice-Hall.

BARTOSCHEK, WALTER. (n.d.) *Gesangstechnik im Lichte neuerer Erkenntnisse.* Berlin: Privately published.

BAST, T. H., AND ANSON, B. J. (1949). *The Temporal Bone and the Ear.* Springfield, IL: Charles C Thomas.

BATES, D. V., AND CHRISTIE, R. V. (1964). *Respiratory Function in Disease: Introduction to the Integrated Study of the Lung.* Philadelphia, W. B. Saunders.

BAUDISSONE, BRUNO (1983). Un nido di memorie: interviste a 40 cantanti lirici. Turin: Edizioni Musicali Scomegna.

BAUM, GÜNTHER (1955). *Die Stimmbildungslehre des Dr. Jean Nadolovitch.* Hamburg: Hüllenhagen & Griehl.

BECKER, WALTER; BUCKINGHAM, RICHARD; HOLINGEN, PAUL H.; KORTUNG, GÜNTHER W.; AND LEDERER, FRANCIS L. (1969). *Atlas der Hals–Nasen–Ohren–Krankheiten.* Stuttgart: Georg Thieme.

BECKMAN, GERTRUDE WHEELER (1955). *Tools for Speaking and Singing.* New York: G. Schirmer.

BEHNKE, EMIL (1880). *The Mechanism of the Human Voice.* London: J. Curwen & Sons.

BERANEK, LEO (1954). *Acoustics.* New York: McGraw-Hill.

BÉRARD, JEAN-BAPTISTE (1775). *L'Art du chant.* Transl. and ed. by Sidney Murray, 1968. Milwaukee, WI: Pro Musica Press.

BERRY, M. F., AND EISENSON, J. (1956). *Speech Disorders.* New York: Appleton–Century–Croft.

BERTONI, GIULIO, AND UGOLINI, FRANCESCO (1944). *Prontuario di pronunzia e di ortografia.* Turin: Istituto del libro italiano.

BILANCONCI, G. (1923). *La voce cantata, normale e patologica.* Rome: Pozzi.

BIRRELL, J. F., ed. (1977). *Logan Turner's Diseases of the Nose, Throat and Ear.* Bristol: Wrights.

BLOCH, BERNARD, AND TRAGER, GEORGE L. (1949). *Outline of Linguistic Analysis.* Linguistic Society of America. Ann Arbor, MI: Edwards Brothers.

BLOOMFIELD, LEONARD (1955). *Language.* New York: Henry Holt.

BÖHME, GERHARD (1972). *Untersuchungs-Methoden der Stimme und Sprache.* Leipzig: J. A. Barth.

———(1974). *Stimm–Sprach und Sprachstörungen.* Stuttgart: Gustav Fischer.

BOLOGNINI, TOMMASO (1982). *Trattato di tecnica del canto dalla pratica antica alla moderna.* Fasano di Puglia: Schena Editore.

BONNIER, PIERRE (1908). *La voix professionnelle.* Paris: Bibliothèque Larousse.

BOONE, D. R. (1977). *The Voice and Voice Therapy.* Englewood Cliffs, NJ: Prentice-Hall.

BOUHUYS, AREND, ed. (1968). *Sound Production in Man: Annals of the New York Academy of Sciences.* New York: New York Academy of Sciences.

———(1977). *The Physiology of Breathing.* London: Grune & Stratton.

BOWEN, WILBER D., AND STONE, HENRY A. (1949). *Applied Anatomy and Kinesiology.* Philadelphia: Lea & Febiger.

BREWER, DAVID J., ed. (1964). *Research Potentials in Voice Physiology.* Syracuse, NY: State University of New York.

BROAD, DAVID J., ed. (1977). *Topics in Speech Science.* Los Angeles: Speech Communication Research Laboratory.

BRODNITZ, FRIEDRICH S. (1953). *Keep Your Voice Healthy.* New York: Harper & Brothers.

———(1971). *Vocal Rehabilitation,* 4th ed. Rochester, MN: American Academy of Ophthalmology and Otolaryngology.

BROWN, RALPH M. (1946). *The Singing Voice.* New York: Macmillan.

BROWN, WILLIAM EARL (1931). *Vocal Wisdom: Maxims of Giovanni Battista Lamperti.* Reprint, 1973. Boston: Crescendo Press.

BROWNE, LENNOX, AND BEHNKE, EMIL (n.d.). *Voice, Song and Speech.* New York: G. P. Putnam's Sons.

BRUNELLI, M. D., AND PITTOLA, E. (1940). *Guida per l'insegnamento pratico della fonetica italiana.* Perugia: Regia l'Università per Stranieri.

BRUSSARD J. F. (1912). *Elements of French Pronunciation.* New York: Charles Scribner's Sons.

BRYCE, D. P. (1974). *Differential Diagnosis and Treatment of Hoarseness.* Springfield, IL: Charles C Thomas.

BUITER, CORNELIUS TEKKE (1976). *Endoscopy of the Upper Airways.* Amsterdam: Excerpta Medica.

BUNCH, MERIBETH (1982). *Dynamics of the Singing Voice.* New York: Springer-Verlag.

BURGIN, JOHN CARROLL (1973). *Teaching Singing.* Metuchen, NJ: Scarecrow Press.

BURROWS, BENJAMIN; KNUDSON, RONALD J.; AND KETAL, LOUISE J. (1975). *Respiratory Insufficiency.* London: Lloyd-Luke [Medical Books].

CALLANDER, C. LATIMER (1948). *Surgical Anatomy.* Philadelphia: W. B. Saunders.

CAMPBELL, E. J. MORAN (1958). *The Respiratory Muscles and the Mechanics of Breathing.* Chicago: Year Book (Medical) Publishers.

CAMPBELL, E. J. MORAN; AGOSTONI, EMILIO; AND NEWSOM DAVIS, JOHN (1970). *The Respiratory Muscles: Mechanics and Neural Control.* London: Lloyd-Luke [Medical Books].

CAPPIANA, LUISA (1908). *Practical Hints and Helps for Perfection in Singing.* New York: Leo Feist.

CARUSO, ENRICO (1913). *How to Sing: Some Practical Hints.* London: John Church.

CARUSO, ENRICO, AND TETRAZZINI, LUISA (1909). *On the Art of Singing.* The Metropolitan Company, Reprint, 1975. New York: Dover Publications.

CATES, H. A., AND BASMAJIAN, J. W. (1955). *Primary Anatomy.* Baltimore: Williams & Wilkins.

CELLETTI, RODOLFO (1983). *Storia del belcanto.* Fiesole: Discanto Edizioni.

CHERRY, COLIN (1957). *On Human Communication.* London: Chapman and Hill.

CHRISTY, VAN A. (1974). *Expressive Singing,* 3d ed. Dubuque, IA: Wm. C. Brown, 2 vols.

_____(1975). *Foundations in Singing,* 3d ed. Dubuque, IA: Wm. C. Brown.

CLIPPINGER, D. A. (1917). *The Head Voice and Other Problems.* Philadelphia: Oliver Ditson.

_____(1929). *Fundamentals of Voice Training.* New York: Oliver Ditson.

COFFIN, BERTON (1980). *Overtones of Bel Canto.* Metuchen, NJ: Scarecrow Press.

COMROE, J. H., JR. (1965). *Physiology of Respiration.* Chicago, IL: Year Book [Medical] Publications.

COMROE, J. H., JR.; FORSTER, R. F.; DUBOIS, A. B.; BRISCO, W. A.; AND CARLSEN, E. (1968). *The Lung,* 2d ed. Chicago: Year Book [Medical] Publications.

COOPER, MORTON (1974). *Modern Techniques of Vocal Rehabilitation.* Springfield, IL: Charles C Thomas.

COTES, JOHN E. (1975). *Lung Function,* 3rd ed. London: Blackwell Scientific.

CRANMER, ARTHUR (1957). *The Art of Singing.* London: Dennis Dobson.

CRITCHLEY, M., AND HENSON, R.A., eds. (1977). *Music and the Brain.* London: Heinemann Medical Books.

CROFTON, JOHN, AND DOUGLAS, ANDREW (1975). *Respiratory Diseases,* 2d ed. London: Blackwell Scientific.

CULVER, CHARLES A. (1956). *Musical Acoustics.* New York: McGraw-Hill.

Cunningham's Manual of Practical Anatomy (1977). Ed. by G. J. Romanes. Oxford: Oxford University Press.

CURRY, ROBERT (1940). *The Mechanism of the Human Voice.* New York: Longmans Green.

CURTIS, H. HOLBROOK (1901). *Voice Building and Tone Placing.* New York: D. Appleton.

DAWSON, JOHN J. (1902). *The Voice of the Boy.* New York: A. S. Barnes.

DE ARMOND, STEPHEN J.; FUSCO, MADELEINE M.; AND DEWEY, MAYNARD M. (1976). *Structure of the Human Brain.* London: Oxford University Press.

DE BOOR, HELMUT; MOSER, HUGO; AND WINKLER, CHRISTIAN (1969). *Siebs Deutsche Aussprache* Berlin: Walter de Gruyter.

DECECCO, J. P., ed. (1967). *The Psychology of Language, Thought and Instruction.* New York: Holt, Rinehart and Winston.

DENES, PETER B., AND PINSON, ELLIOT N. (1963). *The Speech Chain: The Physics and Biology of Spoken Language.* Bell Telephone Laboratories.

DE REUCK, A. V. S., AND O'CONNOR, M., eds. (1962). *Ciba Foundation Symposium on Pulmonary Structure and Function.* London: J. & A. Churchill.

DEYOUNG, RICHARD (1958). *The Singer's Art.* Chicago: DePaul University.

DOSSERT, DEAN (1932). *Sound Sense for Singers.* New York: J. Fischer and Brothers.

DREW, DONALD, AND JENSEN, PAUL J. (1977). *Phonetic Processing: The Dynamics of Speech.* Columbus, Ohio: Charles E. Merrill.

DUEY, PHILIP (1950). *Bel Canto in Its Golden Age.* New York: King's Crown Press.

DUNKLEY, FERDINAND (1942). *The Buoyant Voice Acquired by Correct Pitch-Control.* Boston, C. C. Birchard.

ECKERT-MÖBIUS, H. C. A. (1964). *Lehrbuch der Hals–Nasen–Ohren–Heilkunde.* Leipzig: Georg Thieme.

EGENOLF, HEINRICH (1959). *Die menschliche Stimme: ihre Erziehung, Erhaltung und Heilung,* 2d ed. Stuttgart: Paracelsus.

EIGLER, GERHARD (1966). *Ohren–Nasen–Rachen–und Kehlkopfkrankheiten.* Berlin: Walter de Gruyter.

ELLIS, ALEXANDER (1898). *Speech in Song.* London: Novello.

EMIL-BEHNKE, KATE (1945). *The Technique of Singing.* London: Williams and Norgate.

Enciclopedia Garzanti della musica, ed. by Aldo Garzanti (1974). Milan: Garzanti.

FENN, W. O., AND RAHN, H., eds. (1964). *Handbook of Physiology.* American Physiological Society. Baltimore: Williams and Wilkins.

FFRANGEON-DAVIES, DAVID (1905). *The Singing of the Future.* Reprint, 1960. Champaign, IL: Pro Musica Press.

FIELDS, VICTOR ALEXANDER (1947). *Training the Singing Voice.* New York: King's Crown Press.

_____(1977). *Foundations of the Singer's Art.* Reprint, 1984, New York: NATS Publications.

FILLEBROWN, THOMAS (1911). *Resonance in Singing and Speaking.* Bryn Mawr, PA: Oliver Ditson.

FINK, B. R. (1975). *The Human Larynx: A Functional Study.* New York: Raven Press.

FLETCHER, HARVEY (1953). *Speech and Hearing in Communication.* New York: D. Van Nostrand.

FOREMAN, EDWARD, ed. (1968). *The Porpora Tradition.* Milwaukee, WI: Pro Musica Press.

FORNEBERG, ERICH (1964). *Stimmbildungsfibel.* Frankfurt: Moritz Diesterweg.

FRANCA, IDA (1959). *Manual of Bel Canto.* New York: Coward-McCann.

FRANCIS, CARL C., AND FARRELL, GORDON L. (1957). *Integrated Anatomy and Physiology,* 3d ed. St. Louis, MO: C. V. Mosby.

FRISELL, ANTHONY (1964). *The Tenor Voice.* Boston: Bruce Humphries.

_____(1972). *The Baritone Voice.* Boston: Crescendo Press.

FROESCHELS, EMIL (1933). *Speech Therapy.* Boston: Expression.

_____, ed. (1948). *Twentieth Century Speech and Voice Correction.* New York: Philosophical Library.

_____(1964). *Selected Papers of Emil Froeschels: 1940–1964,* ed. by Helen Beebe and Felix Trojan. Amsterdam: North-Holland Publishing.

FRY, D. B. (1979). *The Physics of Speech.* London: Cambridge University Press.

FUCHS, VIKTOR (1963). *The Art of Singing and Voice Technique.* London: Calder and Boyars.

FUCITO, SALVATORE, AND BEYER, BARNET (1924). *Caruso: Gesangskunst und Methode,* transl. by Curt Thesing. Berlin: Bote & Bock.

FUDGE, ERIK C., ed. (1973). *Phonology.* London: Penguin Books.

FUGÈRE, LUCIEN, AND DUHAMEL, RAOUL (1929). *Nouvelle méthode pratique de chant français par l'articulation.* Paris: Enoch.

FULTON, J. F. A. (1951). *A Textbook of Physiology.* Philadelphia: W. B. Saunders.

GARCIA, MANUEL (n.d.). *Garcia's Complete School of Singing.* (A compilation of editions of 1847 and 1872). London: Cramer, Beale and Chappell.

_____(1849). *Mémoire sur la voix humaine présenté a l'académie des sciences en 1840.* Paris: E. Suverger.

_____(1894). *Hints on Singing,* transl. by Beata Garcia. London: Ascherberg, Hopwood and Crew.

GARDINER, JULIAN (1968). *A Guide to Good Singing and Speech.* London: Cassell.

GESCHEIDT, ADELAIDE (1930). *Make Singing a Joy.* Cincinnati, OH: Willis Music.

GIB, CHARLES (1911). *Vocal Science and Art.* London: William Reeves.

GOLDSCHMIDT, HUGO (1892). *Die italienische Gesangsmethode des XVII. Jahrhunderts und ihre Bedeutung für die Gegenwart.* Breslau: Schlesische Buchdruckerei, Kunst und Verlags Anstalt.

GOODRICH, E. S. (1958). *Studies on the Structure and Development of Vertebrates.* New York: Dover Publications.

GRANT, J. C. BOILEAU (1962). *An Atlas of Anatomy.* London: Baillière, Tindall & Cox.

GRAY, GILES WILKERSON, AND WISE, CLAUDE MERTON (1934). *The Bases of Speech.* New York: Harper & Brothers.

Gray's Anatomy (1980), ed. by Robert Warwick and Peter Williams. Edinburgh: Churchill Livingstone.

GREENE, HARRY PLUNKET (1912). *Interpretation in Song*. Reprint, 1956, London: Macmillan.

GREENE, MARGARET C. L. (1959). *The Voice and Its Disorders*. London: Pitman Medical Publishing.

GÜMMER, PAUL (1970). *Erziehung der menschlichen Stimme*. Kassel: Bärenreiter.

GUNNING, THOMAS BRIAN (1874). *The Larynx: The Source of Vowel Sounds*. Baltimore: American Journal of Dental Science.

HALLE, M.; LUNT, H.; AND MACLEAN, H., eds. (1956). *For Roman Jakobson*. The Hague: Mouton.

HAMMER, RUSSELL A. (1978). *Singing—An Extension of Speech*. Metuchen, NJ: Scarecrow Press.

HARDCASTLE, W. J. (1976). *Physiology of Speech Production: An Introduction for Speech Scientists*. London: Academic Press.

HARPSTER, RICHARD W. (1984). *Technique in Singing*. New York: Schirmer Books.

HAYEK, HEINRICH, ed. (1960–1963). *Toldt-Hochstetter Anatomischer Atlas*. Vienna: Urban & Schwarzenberg, 3 vols.

HAYWOOD, FREDERICK H. (1932). *Universal Song: A Voice-Culture Course*. New York: G. Schirmer.

HEATON, WALLACE, AND HARGENS, C. W., eds. (1968). *An Interdisciplinary Index of Studies in Physics, Medicine and Music Related to the Human Voice*. Bryn Mawr: Theodore Presser.

HEFFNER, R. M. (1950). *General Phonetics*. Madison, WI: University of Wisconsin Press.

HEIKE, GEORG (1972). *Phonologie*. Stuttgart: Metzlerische Verlagsbuchhandlung.

HELMHOLTZ, HERMANN L. F. (1875). *On the Sensations of Tone*, transl. by Alexander J. Ellis. Reprint, 1939. London: Longmans, Green.

HENDERSON, WILLIAM JAMES (1937). *The Art of Singing*. New York: Dial Press.

HERBERT-CAESARI, E. (1936). *The Science and Sensations of Tone*, 2d ed., rev. Reprint, 1968. Boston: Crescendo Publishers.

_____(1965). *The Alchemy of Voice*. London: Robert Hale.

_____(1969). *The Voice of the Mind*. London: Robert Hale.

HERIOT, ANGUS (1964). *The Castrati in Opera*. New York: Da Capo Press.

HERMAN, TONA (1929). *Die Grammatik des Singens*. Vienna: Universal Edition.

HINES, JEROME (1982). *Great Singers on Great Singing*. New York: Doubleday.

HINMAN, FLORENCE LAMONT (1934). *Slogans for Singers*. New York: G. Schirmer.

HIRANO, MINORU (1981). *Clinical Examination of Voice*. Vienna: Springer-Verlag.

HOCHSTETTER, F. *see* Hayek, Heinrich.

HOCKETT, C. F. (1955). *Manual of Phonology*. Bloomington, IN: Indiana University Publications in Anthropology and Linguistics.

HOLLENDER, A. R. (1953). *The Pharynx*. Chicago: Year Book [Medical] Publishers.

HOOPS, RICHARD A. (1960). *Speech Science*. Springfield, IL: Charles C Thomas.

HOWELL, J. B. L., AND CAMPBELL, E. J. MORAN, eds. (1966). *Breathlessness*. Oxford: Blackwell Scientific.

HULBERT, H. H. (1928). *Voice Training in Speech and Song*. London: University Tutorial Press.

HULS, HELEN STEEN (1957). *The Adolescent Voice.* New York: Vantage Press.

HUSLER, FREDERICK (1970). *Das vollkommene Instrument.* Stuttgart: Belsar-Verlag.

HUSLER, F., AND RODD-MARLING, YVONNE (1960). *Singing: The Physical Nature of the Vocal Organ.* London: Faber and Faber.

HUSSON, RAOUL (1960). *La Voix chantée.* Paris: Gauthier-Villars.

JACKSON, C., AND JACKSON, C. L. (1934). *Bronchoscopy, Esophagoscopy, and Gastroscopy,* 3d ed. Philadelphia: W. B. Saunders.

———(1942). *Diseases and Injuries of the Larynx.* New York: Macmillan.

JACOBI, HENRY N. (1982). *Building Your Best Voice.* Englewood Cliffs, NJ: Prentice-Hall.

JAKOBOVITS, L. A., AND MIRON, M. S., eds. (1967). *Readings in the Psychology of Language.* Englewood Cliffs, NJ: Prentice-Hall.

JAKOBSON, ROMAN; FANT, GUNNAR; AND HALLE, MORRIS (1967). *Preliminaries to Speech Analysis.* Cambridge, MA: The M. I. T. Press.

JAMIESON, E. B. (1946). *Illustrations of Regional Anatomy: II. Head and Neck; III. Abdomen,* 6th ed. Edinburgh: E. & S. Livingstone.

JERGER, JAMES, ed. (1963). *Modern Developments in Audiology.* New York: Academic Press.

JONES, DANIEL (1950). *The Phoneme: Its Nature and Use.* Cambridge: Heffner and Sons.

———(1956). *An Outline of English Phonetics,* 6th ed. New York: E. P. Dutton.

JONES, DORA DUTY (1913). *Lyric Diction for Singers, Actors and Public Speakers.* London: Harper & Brothers.

JUDD, PERCY (1951). *Vocal Technique.* London: Sylvan Press.

JUDSON, LYMAN S., AND WEAVER, ANDREW T. (1942). *Voice Science.* New York: Appleton–Century–Crofts.

KAHANE, JOEL C., AND FOLKINS, JOHN F. (1984). *Atlas of Speech and Hearing Anatomy.* Columbus, OH: Charles E. Merrill.

KAISER, LOUISE, ed. (1957). *Manual of Phonetics.* Amsterdam: North-Holland Publishing (for the Permanent Council for the International Congress of Phonetic Sciences).

KANTNER, CLAUDE E., AND WEST, ROBERT (1960). *Phonetics.* New York: Harper & Brothers.

KARR, HARRISON (1938). *Your Speaking Voice.* Glendale, CA: Griffin-Patterson.

KATZ, B. (1966). *Nerve, Muscle and Synapsis.* New York: McGraw-Hill.

KELSEY, FRANKLIN (1950). *The Foundations of Singing.* London: Williams and Norgate.

KEMPER, JOSEF (1951). *Stimmpflege.* Mainz: B. Schott's Söhne.

KENYON, JOHN S. (1953). *American Pronunciation,* 10th rev. ed. Ann Arbor, MI: George Wahr.

KESSLER, H. H. (1950). *The Principles and Practices of Rehabilitation.* Philadelphia: Lea & Febiger.

KLEIN, HERMAN (1923). *An Essay on Bel Canto.* London: Oxford University Press.

KLEIN, JOSEPH J., AND SCHJEIDE, OLE A. (1967). *Singing Technique: How to Avoid Trouble.* Princeton, NJ: D. Van Nostrand.

KNUDSON, CHARLES A., AND CHAPARD, LOUIS (1966). *Introduction to French Pronunciation,* 2d ed. Urbana, IL: Privately published.

KOCKRITZ, HUBERT (1965). *Language Orientation—An Introduction to the Pronunciation of Foreign Languages Based upon the International Phonetic Alphabet.* Cincinnati: Privately published.

KOFLER, LEO (1889). *The Art of Breathing as the Basis of Tone-Production*, 6th rev. ed. New York: Edward S. Werner.

KWARTIN, BERNARD (1952). *Vocal Pedagogy*. New York: Carlton Press.

LABLACHE, LOUIS (n.d.) *Lablache's Complete Method of Singing: or a Rational Analysis of the Principles According to Which the Studies Should Be Directed for Developing the Voice and Rendering It Flexible, and for Forming the Voice*. Boston: Oliver Ditson.

LADEFOGED, PETER (1962). *Elements of Acoustic Phonetics*. Chicago: The University Press.

———(1967). *Three Areas of Experimental Phonetics*. London: Oxford University Press.

———(1975). *A Course in Phonetics*. New York: Harcourt Brace Jovanovich.

LAMPERTI, FRANCESCO (n.d.). *The Art of Singing*, transl. by J. C. Griffith. New York: G. Schirmer.

LAMPERTI, GIOVANNI BATTISTA *see* Brown, William Earl.

LANGE, C. S., AND JAMES, WILLIAM (1921). *The Emotions*. Baltimore: Williams & Wilkins.

LARGE, JOHN W., ed. (1973). *Vocal Registers in Singing*. The Hague: Mouton.

———, ed. (1980). *Contributions of Voice Research to Singing*. Houston, TX: College-Hill Press.

LAWRENCE, VAN L., ed. (1978). *Transcripts of the Sixth Symposium: Care of the Professional Voice*, June 1977. New York: The Voice Foundation.

———, ed. (1979). *Transcripts of the Seventh Symposium: Care of the Professional Voice*, June 1978. New York: The Voice Foundation.

———, ed. (1982). *Transcripts of the Tenth Symposium: Care of the Professional Voice*, June 1981. New York: The Voice Foundation.

———, ed. (1983). *Transcripts of the Eleventh Symposium: Care of the Professional Voice*, June 1982. New York: The Voice Foundation.

LAWRENCE, VAN L., AND WEINBERG, BERND, eds. (1981). *Transcripts of the Ninth Symposium: Care of the Professional Voice*, June 1980. New York: The Voice Foundation.

LAWSON, FRANKLIN D. (1944). *The Human Voice: A Concise Manual on Training the Speaking and Singing Voice*. New York: Harper & Brothers.

LAWSON, JAMES TERRY (1955). *Full-Throated Ease*. New York: Mills Music.

LEFORT, JULES (1892). *L'Emission de la voix chantée*. Paris: Lemoine & Fils.

LEHISTE, ILSE, ed. (1967). *Readings in Acoustic Phonetics*. Cambridge, MA: The M. I. T. Press.

LEHMANN, LILLI (1903). *How to Sing*. New York: Macmillan.

LEHMANN, LOTTE (1946). *More Than Singing*. London: Boosey and Hawkes.

LEMAIRE, THÉOPHILE, AND LAVOIX, HENRI (1881). *Le Chant: ses principes et son histoire*. Paris: Heugel et Fils.

LENNEBERG, E. H. (1967). *Biological Foundations of Language*. New York: John Wiley & Sons.

LERCHE, WILLIAM (1950). *The Esophagus and Pharynx in Action*. Oxford: Blackwell Scientific.

LESSAC, ARTHUR (1967). *The Use and Training of the Human Voice*, 2d. ed. New York: Drama Book Specialists.

LEVIEN, JOHN NEWBURN (n.d.). *Some Notes for Singers*. London: Novello.

LEVIN, N., ed. (1962). *Voice and Speech Disorders: Medical Aspects*. Springfield, IL: Charles C Thomas.

LEWIS, JOSEPH (1940). *Singing Without Tears*. London: Ascherberg, Hopwood and Crew.

LIEBERMAN, PHILIP (1967). *Intonation, Perception and Language.* Cambridge, MA: The M. I. T. Press.

LOHMANN, PAUL (1925). *Die sängerische Einstellung.* Lindau: C. F. Kahnt.

_____(1933). *Stimmfehler–Stimmberatung.* Mainz: B. Schott's Söhne.

LOISEAU, GEORGES (n.d.). *Notes sur le chant.* Paris: Durand.

LUCHSINGER, RICHARD, AND ARNOLD, GODFREY E. (1965). *Voice–Speech–Language,* transl. by Godfrey Arnold and Evelyn Robe Finkbeiner. Belmont, CA: Wadsworth Publishing.

LULLIES, HANS (1953). *Physiologie der Stimme und Sprache.* Berlin: Verlag Julius Springer.

LULLIES, HANS, AND RANKE, O. F. (1953). *Gehör–Stimme–Sprache.* Vienna: Springer-Verlag.

MACKENZIE, SIR MORELL (1884). *A Manual of Diseases of the Throat and Nose, including the Pharynx, Larynx, Trachea, Oesophagus, Nose, and Naso–Pharynx.* New York: William Wood.

_____(1890). *Hygiene of the Vocal Organs.* London: Macmillan.

MACKINLEY, M. STERLING (1910). *The Singing Voice and Its Training.* London: George Routledge & Sons.

MAGRINI, GUSTAVO (1918). *Il canto, arte e tecnica.* Milan: Ulrico Hoepli.

MALMBERG, BERTIL, ed. (1963). *Phonetics.* New York: Dover Publications.

_____(1968). *Manual of Phonetics.* Amsterdam: North-Holland Publishing.

MANCHESTER, ARTHUR L. (1937). *Twelve Lessons in the Fundamentals of Voice Production.* New York: D. Appleton–Century.

MANCINI, GIOVANNI BATTISTA (1774). *Practical Reflections on the Art of Singing,* transl. by Pietro Buzzi, 1907. Boston: Oliver Ditson.

MANÉN, LUCIE (1974). *The Art of Singing.* London: Faber Music.

MARAFIOTI, P. MARIO (1922). *Caruso's Method of Voice Production: The Scientific Culture of the Voice.* New York: D. Appleton.

MARCHESI, MATHILDE (1901). *Ten Singing Lessons.* New York: Harper & Brothers.

_____(1903). *Theoretical and Practical Vocal Method.* Reprint, 1970. New York: Dover Publications.

MARCHESI, SALVATORE (1902). *A Vademecum.* New York: G. Schirmer.

MARI, NANDA (1970). *Canto e voce.* Milan: G. Ricordi.

MARSHALL, MADELEINE (1953). *The Singer's Manual of English Diction.* New York: G. Schirmer.

MARTIENSSEN-LOHMANN, FRANZISKA (1923). *Das bewusste Singen.* Leipzig: C. F. Kahnt.

_____(1943). *Der Opernsänger.* Mainz: B. Schott's Söhne.

_____(1963). *Der wissende Sänger.* Zurich: Atlantis-Verlag.

MARTINET, A. (1955). *Phonology as Functional Phonetics.* The Philosophical Society. Oxford: Blackwell.

MARTINO, ALFREDO (1953). *Today's Singing,* rev. ed. New York: Executive Press.

MASSENGILL, R. (1966). *Hypernasality: Considerations in Causes and Treatment Procedures.* Springfield, IL: Charles C Thomas.

MAURICE-JACQUET, H. (1947). *The Road to Successful Singing.* Philadelphia: Oliver Ditson.

MCALLISTER, A. H. (1937). *Clinical Studies in Speech Therapy.* London: University of London Press.

MCBURNEY, J. H., AND WRAGE, E. J. (1953). *The Art of Good Speech.* Englewood Cliffs, NJ: Prentice-Hall.

McClosky, David Blair (1959). *Your Voice at Its Best.* Boston, MA: Little, Brown.

McKensie, Duncan (1956). *Training the Boy's Changing Voice.* New Brunswick, NJ: Rutgers University Press.

McKerrow, Janet (1925). *The Vocal Movements.* London: Kegan, Paul, Trench, Trubner.

McKinney, James (1982). *The Diagnosis and Correction of Vocal Faults.* Nashville, TN: Broadman Press.

Meano, Carlo (1964). *La voce umana nella parola e nel canto.* Milan: Casa editrice ambrosiana.

Melba, Dame Nellie (1926). *Melba Method.* London: Chappell.

Mellalieu, W. Norman (1905). *The Boy's Changing Voice.* Reprint, 1966. London: Oxford University Press.

Miller, Dayton Clarence (1916). *The Science of Musical Sounds.* New York: Macmillan.

Miller, Frank E. (1913). *The Voice, Its Production, Care and Preservation.* New York: G. Schirmer.

_____(1917). *Vocal Art–Science and Its Application.* New York: G. Schirmer.

Miller, Richard (1977). *English, French, German and Italian Techniques of Singing.* Metuchen, NJ: Scarecrow Press.

Miller, William Snow (1947). *The Lung,* 2d ed. Springfield, IL: Charles C Thomas.

Mills, Wesley (1908). *Voice Production in Singing and Speaking,* 2d ed. Philadelphia: J. P. Lippincott.

Minifie, Fred D.; Hixon, Thomas J.; and Williams, Frederick (1973). *Normal Aspects of Speech, Hearing, and Language.* Englewood Cliffs, NJ: Prentice-Hall.

Mori, Rachele Maragliano (1970). *Coscienza della voce nella scuola italiana di canto.* Milan: Edizioni Curci.

Moriarty, John (1975). *Diction.* Boston: E. C. Schirmer Music.

Morley, M. E. (1957). *The Development and Disorders of Speech in Childhood.* Baltimore: Williams & Wilkins.

Moses, Paul J. (1954). *The Voice of Neurosis.* New York: Grune & Stratton.

Murphy, A. T. (1964). *Functional Voice Disorders.* Englewood Cliffs, NJ: Prentice-Hall.

Myer, Edmund J. *The Voice from a Practical Stand-Point.* New York: Wm. A. Pond (n.d.).

Myerson, M. C. (1964). *The Human Larynx.* Springfield, IL: Charles C Thomas.

Nadoleczny, M. (1923). *Untersuchungen über den Kunstgesang.* Berlin: Verlag Julius Springer.

Nagel, Wilhelm (1909). *Handbuch der Physiologie,* Vol. 4. Braunschweig: Vieweg.

Negus, Sir Victor E. (1928). *The Mechanism of the Larynx.* Reprint, 1931. St. Louis, MO: C. V. Mosby.

_____(1949). *The Comparative Anatomy and Physiology of the Larynx.* Reprint, 1962. New York: Hafner Publishing.

Neidlinger, W. H. (1903). *A Primer on Voice and Singing.* Chicago: Rand, McNally.

Nervina, Viola (1953). *Voice Production in Singing.* London: Hutchinson's Scientific and Technical Publications.

Nicolaus, Gertrud (1963). *Die Gesetzmässigkeit der richtigen Vokalbildung jeder Tonhöhe als Vorbedingung für Schönheit und Dauer der Stimme.* Berlin: Privately published.

OGDEN, ROBERT MORRIS (1930). *Hearing.* New York: Harcourt, Brace.

O'NEILL, J. M., ed. (1941). *Foundations of Speech,* rev. ed. New York: Longmans, Green.

ORR, F. W. (1938). *Voice for Speech.* New York: McGraw-Hill.

ORTON, JAMES L. (1945). *Voice Culture Made Easy,* 3d. ed. London: Thorsons.

OSGOOD, CHARLES E., AND SEBECK, THOMAS A. (1965). *Psycholinguistics.* Bloomington, IN: Indiana University Press.

OSTWALD, PETER, (1963). *Soundmaking Acoustic Communication of Emotion.* Springfield, IL: Charles C Thomas.

PAFF, C. (1973). *Anatomy of the Head and Neck.* Philadelphia: W. B. Saunders.

PAGET, SIR RICHARD (1930). *Human Speech.* New York: Harcourt.

PANCOAST, H. K.; PENDERGRASS, E. P.; AND SCHAEFFER, J. P. (1940). *The Head and Neck in Roentgen Diagnosis.* Springfield, IL: Charles C Thomas.

PANZÈRA, CHARLES (1957). *L'Amour de chanter.* Paris: Henry Lemoine.

PERNKOPF, EDUARD (1963; 1964). *Atlas der topographischen und angewandten Anatomie des Menschens,* Vol. I; Vol. II. Munich: Urban & Schwarzenberg.

PETERFALVI, JEAN-MICHEL (1970). *Recherches expérimentales sur le symbolisme phonétique.* Paris: Centre nationale de la recherche scientifique.

PETERSON, PAUL W. (1966). *Natural Singing and Expressive Conducting.* Winston-Salem, NC: John F. Blair.

PEYROLLAX, MARGUERITE, AND BARA DE TROVA, M.-L. (1954). *Manuel de phonétique et de diction françaises.* Paris: Librairie Larousse.

PFAUTSCH, LLOYD (1971). *English Diction for the Singer.* New York: Lawson-Gould Music.

PFAUWADEL, MARIE CLAUDE (1981). *Respirer, Parler, Chanter.* Paris: Le Maneau Editeur.

PIKE, KENNETH (1945). *Phonetics.* Ann Arbor, MI: University of Michigan Press.

———(1947). *Phonemics.* Ann Arbor, MI: University of Michigan Press.

PLEASANTS, HENRY (1966). *The Great Singers.* New York: Simon and Schuster.

PLEASANTS, JEANNE VARNEY (1962). *Pronunciation in French,* transl. by Esther Egerton. Ann Arbor, MI: Edwards Brothers.

PORTER, RUTH, ed. (1970). *Breathing: Hering–Breuer Centenary Symposium* (Ciba Foundation). London: J. & A. Churchill.

POSTAL, P. M. (1968) *Aspects of Phonological Theory.* New York: Harper & Row.

POTTER, RALPH K.; KOPP, GEORGE A.; AND GREEN, HARRIET C. (1947). *Visible Speech.* New York: D. Van Nostrand.

PRESSMAN, JOEL J., AND KELEMAN, GEORGE. (1955). *Physiology of the Larynx,* rev. by J. A. Kirchner, 1970. Rochester, MI: American Academy of Ophthalmology and Otolaryngology.

PROCTOR, DANIEL F. (1980). *Breathing, Speech and Song.* Vienna: Springer-Verlag.

PROSCHOWSKY, FRANTZ (1923). *The Way to Sing.* Boston: C. C. Birchard.

PUNT, NORMAN A. (1979). *The Singer's and Actor's Throat,* 3rd ed. London: Heinemann Medical Books.

QUIRING, DANIEL P., AND WARFEL, JOHN H. (1967). *The Head, Neck and Trunk.* Philadelphia: Lea & Febiger.

RAMA, SWAMI; BALLENTIN, R; AND HYMES, A. (1981). *Science of Breath,* 3d printing. Honesdale, PA: Himalayan International Institute of Yoga Science and Philosophy.

RANDEGGER, ALBERTO (1880). *Singing.* London: Novello, Ewer.

RANKE, OTTO F., AND LULLIES, HANS (1953). *Gehör–Stimme–Sprache.* Berlin: Springer-Verlag.

RASMUSSEN, A. T. (1952). *The Principal Nervous Pathways.* New York: Macmillan.

RASMUSSEN, G. L., AND WINDLE, W. F., eds. (1960). *Neural Mechanism of the Auditory and Vestibular Systems.* Springfield, IL: Charles C Thomas.

RAUBICHECK, L.; DAVIS, E. H.; AND CARLL, L. A. (1936). *Voice and Speech Problems.* New York: Prentice-Hall.

REANEY, PERCY H. (1923). *Elements of Speech Training.* London: Methuen.

REID, CORNELIUS L. (1950). *Bel Canto: Principles and Practices.* New York: Coleman-Ross.

_____(1965). *The Free Voice.* New York: Coleman-Ross.

_____(1975). *Psyche and Soma.* New York: Joseph Patelson Music House.

REUSCH, FRITZ (1956). *Der kleine Hey—Die Kunst des Sprechens.* Mainz: B. Schott's Söhne.

RÉVÉSZ, GEZA (1946). *Ursprung und Vorgeschichte der Sprache.* Bern: Francke.

_____(1954). *Introduction to the Psychology of Music,* transl. by G. I. C. de Courcy. Norman, OK: University of Oklahoma.

RICE, WILLIAM (1961). *Basic Principles of Singing.* Nashville, TN: Abingdon Press.

RIGAULT, ANDRÉ, AND CHARBONNEAU, RENÉ, eds. (1972). *Proceedings of the Seventh International Congress of Phonetic Sciences.* The Hague: Mouton.

ROGERS, CLARA KATHLEEN (1927). *Clearcut Speech in Song.* Boston: Oliver Ditson.

ROMA, LISA (1956). *The Science and Art of Singing.* New York: G. Schirmer.

ROMANES, G. J., ed. (1967). *Cunningham's Manual of Practical Anatomy,* Vol. III. *Head and Neck and Brain.* London: Oxford University Press.

_____(1977). *Cunningham's Manual of Practical Anatomy,* Vol. II. *Thorax and Abdomen.* London: Oxford University Press.

ROOT, FREDERIC W. (1896). *The Polychrome Lessons in Voice Culture.* New York: Fillmore Brothers.

ROSE, ARNOLD (1962). *The Singer and the Voice.* London: Faber and Faber.

ROSENTHAL, HAROLD (1966). *Great Singers of Today.* London: Calder and Boyars.

ROSEWALL, RICHARD B. (1961). *Handbook of Singing.* Reprint, 1984. Evanston, IL: Summy-Birchard.

ROSS, WILLIAM ERNEST (1948). *Sing High, Sing Low.* Bloomington, IN: Indiana University Bookstore.

_____(1954). *Secrets of Singing.* Bloomington, IN: Privately published.

ROSVAENGE, HELGE (1969). *Leitfäden für Gesangsbeflissene.* Munich: Obpacher.

ROUSSELET, L'ABBE P. J. (1924; 1925). *Principes de phonétique expérimentale,* Vol. I; Vol II. Paris: H. Didier.

RUSH, JAMES (1821). *The Philosophy of the Human Voice: Embracing Its Physiological History; Together with a System of Principles by Which*

Criticism in the Art of Elocution May be Rendered Intelligible; and Instruction, Definite and Comprehensive, in Which is added a Brief Analysis of Song and Recitative. Philadelphia, PA: Maxwell.

RUSHMORE, ROBERT (1971). *The Singing Voice.* New York: Dodd, Mead.

RUSSELL, GEORGE OSCAR (1928). *The Vowel.* Columbus, OH: The Ohio State University Press.

_____(1931). *Speech and Voice.* New York: Macmillan.

RUSSELL, RITCHIE W., AND DEWAR, A. J. (1975). *Explaining the Brain.* London: Oxford University Press.

RUSSELL, WILLIAM (1882). *Orthophony, or Vocal Culture.* Boston: Houghton Mifflin.

SABLE, BARBARA KINSEY (1982). *The Vocal Sound.* Englewood Cliffs, NJ: Prentice-Hall.

SALZER, F. (1962). *Structural Hearing.* New York: Dover Publications.

SAMOILOFF, LAZAR S. (1942) *The Singer's Handbook.* Philadelphia: Theodore Presser.

SAWASHIMA, MASAYUKI, AND COOPER, FRANKLIN S., eds. (1977). *Dynamic Aspects of Speech Production.* Tokyo: University of Tokyo Press.

SCHANE, SANFORD A. (1973). *Generative Phonology.* Englewood Cliffs, NJ: Prentice-Hall.

SCHEMINZKY, FERDINAND (1943). *Die Welt des Schalles.* Vienna: Deutsche Vereinsdruckerei.

SCHIØTZ, AKSEL (1969). *The Singer and His Art.* New York: Harper & Brothers.

SCHLAFFHORST, CLARA, AND ANDERSON, HEDWIG (1928). *Atmung und Stimme.* Wolfenbüttel: Möseler Verlag.

SCHMAUK, THEODORE E. (1890). *The Voice in Speech and Song.* New York: John B. Alden.

SCHMIDINGER, JOSEF (1970). *Belcanto im zwanzigsten Jahrhundert.* Vienna: Privately published.

SCHUBERT, EARL D. (1980). *Hearing: Its Function and Dysfunction.* Vienna: Springer-Verlag.

SCHULTZE, OSCAR (1935). *Atlas und kurzbefasstes Lehrbuch der topographischen und angewandten Anatomie,* ed. by W. Lubosch. Munich: J. F. Lehmanns Verlag.

SCHUMACHER, WALTER (1974). *Voice Therapy and Voice Improvement.* Springfield, IL: Charles C Thomas.

SCHUTTE, HARM KORNELIUS (1980). *The Efficiency of Voice Production.* Groningen: State University Hospital.

_____, ed. (1981). *Congress Proceedings and Abstracts of the IXth Congress of the Union of European Phoniatricians.* Amsterdam: Vrije Universiteit.

SCOTT, CHARLES KENNEDY (1954). *The Fundamentals of Singing.* London: Cassell.

SCOTT-BROWN, W. G. *see* Ballantyne and Groves.

SCRIPTURE, E. W. (1902). *The Elements of Experimental Phonetics.* New York: Charles Scribner's Sons.

SEASHORE, CARL E. (1947). *In Search of Beauty in Music: A Scientific Approach to Musical Aesthetics.* New York: Ronald Press.

SEILER, EMMA (1875). *The Voice in Singing.* Philadelphia: J. B. Lippincott.

SGUERZI, ANGELO (1978). *Le stirpi canore.* Bologna: Edizione Bongiovanni.

SHAKESPEARE, WILLIAM (1921). *Plain Words on Singing.* Bryn Mawr, PA: Oliver Ditson.

_____(1921). *The Art of Singing.* Bryn Mawr, PA: Oliver Ditson.

SHAW, GEORGE BERNARD (1955). *Shaw on Music.* ed. by Eric Bentley. Garden City, NY: Doubleday.

SHAW, W. WARREN (1930). *Authentic Voice Production.* Philadelphia: J. B. Lippincott.

SHELDON, W. H. (1940). *The Varieties of Human Physique.* New York: Harper & Brothers.

SIEBER, FERDINAND (1872). *The Art of Singing,* transl. by F. Seeger. New York: William A. Pond.

SIEBS, Th. *See* de Boor et al.

SIMPSON, JOHN F.; BALLANTYNE, J.; CHALMERS, J.; ROBERT, IAN G.; AND EVANS, CHARLES HAROLD (1957). *A Synopsis of Otorhinolaryngology.* Bristol: John Wright & Sons.

SLATER, DAVID D. (n.d.). *Vocal Physiology and the Technique of Singing: A Complete Guide to Teachers, Students and Candidates for the A.R.C.M., L.R.A.M., and All Similar Examinations.* London: J. H. Harway.

SPALTEHOLZ, WERNER (1932–1933). *Handatlas der Anatomie des Menschens.* 13th ed., 3 vols. Leipzig: S. Hirzel-Verlag.

STAMPA, ARIBERT (1956). *Atem, Sprache und Gesang.* Kassel: Bärenreiter Verlag.

STANISLAVSKI, CONSTANTIN, AND RUMYANTSEV, PAVEL (1975). *Stanislavski on Opera,* transl. and ed. by Elizabeth Reynolds Hapgood. New York: Theatre Arts Books.

STANLEY, DOUGLAS (1929). *The Science of Voice.* New York: Carl Fischer.

_____(1933). *Your Voice, Its Production and Reproduction.* New York: Pitman Publishing.

_____(1945). *Your Voice—Applied Science of Vocal Art.* New York: Pitman Publishing.

STETSON, RAYMOND H. (1945). *Bases of Phonology.* Oberlin, OH: Oberlin College Press.

STEVENS, KENNETH N., AND HIRANO, MINORU (1981). *Vocal Fold Physiology.* Tokyo: University of Tokyo Press.

STEVENS, STANLEY S., AND WARKOFSKY, GEORGE (1965). *Sound and Hearing.* New York: Time Books.

STEWARD, G. W., AND LINDSAY, R. B. (1930). *Acoustics.* New York: Van Nostrand.

STUBBS, G. EDWARD (1908). *The Adult Male Alto or Counter-Tenor Voice.* London: Novello.

SUNDBERG JOHAN, ed. (1981). *Research Aspects on Singing.* Stockholm: The Royal Swedish Academy of Music.

SUNDERMAN, LLOYD F. (1970). *Artistic Singing: Its Tone Production and Basic Understandings.* Metuchen, NJ: Scarecrow Press.

TARNEAUD, JEAN (1941). *Traité pratique de phonologie et phoniatrie.* Paris: Librairie Maloine.

_____(1957). *Le Chant, sa construction, sa destruction.* Paris: Librairie Maloine.

THOMAS, FRANZ (1968). *Die Lehre des Kunstgesanges nach der altitalienischen Schule.* Berlin: Georg Achterberg Verlag.

THORNE, BARRIE, AND HENLEY, NANCY M., eds. (1975). *Language and Sex: Difference and Dominance.* Rowley, MA: Newbury House Publishers.

THORPE, CLARENCE R. (1954). *Teach Yourself to Sing.* London: The English Universities Press.

TOLDT, C. *see* Hayek.

TOSI, PIER FRANCESCO (1743). *Observations on the Florid Song,* transl. by J. E. Galliard. London: J. Wilcox.

TRAVIS, L. E., ed. (1917). *Handbook of Speech Pathology.* Reprint, 1957. New York: Appleton–Century–Crofts.

TROJAN, FELIX (1948). *Der Ausdruck von Stimme und Sprache.* Vienna: Verlag Maudrich.

TRUBETZKOY, N. S. (1969). *Principles of Phonology,* transl. by Christiane A. M. Baltaxe. Berkeley, CA: University of California Press.

TRUSLER, IVAN, AND EHRET, WALTER (1972). *Functional Lessons in Singing,* 2d ed. Englewood Cliffs, NJ: Prentice-Hall.

TURNER, A. L., ed. (1927). *Diseases of the Nose, Throat and Ear.* New York: William Wood.

TYNDALL, JOHN. *Sound.* (1888). New York: D. Appleton–Century.

ULRICH, BERNHARD (1910). *Concerning the Principles of Vocal Training in the A Cappella Period, and Until the Beginning of Opera (1474–1640),* transl. by John Seale. Reprint, 1973. Minneapolis, MN: Pro Musica Press.

URIS, DOROTHY (1971). *To Sing in English.* New York: Boosey & Hawkes.

VAN BORRE, THOORIS (1927). *Le Chant humain.* Paris: Madédée Legrand.

VAN DEINSE, J. B., AND GOSLINGS, V. R. O. (1982). *The Technique of Singing: A Comparative Study.* The Hague: Government Publishing House.

VAN DUSEN, C. R. (1953). *Training the Voice for Speech.* New York: McGraw-Hill.

VANNINI, VINCENZO (1924). *Della voce umana.* Florence: Tipografia Barbera.

VAN RIPER, CHARLES, AND IRWIN, JOHN W. (1958). *Voice and Articulation.* Englewood Cliffs, NJ: Prentice-Hall.

VENNARD, WILLIAM (1967). *Singing: The Mechanism and the Technic,* 5th ed. New York: Carl Fischer.

VIËTOR, WILHELM (1918). *Elements of Phonetics: English, French and German,* transl. by Walter Ripman. New York: E. P. Dutton.

VON BÉKÉSY, GEORG (1960). *Experiments in Hearing,* transl. and ed. by E. G. Weaver. New York: McGraw-Hill.

VON MEYER, GEORG HERMANN (1884). *The Organs of Speech.* New York: D. Appleton–Century.

VOORHEES, IRVING WILSON (1923). *Hygiene of the Voice.* New York: Macmillan.

WARMAN, E. B. (1889). *The Voice: How to Train It and Care for It.* Boston: Lee and Shepard.

WATERS, CRYSTAL (1930). *Song: The Substance of Vocal Study.* New York: G. Schirmer.

WEAVER, E. G., AND LAWRENCE, M. (1954). *Physiological Acoustics.* Princeton, NJ: Princeton University Press.

WEER, ROBERT LAWRENCE (1948). *Your Voice.* Los Angeles, CA: Privately published.

WEISS, D. A., AND BEEBE, HELEN (1950). *The Chewing Approach in Speech and Voice Therapy.* Basel: S. Karger.

WELLS, J. C., AND COLSON, GRETA (1971). *Practical Phonetics.* London: Pitman Publishing.

WEST, ROBERT; ANSBERRY, M.; AND CARR, ANNA (1957). *The Rehabilitation of Speech.* New York: Harper & Brothers.

WESTERMAN, KENNETH N. (1949). *Emergent Voice.* Ann Arbor, MI: Privately published.

WHITE, ERNEST G. (1909). *Science and Singing.* Reprint, 1969. Boston: Crescendo Publishers.

———(1938). *Sinus Tone Production.* Reprint, 1970. Boston: Crescendo Publishers.

WHITLOCK, WELDON (1967). *Facets of the Singer's Art.* Champaign, IL: Pro Musica Press.

———(1968). *Bel Canto for Twentieth Century.* Champaign, IL: Pro Musica Press.

———(1975). *Profiles in Vocal Pedagogy.* Ann Arbor, MI: Clifton Press.

WILCOX, JOHN C. (1945). *The Living Voice.* New York: Carl Fischer.

WINCKEL, FRITZ (1968). *Music, Sound, and Sensation: A Modern Exposition,* transl. by Thomas Binkley. New York: Dover Publications.

WISE, CLAUDE MERTON (1957). *Applied Phonetics.* Englewood Cliffs, NJ: Prentice-Hall.

WITHERSPOON, HERBERT (1925). *Singing.* New York: G. Schirmer.

WOLF, ARTUR (n.d.). *Criticism of One-Sided Singing Methods: Problems of Voice-Building and Their Solution,* translated by Bert Jahr. New York: Irene Tauber.

WOOD, ALEXANDER (1941). *The Physics of Music,* rev. ed. by J. M. Bowsher, 1961. London: Methuen.

WOODBURY, ISAAC BAKER (1853). *The Cultivation of Voice Without a Master.* New York: J. J. Huntington.

WORMHOUDT, PEARL SHINN (1981). *Building the Voice as an Instrument.* Oskaloosa, IA: William Penn College.

WUNDT, W. M. (1908). *Principles of Physiological Psychology.* New York: Macmillan.

YOUNG, GERALD M. (1956). *What Happens in Singing.* New York: Pitman.

ZEMLIN, W. R. (1981). *Speech and Hearing Science: Anatomy and Physiology,* 2d ed. Englewood Cliffs, NJ: Prentice-Hall.

ZUCKERMAN, SIR SOLLY (1961). *A New System of Anatomy.* London: Oxford University Press.

ZUIDERMA, GEORGE D., ed. (1977). *The Johns Hopkins Atlas of Functional Anatomy.* London: Baillière Tindall.

Subject Index

Abdomen, 10, 12, 20, 23, 24, 25, 26, 27, 28, 30, 31, 32, 33, 38, 41, 42, 265, 277–78
"Abdominal" vibrato, 184, 185, 190, 191
Acoustic at-rest posture, 69, 97
Acoustic energy, 50
Aditus laryngis, 248
Aerodynamics, 2, 20, 22
aggiustamento, 150, 151, 155, 156, 157–60, 165
Agility, 19, 32, 37, 40, 41, 42, 43–47
Air pressure, 2, 20, 23
Airflow, 2, 7, 13, 14, 20, 22, 23, 37, 41, 48, 56, 152, 172, 257, 290, 292, 293
Alveoli, 269
Anal sphincteral closure, 38
Anterolateral abdominal wall, 25, 26, 27, 28, 33, 37, 94, 191, 275–78
Antihistamines, 230, 231
appoggio, 23, 24, 25, 29, 38, 41, 61, 126, 184, 186, 187
arrotondamento, 156, 158
Articulatory system, 48, 52, 53, 69, 293
Aryepiglottic folds, 245, 248
Arytenoid cartilages, 23, 48, 49, 245
Arytenoid muscle, 245
Associative function, 198
Atmospheric pressure, 20
Attack (*see* Onset)
Auditory monitoring, 198
Axial alignment, 30

Baritone, 117, 119, 123, 125, 155
Bass, 123
basso profondo, 116
Bauchaussenstütze, 237–38
bel canto, 150, 194, 196, 216
Bell register (*see* Flageolet voice)
Bellows analogy, 22
Bernoulli principle, 22, 23
"Belly breathing," 278
"Breaks" and "lifts," 15, 115, 118
Breath energy, 36, 108–109
Breath management, 18, 19, 20, 22, 23, 25, 28, 29, 30, 33, 34, 37, 38, 39, 94, 114, 172–73, 270, 278
Breath mixture, 108, 119, 172, 177, 179
Breath renewal, 10, 12, 14, 25, 29, 31, 32, 34, 35, 36
Breathiness, 3, 8, 15, 177
Breathing, 5, 12, 24, 26, 28, 30, 31, 33, 34, 36, 38, 266, 267

Bronchi, 269
Buccinator, 67
Buccopharyngeal posture, 58, 59, 60, 64, 74, 94

"Call" of the voice, 116–18
cantare come si parla, 74
Cervical vertebrae, 153, 154
Chest, open, 136
Chest mixture (female), 136–41
Chest posture, 29, 30, 278
Chest register (male), 116–17
Chest voice (female), 33, 115, 133, 136
Chest wall muscles, 23
Chewing, 233–35
Clavicular breathing, 28, 29, 267
Coloratura soprano, 133, 134, 148, 161, 178
Communication in singing, 201, 204
Complemental breath, 278, 279
Consonants, voiced and unvoiced, 293–96
Constrictor pharyngis, inferior, medius, and superior, 65, 285
Contralto, 133, 135, 136, 137
Conus elasticus, 246, 247
copertura, 156
Corniculate cartilages of Santorini, 245
Corniculate pharyngeal ligaments, 248
Costals, 22, 26, 34, 265
Coughing, 232–33
Counter-tenor, 123–125
Coupled consonants, 106–107
"Covering," 150–151, 152, 153–55, 158
Cricoarytenoid muscles, 2, 244
Cricoid cartilage, 243, 244, 245, 285
Cricothyroid ligament, 67, 248
Cricothyroid muscle, 2, 27, 118, 133, 136, 184, 185, 192, 198, 244, 245, 255, 257, 287–90
Cricotracheal ligament, 246
Cricovocal ligament, 246
Cuneiform cartilages of Wrisberg, 245

Damping, 291–92
Deckung, 156
Deltoid muscle, 273
Diaphragm, 23, 24, 30, 33, 34, 40, 191, 262, 264, 265, 267
Diet, 219, 237–38
Digastric muscle, 249, 250, 251
Diphthongization, 90
Dorsal muscles, 25, 38, 272

Name Index